WITHDRAWN

# THE EMANCIPATION OF
# FRENCH INDOCHINA

# The
# Emancipation of
# FRENCH
# INDOCHINA

෫෨෫෨෫෨෫෨෫෨෫෨

DONALD LANCASTER

*Issued under the auspices of the*
*Royal Institute of International Affairs*

## OCTAGON BOOKS

A DIVISION OF FARRAR, STRAUS AND GIROUX

New York    1974

*Reprinted 1975*
*by special arrangement with Oxford University Press, Inc.*

OCTAGON BOOKS
A Division of Farrar, Straus & Giroux, Inc.
19 Union Square West
New York, N. Y. 10003

Library of Congress Cataloging in Publication Data

Lancaster, Donald.
    The emancipation of French Indochina.

    Reprint of the ed. published by Oxford University Press, London.

    Bibliography: p.
    Includes index.
    1. Indochina, French—History.    I. Title.
[DS541.L28    1975]                    959.7′03                    74-23161
ISBN 0-374-94719-8

Manufactured by Braun-Brumfield, Inc.
Ann Arbor, Michigan

Printed in the United States of America

*To my nephew*
JOHN

# PREFACE

THE following account of the French intervention in Indochina and of the events leading up to the fall of Dien Bien Phu in May 1954 is based on information contained in the books listed in the attached bibliography, on material in the Press Archives in Chatham House, and also on innumerable discussions with Vietnamese nationalists, whose friendship I gained while serving on the staff of the British Legation in Saigon during the years 1950–4, and with French officials and journalists. Here opportunities also occurred to observe from a respectful distance the French and Indochinese personalities responsible for the conduct of civil and military affairs.

The appreciation then acquired of the issues at stake, genuine respect and affection for both the French and Vietnamese peoples, and some personal experience of the harsh realities of war represented the slender baggage with which I embarked upon what turned out to be a considerable task. But I was sustained by nostalgic memories of vast skies arched over opulent deltas, broad rivers bearing their tribute of alluvium and *luc binh* to the sea, of noble uplands and tropical forests serving as a backcloth to a majestic coastline: landscapes animated by naked children cheerfully splashing around like glistening fish in what seemed their natural element, or perched on the back of water-buffaloes in a state of almost mystic communion with those dignified and rather fearsome beasts, and by country folk in conical hats, with twin baskets suspended from their shoulders, trotting diligently along dust tracks and dykes to distant villages screened by bamboos and areca palms. A country inhabited by men with delicate, almost flowerlike hands and subtle minds and by women elegant and perennially young: a fluid people, expert at nuances, who were often bewildered and even outraged by the European capacity for incisive thought and brutal action.

The complexity of the subject has prevented me, however, from devoting the same attention to events in each of the three Indochinese states formerly associated in the French Union; and whereas the French occupation of Vietnam is dealt with at some length, events in Cambodia and Laos, forming the lateral panels of the triptych, have been treated in a perfunctory fashion which does scant justice to the past greatness and present status of these kingdoms. However, in spite of its limitations, this book may serve to remove certain misconceptions sedulously fostered by Communist propaganda in regard to a war fought over extraordinarily difficult terrain by French-officered troops, who had been furnished neither with the means to achieve victory nor adequate reasons to continue the struggle: a war redeemed by the high morale and the spirit of self-sacrifice displayed by the contending forces.

Finally, I wish to express my grateful thanks to Miss Hermia Oliver, whose suggestions and unstinted help in revising the manuscript have been invaluable, and to the staff of the Library and Press Archives at Chatham House. I am also indebted to my Vietnamese friends for their aid and encouragement.

*London,*
*December 1959*

# CONTENTS

# PART III

# THE STRUGGLE WITH THE VIET MINH

# ABBREVIATIONS

*CSM :*      *Christian Science Monitor*

Cole :      A. B. Cole, ed., *Conflict in Indo-China and International Repercussions; a Documentary History, 1945–1955.* Ithaca NY, Cornell University Press, 1956.

*DSB :*      *Department of State Bulletin.*

EDC :       European Defence Community.

IMTFE :     International Military Tribunal, Far East, Tokyo, 1946–8: *Record of Proceedings, Exhibits, Judgment, Dissenting Judgments,* etc. (mimeo.).

*J.O.*        *Journal Officiel.*

*NCNA :*      *New China News Agency.*

*NYHT :*      *New York Herald Tribune.*

*NYT :*       *New York Times.*

RIIA,

*Documents :* Royal Institute of International Affairs, *Documents on International Affairs.*

# Part I

## THE ARRIVAL OF THE EUROPEANS

# I

# Introduction

THE promontory forming the south-eastern extremity of Asia includes the Indochinese states of Vietnam, Cambodia, and Laos. These states, which lie within the Tropic of Cancer and are known collectively as Indochina, occupy its eastern part and cover an area of some 285,000 square miles.

Indochina's eastern seaboard, which is part of Vietnam, uncoils over a distance of 1,200 miles in the shape of the letter S, of which the Red river delta forms the north-eastern part. This delta is linked by a chaplet of coastal plains with that of the river Mekong in the south. Both these rivers rise in China and flow through Indochina's mountainous northern region, which extends southwards to merge into the Annam chain, a dorsal range of mountains running parallel to the coast, which forms the watershed between the Mekong and the coastal plains. This mountain chain drops steeply on its eastern side in a tangle of vegetation to the China Sea, while to the west it falls in a series of savannah-like plateaux to the river Mekong.

The Mekong and the Red rivers have played an important part in the geological formation of the country. The Red river is the principal architect of the Tongking delta, which was in geologically recent times a gulf, and the alluvial deposits of the Mekong river have created, except for the restricted watershed of the river Donnai, the whole area between the foothills of the Annam chain and the shores of the Gulf of Siam, a region which was also formerly a gulf.[1]

The Indochinese peninsula was first inhabited by peoples akin to the Australian aborigines and the Negroid Papuans of Melanesia, who were displaced and partially absorbed by Indonesian peoples from the north. Most of these Indonesian peoples later moved on and settled in the Malay peninsula and the islands of the Indian archipelago, while the remainder were either absorbed by another wave of emigrants or forced to seek refuge in the hills and mountains. These surviving Indonesian

[1] The Great Lake (Tonle Sap), situated about eighty miles north of Phnom Penh, represents the remains of this gulf.

2

tribes, who are called 'savages' or Mois by the Vietnamese, Phnong by the Cambodians, and Khas by the Lao, are now to be found for the most part on the plateaux and in the forests of the Annam mountain chain, where they cultivate 'dry' rice, millet, and some tobacco in forest clearings prepared before the rainy season by felling the timber which is then burnt to fertilize the soil; a procedure which has to be repeated after a year or two in another part of the forest. The tribes supplement their diet with game, which is hunted with a primitive form of crossbow, with fish from the mountain streams, and forest fruits.

The Mois, in spite of evidence in some tribes of intermarriage with their less comely predecessors on the peninsula, are a handsome, bronze-skinned people akin to the Dyaks of Borneo and the Bataks of Sumatra. They wear a loin-cloth or sarong, and adorn themselves with metal necklaces and, in some tribes, with rings or bone plugs inserted in the lobes of the ears. Their habits, social organization, and religious beliefs are as simple as their dress. The Mois recognize the authority of tribal chieftains and live for the most part communally in 'longhouses' raised on piles, which are shared between a number of interrelated families, while their religious needs are catered for by Shamans, or sorcerers skilled in propitiating the forces of nature and the spirits of the dead. These Shamans are popularly credited with the possession of uncanny powers; and the destructive capacity of the most eminent members of this fraternity, the Sadet of Water, and the Sadet of Fire, who belong to the Jarai tribe, was formerly regarded with apprehension even by the rulers of powerful kingdoms who sought to propitiate these malefic beings with gifts.

Although they are resolutely averse to routine work in any form, the Mois perform communal tasks with gusto, and are of a convivial and hospitable disposition, welcoming opportunities to broach the great earthenware jars used for the storage of rice-wine, the contents of which are then imbibed ceremoniously through hollow bamboo rods.

### FUNAN AND CHAMPA

The existence of the Moi tribes was first reported by Chinese emissaries who visited a kingdom in the Mekong delta called Funan in the third century A.D. This kingdom had probably been founded some two or three hundred years before by sea-farers from India, who intermarried with the Indonesian tribal populations and established trading stations in a coastal area which was then a staging post on the sea route to China. By the second century A.D. the territories of this kingdom included the Mekong delta to the south of the Tonle Sap and the coastal plains as far north as Cam Ranh Bay. The Funanese king was also the acknowledged leader of a confederation of Indianized states, which stretched westward to the Gulf of Martaban and down to the Kra peninsula.

At the beginning of the fifth century the spread of Hindu culture and religious beliefs was promoted by the election to the throne of a Brahman, whose accession seems to have led to a fresh influx of emigrants from South India, including members of the Brahmanic priestly caste, with the result that Sivaism and Vishnuism, together with Mahayana Buddhism, replaced the more primitive indigenous beliefs. Sivaism was adopted at that time as the official state cult. This cult, in recognition of the fact that Siva is both the great destroying and dissolving force but also the reproductive power which is perpetually restoring that which has been destroyed, is symbolized by the Linga or phallus, represented as a vertical cylinder on a square base, and this was installed in a temple on a hill near the capital.

Meanwhile another Indianized kingdom, known to the Chinese as Lin Yi and later as Champa, had been founded on the coastal plains of central Indochina. This kingdom was populated by an Indonesian people called the Chams, who may have reached the sea from across the Annam mountain chain, and have been settled in the Mekong valley to the north of the Cambodian town of Stung Treng. After raiding the Chinese province of Giao Chi, which then included the coastal plains down to the Col des Nuages, the Chams founded a principality in the southern half of the Chinese commandery of Je Nan in A.D. 192 and, when they were expelled from this region in the middle of the fifth century, they transferred their capital to a site near Fai Fo.

Although they proved disquieting neighbours for the Chinese, whom they harried incessantly, the Chams, who possessed a common frontier with Funan near Cam Ranh Bay, maintained friendly relations with the southern kingdom: relations based perhaps on common religious beliefs and conceptions of government derived from India. But the occupation of the coastal plains appears to have weakened their hold over the Cham-inhabited territory to the west; and at some time during this period the Chams in this region were evicted or absorbed by the Khmers, who founded a kingdom called Chenla on the middle reaches of the Mekong. This kingdom was at first a vassal state of Funan, but towards the middle of the sixth century a king of Chenla, who claimed descent from a Brahman hermit, Kambu Suryavamsa, and an Apsaras, or celestial nymph named Mera, rebelled against his suzerain, and during the next 100 years his successors annexed Funan and conquered the territories to the north and west of their kingdom. Chenla soon fell a victim to dynastic disputes, however, with the result that, by the beginning of the eighth century it was partitioned between two rival principalities known respectively as Upland and Maritime Chenla.

This partition took place at a time when the coastal regions of Indochina were being devastated by pirate raids from the Malay peninsula and from Java, where a powerful kingdom, that of the Sailendra Kings of the Mountain, was founded probably in the latter half of the century. Shortly after the rise of this kingdom the reigning Sailendra monarch appears to have invaded Maritime Chenla where, after seizing the capital, he captured and beheaded the king. This disaster seems to have been followed by a period of anarchy, but after a while a Khmer prince who had been living in Java returned and established his capital near Kompong Cham on the lower Mekong, where he proclaimed himself king of Kambujadesa, or 'land of the Kambuja', under the reign-name of Jayavarman II. He then proceeded to subdue the regions around the Great Lake, and when this had been done moved his capital to the northern shore, which was to become the capital region of the Khmer Empire. Later he again transferred the seat of government north-east to a plateau in an isolated group of hills, the Phnom Kulen, where a ceremony of great consequence for the future of the kingdom took place in A.D. 802. This ceremony, which was performed by a learned Brahman, freed Kambujadesa from the suzerainty of the Sailendra kings, invested Jayavarman with the authority of a Chakravartin or, in the language of Hindu mythology, of a controller of the universal Dharma with a status equivalent to that of a demiurge, and made him cosubstantial with the god Siva. This mystical union was symbolized by the consecration of a gold linga, which thereafter became the centre of the state cult of the Deva-raja or 'God-King'.

After some years Jayavarman II moved his capital back from the Kulen hills to the shore of the Great Lake and brought with him the gold linga or, in the language of temple inscriptions, the 'God-King'. Although the territories over which he was reigning at the time of his death do not appear to have included Upland, or even the whole of Maritime Chenla, Jayavarman II had nevertheless secured possession of the region around the Great Lake, which was to become the centre of a great empire. For he was succeeded by capable and warlike kings who had extended the frontiers of Kambujadesa by the latter half of the tenth century to include all of present-day Cambodia and Cochin-China and probably the territory stretching in the west to the Menam and in the north to Vientiane, while a buttress of vassal kingdoms, extending from the Shan States southward to the Kra peninsula, acknowledged the suzerainty of the Khmer monarch.

The revenues derived from these territories, together with the loot and slaves acquired in their wars, enabled the Khmer rulers to perpetuate the extravagant cult of the God-King. This cult imposed upon each successive monarch the task of erecting in his capital region, which was named Angkor,[2] a steep-sided stone pyramid of majestic proportion, lavishly adorned with sculpture both in the round and in bas-relief, and usually crowned by a quincunx of sanctuary towers or prasats, four of which occupied the corners of the top platform, while the fifth, which was centrally placed and dominated the others, enshrined the image of the royal procreative power: this edifice served for the celebration of his cult during his lifetime and as the repository for his ashes after his death. Moreover, as the pyramid temple symbolized Mount Meru, the abode of the gods, which was, according to Hindu cosmography, the navel of the universe, the shrine of the reigning God-King had likewise to be erected in the centre of the capital: a requirement which entailed periodic shifts in the site and frequent alterations to the lay-out of Angkor.

[2] 'Angkor' is a corruption of the Sanskrit word 'Nagara' meaning walled, or capital, city.

But the subjects of the God-King were sometimes diverted from the unending task of erecting pyramid temples to more productive labour, for the God-King was required to fulfil the functions of the ancient gods of the soil and assure the fertility of the land around his mountain dwelling which symbolized the universe in microcosm. This led to the construction of two immense reservoirs measuring some five miles in length and about a mile in breadth, the water being used by an elaborate system of canals, channels, and rivulets, to irrigate the spacious plain around Angkor during the dry season. Nevertheless, the onerous cult of the God-King and the alienation of vast tracts of land and innumerable villages in the form of endowments to perpetuate the cult of a deceased monarch, together with incessant wars and dynastic disputes, were soon to sap the economic foundations of an empire which seemed destined for a longer lease of power.

In the twelfth century the Khmer Empire became involved in a series of indecisive wars with Champa; and in 1177 a Cham fleet, piloted by a shipwrecked Chinese mariner, sailed up the Mekong, crossed the Great Lake, and attacked Angkor, which was captured and sacked. Although the Khmers recovered from this disaster and, under the leadership of an exiled Buddhist prince who took the reign-name of Jayavarman VII, reconquered the lost territories and occupied Champa itself, the victory was followed by a mass conscription of labour for an ambitious building programme, including the erection of pyramid temples dedicated to the posthumously deified parents of the monarch and the construction of monasteries, hospitals, rest-houses, bridges, and roads throughout the Empire, while the capital itself, which was renamed Angkor Thom or Angkor the Great, was enclosed within laterite walls and surrounded by a moat. Each wall was 25 feet high and 2 miles long and backed by a massive earth rampart, while five monumental gateways, each approached across a stone causeway, gave access to the city.

These herculean tasks appear to have finally discouraged and exhausted the Khmers, who were shortly to be threatened by a fresh danger from the north, where the Thai peoples had been moving down the river valleys from south-west China for centuries. One of these peoples, the Lao Thai, who had settled in the valley of the Upper Mekong, where they enslaved the Indonesian tribal population, the Khas, were then infiltrating across the Korat plateau and down the Mekong towards the Khong Falls, while another group, called 'Syam' by their neighbours, had reached the Menam and were settled on its upper and middle reaches.

About the middle of the thirteenth century a Syam chieftain attacked the town of Sukothai, expelled the Khmer Governor, and proclaimed himself king, and in the latter half of the century a son of the king, Rama Khamheng, conquered the watershed of the Menam and forced the rulers of the principalities situated between the Salween and the Mekong to pay him homage. But in 1349 Sukothai's paramountcy was successfully challenged by a Thai prince established on the right bank of the river Suphan; and in the following year this prince moved his capital to Ayuthya, a small island on the lower reaches of the Menam.

The foundations of a strong and aggressive kingdom in this region represented a threat to the Khmer homelands around the Great Lake, and from that time onwards the two kingdoms were continually at war with each other. Finally, in 1430, the Siamese captured and sacked Angkor Thom. Although the Khmers soon regained possession of their capital, the decision was taken two years later to move the seat of government south of the Great Lake. This move appears to have been based on strategic considerations and also on the fact that the upkeep of the great temples in the region had become an intolerable burden to the impoverished kingdom. Moreover the Khmer people had themselves abandoned the worship of the Brahmic gods, and adopted Hinayana Buddhism, a religion which had probably been introduced into the country by refugees from the Lower Menam during the latter half of the thirteenth century. Their adoption of this faith can occasion no surprise, as a religion which instructed its adepts to renounce earthly ambitions and social strivings and exalted the serenity of mind attained by the elimination of desire must have seemed well adapted to the needs of a people who had worn themselves out in the service of a God-King. But although Angkor Thom and the outlying temples were abandoned to the jungle, the Khmer kings still visited the region now and then, either to hunt or to wage war upon their neighbours, while a small troupe of Buddhist monks were soon in occupation of Angkor Wat, which is the largest and also the most accessible of the Khmer temples.

The establishment of the capital at Lovek, however, did not mark the end of the kingdom's independence, and in 1564 a Khmer force invaded the Menam delta and laid siege to Ayuthya. Thirty years later the capture of Lovek by the Siamese reduced the once far-flung and powerful empire to the position of a vassal state, which was known as Camboxa or Cambuja by the Spanish and Portuguese missionaries, adventurers, and traders who were soon to arrive from Malacca and the Philippines.

## LAN XANG

The long struggle between Ayuthya and Angkor was to lead to the rise of a Lao kingdom in the Mekong valley founded by a prince named Fa Ngoum, who had spent most of his youth in exile at Angkor where his education had been entrusted to a learned Buddhist monk. Fa Ngoum when he reached manhood managed to enlist the support of the Khmer monarch, was given his daughter in marriage, and sent at the head of an army to make good his claim to the principality of Muong Swa on the Upper Mekong in 1353. Successful in this enterprise, the prince compelled the Lao princes in the Mekong valley to pay him homage and, having consolidated his authority by the capture of Vientiane, proclaimed himself King of Lan Xang or 'the country of a million elephants' in 1355. He then asked the King of Angkor to assist him in propagating Hinayana Buddhism among his subjects, and in 1358 a party of Buddhist missionaries, whose baggage included the sacred books of the Buddhist Canon and a statue (prabang) of the Buddha presented by a king of Lanka (Ceylon) to a Khmer monarch in the eleventh century, were sent to Muong Swa. The arrival of the statue was considered so auspicious that it was adopted as the palladium of the kingdom, and the capital was renamed in its honour 'Luang Prabang' (the town of the prabang). Fa Ngoum's military capacities, however, failed to reconcile his subjects to the oppressive nature of his rule, and after reigning for twenty years he was compelled to abdicate in favour of his son, Oun Hueun.

His successor proceeded to consolidate his authority and to

provide himself with the means to resist attack. He was faced with a considerable task, however, since Lan Xang possessed neither access to the sea nor a fertile central region which would have provided a suitable site for the capital. Moreover, although the Mekong valley represented Lan Xang's heartland, its course was obstructed by rapids and rocks which, by isolating the population along its navigable reaches from contact with their kinsmen living up- and down-stream, encouraged the growth of regional particularism.

In 1376 Oun Hueun ordered a census of males to be taken. The valid male population were then enrolled in militia units placed under the command of regional governors, or Chao Muong, who were required to maintain them out of local revenues: an arrangement which invested the Chao Muong, whose office tended to become hereditary, almost with the authority of a vassal prince, for they were left undisturbed to administer their regions through officials whose functions were similar to those of the court dignitaries, and were merely required to remit to Luang Prabang a fixed contribution amounting to half the local crop every third year. Thus although the King of Luang Prabang was styled 'the Master of Life' and ruled as an absolute monarch, his powers were in effect circumscribed by the authority vested in the regional governors and also by the semi-elective form assumed by the monarchy, since on the death of a king the viceroy, who was invested with the high-sounding title of Chao Maha Oupahat and frequently deputized for the king himself, was required, at least in theory, to convene a meeting of the great dignitaries who would then proceed to elect a successor; the choice being restricted, however, to princes of the royal house.[3]

In 1563 the seat of government was moved from Luang Prabang, which is inaccessible during certain months of the year, to Vientiane. This new capital was captured and occupied by the Burmese some years later, and although it was soon

[3] The royal house of Lan Xang claimed descent from Khoun Barom, who may have been a member of a princely family sent from Yunnan to direct and organize the Thai infiltration southwards. This legendary personage, who arrived on the banks of the Mekong on a white elephant, accompanied by two wives and an escort of civil servants, pages, musicians, maids of honour, and tirewomen, is reported to have brought with him regalia both for his own coronation and for that of his seven sons, who were predestined to found and rule over the Thai principalities of South East Asia.

evacuated by the invaders, the incursion marked the beginning of a troubled period during which the Burmese, profiting from a dynastic crisis, were able to impose their suzerainty over the kingdom. But the loss of independence failed to unite Lan Xang, and rival claimants continued to fight for the throne. Finally, an able monarch, Souligna Vongsa, succeeded in restoring unity and independence in 1637. During his reign in 1641 a Dutch trading mission was sent to Vientiane, led by a merchant named Gerrit Wuysthoff who wrote an account of his journey,[4] describing Lan Xang as a country endowed with natural wealth inhabited by a carefree, pleasure-loving people and ruled over by a monarch who maintained a luxurious and splendid court. On Souligna Vongsa's death in 1694 the succession was again disputed between rival claimants, with the result that three kingdoms were set up in the regions of Luang Prabang, Vientiane, and Champassak (Bassac) respectively.

The partition of Lan Xang led to internecine strife among the rulers which weakened their power to resist a foreign invader still further, and in 1778 the Siamese profited from this state of affairs, to impose their suzerainty upon them. In 1826 the King of Vientiane, Chao Anourouth, made a final attempt to free himself from Siamese domination and marched on Bangkok at the head of an army. But his troops were dispersed, and in the following year the Siamese, after capturing and sacking Vientiane, devastated the surrounding countryside and deported the population of the once opulent kingdom across the Mekong to the Korat plateau. The destruction of Vientiane left Luang Prabang open to Siamese attack, and the king in his perplexity turned to the Vietnamese Emperor for support; sending an embassy across the Annam mountain chain to the court of Hué in 1831, with the traditional gift of gold and silver flowers in token of vassalage. The dispatch of this embassy represented an acknowledgement of the paramount position which the Vietnamese now held in the peninsula, a position that had been acquired by the success of Vietnamese efforts to absorb the territories of their Indianized neighbours.

---

[4] 'Journael ofte daegelijcze aenteeckening van de reijse uijt het rijck van Cambodia naer der Lauwen landt, gehouden door den ondercoopman Gerrit Wuijsthoff', in Linschoten-Vereeniging, *De Oost-Indische Compagnie in Cambodja en Laos*, ed. by H. P. N. Muller (The Hague, 1917), pp. 149–229.

## GIAO CHI

The Vietnamese who had been cradled in the Red river delta appear to represent the result of cross-breeding between Indonesian tribal peoples and later Thai and Mongoloid emigrants from the north; a process which took place between the second century B.C. and the tenth century A.D., when Tongking and North Annam formed the Chinese border province of Giao Chi. The inhabitants of the Red river delta during this period adopted the agricultural methods used in South China, and also Chinese administrative methods, culture, and religious beliefs.

After conquering this area, which consisted at that time mostly of swamps and forests infested with wild beasts and crocodiles, the Chinese contented themselves at first with exacting tribute from the population, who continued to be ruled by their chieftains. But the arrival of emigrants from the central provinces of the great Han Empire, who were for the most part political exiles, landless men, and fugitives from justice, together with an increasing tendency on the part of Chinese officials to intervene directly in administrative matters, aroused popular resentment which culminated, in A.D. 40, in an insurrection led by the widow of a local chieftain, Trung Trac, whose husband had been put to death on the orders of a Chinese governor. After overwhelming the garrisons, Trung Trac and her sister Trung Nhi proclaimed themselves joint sovereigns of the liberated territory, but their reign was brief since in the following year an expeditionary force under the command of a veteran general was dispatched to reconquer the lost province, and in A.D. 43 the Trung sisters, with their army dispersed, were driven to commit suicide in the waters of the river Day. Nevertheless these warrior queens were to become symbols in Vietnamese legends of resistance to foreign oppression, and in later centuries pagodas were dedicated to their cult, while their memory continues to be celebrated to this day by artists and craftsmen who portray the sisters in watercolours, lacquer, or embroidery mounted on richly caparisoned elephants, amid a flurry of parasols, leading their troops into battle against the invaders.

The suppression was severe, and the chieftains implicated in the revolt were executed, degraded, or exiled, together with their families, to South China, while garrisons were established

at strategic points and a policy of assimilating the local population with the Chinese was pursued with vigour, a process
hastened by the adoption of the Chinese ideographic script and
system of education. Although the Vietnamese proved diligent
pupils, their industry and ability were inadequately recompensed; it was not till the end of the Chinese occupation that
they were allowed to compete on a footing of equality for entry
into the Chinese administrative service. Invidious distinctions
of this nature, which revealed Chinese contempt for a subject
and still barbarous people, together with some official rapacity
and the persistence of certain popular superstitions and customs,
including those of tattooing the body, coating the teeth with
black lacquer, and chewing betel nut, served to keep alive the
memory of their lost independence among the inhabitants of the
Red river delta.

The Chinese occupation survived the collapse of the Han
dynasty and the ensuing period of confusion, which ended with
the establishment of the Tang dynasty in A.D. 618. The liberal
policies and cosmopolitan outlook of the new rulers who
advanced the frontiers of the Empire to the shores of the
Caspian Sea, combined with the rise of a mercantile power, the
Sumatran kingdom of Srivivaja, which put down piracy in the
Malacca Straits, stimulated international trade and increased
the prosperity of South East Asia. The province of Giao Chi,
which was renamed the Protectorate-General of Annam, or the
'Pacified South', derived considerable advantage from this.
The population increased, the reclamation and settlement of
the Red river delta was pursued with vigour, and villages were
built similar to those which still ride, compact and raftlike,
on the deltaic plain behind a protective screen of bamboos and
areca palms. However, the disorders preceding the fall of the
Tang dynasty caused the Vietnamese to realize that in the
event of raids by mountain tribes or an attack from the sea the
Protectorate-General would have to rely upon its own resources,
and in 906 the Chinese Governor was driven out and replaced
by a local dignitary, the popular choice being later confirmed
by the last Tang Emperor.

During the next sixty years the Red river delta became the
prey of rival chieftains until in 968 one of their number, Dinh
Bo Linh, defeated his rivals and proclaimed himself king and
first Emperor of the Dinh dynasty (968–980). Dinh Bo Linh

then established the basis of future relations with China by sending an embassy to the Sung Emperor, who had just restored national unity, with a request that his authority over this outlying province should be officially confirmed. This embassy, after rejecting the rank of 'Governor' at first proposed for their sovereign, agreed to accept on his behalf the title 'Vassal King' and to remit the customary triennial tribute to the Chinese court. Formal acceptance of Chinese suzerainty was tempered by a tacit understanding that no attempt would be made to reassert Chinese authority over the lost territory. Moreover, although the ruler of the province of Giao Chi ranked as a vassal prince at the Chinese court, he was at liberty —if he should desire to perpetrate such a solecism—to style himself 'Emperor' in his relations with his subjects and also in his dealings with the barbarians on the fringes of the Chinese world.

The throne of the first Emperor of the Dinh dynasty was usurped by one of his generals, and it was not until 1010 that a stable dynasty was established in Annam. This dynasty—that of the Ly (1009–1225) was to provide the new state with public revenues, with an army, and with an administrative service, while the draining and settlement of the Red river delta was completed, dykes constructed, and the capital moved to Thang Long (Hanoi) in the centre of this rich agricultural area. Also under this dynasty a Chinese invasion of Tongking was repulsed, while the coastal plains down to the 17th parallel of latitude were annexed.

These two events indicated the future course of Vietnamese history, for the dynasties who succeeded each other upon the throne of Annam were faced with the dual task of defending the Red river delta against recurrent Chinese invasions and of making land available for the surplus population. Although the narrow coastal plains to the south were suitable for Vietnamese settlers, this territory was in the possession of a bellicose race of Indonesian origin and Indian culture, the Chams, who supplemented the agricultural resources of the area by trade and piracy. Consequently from the tenth to the seventeenth century the Vietnamese monarchs were engaged in a succession of wars which ended in the annexation of the Cham kingdom and the destruction of the Cham race.[5]

[5] Some 20,000 Chams still live in mud villages to the west of Phan Rang and near Phan Ri.

In 1225 the throne was usurped by the Tran dynasty, who were related by marriage to the Ly. The Tran kings at first turned their attention to administrative reforms and to the construction of dykes between Thang Long and the sea, but the disturbed state of Asia, where the armies of Genghis Khan were causing widespread destruction led them also to re-organize the army and to build a fleet. Fears of an invasion proved well founded: in 1257 a Mongol army which had conquered the Thai principality of Nanchao in western Yunnan advanced down the Red river valley and sacked the capital.

Tongking was again invaded in 1284, but although the whole country, with the exception of Thanh Hoa province, was over-run in the short space of two months by an immense army, the Mongols—who were harassed by guerrilla fighters, short of supplies, decimated by sickness, and perplexed by the difficulty of operating in a country where waterways replaced roads—proved unable to consolidate their conquest, and after suffering a reverse in the Red river delta withdrew to China. Although a third invasion took place three years later, the Mongols were on this occasion compelled to withdraw following the destruc-tion of a fleet which was bringing supplies to their armies. The Tran monarch then sent an embassy to Kublai Khan, the founder of the Yuan dynasty, and in return for homage and tribute peace was made and the former relations established with China.

Throughout the following century Chams and Vietnamese were engaged in a prolonged and inconclusive struggle during which the territory to the north of Tourane was annexed by the Vietnamese; on two occasions the Chams were able to invade Tongking. The devastation caused by these invasions aroused popular discontent and undermined the prestige of the dynasty, and in 1400 an ambitious regent, Le Qui Ly, profited from this disaffection to usurp the throne. Le Qui Ly, who adopted the name of Ho for his dynasty, then sent an embassy to the Chinese Emperor to announce his succession. The Emperor whose dynasty—the Ming—had driven out the Mongols, acting on the assurance that the Tran were extinct, agreed to recognize the usurper and invested him with the title of 'Vassal King', but in 1404 the arrival of a Tran pretender at his court pro-vided the Ming Emperor with a pretext to intervene in the affairs of the former Protectorate-General, and in the autumn of 1406 Chinese armies invaded Tongking and captured Thang Long. The invaders, who provoked defections by announcing that they intended merely to restore the Tran dynasty, completed their occupation of Annam by the spring of the following year. The conquered territory was then formally incorporated in the Empire and administered by officials who took drastic steps to enforce conformity with Chinese usages and customs. This policy, combined with the financial exactions of these officials, soon aroused popular resentment and in 1418 a wealthy landowner, Le Loi, raised the standard of revolt in Thanh Hoa province. At first Le Loi, who established his headquarters in wooded hill country, confined his activities to attacking supply columns and lightly held enemy positions, but in spite of these cautious tactics the position of his guerrilla force, which was twice dispersed by the Chinese and often faced with starvation, remained precarious. Finally, with the assistance of other guerrilla bands who had been operating independently against the Chinese, he was able to gain possession of the provinces of Thanh Hoa and Nghe An, and from this base he proceeded to attack the garrisons in the Red river delta.

The issue of the long war was decided in 1427, when the Chinese armies sent to the relief of the besieged garrison in Thang Long were defeated. Nevertheless after the Chinese troops and officials had left Tongking Le Loi sent an embassy to pay homage to the Chinese Emperor and resumed the triennial payments of tribute. This haste to re-establish amicable relations with a powerful neighbour was inspired by the desire to discourage further invasions and also by the fact that Annam remained a cultural dependency of China, for together with the Chinese legal code and calendar the Vietnamese had adopted Chinese political institutions and administrative methods.

### THE EMPIRE OF ANNAM

Under the Le dynasty, Vietnamese institutions assumed the form which they were to retain until the French conquest. The monarchy was both a ritual and an absolute monarchy: the 'First August Head', or Emperor, discharged the dual office of head of the state and sovereign pontiff, who in his capacity as 'Son of Heaven' was the representative of the divine power on earth, and in his role as 'Father and Mother' of his people was required to intercede with this power on behalf of his people. Although he could thus demand unquestioning obedience, the monarch also assumed personal responsibility for natural and political calamities, which he was accustomed to ascribe to some personal defect of character, or to some mistaken action on his part. Succession to the throne was by primogeniture; and the eldest son of the monarch's principal consort, who was the only member of the harem to have official status, usually succeeded his father, although sometimes a son who did not possess this qualification was designated as heir during his father's lifetime.

The monarch was assisted in the task of governing by six administrative departments—personnel, finance, rites, justice, armed forces and public works—and the activities of the administrative service were supervised by a tribunal of censors, who were chosen for their personal integrity and moral worth: these censors were also supposed to bring causes of popular discontent to the Government's attention and to rebuke court dignitaries and even the monarch himself for any failure to conform to Confucian precepts.

Officials staffing the administrative service—the mandarins—were divided into nine grades and recruited by a complicated system of examinations, in which knowledge of the Chinese classics, ability to write rhymed prose and verse, and skill at drafting edicts and official regulations were demanded of the candidate. The first step towards an administrative career was for the candidate to present himself at a preliminary examination, which took place each year in the provincial administrative centres. The survivors of this elementary test were then able to compete in examinations, which were held at three-yearly intervals in the regional capitals. These examinations were regarded as events of national importance and attracted thousands of candidates, who were segregated in an enclosure known as 'the Scholars' Camp', for one or two weeks. Successful candidates, who represented about 2 per cent. of the entrants, were awarded the diploma either of Bachelor or Master of Letters, and were thereby qualified to compete for that of Doctor or Professor of Letters in the examinations which took place likewise at three-yearly intervals in Thang Long. Here the recipients of these coveted diplomas were usually offered posts in the administrative service and became mandarins, while the obscure but honourable teaching profession absorbed most of the remainder. The acquisition of a diploma entitled the holder to consider himself a member of the 'Scholar Class', which was responsible for public administration and also for the education of Vietnamese youth.

The authority of the mandarins was limited, however, by a tendency under the Tran and Le dynasties to withdraw administrators from the village communities and to leave these communities to manage their own affairs through a Council of Notables who were responsible for public order, the execution of official decrees, and the collection of taxes; they were also required to keep a register containing particulars of the local population, these particulars being required to assess the fiscal contribution and also the quota of conscripts to be furnished by the community. The conscripts who were raised in this way either joined locally based territorial units, or were posted to the Imperial Guard, which was stationed in the capital. These units were officered by a hierarchy of military mandarins, who were divided into nine grades and recruited by competitive examinations, in which candidates for a commission were required to display physical aptitude for their profession and also some knowledge of the Chinese classics.

The army, which had been reduced to 100,000 men after the defeat of the Ming, was used in 1432 to suppress a rising in the mountainous region of Tongking, while it was again employed, forty years later, to invade Champa. This invasion was led by the king, Le Thanh Tong, and resulted in the final destruction of the Cham kingdom and the annexation of Cham territory situated to the north of Cape Varella. Eight years later another expedition against the Lao principalities in north-west Indochina led to the capture of Luang Prabang, the capital of the Lao kingdom of Lan Xang, and to the first appearance of a Vietnamese army on the banks of the river Mekong. After the death of Le Thanh Tong (1487) the power and prestige of the dynasty declined due to the accession of a series of debauched and incompetent monarchs, and in 1527 a general, Mac Dang Dung, after suppressing the contending factions in the name of the reigning Le monarch, usurped the throne.

The usurper was faced with the danger that the events which had marked the fall of the Tran dynasty would be repeated, for the Chinese emperor proved reluctant to confirm the legitimacy of the new dynasty. However, Mac Dang Dung was able to avert the threatened invasion by appearing at the frontier in person accompanied by forty-two members of his family bearing the registers containing particulars of the national revenue; and Chinese doubts about the legitimacy of the dynasty were finally laid at rest, after a distribution of bribes, by the cession of certain frontier districts, and the readiness of the usurper to accept the rank of 'Governor' instead of the title of 'Vassal King', with which the Vietnamese rulers had hitherto been invested. But although the Chinese had consented to be bought off, Mac Dang Dung had still to contend with the popular reluctance to recognize his authority. The dispossession of the Le dynasty, whose deeds had been enshrined in the national legend by the *literati* attached to their court, was generally resented, and in 1532 a Le pretender was proclaimed in the mountainous region bordering Thanh Hoa province by a general, Nguyen Kim.

The progress of the revolt was slow, but after a series of military successes the 'loyalists' established their control over the provinces of Thanh Hoa and Nghe An in 1543, and although Nguyen Kim died the leadership of the Le forces was assumed by his son-in-law, Trinh Kiem, who continued for the next twenty-five years to launch attacks in the delta and to repulse attempts by the Mac to recover the lost provinces. In 1592 Le armies under the command of Trinh Tung, who had succeeded his father Trinh Kiem, captured Thang Long and restored the Le dynasty, but although a Le monarch again reigned in Thang Long, Trinh Tung continued to govern the country, confining the sovereign to the discharge of his ritual and representative functions. Trinh Tung's refusal to divest himself of his authority alarmed his kinsman, Nguyen Hoang, who was the son of the general who had first championed the Le cause, and in 1600 he obtained permission to retire from the court to the southern provinces of Quang Tri, Thuan Thien, and Quang Nam, which were to become an appendage of his family. Nguyen Hoang's departure from Thang Long led to the partition of the kingdom into two principalities, named by the European traders and missionaries whose arrival was imminent Tongking and Cochin-China respectively. Although the Nguyen lords of Cochin-China continued to profess allegiance to the Le monarch, this allegiance was tempered by the objection that the suzerain had been illegally sequestrated by the Trinh, and after 1620 they refused to send the customary tribute.

The scission of the kingdom into rival principalities was brought about by the territorial expansion which had taken place at the expense of the Cham kingdom, resulting in the inclusion within the national frontiers of a coastal strip of territory consisting of a succession of narrow coastal plains backed by the dense forests of the Annam chain and separated from each other at several points by mountain spurs. Although the difficulty of administering this territory from Thang Long favoured a measure of local autonomy, the failure of the Trinh princes, who ruled over the wealthier and more populous part of the country, to prevent the establishment of an independent principality in the south may have been due partly to the presence in Tongking of representatives of the Mac dynasty, who maintained themselves, with Chinese assistance, in a principality centred around Cao Bang until 1676. The fact that the Nguyen, basing their defence on a system of fortifications in the vicinity of Dong Hoi, were able to bring to bear upon an attacking force cannons of a calibre superior to those which the Trinh could transport from their arsenal in Thang Long across the innumerable water-courses to Dong Hoi and to maintain the upper hand at sea may also have contributed to their successful resistance. Thus although the southern principality was attacked on seven occasions between 1627 and 1673 by the Trinh with vastly superior forces, from the security of their fortifications the Nguyen were able to scatter the hordes of infantry and elephants brought into line against them.

After the failure of their attack in 1673 the Trinh abandoned for a century further attempts to subdue the southern principality and turned their attention to the administrative reorganization of Tongking, while their military activities were confined, after the fall of the Mac principality, to reimposing Vietnamese suzerainty over the Lao kingdom of Vientiane. Meanwhile the Nguyen lords of Cochin-China were able to devote themselves to the territorial expansion of the principality southwards since after completing their absorption of Cham territory Vietnamese settlers were now infiltrating into the Khmer lands of the Mekong delta, and by the dual process of infiltration and settlement the frontiers of Cochin-China were extended, by the middle of the eighteenth century, to the shores of the Gulf of Siam and to the limits of the area which today constitutes South Vietnam.[6]

[6] South Vietnam was known as Lower Cochin-China to European traders and missionaries.

# II

# European Missionaries and Traders

WHILE the energies of the Vietnamese people were thus absorbed by the prolonged and inconclusive struggle between the Trinh and Nguyen princes, the Portuguese maritime power, which had established itself in India and South East Asia during the first half of the sixteenth century, continued its expansion eastwards and founded in 1557 a trading station at Macao on the Chinese mainland.

At first the traders and Jesuit missionaries peopling this distant outpost showed little interest in the Indochinese peninsula since their attention had been diverted by the favourable reception that both traders and missionaries were receiving in Japan. In 1614, however, after inquiries by the Japanese rulers had led them to suppose that Portuguese commercial and proselytizing activities constituted a threat to national independence, an imperial decree was issued banishing Jesuit missionaries from the Japanese islands. This decree compelled the Jesuits, who had founded a seminary at Macao, to turn their attention to other missionary fields.

In the same year a Portuguese merchant who had returned to Macao from trading in Cochin-Chinese waters drew the attention of the Jesuit Fathers to the hopes that might be entertained of converting the inhabitants of Cochin-China to the Christian faith, a suggestion which thus found the Jesuit Superior in Macao in a receptive mood. In the following year mass was celebrated on Easter Day in Tourane harbour by two Jesuit Fathers who had arrived on board a merchant ship.[1]

The headquarters of the mission were established in the same year at Fai Fo, a port some twenty miles south of Tourane, which was then the commercial centre of the Nguyen principality and frequented, from February till April, by Chinese and Japanese traders who exchanged porcelain, paper, tea, weapons, sulphur, saltpetre, lead, copper, woollen and cotton goods, silver coins and bars, for silk, precious woods, including

[1] One of these priests, Father Buzomi, was destined to remain in Cochin-China for twenty-four years.

eagle and camphor wood, sugar, musk, cinnamon, pepper, rice, and edible sea-birds' nests. The missionaries, who were welcomed by a group of Japanese Christians, lost no time in starting to evangelize the Vietnamese. Their labours proved fruitful, and by the following year 300 had been baptized.

The success achieved in the southern principality encouraged the Superior of the Jesuit Order to establish a mission in Tongking; and in 1627 a Jesuit missionary, Father Alexandre de Rhodes, was sent there. This missionary, who was well received by the Trinh lord in Hanoi, was able to make a number of converts among the families attached to the court, but the success of the missionaries alarmed the Vietnamese official class, who recognized that the new religion, with its accent on personal salvation, was incompatible with Confucian precept, and the women and staff of the royal harem, whose anxiety was aroused by the Christian approach to the institution of marriage. The Vietnamese rulers themselves also appear to have been conscious of the danger that the conversion of their subjects represented for the state, but as they were unable to establish the exact degree of interdependence between European traders and European priests, they feared that if they were to refuse to allow missionaries to land or were to cause them to be expelled or executed, they might deprive themselves by such action of the weapons and other products of European ingenuity and skill which served to promote the success of their armies and to enhance the splendour of their court. The presence of missionaries thus represented in their eyes a gauge of the good intentions of the trading community in Macao towards them. The early Jesuit missionaries, who were well versed in the ways of Eastern courts, were also careful to ingratiate themselves on their arrival by presenting gifts well calculated to appeal to a curious or jaded princely taste: gifts such as clocks or richly bound books printed in Chinese characters. Moreover, being abreast of scientific development, they were able on occasion to foretell an eclipse or to act in the delicate capacity of personal physician to the local ruler.

The collapse of the Portuguese maritime empire in the middle of the seventeenth century introduced another element which further confused the Vietnamese in their attempt to assess the power and significance of the West. In 1633 the first Dutch trading vessels from Batavia called at Fai Fo, where their arrival caused considerable displeasure to the Portuguese traders and missionaries. The Dutch also obtained permission, in 1637, to open a factory in Tongking.

Meanwhile, in spite of intermittent persecutions and some expulsions, the Jesuits in Cochin-China and Tongking proved so successful that they were soon in urgent need of assistance, and in 1645 Father Alexandre de Rhodes, who had been sent to Cochin-China after being expelled from Tongking,[2] went to Rome to explain the needs of the Catholic missions in Indochina. Here this enterprising priest availed himself of the opportunity to suggest that these needs could best be met by the ordination of Vietnamese priests by European bishops directly responsible to the Sovereign Pontiff,[3] but although this proposal was well received, a final decision was delayed out of consideration for the offence that the dispatch to the Far East of bishops directly appointed by, and responsible to, the Pope would cause the Portuguese.

Meanwhile Father Alexandre, who was himself a native of the Papal Comtat of Avignon, went to France in order to recruit personnel and to raise the necessary funds for the maintenance of these prelates. His appeal aroused interest in Paris since France was then entering upon a period of national expansion. The nobility and the merchant class thus welcomed an opportunity to establish a claim to intervene in a sphere of activity in which the Spanish and Portuguese had hitherto enjoyed a monopoly. Candidates for the episcopate were soon forthcoming and sufficient funds were subscribed for the maintenance of their dignity, but the Congregation for the Propagation of the Faith hesitated to give effect to the proposal. However, finally, in 1658, two French priests, François Pallu and Lambert de la Motte, were raised to the episcopate as bishops

[2] Father Alexandre later perfected a romanized script for the Vietnamese language.

[3] Portugal, in virtue of the Papal Bull of 1493, which established a line of demarcation between Spanish and Portuguese influence throughout the world,' claimed the right of ecclesiastical patronage throughout the Far East. It was apparent, however, by 1645 that the evangelization of this vast region was beyond the capacity of a small European power which had already overreached itself. Pope Gregory XV had already indicated that he was aware that the Portuguese right of patronage in the Far East should be circumscribed in the interests of Christendom, and had set up, in 1622, a Congregation for the Propagation of the Faith, composed of thirty cardinals, two bishops, and a secretary, who were charged with the task of asserting direct control over the whole field of missionary endeavour among heretics and the heathen.

of the extinct sees of Heliopolis and Beryte,[4] and appointed Vicars Apostolic of Tongking and Cochin-China respectively. The bishops were instructed to remain in close liaison with Rome and to base their conduct on the principle that the institution of Vicars Apostolic was primarily intended to hasten the formation of a native clergy from whose ranks bishops would be recruited in due course. They were also advised to adopt an attitude of prudent reserve towards political developments and matters of purely local interest in their vicariates and to show respect for the civilizations with which they would be in contact. After the Vicars Apostolic had left for the Far East a seminary was opened in Paris where priests were prepared for missionary work in that part of the world. This foundation later developed into the Society of Foreign Missions and assumed general responsibility for French missionary activities overseas.

Meanwhile the Vicars Apostolic, who appear to have been persuaded that the success of the enterprise would depend to some extent on the development of trade with France, had actively encouraged the formation of a 'China Company' with a charter which contained a formal acknowledgement of the commercial *cum* religious considerations inspiring the founders,[5] and when this Company failed to raise sufficient capital to embark on trading ventures in the Far East, Pallu and Lambert de la Motte drew the attention of the French East India Company[6] to the advantages which would be derived from the establishment of a factory in Tongking. However, the hostility then being shown by the Nguyen and Trinh princes towards European missionaries compelled the French bishops to establish themselves in Siam, where a general seminary for Asian priests was opened in 1666. After a Burmese invasion in 1765, this seminary was moved first to Hon Dat in Cochin-China and from there to Pondicherry.

---

[4] Extinct sees were chosen in order to mitigate the offence which the consecration of these bishops would cause the Portuguese.

[5] The charter included a clause to the effect that, as the principal object which had inspired the promoters was the desire to provide a passage for the bishops and their suite to enable them to work for the glory of God and the conversion of the heathen in the Empire of China, the kingdoms of Tongking, Cochin-China, and the adjacent islands, the aforesaid bishops should see that Company monies were not misappropriated and that sales and purchases were correctly entered in the appropriate ledgers by the Company's agents (quoted by J. Chesneaux, *Contribution à l'histoire de la nation vietnamienne* (1955), p. 55).

[6] Founded in 1664.

During the eighteenth century European trade with Indo-china lost much of its importance, partly due to a decision by the Trinh princes to abandon further attempts to conquer the southern principality by force of arms, and partly because of an increase in restrictions on foreign trade.[7] In 1697, therefore, the East India Company closed its factory in Tongking, while similar action was taken by the Dutch in 1761; thereafter European trade with Indochina was limited to occasional visits by merchant vessels from Macao and Batavia. By the eighteenth century missionary activities in Indochina had also lost much of their initial impetus since although the French Vicars Apostolic had succeeded, by the middle of the century, with papal support, in imposing their authority over the missionaries belonging to the regular orders—who had been reluctant at first to recognize the supersession of the Portuguese right of ecclesiastical patronage—lack of funds and a dearth of vocations in France now hampered their efforts.[8] Nevertheless, in spite of recurrent and on occasion severe persecution, the Vietnamese Christian community was estimated by the middle of the century to number 300,000.

## THE BISHOP OF ADRAN

In the last quarter of the century Vietnam became the theatre of a protracted and savage civil war which ravaged both the northern and the southern principality. This war, known as the Tay Son revolt, began in the mountainous region of Central Annam, whence it spread to the coastal plains; in 1773 the Tay Son, under the leadership of three brothers, Nhac, Lu, and Hué, who assumed the auspicious patronymic of Nguyen, captured Qui Nhon.[9]

Profiting from these disturbances the Trinh prince then

---

[7] The decline in commercial activities may also be ascribed to recognition on the part of the European traders themselves that the commercial potentialities of Indochina were limited and that Chinese merchants were more advantageously placed to cater for the limited popular demand for foreign, and particularly for Chinese, products.

[8] In 1774 the suppression of the Society of Jesus, which had been the first and the most active religious body engaged in missionary work in Indochina, enabled the French missionaries to extend their influence and activities.

[9] Tay Son seems to have been the name of the region around An Khe, where the rebels were first based.

invaded the southern principality and after overrunning the defences at Dong Hoi occupied Hué in 1775. In the following year the surviving supporters of the Nguyen dynasty were defeated in Lower Cochin-China by the Tay Son, who captured Gia Dinh (Saigon). Some years later, the youngest and most brilliant of the Tay Son brothers, Nguyen Hué, was encouraged by a dynastic dispute in Tongking to attack the northern principality, and after defeating the Trinh armies he proclaimed himself emperor. Meanwhile the Nguyen cause was represented by a claimant, Nguyen Anh, who lived the adventurous life of an outlaw in the mangrove swamps of the Ca Mau peninsula, and among the islands in the Gulf of Siam. During his wanderings the prince was sheltered and assisted by the Apostolic Vicar of Cochin-China, Mgr. Pigneau de Behaine, titular Bishop of Adran, who was then living at Ha Tien. The meeting between the Bishop and the Nguyen pretender was to have important political consequences, for Pigneau, who was a man of sanguine temperament, espoused the pretender's cause with zeal, and in spite of the consequences that such advice might entail for the Christian communities urged him to enlist France's aid against the Tay Son.

In 1784 Nguyen Anh, who was then a refugee in Siam, finally resigned himself to this course of action and after entrusting his heir, Prince Canh, who was then a child of four, together with the great seal of the principality to his care, authorized the Bishop to negotiate a treaty with the French Government. Pigneau then went to Pondicherry, and after a fruitless attempt to enlist the support of the Governor-General of the French settlements, he embarked, together with the prince and his suite, for Lorient, where his arrival in 1787 embarrassed the French Government. But the young prince in his exotic garb with his aura of misfortune, and flanked by his portly and dignified preceptor, formed a *tableau vivant* which aroused interest and sympathy at the court and in the Paris salons, while the Bishop's persuasive powers finally overcame the hesitations of a perplexed monarch and the reluctance of a bankrupt Government to embark on such an undertaking. In November 1787 a treaty was signed by the Count of Montmorin, the Foreign Minister, on behalf of Louis XVI, and by Pigneau on behalf of the King of Cochin-China, in which the former undertook to restore the latter to his throne in return for certain territorial concessions and the monopoly of European trade. However, the execution of this undertaking was entrusted to the Commander-in-Chief of the French establishments in India, who was privately informed that if he should consider it impracticable, he was at liberty to countermand the expedition.[10]

On his return to Pondicherry Pigneau, whose integrity and singleness of purpose had prevented him from divining these instructions, was soon in conflict with the Commander-in-Chief, whose refusal to go to the assistance of the dispossessed Cochin-Chinese prince bewildered and angered him. Finally, in 1789, the Bishop decided to act on his own initiative; and with such financial resources as he could raise from the merchant communities of Pondicherry and Mauritius he left for Cochin-China accompanied by about 100 French volunteers, who were for the most part naval personnel. On his arrival he was warmly welcomed by Nguyen Anh, who had profited in the preceding year from an outbreak of internecine strife among the Tay Son brothers to recapture Saigon and the provinces of Lower Cochin-China. Acting on the Bishop's advice, Nguyen Anh then employed some of the French volunteers to train his army, while others were entrusted with the tasks of supervising the construction of fortifications, founding field-pieces, and building ships which were similar to those in commission in European navies. The exact contribution made by the French volunteers to the final victory of the Nguyen cause is, however, difficult to establish since the majority, exhausted by the climate and disgruntled by the conditions of service and the low rates of pay, soon returned to India. But the conquest of Annam between the years 1791 and 1801 in a series of short campaigns in which Cochin-Chinese land forces equipped with field artillery co-operated effectively with a Cochin-Chinese fleet may probably be ascribed to their credit.

In 1799 Pigneau died at the siege of the Tay Son stronghold of Qui Nhon, but his death did not affect the outcome of the war since he had been predeceased by the ablest of the Tay Son brothers, Nguyen Hué, and the fortunes of war were no more to desert the Cochin-Chinese banners. The Bishop, whose robust constitution had been undermined by a liver disease, is

---

[10] It would thus seem that the treaty of 28 November 1787 represented in the eyes of the French Government merely a way of getting rid of the eloquent and strong-minded prelate.

reported to have regarded his approaching end as a release from his delicate position, since after his return to Saigon he had reluctantly assumed the role of counsellor in both civil and military affairs to Nguyen Anh. His position during the last ten years of his life must consequently have been unenviable: having committed himself irrevocably to the Nguyen cause, he was compelled to engage in activities which were both incongruous and a cause of scandal to the missionary priests of the regular orders.[11]

In spite of disagreements and misunderstandings, the French prelate and the Asian prince had nevertheless remained friends, and although Pigneau's affection for the irresolute, emotional, and tight-fisted prince had been sorely tried, Nguyen Anh for his part appears to have valued the advice and appreciated a friendship from which he had most to gain, as he had obtained at small cost to himself the technical assistance that he required, whereas the Bishop, whose justification for his intervention in Cochin-Chinese internal affairs had been based on the hope that his action would lead to the installation of a Christian prince upon the throne, admitted on his death-bed that this hope had proved vain.[12] Nevertheless the Bishop's role in the Tay Son revolt had at least demonstrated that French military intervention might provide an alternative to the commercial relations on which the Vicars Apostolic had hitherto founded their hopes of evangelizing Indochina.

In 1801 Nguyen Anh completed the rout of his enemies and captured Hanoi, where he proclaimed himself Emperor under the reign-name of Gia Long. This choice of reign-name reveals the achievement by which he wished to be remembered by posterity: that of the Emperor who had united the Vietnamese lands, which stretch from the southern capital of Gia Dinh, or Saigon, to the northern capital of Thanh Long, or Hanoi. As successor to Nguyen Hué, the youngest of the Tay Son brothers, whose authority had been formally recognized by the Chinese Emperor, Gia Long then dispatched envoys to Peking in 1802, to announce his victory and to request that he in turn should be invested with the title of Vassal King by his imperial suzerain. This was done in the following year when a Chinese

---

[11] Following the suppression of the Society of Jesus in 1774, Spanish priests belonging to the Dominican Order had replaced the Jesuit missionaries.
[12] Prince Canh died in 1801.

embassy bearing a new tributary seal arrived in Tongking.[13] Gia Long, who established his residence at Hué, which became the capital of the empire, was to devote his reign to alleviating the general distress caused by the war, and to organizing the administration of the empire. Particularist tendencies were recognized by setting up Governments-General in Lower Cochin-China and in Tongking under the authority of Viceroys, and the decimated ranks of the civil service were filled by reappointing those mandarins who had served the Trinh prince and by the resumption of the competitive entrance examinations. The revenues of the newly constituted state continued to be derived from the traditional taxes, and the financial contribution of the rich provinces of Lower Cochin-China was increased by a census of the population and a regional cadastral survey designed to establish the acreage under cultivation.

The reign of the Emperor Gia Long is principally remarkable for the number and importance of the public works undertaken. Repairs were carried out to the system of dykes in Tongking and arrangements made for their maintenance; communications were improved by the completion of a road from Hanoi to Saigon, a distance of some 1,300 miles, while relays of messengers were recruited and staging posts established to enable the central Government in Hué to maintain contact with the local authorities in Tongking and Cochin-China. The principal strategic centres were also secured by the construction of vast and elaborate fortifications similar to those built under the supervision of the French volunteers, who had served as mercenaries against the Tay Son. Although the erection of these fortifications, which was carried out by impressed and unpaid labour, is reported by French missionaries to have provoked much popular discontent, the royal authority was sufficiently well established on Gia Long's death in 1820 for him to transmit the throne to his fourth son, Minh Mang.[14]

---

[13] Whereas Le Loi had named the territories over which he ruled Dai Viet, or the Great [country of the] Viet, Gia Long changed this name on his accession to that of Vietnam, or the [country inhabited by] the Viet of the South. The Chinese, however, continued to refer to the area as Annam, or the Pacified South.

[14] The tomb which the Emperor built for his last resting place represents a final tribute to the French volunteers who accompanied the sanguine Bishop of Adran on his return to Cochin-China. In a site of melancholy beauty, the founder of the dynasty has chosen to lie, with his Empress beside him, in a bleak quadrangle

## THE EMPEROR MINH MANG

The Emperor Minh Mang, whose reign marks the apogee of the Nguyen dynasty, was to complete the unification of the Vietnamese lands by extending a uniform administrative system to the three regions which formed the empire. The creation of a strong and centralized state also enabled the Vietnamese to reassert their influence in Cambodia, and in the Laotian principalities where the Siamese, profiting from the protracted civil war, had been able to secure a predominant position. Nevertheless, although the reign of Minh Mang appeared to represent a period of national revival, the country was not in fact to escape the intellectual and economic stagnation which paralysed states ruled according to Confucian principles during the nineteenth century.

Minh Mang's accession had been regarded with dismay by the European missionaries, who had profited from his predecessor's tolerance to increase their activities throughout the country. It was well known that Minh Mang, who was conservative in his tastes and attached to the cultural heritage received from China, was opposed to the spread of Christianity among his people. However, the new Emperor was preoccupied during the first years of his reign with the task of securing his throne and imposing his authority, and he concealed for some years his intentions in regard to the Catholic missions. Finally, in 1825, on hearing a report that a French missionary had landed clandestinely at Tourane, he promulgated an edict enjoining provincial governors to prevent a recurrence of such incidents on the grounds that 'the perverse religion of the Europeans corrupts the heart of man'. This edict was welcomed by the official class, who shared the Emperor's conviction that a religion which compelled its adepts to abandon ancestor worship and traditional ritual observances constituted a threat to the existence of the state.

The impending persecution was only postponed by the action of Le Van Duyet, the Viceroy of Lower Cochin-China, who intervened in favour of the Christian communities. On the death of this influential Viceroy, however, Minh Mang was able to take measures to eradicate the Catholic faith from his

protected by strong and unadorned walls which recall to mind some fort of minor strategic importance in a French frontier zone.

dominions, and by an edict promulgated in 1833 the profession of Christianity was declared a crime punishable by death, while orders were issued that buildings which had served either for the celebration of the mass, or to house Catholic priests should be demolished. The implementation of this edict was to result in the execution, imprisonment, or exile of a number of European missionaries.

In July of that year Le Van Duyet's adopted son, Le Van Khoi, raised the standard of revolt in Lower Cochin-China. The rising, which is reported to have received some support from the local Christian communities, was at first successful, but this success proved short-lived and the rebels were soon forced to take refuge in Saigon, which fell to Minh Mang's armies in 1835. The presence among the captives of a French missionary, Father Marchand, who is alleged to have acted as counsellor to the rebels, confirmed Minh Mang in his suspicions regarding the subversive activities of European missionaries and the dubious loyalty of his Christian subjects. Consequently in 1836 a further edict closed Vietnamese ports, with the exception of Tourane, to European shipping, while the death penalty was decreed against foreign missionaries discovered in the country.

Towards the end of his reign the activities of European powers in Far Eastern waters caused Minh Mang some misgivings, and in 1840 a delegation was sent to Europe in order to investigate European intentions towards Vietnam. Although the arrival of the Vietnamese mandarins in France aroused popular interest, their attempt to negotiate a commercial treaty, which constituted the ostensible motive for their visit, failed, this failure being ascribed to the Directors of the Society of Foreign Missions[15] who successfully checkmated the delegation's efforts. Despite the fact that the French Government was reluctant at that time to admit the existence of any national obligation to protect missionaries from the perils to which they exposed themselves, the recognition by Pope Gregory XVI of French primacy in the Far Eastern missionary field in 1839, together with a revival of national interest in missionary activities, had placed the Society in an influential position.

Minh Mang's death in 1842 led to no improvement in the lot of the Christian communities, but his successor, Thieu Tri,

[15] The Society of Foreign Missions had been re-established after the Revolution.

alarmed by the establishment of the British at Hong Kong, hesitated to have missionaries put to death for fear that such action might provoke European intervention.

Meanwhile the success of British efforts to open the Chinese market to European trade had caused the French Government to station a naval squadron in the China Seas with orders to protect French missionaries, if such action could be carried out without exposing the French flag to possible affront and without resorting to force. These instructions were interpreted in the widest sense by French naval officers serving in the Far East since in spite of the changes brought about by the Revolution, the French navy remained as a body attached to the Catholic faith and retained a traditional belief in the importance of expansion overseas; these sentiments were, moreover, reinforced by the fact that the possession of a naval base where vessels operating in Far Eastern waters could be refitted represented an urgent naval requirement. Accordingly in 1843 the commanding officer of a French corvette, who had heard that five missionaries were imprisoned at Hué, proceeded on his own initiative to Tourane, where he presented a demand for their release to the local mandarins. Although this demand was officially rejected Thieu Tri, impressed by the tenacity and threats of reprisal proffered by this officer, feigned an impulse of 'immense benevolence' and liberated the captives. Two years later a similar intervention carried out on the orders of the Admiral commanding the French naval squadron resulted in the release from prison, against a receipt in due form, of Mgr. Lefebvre, the coadjutor to the Vicar Apostolic of Annam.

In 1847 the French Commander-in-Chief in person visited Tourane on board the frigate *La Gloire*, escorted by a corvette, *La Glorieuse*, to demand the release of the undaunted Mgr. Lefebvre, who had again been arrested following his clandestine return to the country. On this occasion, however, the French naval force found five Vietnamese corvettes built on European lines in the harbour, while the local mandarins refused to accept a letter in which the Commander-in-Chief informed the Emperor of Annam that permission had been accorded by his suzerain the Chinese Emperor for the Christian religion to be practised within his dominion, and requested that Vietnamese Christians should be granted a similar privilege.

The deadlock finally provoked the French into sending

boarding-parties, who removed the sails from the corvettes, and some days later, acting on the assumption that they were about to be attacked, the French opened fire upon the Vietnamese vessels. The engagement, in which untrained Vietnamese crews, serving guns which were both outclassed and in many cases unserviceable, proved unable 'in spite of their despair' to retaliate effectively, resulted in the destruction of the five corvettes with heavy loss of life. After this action the French Commander-in-Chief, who now realized that he was unable to compel the Emperor to grant concessions to his Christian subjects, sailed away and left the missionaries and Christian communities to face the extreme displeasure of Thieu Tri, who in an outburst of hysterical rage ordered that all articles from Europe in his palace should be smashed, and personally assisted in this work of destruction.

On Thieu Tri's death at the end of 1847 his successor, Tu Duc, seemed ready to adopt a more tolerant attitude towards the missionaries. In 1851, however, the Emperor, who had reason to suppose that his elder brother was seeking to enlist European support for his claims to the throne, promulgated an edict placing a price on the head of the mission priests.

Meanwhile, following the overthrow of the Orléans dynasty in France, the Prince-President Louis Napoleon had been able, with Catholic support, to prepare the way for the proclamation of the Second Empire in December 1851. The new régime was to provide more effective support for French missionary activities and to adopt a policy which was to lead to the conquest of Indochina. However, before resorting to force the French Government made a final attempt to open the country to French trade and to secure freedom of worship for Vietnamese Christians by peaceful means. But as the arrival of the diplomatic mission charged with conducting these negotiations had been preceded by a naval bombardment of the harbour forts at Tourane, this attempt proved abortive, and the French envoy, Charles de Montigny, was able to do no more than warn the Vietnamese authorities that the persecution of the Christian minority would entail grave consequences. The shelling of the forts at Tourane combined with the failure of the attempt to negotiate a settlement filled the missionaries with foreboding; they had learnt to their cost that isolated action by naval forces operating along the coast of Vietnam served only to increase the danger of their position. These fears proved well founded, for in 1857 another imperial edict led to an intensification of the persecution.[16]

## MISSIONARY INFLUENCE

Although most of the missionaries disclaimed any desire to influence French policy some of the Vicars Apostolic, mindful of the precedent set up by the Bishop of Adran, were tempted to pursue the secular dream of placing a Christian prince upon the throne of Annam. Mgr. Pellerin, the Vicar Apostolic of Upper Cochin-China, belonged to the more forceful school of missionary thought, and in 1856, when he heard that the captain of a French corvette at Tourane required an interpreter, he set out to offer his services. In this capacity he was present at the ensuing meeting between de Montigny and the mandarins, and following the Vietnamese refusal to negotiate he went to Hong Kong where, with the approval of the coadjutor of the Society of Foreign Missions, he took passage to Europe.

Pellerin's arrival in Paris proved opportune since a special Commission had been set up in the spring of 1857 to consider the advisability of occupying a base on the Cochin-China coast. After examining the international implications of such an action, and listening to the evidence of missionaries, including Pellerin, the Commission decided unanimously that it was morally, politically, and commercially in French interests to occupy without delay three towns in Cochin-China. The Commission did not advise any annexation of territory but favoured the maintenance of the reigning dynasty under French protection.

The French Government decided to act on these recommendations, and in November Admiral Rigault de Genouilly, commanding the French naval division in the Pacific, was ordered to occupy and garrison the port and village of Tourane. The Admiral was given no definite instructions in regard to the nature of the relations that he should then establish with the

[16] Montezon and Estave, *Missions de la Cochinchine et du Tonkin* (1858), quoted in G. Taboulet, *La Geste française en Indochine* (1955), i. 398. The persecutions between October 1853 and July 1857 are reported to have claimed a total of 95 victims, 44—including six Europeans—being martyred in Cochin-China, while 51, including eight Europeans, were martyred in Tongking.

Vietnamese Government, and it was left to his discretion to decide whether future relations between France and Annam should be governed by a treaty or whether national interests would best be served by establishing a protectorate. The signing of the Treaty of Tientsin in June 1858 enabled Rigault de Genouilly to carry out these instructions, and a combined Franco-Spanish squadron of fourteen ships finally appeared off Tourane in September of that year.[17]

[17] The Spanish contingent, consisting of a sloop and 1,000 Spanish-officered Filipino troops, had joined the French force in order to avenge the martyrdom in Tongking of Mgr. Diaz, an elderly Spanish Vicar Apostolic.

# III

# The Conquest

THE Franco-Spanish force was able to silence the harbour forts and occupy the village of Tourane without difficulty, but Pellerin, who appears to have accompanied the expedition in the capacity of a recruiting sergeant, failed to raise a labour force from among the local Christian communities, and the intelligence which he obtained concerning the enemy intentions proved to be inaccurate. Moreover the Bishop adopted a critical attitude towards the conduct of the military operations, blamed the Admiral for his initial hesitation to attack Hué, and recommended that the local stalemate should be broken by an attack on Tongking: a recommendation based on his assumption that the Christian communities, and indeed the whole population, exasperated by the oppression of the mandarins and loyal to the dispossessed Le dynasty, would rise to support the invaders. This proposal was rejected and its author, whose failure to indicate the nature of the difficulties that the expeditionary force would encounter at Tourane had caused general irritation, was shipped back to Hong Kong.

In February 1859 Rigault de Genouilly re-embarked the bulk of his troops for an attack on Saigon, for he calculated that the occupation of Lower Cochin-China, which supplied 80,000 tons of grain yearly to Annam, would prove a valuable asset and would compel the court of Hué to negotiate a settlement. The attack was successful, and after the destruction of the forts guarding the entrance to the Donnai river Saigon fell to the invaders. A small garrison consisting of 800 French and 100 Filipino troops was then installed in part of the captured fortifications, while Rigault de Genouilly himself, together with the main force, moved back to Tourane, where negotiations were opened with the court. These negotiations made little progress, however, and when it became apparent that the French would be required to furnish a contingent for impending military operations against China, the decision was taken to evacuate Tourane, an operation which was completed by March 1860.

The ratification of the Treaty of Peking in October of that

year enabled a French force under the command of Admiral Charner to go to the relief of Saigon, where the garrison was besieged by an army made up of regular troops, contingents of volunteers, and soldier settlers whose colonization of Lower Cochin-China had been encouraged by the Nguyen rulers. In February 1861 Charner's fleet, transporting a force of 4,000 men, again forced the passage of the river Donnai and arrived at Saigon. After evicting a Vietnamese force from their entrenchments, Charner's troops proceeded to occupy the approaches to the town, and the area under French control was extended in April by the seizure of My Tho, a town commanding one of the mouths of the river Mekong.

Towards the end of the year Charner handed over his command to Admiral Bonard, who was to become the first Governor of Cochin-China.[1] The new Commander-in-Chief improved the French position by occupying the provinces of Bien Hoa and Baria, and in March 1862 French forces captured the town of Vinh Long, situated on a large island in the Mekong delta, which had become a centre of Vietnamese resistance.

Meanwhile the disturbed state of Tongking, where government forces were powerless to arrest the progress of a revolt, combined with the embarrassment caused by the loss of rice supplies from the south, finally induced the court of Hué to negotiate, and a delegation invested with full powers was sent to Saigon where a treaty was signed in June 1862. By its terms France acquired the three eastern provinces of Cochin-China, together with the island of Poulo Condore, while French naval and merchant vessels were accorded free passage up the Mekong river to Cambodia; Roman Catholic missions were authorized to propagate their faith, and both France and Spain were given the right to trade in the ports of Tourane, Ba Lat, and Quang Yen. The Vietnamese Government also undertook to cede no territory to a foreign power without French consent and to pay an indemnity calculated in a Mexican silver coin, the piastre, which had a wide circulation in the Pacific area.

[1] After the conquest Lower Cochin-China became known to the French as Cochin-China, while the central portion of the truncated empire was called Annam, the name formerly used to describe the three regions or *Ky*, comprising Tongking, Cochin-China, and Lower Cochin-China, over which the Emperors had ruled.

## THE FRENCH ADMIRAL-GOVERNORS

The administration of the ceded provinces presented a considerable problem to the French admirals who were to govern the new colony, for the mandarins, in obedience to instructions from Hué, had withdrawn. The admirals were thus faced with the task of administering an area where the only remaining unit was represented by the village commune. The problem was solved by seconding naval officers, who were paid handsome salaries and were put in control of the local functionaries. Known as 'inspectors of indigenous affairs' these officers were responsible for administrative, judicial, and financial matters within their respective districts, but as they possessed only a sketchy knowledge of the language and local customs they were compelled to rely upon Vietnamese interpreters and clerks, whose readiness to serve the French authorities was in many cases inspired by questionable motives. The Admiral-Governors were also hampered in their administrative task by the need to raise substantial revenues in order to reconcile French political opinion to the retention of the conquered territory.

Since the Vietnamese monarch, Tu Duc, was reluctant to resign himself to the loss of this territory, he resolved to try to recover the lost provinces by negotiating a settlement with the French Government, and in June 1863 an imposing delegation embarked for France. Their arrival was well timed, as French intervention in Mexico was then threatening to involve France in large-scale military operations in Central America. Moreover the Vietnamese proposals were backed up by a naval officer, Captain Aubaret, who occupied the post of chief inspector of indigenous affairs in Saigon. This officer submitted a report to Napoleon III in which, after forecasting that the administration of the three provinces would involve the French authorities in difficulties, he proposed that the French Government should return the captured territory to the Vietnamese and limit the French occupation to Saigon, Cap St. Jacques, and the control of the river Donnai. In compensation France would demand the payment of a perpetual tribute. These recommendations were adopted by the French Government; and Aubaret was instructed to negotiate a treaty with the court of Hué on these lines, but although the proposed treaty was in fact negotiated and signed, the combined opposition of the

French Admiralty and shipping and commercial interests proved sufficiently powerful to prevent its subsequent ratification by the French National Assembly.

Meanwhile popular resistance to the French occupation continued to be represented by armed bands who received clandestine support from the provinces of West Cochin-China, which remained under Vietnamese administration. In June 1867, therefore, French forces under the command of Admiral de La Grandière occupied the western provinces of Vinh Long, An Giang, and Ha Tien, which were then annexed to the colony. The despair of Tu Duc at this further loss of territory is revealed in an imperial edict promulgated at that time, in which he expressed his personal grief and profound concern at his inability to formulate a policy capable of redressing the situation.

There have never been so many disastrous events as in our times [lamented the Emperor]; there have never been such great misfortunes as have happened this year. . . . Above me I fear the decrees of Heaven, and when I look beneath me, compassion for the people weighs on me day and night. I tremble and blush at one and the same time while I assume without faltering all the odium for these misfortunes, so that the people shall bear no part of the responsibility. But before atonement can be made fresh calamities assail us. Truly one does not know what to say, or what to do in order to help the subjects of this kingdom.[2]

## THE FRENCH PROTECTORATE OVER CAMBODIA

The occupation of West Cochin-China left the French in sole possession of an open and disputed frontier with Cambodia, and Bonard had been quick to appreciate the danger which the occupation of this weak buffer kingdom by a hostile power would represent for the French colony: a danger which had also been stressed by his unofficial political adviser, Mgr. Miche, the Vicar Apostolic of Cambodia, who had been engaged for some years past in persuading the Cambodian monarch that he would derive great benefit from a close association with France. Miche was also of the opinion that France had acquired, together with the Cochin-Chinese provinces, suzerainty over Cambodia since in the seventeenth century the Nguyen lords

[2] Quoted by Chesneaux, pp. 119–20.

had profited from the recurrent dynastic disputes in the neighbouring kingdom to impose their overlordship upon the Cambodian kings and to wrest from them the deltaic plains of
Cochin-China.

Vietnamese claims to suzerainty over Cambodia had been
disputed, however, by the Siamese; and after a century and a
half of intermittent and inconclusive strife, during which the
Siamese had compensated themselves for Vietnamese territorial
gains by extending their jurisdiction over the provinces of
Battambang, Sisophon, and Siem Reap (Angkor), a treaty had
been signed by the rival monarchs in 1845. This stipulated that
Vietnamese and Siamese troops should be withdrawn from
Cambodian soil, confirmed the Siamese in possession of the
provinces of Stung Treng, Tonle Repou, and Mlu Prey, which
they had occupied in 1814, and imposed their dual suzerainty
upon the Cambodian king.

The French occupation of Cochin-China had now destroyed
this uneasy arrangement, and the Siamese further reinforced
their position in 1862 by restoring the Cambodian king,
Norodom, to his throne, from which he had been evicted after a
brief reign. Accordingly in September of the same year Bonard
profited from an official inspection in the provinces of My Tho
and Vinh Long to continue his journey to Udong, where he
paid his respects to Norodom. This action was followed up in
June 1863 by his successor, de La Grandière, who decided,
without consulting the French Government, to establish a
naval station in Cambodia and sent a sloop, the *Gia Dinh*, under
the command of an energetic officer, Lt. Doudart de Lagrée,
to Udong with orders to make a geological survey and establish
contact with the king.

The dispatch of the sloop proved timely and served to
strengthen the hand of Miche, who was then engaged, unknown
to de Lagrée, in secretly negotiating with the king for the
establishment of a French protectorate. By July 1863 the
negotiations were sufficiently far advanced for de La Grandière
to pay a visit to Udong, where a treaty was signed on 11 August,
'transforming' French suzerain rights into a protectorate. But
as the Admiral-Governor had merely been authorized by the
French Government to take soundings, the signatories agreed
that the treaty should remain secret until it had been ratified
by the French emperor.

Discretion was not, however, a characteristic either of the debonair monarch or of his entourage, with the result that the Siamese Resident was soon informed of the situation and carried out an effective counter-move. This took the form of a second secret treaty formally entrusting Siam with Cambodia's defence and internal security, which Norodom was persuaded to sign in the capacity of a viceroy, or governor—a status which automatically invalidated the French treaty. Moreover the Siamese insisted that Norodom's coronation should take place in Bangkok, where he had deposited the regalia on his flight from Udong.

In March 1864 Norodom agreed to this condition and, disregarding de Lagrée's stern warning that his departure would be the signal for the French to occupy his capital, set out for Siam; the French officer then landed a naval party, hoisted the tricolour flag over the palace, and fired a salute of twenty-one guns. This resolute action, which was supported by the arrival of reinforcements consisting of three gun-boats and a party of 100 marines, alarmed the king, who abandoned his journey and returned in haste.

Meanwhile de La Grandière's treaty had been ratified in December 1863 and the Siamese Government, disturbed by the expansion of British influence in South East Asia, decided to abandon a policy which threatened to bring them into conflict with the French. They therefore agreed to return the regalia to Udong, where Norodom was crowned in June 1864. A treaty was then negotiated which was signed on 15 July 1867: by its terms Siam renounced all claims to suzerainty over Cambodia and recognized the French Protectorate, while France formally confirmed Siam in possession of the provinces of Battambang, Sisophon, and Siem Reap.[3]

The settlement gave the French a free hand to bring order and settled government to a kingdom which had been reduced by centuries of invasion and civil war to a state bordering on anarchy. But although the seat of government was moved in the same year from Udong to a more accessible site, the Quatre Bras at the mouth of the Tonle Sap, Norodom showed marked reluctance to institute the necessary reforms, dissipated the public revenues, and eluded all attempts by the French Resident

[3] These provinces were later restored to Cambodia under agreements signed in 1904 and 1907 respectively.

to bring him to book. Finally, on the night of 17–18 June 1884, the Governor of Cochin-China, M. Thomson, accompanied by an armed guard, surprised the king in his palace and obtained his signature to a convention which deprived him of control over public revenues, customs, and public works, and provided him with a fixed civil list. This drastic action not unnaturally aroused resentment and led to widespread unrest, and two years later the French renounced the advantage they had gained and agreed to observe the terms of the treaty of 1863.

## THE FRENCH PROTECTORATE OVER ANNAM AND TONGKING

The establishment of a French protectorate over the lower reaches of the Mekong aroused interest in this great river, which was believed to represent a route to the rich land-locked provinces of South China. Permission was therefore obtained from Paris for an attempt to be made to map its course and discover its source, and in 1866 an expedition set out from Saigon under the leadership of Doudart de Lagrée. The explorers endured great hardship, which resulted in de Lagrée's death from illness and exhaustion in March 1868, but although the search for the Mekong's source was abandoned, the expedition was at least able to discover that whereas the Mekong was not navigable, the Red river probably offered an alternative route to the Chinese province of Yunnan. This discovery drew the attention of the authorities in Saigon and also of business interests in France to the commercial possibilities of the populous Red river delta, and led a French merchant-adventurer and arms trafficker, Jean Dupuis, to make an attempt to open this route to trade. Dupuis had made an arms deal with a Chinese military commander engaged in suppressing a revolt of the Moslem population in western Yunnan, and he decided to ship a consignment of war material which he had contracted to deliver by way of the Red river. In order to facilitate the passage of these arms through Tongking, the Chinese general provided him with a *laissez-passer* addressed to the local Vietnamese authorities. Dupuis then returned to France to procure this war material and to interest the French Admiralty in his venture, but, although he received no official encouragement in Paris, he was assured, on his arrival in Indochina, by the

Governor of Cochin-China *per interim*, that a naval vessel would be sent at regular intervals to Tongking to check up on the progress of his expedition.

Accordingly, in November 1872 Dupuis appeared with a flotilla consisting of two gun-boats, a launch, and a large junk in one of the mouths of the Red river, and asked permission to proceed upstream to the Chinese frontier. The Vietnamese authorities with some justification refused to recognize the validity of the *laissez-passer* furnished by the Chinese military commander in Yunnan, but Dupuis nevertheless sailed up the river to Hanoi, where his arrival caused great excitement. The mandarins then tried to persuade Dupuis to renounce his project, enlisting for this purpose the good offices of Mgr. Puginier, the Vicar Apostolic of West Tongking. Finally, in January 1873 Dupuis, ignoring these official remonstrances, left Hanoi and successfully overcame all the obstacles placed in the way of his passage upstream. Three months later he crossed the Chinese frontier and, after delivering the consignment of war material, returned by the same route to Hanoi, where he announced his intention of again proceeding to Yunnan with a cargo of salt. Alarmed by the manifest inability of their representatives in Tongking either to prevent or to discourage this enterprise, the court of Hué then appealed to the French authorities in Cochin-China for help in evicting the intruder.

This gave Admiral Dupré, the Governor of Cochin-China, the opportunity to intervene, and he dispatched a force of about 200 sailors and marines to Tongking, under the command of Francis Garnier, a naval lieutenant on half-pay, who had played a distinguished part in the exploration of the river Mekong. Garnier was instructed to act as arbitrator in the dispute between Dupuis and the Tongkingese authorities and 'to protect commerce in opening the country and its river to all nations under the protection of France'.[4] On his arrival in Hanoi Garnier was soon involved in a dispute with the Vietnamese authorities, as he insisted that he had come to supervise the opening of the Red river to international commerce, but the Vietnamese maintained that he had been sent to remove Dupuis. Official relations finally deteriorated to such an extent that Garnier, considering that the safety of his force was threatened by Vietnamese military preparations, stormed and

[4] Le Thanh Khoi, *Le Viet-Nam* (1955), p. 374.

captured the Hanoi citadel. Then with the small military force at his disposal he proceeded to capture the delta towns of Phu Ly, Hai Duong, Ninh Binh, and Nam Dinh. On 21 December Garnier was killed in a skirmish outside Hanoi, and Dupré, who had now (January 1874) received instructions from the French Government to the effect that no offensive operations were to be undertaken in Tongking, was compelled to return his embarrassing conquest, an action which delivered the Christian communities who had contributed towards the success of the operation into the hands of the Hué Government.[5]

Nevertheless Garnier's successful operations in Tongking had alarmed the Emperor Tu Duc, who signed on 15 March 1874 a treaty of 'peace, friendship, and perpétual alliance' at Hué. This treaty established an ill-defined form of French protectorate, for the Empire of Annam undertook to align its foreign policy with that of France, and recognized French sovereignty over the lost provinces of Cochin-China, while a French Resident, with the rank of Minister, was to be accredited to the court. The ports of Qui Nhon, Haiphong, and Hanoi were also to be made available to French vessels and the Red river was to be opened to navigation between the Chinese frontier and the sea.

With its prestige impaired, however, the Vietnamese Government proved incapable of re-establishing its authority in Tongking, where bands of Chinese irregulars, representing the remnants of the military forces who had fought for the Taipings in South China, were in control of the frontier region. The Emperor of Annam, who did not consider that the treaty with France had affected his position as vassal of the Chinese Emperor, therefore appealed to Peking for assistance against these intruders, and in response to this appeal Chinese regular troops moved into the provinces of Lang Son, Cao Bang, Thai Nguyen, and Bac Ninh.

Alarmed by this situation the French Government authorized Le Myre de Vilers, the Governor of Cochin-China, to reinforce the contingent guarding the French concession in Hanoi and in March 1882 he dispatched two companies of marines under Captain Rivière, the Commander of the naval division in Cochin-China, who was instructed to bear in mind that his force was intended primarily to protect the French consulate from surprise attack, while the extension of French influence in

[5] A. Thomazi, *La Conquête de l'Indochine* (1934), p. 132.

Tongking was to be achieved by political and pacific means. Shortly after his arrival, however, the hostility of the Vietnamese Governor, combined with the reinforcements of the local garrison and evidence that repairs were being carried out to the fortifications, convinced Rivière that his small force was exposed to the danger of a surprise attack. On 25 April, therefore, he attacked and captured the citadel. The ensuing sequence of events followed closely the pattern of Garnier's brief campaign in the Red river delta, for Nam Dinh and the site of the anthracite mines at Hon Gay were occupied by detachments of French troops in 1883 and on 19 May of that year Rivière himself was killed in the course of an engagement with Chinese 'irregulars' near Hanoi.

On this occasion, however, Rivière's action was to lead to the French occupation of Tongking since shortly before his death the French National Assembly had voted a supplementary credit for the dispatch of a force of 3,000 metropolitan troops to Indochina, while the appointment was announced of a civilian Commissioner-General, who was entrusted with the task of organizing the protectorate. On 30 July 1883 this Commissioner-General, Dr. Harmand, met Admiral Courbet, commanding the naval division in Tongking, and General Bouët, Senior Commandant in Saigon, in Haiphong, where a plan of operations was drawn up. This was designed to evict the enemy from their fortified positions between the river Day and the Red river, while Courbet carried out a seaborne attack upon the forts at Thuan An which commanded the approaches to Hué, on 20 August. After the fall of these forts, the Vietnamese Government requested an armistice, and on 25 August a treaty was signed whereby the court of Hué formally recognized the French Protectorate.

Before the French attack the death of the Emperor Tu Duc on 17 July 1883 had opened a prolonged dynastic crisis, since two of the Regents appointed by the deceased Emperor, Nguyen Van Tuong and Ton That Thuyet, now sought to place upon the throne a prince who would be both subservient to their authority and prepared to offer resolute opposition to the French. The Emperor's heir Duc Duc, who was not considered to offer the necessary guarantees, was therefore deposed and immured in a pavilion to die of hunger and thirst, while his successor, Hiep Hoa, was bludgeoned to death with wooden staves on the suspicion that he was engaged in negotiating with the French. The terrible Regents then selected a boy of 14, Kien Phuc, who had to be dragged from under a bed to occupy the blood-stained throne of Annam.[6] Meanwhile in Tongking the French expeditionary force, with the assistance of interpreters, coolies, and militia provided by the Christian communities,[7] captured the town of Son Tay at the end of the year.

In May 1884 by the Convention of Tientsin the Chinese Government also recognized the French Protectorate over Vietnam and undertook to withdraw the Chinese garrisons from Tongking, and on 6 June a second Franco-Vietnamese treaty was signed at Hué, confirming the French Protectorate over Annam and Tongking. By the terms of this treaty Annam was allowed to retain a measure of internal administrative autonomy, while Tongking was to be controlled by French Residents established in the provincial towns, where they would exercise the right of general supervision over the Vietnamese administration. A Resident-General charged with the implementation of these arrangements was to reside in the citadel of Hué, where he would have the privilege of being received in private audience by the Emperor.

Following the signing of this treaty an engagement between a French military column near Lang Son and Chinese regular troops led to an outbreak of general hostilities against China during which Courbet occupied Kelung, destroyed the Chinese fleet, and blockaded Formosa. In June 1885 a second treaty was signed at Tientsin, which contained some amplifications to the treaty signed in the previous year. Nevertheless the Regents, who had now disposed of the young Emperor Kien Phuc probably by poison, and enthroned his younger brother, Ham Nghi, still refused to resign themselves to the loss of national independence and with the support of the 'scholars' and some of the court officials made preparations to resist the French by force. These preparations included the construction of a stronghold in the hinterland of Quang Tri province to serve as a refuge for the court.

On 2 July 1885 General de Courcy, who had been appointed Commander-in-Chief, Governor of Tongking, and Resident-General in Annam, arrived at Hué, with an imposing escort of

[6] *Bull. de la Société des Amis du Vieux Hué*, April-June 1944.
[7] Chesneaux, p. 131.

Zouaves, to present his credentials to the Emperor. The General, who was unversed in the subtleties of Chinese etiquette, immediately insisted that he should be allowed to proceed to an audience with the Emperor, accompanied by his escort, through the central portal of the 'Bull Gate' of the imperial city, which was traditionally reserved for the exclusive use of the emperor and ambassadors from Peking. Although the court was prepared to allow the General and his staff to use this entry, it was reluctant to concede such a privilege to the escort. De Courcy's refusal to withdraw a demand which would have entailed an inconceivable breach of etiquette was thus ascribed to a deliberate intention to humiliate the court, and the Regents decided to launch a surprise night attack upon the French on 4 July.

The attack failed and the young Emperor, the Queen Mother, and the Regent, Ton That Thuyet, escorted by 5,000 soldiers and pursued by a party of 50 French marines, fled from the imperial city to the mountainous region of Thanh Hoa and Ha Tinh where for three years guerrilla forces continued to resist French attempts to capture the fugitive monarch. Meanwhile the French troops proceeded to loot the royal palaces, to plunder the treasury, to burn the government archives, and to cause great damage to the state press. The flight of the Emperor from Hué was the signal for a general massacre of Christians throughout Annam, where they had aroused popular resentment by their readiness to act as guides and informants to the French forces.

Although Ham Nghi was able to evade capture until November 1888, de Courcy installed upon the throne one of his brothers. This young man, Dong Khanh, whose reign was regarded as a usurpation by the majority of his subjects, died in 1889, when at the instigation of senior court officials the throne was given to a member of an elder branch of the dynasty. This Emperor, Thanh Thai, was a son of Duc Duc who had been immured and starved to death after a reign of three days. The new sovereign, who had spent most of his life in prison, was eleven years old at the time of his accession. He is described by Marshal Lyautey,[8] who visited the court in 1896, as a slim and elegant youth possessed, on occasion, of great dignity and of an inquiring turn of mind, but deprived of effective power,

[8] Pierre Lyautey, *Lettres du Tonkin et de Madagascar* (1920), ii. 61–62.

and with his activities confined to the vicinity of Hué, Thanh Thai expended his energies and high spirits in fantastic pranks and in the exercise of a sadistic tyranny over the women of his harem: behaviour which led to his summary deposition in 1907. His successor, Duy Tan, was selected from among Thanh Thai's numerous progeny by the French military doctor at Hué on the grounds of his physical fitness for the throne.[9]

PAVIE AND LAOS

After the establishment of a protectorate over Annam in 1884, the French set up defence posts along the watershed of the Annam mountain chain, and from this vantage-point they were able to appreciate the strategic importance and potential economic interest of the western slopes which fell in a succession of plateaux to the middle reaches of the Mekong. But the political climate in France was now unfavourable to the acquisition of colonial territory since public opinion, always hostile to the expense and dispersal of military forces entailed by France's expansion overseas, had been greatly alarmed by the difficulties which the expeditionary corps had encountered in Tongking during the spring of 1885. Thus other methods had to be devised to incorporate this region within the frontiers of French Indochina. The agent who was to be principally responsible for bringing the middle and upper reaches of the Mekong under French control was an official employed by the Cochin-Chinese Postal and Telegraph Services named Auguste Pavie. He had been stationed for a number of years at the Cambodian port of Kampot, where his kindly nature and simple ways endeared him to the population. But in addition to natural benevolence, Pavie was endowed with energy, stamina, and an inquiring turn of mind; and while employed in supervising the installation of a telegraph line between Phnom Penh and Bangkok he had collected a mass of data on the flora, fauna, and history of this little-known region: data which were later incorporated in a series of articles and published in a Saigon review.

Le Myre de Vilers, whose appointment as the first civilian Governor of Cochin-China had been due to the French Government's desire to have done with the policy of the *fait accompli* and the strong-arm administrative methods of the

⁹ R. Dorgelès, *Sur la route mandarine* (1929), pp. 137–44.

Admiral-Governors, read these articles with interest and, appreciating that the author possessed the qualities now required to reconcile the local populations to French rule, decided to employ him in some more appropriate capacity. In 1885, therefore, Pavie was sent to France with a party of young Cambodians who had been selected to form the nucleus of a school for colonial peoples; and in Paris he was offered, on the recommendation of Le Myre de Vilers, and to the surprise of officials at the Quai d'Orsay, the post of vice-consul at Luang Prabang,[10] together with the leadership of an expedition sponsored by the French Admiralty and the Postmaster General to explore the region situated between Luang Prabang and the Red river delta.

This region, which was then causing the military authorities in Tongking some disquiet, forms an integral part of the mountain ranges of south and south-west China, and is cleft in its western section by the precipitous valleys of the Mekong's tributary streams, while to the east it comprises Indochina's highest mountain, the Fan Si Pan, the plateaux of Son La and Moc Chau, and the valley of the Black river, which flows through gorges on its upper and lower reaches to join the Red river at Vietri. The inhabitants are for the most part Thai peoples, who live in the valleys and on the plateaux and are distinguished by the colour or style of dress worn by the women of the different communities; the mountains are sparsely settled by Indonesian tribal groups, the A-Kha and the Man, who appear to have arrived from their homeland in China sometime in the sixteenth century.

During the nineteenth century this scattered population was assailed first by aggressive emigrants from south-east China, the Meos, and later by armed bands representing the broken remnants of the Taiping armies, who were to be reinforced, after 1874, by the survivors of the Moslem revolt in western Yunnan: these armed bands were called Hos, or Chinese, by the local population. In 1872 the Hos devastated the Tran Ninh plateau, and after raiding the region around Vientiane infiltrated northwards into the isolated kingdom of Luang Prabang, which was soon reduced to a state of anarchy. Thereupon the king, Oun Kham, finding himself unable to expel the invaders

---

[10] The creation of a French vice-consulate at Luang Prabang was sanctioned by a Franco-Siamese provisional agreement of 7 May 1886.

appealed for help to his Siamese suzerain, who dispatched a military force to his assistance in 1883. But in return for this aid the Siamese imposed their tutelage upon the Lao king, installed advisers at his court, and sent troops into the mountainous region where military posts were established as far east as the Black river valley.

The Siamese advisers at Luang Prabang were thus able to ensure Pavie a frigid reception when he arrived in February 1887, and they succeeded in isolating him from the court and restricting his contacts with the local population. However, this state of affairs did not last long, since at the approach of the rainy season the Siamese troops withdrew, taking with them a number of hostages, including four brothers of Deo Van Tri, a powerful Ho chieftain installed at Lai Chau. Their departure was the signal for Deo Van Tri, who was incensed at the manner in which his brothers had been seized, to descend upon the defenceless capital at the head of an armed band. At this time of crisis Pavie was able to render invaluable service by rescuing the king from the clutches of Tri's partisans and assisting him to escape to Pak Lay. Pavie's presence of mind and concern for the wounded earned him Oun Kham's gratitude, and in the absence of the Siamese advisers, who had decamped in good time from the threatened capital, he was able to persuade the king that a French protectorate offered an acceptable alternative to a Siamese occupation.

In January of the following year Pavie set out from Luang Prabang to meet a French column advancing from the Red river delta. The rendezvous took place at Tuan Giao, and measures were then decided upon for the pacification of the region, which included the establishment of military posts at Lai Chau, Son La, and Van Bu respectively, and the use of persuasion rather than force to obtain the submission of the Thai chieftains. After accompanying the column to Son La, Pavie returned to Luang Prabang, whence he set out again in April for Hanoi. On his arrival there he was entrusted by the military authorities—doubtless impressed by his physical stamina, knowledge of the local languages, and ability to acquire the support of the local populations—with further responsibilities: these included the task of supervising the pacification of the Thai cantons in the Black river area and that of investigating the situation on the middle reaches of the

Mekong, where Siamese troops were reported to be infiltrating into the Cam Mon region, which had been attached to the Crown of Annam following the destruction of Vientiane in 1828.

On his return to Luang Prabang Pavie, acting in his capacity of pacificator, received the local Siamese delegate near Dien Bien Phu; and at a ceremony attended by the local chieftains, the latter formally renounced all claims to suzerainty over the area in the name of his government. After this ceremony Pavie went on to Luang Prabang; and, after a brief delay due to the after effects of malaria, he left to carry out the second part of his mission in February 1889. The journey proved arduous and, on reaching the Cam Mon region, Pavie informed the local Siamese official with some asperity that the presence of Siamese troops in the area constituted an invasion of territory which was under French protection. He warned him, therefore, to refrain from activities calculated to embarrass the garrison of a French post, which was about to be set up at Napé. The indomitable vice-consul then proceeded on his way to Hanoi.

The nature of the intelligence obtained in the course of his travels now led Pavie to propose that a topographical and ethnological survey should be carried out in the territories on the left bank of the Mekong, a proposal based on the belief that this would produce evidence calculated to refute Siamese claims to sovereignty over the area. The French authorities in Tongking, conscious of his ability to secure considerable advantages at small cost to the French taxpayer, fell in with this proposal and suggested to the Minister for Foreign Affairs that Pavie should be recalled for consultations to Paris. These consultations led to the decision to extend the scope of the proposed surveys to include an assessment of the mineral wealth and commercial possibilities of the disputed territories.

In November 1889 Pavie returned to Indochina to take over the leadership of the mission entrusted with these tasks, and after breaking his journey in Bangkok to inform the Siamese Government of French intentions, he proceeded to Hanoi, where he assumed his new responsibilities with enthusiasm. The members of the mission were divided into groups, each group being assigned a specific area, while Pavie himself took over the job of reconnoitring the Chinese border: an area where Deo Van Tri, the paramount Thai chieftain, was then

awaiting his arrival to submit to the French authorities. The
ceremony took place on 7 April 1889, and Pavie managed by
an adroit display of tact and affability to gain the chieftain's
confidence and friendship. After some weeks spent in Deo Van
Tri's company, Pavie left for Luang Prabang, where he was
joined in the course of the following weeks by the other members
of the mission, who had been instructed to assemble there,
before the onset of the rainy season, in order to collate the
information collected in their respective areas. In October the
groups dispersed and Pavie travelled down the Mekong on his
way to Saigon and Bangkok, where he was to discuss the border
question with the Siamese authorities. But exasperated by the
dilatory tactics to which the Siamese resorted, and forewarned
of their intention to strengthen their hold over the disputed
territories, he soon broke off the discussions and left for Hanoi,
where he advised the military authorities to be on their guard
against frontier incidents. After delivering this warning, he
set out accompanied by Deo Van Tri, for the Chinese frontier
region. During his absence the authorities in Tongking appear
to have decided to precipitate matters, and on his return to
Hanoi in June 1891 Pavie was sent to voice their misgivings in
Paris, and to urge the Government to adopt a 'policy appropriate to the circumstances'. The Ministry for Foreign Affairs
proved attentive to his arguments and decided to entrust Pavie
with the task of implementing the policy which he recommended. In February 1892, therefore, the French Consulate
in Bangkok was raised to a legation, Pavie being appointed
chargé d'affaires with the rank of consul-general.

The appointment of their redoubtable adversary to this post
must have filled the Siamese Government with misgivings.
Nevertheless Pavie was received with flattering attentions when
he arrived there in June. But after a promising start, the
negotiations made little progress and all attempts to break the
deadlock were courteously eluded. Finally, in September,
minor incidents in the Mekong valley, involving French traders
and a French official, provided a pretext for a resort to force.

The occupation of the disputed territory on the left bank of
the Mekong took the form of a pacification, and was carried
out by columns made up of colonial and militia troops under
the command of French civilian officials. These columns
advanced up the Mekong from Kratie and from Lao Bao and

Vinh respectively; and although the occupation of the islands at the Khong Falls led to fighting, little resistance was encountered elsewhere. But in spite of their inability to oppose the French advance, the Siamese still took no steps either to evacuate the region or to negotiate a settlement. This procrastination exasperated the French, who were inclined to ascribe Siamese behaviour to British machinations in Bangkok. After the assassination of a police inspector by a Siamese official at Cam Mon in July 1893, the Admiral commanding the French naval squadron in the Far East was ordered to proceed up the Menam to Bangkok and, in the face of fire from the batteries of a coastal fort and nine gun-boats, two French cruisers forced the pass at Paknam and reached the capital; impressed by this display of determination, the Siamese Government accepted a French ultimatum some days later.

By the treaty of 3 October 1893 Siam renounced all claims to suzerainty over the territories on the left bank of the Mekong, a renunciation which stopped further Siamese encroachments in this region and secured the coastal plains of Annam against attack. But the decision to accept the Mekong as the frontier separated the Lao population on the left bank of this river from the bulk of their kinsmen settled on the Korat plateau, and enabled the Bangkok Government to annex, without more ado, most of the vassal kingdom of Champassak and part of the kingdom of Luang Prabang; and although some of the lost territory was to be restored by the convention of 25 March 1907, the Lao population who now accepted French rule did so with a sense of grievance.

In 1894 Pavie, who is reported to have indicated this objection to the treaty, was appointed Commissioner-General at Luang Prabang and entrusted with the task of supervising the occupation and administrative organization of the newly acquired territories, a task which he combined with that of establishing, in co-operation with a Chinese and a British boundary commission respectively, the frontiers with China and Burma. He completed this mission in September of the following year, but before his return to France he was able to inform the King of Luang Prabang that the French Government had officially confirmed him in his dynastic rights and privileges. Although the confirmation, which represented the fulfilment of his promises to Oun Kham in June 1887, must have gratified this shrewd but sentimental pioneer and empire-builder, the decision to accord the King of Luang Prabang the status of a protected sovereign led nevertheless to the maintenance of partition by setting up two separate régimes in Lao-inhabited territory, since the provinces which had formed part of the kingdoms of Vientiane and Champassak were treated as French colonial territory. In practice, however, after the constitution of an Indochinese Federation in 1907, French officials tended to ignore this distinction and treated the area which was named Laos as a single political and administrative unit.

# Part II
## FRENCH INDOCHINA

# IV

# Aspects of the French Protectorate

In 1887 a French government decree established a general budget for the countries comprising the Indochinese Union. This budget, which was intended principally to defray military expenditure in Tongking, was to derive its resources from revenue provided by the local customs, post and telegraph services, and from subsidies furnished both by the Cochin-Chinese budget and by the French Government itself. The decree also set up a Government-General to supervise the expenditure of these funds, and in May of that year the appointment of a Governor-General, who was responsible to the Ministry for the Navy and Colonies, was announced.[1]

On the fall of the French Government in the following year the provisions for this budget were suppressed, an action ascribed to agitation on the part of interested parties in the colony of Cochin-China which, being the richest of the territorial divisions, would have contributed most to its funds. However, the successful outcome of this agitation established a dangerous precedent, for French administrators responsible for the implementation of unpopular measures were liable henceforth to find themselves exposed to scurrilous attacks in the Saigon press, while their authority might be undermined by political intrigues in Paris involving powerful commercial and financial groups who had come to look upon Indochina as their fief. Thus the provision of funds to meet military expenditure in Tongking continued to present a problem for successive Governors-General until the appointment in 1897 of Paul Doumer. This energetic and influential Governor-General was to show that Indochina could be a source of profit to commercial and financial interests, without cost to the French taxpayer,[2] by providing the country with a uniform administrative service, with ample public revenues, and with economic equipment which compared favourably with that of other countries in South East Asia.

[1] A separate Ministry for the Colonies was established in 1897.
[2] Chesneaux, p. 152.

In Tongking direct and centralized administration was brought about by doing away with the office of Viceroy, which had been established in 1887, the functions of this Vietnamese official being vested in the French Senior Resident at Hanoi. The authority of the Emperor of Annam was further diminished by depriving the traditional organ of government, the Co-Mat, of executory powers, which were vested in a Council of Ministers whose deliberations were presided over *ex officio* by the French Resident at Hué. French Residents responsible for the collection of taxes and local expenditure were also installed in provincial towns in Annam. Similar measures designed to curb the royal power and to substitute direct French administration for the traditional local autonomy were likewise taken in Cambodia and the kingdom of Luang Prabang in Laos, and in Cochin-China the powers of the Colonial Council were curtailed.[3]

These increased administrative commitments became the responsibility of a French-staffed Indochinese civil service which assumed the direction of customs and excise, public works, agriculture and commerce, posts and telegraphs, and civil affairs. However, the creation of a French administrative service resulted in the local population being saddled with two complete and juxtaposed administrative services,[4] an arrangement which entailed a considerable drain on the local budgets.[5] The financial reorganization accomplished by Doumer thus represented an indispensable supplement to these administrative reforms. It included the establishment of a federal budget which derived its resources from customs and excise and from state monopolies on alcohol, salt, and opium, which proved so lucrative that federal revenues doubled in the space of ten years.[6] The yield from land and poll-taxes proved equally buoyant, and at the end of Doumer's five-year term of office the Vietnamese contribution to public expenditure had

[3] The Colonial Council of Cochin-China had been set up in 1880. The Councillors, who represented French commercial interests and those of the administrative service, were empowered to decide on optional expenditure included in the draft proposals for the budget.

[4] Lyautey, *Lettres du Tonkin*, i. 72.

[5] A French civil servant was estimated to cost five to eight times more than a locally recruited employee (Le Thanh Khoi, p. 414). In consequence, salaries represented more than 75 per cent. of the cost of running the Indochinese Post and Telegraph Services in 1906 (Chesneaux, p. 158).

[6] Ibid. p. 155.

increased from an estimated 35 million gold francs at the time of the French conquest to 90 million gold francs.[7]

The flourishing state of Indochina's finances enabled a loan of 200 million francs to be floated in France, which was used to provide the country with some of the economic equipment of a modern state. The construction of a railway system was begun to link Hanoi with Saigon and the port of Haiphong with Kunming, the capital of the land-locked Chinese province of Yunnan. Roads were built, and the equipping of the ports of Saigon, Haiphong, and Tourane was completed. But the increased fiscal burden imposed upon the population to pay for these developments entailed much hardship.[8]

The impetus given to economic development under Doumer's Governor-Generalship was also to provide Indochina with 1,700 miles of railway track and an admirable system of roads.[9] Moreover, the dredging and draining operations undertaken in the Transbassac—Cochin-China south of the Bassac river— were to result in some 4½ million acres of new land being brought into cultivation during the period 1880 to 1937. This vast increase in the area of cultivated land was reflected in rice exports from Saigon, which increased during the same period from 284,000 to 1,548,000 tons.[10]

French enterprise was also responsible for introducing the rubber tree—*hevea brasiliensis*—into Indochina, and in 1905 the first large plantation, that of Suzannah, was established on 'red lands' near Saigon.[11] The success achieved by the rubber planters aroused French interest in the plateaux of Lang Biang, Darlac, and the Bolovens, which contained wide areas of basaltic soil. This sparsely populated region had hitherto been neglected by the Vietnamese, who were reluctant to abandon the cultivation of rice on the coastal plains and had been discouraged by the prevalence of malaria. Under the direction of the Pasteur Institute measures were taken which, by reducing

[7] Ibid.
[8] The consumption of rice per head fell from 620 lb. a year in 1900 to 400 lb. in 1937; although the price of salt quintupled between 1899 and 1906, the revenue from this monopoly barely doubled (Chesneaux, pp. 180 and 154).
[9] Charles Robequain, *The Economic Development of French Indo-China* (1944), p. 99.
[10] Ibid. p. 220.
[11] By 1938 rubber production had risen to 60,000 tons and accounted, together with rice and maize, for 78 per cent. of the total value of Indochinese exports (ibid. p. 204).

the danger of infection, opened these potentially fertile areas to settlement. Indochina's mineral wealth likewise attracted French investors, particularly during the boom years from 1926 to 1929, and a French mining company started to exploit the fabulously rich anthracite deposits in east Tongking, soon after the conquest.[12] Industrial development was, however, hampered by Indochina's association with France since French interests were naturally reluctant to lose a profitable market and did little to promote the rise of local industries. Nevertheless, before the depression processing industries were estimated to be employing 86,000 workers; these included rice mills in Cholon, distilleries at Hanoi, Nam Dinh, Hai Duong, Cholon, and Phnom Penh, and cotton mills at Nam Dinh.

French commercial interests in Indochina were first represented by enterprising merchants who came to Saigon to cater for the needs of the expeditionary force, and within a few years rice started to be shipped from the conquered territory with the assistance of Chinese intermediaries. As soon as this export trade developed the Comptoir National d'Escompte of Paris, which was already established in other French colonies, set up a branch in Saigon and when this credit house proved unable to cope with local requirements, in January 1875 the Bank of Indochina was founded with the support of a consortium of banking houses, including the Banque de Paris et des Pays Bas.

The new bank, which was granted later in the year the privilege of issuing currency for a period of twenty-five years, was also a discount and commercial bank, and after the creation of the Government-General in 1887 it assumed the functions of official paymaster and acted on behalf of the Government-General in its dealings with the French treasury. The Bank of Indochina, which was to become known throughout the Far East as the 'French Bank', was soon firmly established, and like the Society of Foreign Missions was able to pursue a long-term policy directed towards predetermined ends. This ability placed it at an advantage in its dealings with the French administration, who were compelled to take into account the effect of ministerial changes in Paris. Moreover the Bank soon extended the field of its activities to Japan, to the

[12] In 1938 the output from these mines was 2,335,000 tons (*Annuaire des États Associés*, 1953, p. 90).

French establishments in India, to French possessions in the Pacific area, and to China, where it was to enjoy almost a monopoly of French banking.

The Bank's policy in Indochina gave rise to some criticism on the grounds that when more profitable business could be had elsewhere it neglected its Indochinese interests; it was also accused of being parsimonious in giving credit, of charging high interest rates, and of treating defaulting clients with undue severity. During the period following the First World War, the Bank profited from an influx of French capital to lay the foundations of a financial empire embracing most aspects of Indochina's economic development; and in 1931 its privilege of issuing bank notes in Indochina, French possessions in the Pacific area, French India, and French Somaliland was renewed for a further period of twenty-five years. The French Government availed itself of this opportunity to acquire a 20 per cent. interest in the Bank, together with the right to nominate six of the twenty Directors.

If it was not considered to act always in the best interests of Indochina, the Bank was quick on occasion to exploit the achievements of enterprising French settlers, who played an important part in the economic development of the country.[13] These settlers, who were frequently of peasant origin and included many discharged n.c.o.'s and soldiers, had first been attracted by the agricultural possibilities of the deltaic plains of Cochin-China and Tongking, where they acquired land either by government grant or by purchase.[14] Later they were to break new ground by planting tea and coffee on a commercial scale on the borders of the Tongking delta and in Annam, and although many difficulties were encountered the experience gained encouraged companies with large financial resources to engage in similar activities in the uplands of South Annam and in Cochin-China.

Private enterprise was also responsible for the creation of the first rubber plantations at the beginning of the century near

[13] In 1937 the European community consisted of 10,779 members of the French armed forces and 3,873 government officials, who were employed for the most part in the administrative services, the customs or the police; while some 3,561 Europeans represented the liberal professions or were engaged in banking, insurance and trade (Robequain, p. 29).

[14] Before the outbreak of war in 1939 74,000 acres in Tongking, and 247,000 acres in Cochin-China were in French ownership (ibid. p. 190).

Saigon. The subsequent development of the great rubber estates in Cochin-China and Cambodia was founded on the initiative of pharmacists, clerks, and magistrates in Cochin-China, who had first been attracted by the financial possibilities of the *hevea brasiliensis*,[15] and had been prepared to devote their leisure and their savings to planting these trees. But the settlers and the prospectors who travelled through the unexplored and unhealthy interior were an unruly and vociferous section of the European community, and were quick to resent any lack of willingness on the part of the administration to help them in their enterprises or any official attempts to interfere with their activities. In consequence, French administrators were inclined to view the strenuous and frequently meritorious attempts of these troublesome individualists to develop the country with uneasiness and disfavour. Nevertheless the administrators themselves were not immune from criticism. Having been recruited in some cases merely on the recommendation of a French deputy who wished to be of service to his electors, they did not always possess the administrative capacity or tact necessary to discharge their functions. Indeed, the failure of the administrative service to maintain French moral prestige not only at the courts of the Indochinese sovereigns but also in distant and inaccessible provinces must be considered a contributory cause of the widespread discontent with French rule, which was to culminate in the rising of August 1945, and in 1946 H. M. Bao Dai, in an interview with a press correspondent, was to complain that before the overthrow of the French régime colonial administration in Annam had completely broken down; a break-down which he attributed to the fact that the French civil servants, who were both in excess of requirements and often unsuited to the positions they occupied, had constituted a sort of mafia which was inspired by the 'colonialist' spirit and opposed to all reform.[16]

[15] Robequain, pp. 202-3.
[16] *Combat*, 15 Oct. 1946. A similar complaint had been made in the previous year by a Laotian Cabinet Minister who listed at the head of national grievances against the French Protectorate the fact that its local representatives had been chosen with insufficient care (P. Gentil, *Sursauts de l'Asie* (1950), p. 30).

## ECONOMIC BURDENS OF THE PROTECTORATE

Vietnamese reluctance to accept French rule was based on emotional and practical grounds. Emotionally the Vietnamese naturally regretted the loss of independence, which they attributed to the superior technical means at the disposal of the French rather than to the possession of cultural or moral pre-eminence. This reluctance to accept French tutelage was reinforced by the political disabilities and economic burdens occasioned by the Protectorate. These burdens were shouldered principally by the rural population, and the fiscal demands, together with the high birth-rate, led to the progressive pauperization of the countryside, a process illustrated by the fact that rural indebtedness in Cochin-China alone increased from 31 million piastres in 1900 to 134 million piastres in 1930.[17] As security for debt was usually represented by mortgages on land at interest rates of from 3 to 10 per cent. per month,[18] smallholders who had been compelled to borrow money in order to meet some natural or personal calamity were frequently unable to pay off mortgages and had their land expropriated.

In addition, although a vast acreage was reclaimed in the Transbassac, the rural population was given little opportunity to acquire holdings in this area since the land was sold at auction and subsequently leased to peasant farmers, or *ta dien*, at rents amounting to about 40 per cent. of the yield. The rural population also suffered from the disruption of the traditional administrative system, which had led to the disappearance of the 'scholars' who, in spite of their shortcomings, had enjoyed popular respect, while their extinction had resulted in the closing of the village schools, and although public education was finally reorganized in 1920, the rural population had meanwhile become illiterate.

In fact the French occupation brought little positive benefit to the rural communities. In spite of an ambitious programme of public works, the peasant continued to farm his land with the traditional agricultural implements, to live in the closed economy of his village, and to use the ancient dust tracks across the deltaic plains; he would thus seem to have paid a high price for protection from foreign invasion and for increasing

[17] Paul Bernard, *Problème économique en Indochine*, quoted by Chesneaux, p. 166.
[18] Le Thanh Khoi, p. 422.

immunity from epidemics, which probably represented the principal benefits derived from the French occupation. The French had, however, provided the surplus rural population in Tongking and North Annam with some prospect of alternative employment, either on the plantations in the south or in the anthracite mines and cotton mills of Tongking. The recruitment of a labour force for the rubber plantations was organized by Vietnamese intermediaries who derived large profits from these activities. In 1927 the Government-General attempted to check the abuses to which this system had given rise by appointing inspectors to supervise the embarkation of coolies in the northern ports and to ensure that proper accommodation was provided for them in the south, where conditions on the plantations had aroused criticism.

Labour conditions in Tongking were also unsatisfactory. Whereas 75 per cent. of the labour employed in the Nam Dinh cotton mills consisted, in 1953, of women and children, or girls and boys between the ages of 14 and 18,[19] the miners in the Tongking anthracite mines, including boys of 10, worked under conditions which aroused the compassion and misgivings of a visiting journalist who was, however, perhaps unaware that the employment of child and 'sweated' labour was then general throughout the Far East.[20] Thus in spite of the plight of many landless peasants in Tongking and North Annam, the recruitment of labour for industry and for the plantations proved difficult, and those recruited remained nostalgically attached to their village communities to which they returned with alacrity when their contract had expired.

## THE RISE OF A MIDDLE CLASS

One consequence of the Protectorate was that the economic developments sponsored by the French produced certain social changes which led to the rise of a Vietnamese middle class. The nucleus of this class was formed when, following the flight of many village communities at the time of the conquest, the lands thus abandoned were declared vacant and sold to defray the cost of the occupation; the purchasers in some cases being Vietnamese who had co-operated with the French. Vietnamese

[19] Robequain, pp. 280–1.
[20] Dorgelès, pp. 89–96.

were also to acquire by purchase from the French administration a share in the territories opened up for rice cultivation in the Transbassac, and by leasing this land in parcels of 12 or 24 acres to peasant farmers, they were able to accumulate capital which they then loaned at usurious rates of interest against mortgages on land. The revenues of this middle class were thus principally derived from land and usury.[21]

Attempts by the Vietnamese to expand their activities into banking, commerce, and industry met, however, with scant success since banking, industrial development, and the production of rubber were a jealously guarded French preserve, and the rice-busking mills, inland transport—with the exception of the railways—and the bulk of the export trade remained firmly in the hands of the Chinese, whose traditional skill and knowledge proved a sufficient defence against Vietnamese encroachments. Nevertheless, in spite of these restrictions on their economic activities the ownership of land provided the middle class with the means to provide their children with an education which would qualify them to assume an increasing share in local administration and in the conduct of national affairs, although the educational facilities provided by the French authorities were not designed to hasten the formation of this *élite*: in 1924 only some 6,200 boys and 1,000 girls out of some 600,000 children of school age were receiving an education,[22] while higher education was limited until 1918 to a combined faculty of medicine and pharmacy at Hanoi.[23] The Vietnamese, who traditionally attach great importance to the acquisition of diplomas and degrees, therefore complained not only that these facilities were inadequate but that they revealed an obvious intention on the part of the protecting power to train them merely to fill subordinate positions in the administrative service and to discharge routine commercial and financial tasks. In consequence, many families who were reluctant to accept this situation sent their children to be educated in France.

The existence of a restive and disgruntled middle class who considered that they were being cheated out of the positions of influence and profit to which they could legitimately aspire

[21] Robequain, p. 86.
[22] Chesneaux, p. 196.
[23] A law faculty was later added, together with technical colleges affiliated to Hanoi University, where diplomas in public administration, agriculture, veterinary science, and public works could be acquired.

stopped the French administration from relaxing the security measures introduced at the time of the conquest. The protection of French interests remained the responsibility of an omnipresent Security Service. Vietnamese who wished to leave the region in which they were domiciled had to obtain a passport, while an exit visa was required to go abroad. Mail was censored, domiciliary visits were carried out by police or customs officials without a warrant, and the Governor-General was empowered to intern Vietnamese without trial and to sequestrate their property for a period of ten years.[24] The allegation in clandestine Communist tracts that Indochina was a prison thus had some justification, and even moderate nationalists who were anxious to find a pacific solution to these difficulties complained that Vietnamese were treated like aliens in their own country.[25]

## LAOS AND CAMBODIA

Cambodia and the Lao-inhabited territories on the right bank of the Mekong were administered by methods similar to those employed in Tongking and Annam: methods which however proved less destructive to accepted values and the traditional way of life in these Indianized countries. But the organization of the Protectorate in Cambodia was delayed for some years by a revolt clandestinely encouraged by King Norodom, who resented the means employed to secure his agreement to the surrender of his prerogatives. Finally, in 1891, the terms of the Franco-Cambodian Convention of 1884 were implemented, and French Residents and Deputy Residents were established in the provinces to supervise the local Cambodian officials and to maintain public security and collect the taxes. A Resident-General was also installed in Phnom Penh, who presided *ex officio* over cabinet meetings and countersigned the measures decided upon. But in spite of French tutelage, the prestige of the throne remained almost unimpaired in popular esteem. This was due partly to the fact that the monarch, whose person was sacred, had inherited some of the mystic attributes of the Angkor kings; and his palace still symbolized, in the eyes of his adoring subjects, the navel of the world and the capital

[24] Chesneaux, pp. 192–3.
[25] Le Thanh Khoi, p. 407.

the universe in microcosm. Further evidence of the divine origin of the monarchy was afforded by the presence at court of descendants of the priestly families—the Baku Brahmans—who had formerly celebrated the onerous cult of the God-King. These Brahmans still performed certain rites and had the custody of the regalia, including the Sacred Sword which had allegedly belonged to Jayavarman II, the founder of the Khmer Empire. Besides the prestige derived from his divine predecessors, the monarch's position was further reinforced by his role as official head of both the Thommayut and Mohanikay Buddhist sects, a role which included the prerogative of nominating the Superior of both these influential monastic orders.[26]

Thus although stripped of his temporal power, the king remained in possession of his religious attributes and prerogatives and could count on the support of the Buddhist hierarchy and of the bonzes, who were responsible for instructing male children in the tenets of Hinayana Buddhism; and these assets proved sufficient to retain the loyalty of his subjects. Moreover, the king's position was strengthened by the fact that under the Protectorate the pattern of Cambodian life remained practically unchanged. For the bulk of the population, estimated to include at least 80 per cent. of the available manpower,[27] continued to cultivate small family holdings of ten acres or less: a state of affairs made possible by ample reserves of arable land.[28]

But although the French authorities failed to take positive measures to rouse the somewhat indolent Cambodian people from the indifference and patient acquiescence in misfortune born of historic calamities and fostered by the teachings of Hinayana Buddhism, some important reforms were nevertheless carried out. These included the abolition of slavery for debt, the codification of the ancient Khmer laws, and the institution

[26] The Thommayut sect ('those attached to the doctrine') was first introduced into Cambodia from Siam in 1864, and now numbers some 1,600 bonzes, who are to be found either in Phnom Penh or in certain provincial towns. This lack of numerical importance is compensated, however, by the fact that the sect traditionally enjoys the support of the King and the royal family. The Mohanikay sect ('great congregation') comprises 90 per cent. of the Buddhist clergy and staffs 2,500 out of Cambodia's 2,650 pagodas (T. FitzSimmons, ed., *Cambodia* (1957), pp. 299–301).

[27] Ibid. p. 178.

[28] Only some 10 per cent. of Cambodia's 44 million acres of potentially fertile land are under continuous cultivation (ibid. p. 192).

of an impartial system of justice. Public health also benefited from the foundation of hospitals in Phnom Penh and in the provincial towns and the setting up of infirmaries, maternity centres, dispensaries, and first-aid posts in rural areas, while educational facilities were improved by the opening of state primary schools for children of both sexes and by measures taken to initiate the bonzes employed in village pagoda schools in modern teaching methods. Cambodia also derived advantage from the ambitious programme of public works sponsored by the Government-General. Phnom Penh was laid out on a spacious scale and provided with a river port capable of handling small ocean-going vessels, a fairly good network of roads was built, and a railway was opened in 1935 linking the capital to Battambang and the frontier village of Mongkolborey. But these benefits from French rule were offset by the legal cover and economic incentive afforded Vietnamese and Chinese alike to establish themselves in the country. Thus, whereas Vietnamese were employed as clerks in the French-staffed civil service and in French business houses, and allowed to set themselves up on their own account as artisans and shopkeepers in Phnom Penh, the local Chinese community, reinforced by an influx of their countrymen, profited from the Cambodian distaste for commerce and lack of business acumen to engage in economic activities on an extensive scale in the capacity of itinerant merchants, managers of general stores, contractors, retail dealers, rice brokers, money-lenders, bankers, and owners of road transport, fishing vessels, and pepper plantations situated on the shores of the Gulf of Siam.[29]

Similar activities were engaged in by the Vietnamese and Chinese who settled in the Lao provinces during this period, and in 1945 50,000 Vietnamese were working as clerks, artisans, shopkeepers, and market gardeners in and around the towns along the Mekong, and from 5,000 to 6,000 Chinese were playing an important part in the economic life of these regions. However, trade in these provinces was restricted by a tendency on the part of the scattered population to cater merely for their own needs, and by the absence of transport facilities.[30]

[29] FitzSimmons, pp. 43 and 45.

[30] Route Coloniale No. 13, linking Luang Prabang to Saigon, was finally opened to traffic in 1945. But the uprising later in the year led to the destruction of many bridges and culverts, with the result that long stretches of the road became unusable. The railway line between Tan Ap and Thakhek, designed to facilitate

The contribution of the Lao provinces to Indochina's export trade was therefore modest, amounting to no more than 1 per cent. in 1939, and although tin was mined in Cam Mon province and coffee was planted on the Bolovens plateau, the opium crop, estimated to amount to between 40 and 100 tons, which was harvested by the Meos in the mountainous region, represented the country's principal source of revenue until 1945.

Following the signing of the Franco-Siamese treaty of 3 October 1893, the newly acquired territories were placed at first under the authority of Senior Military Commanders, who set up headquarters at Khong and Luang Prabang respectively. But six years later administrative responsibility for the area was transferred to a Senior Resident, who was assisted in his task by French Residents appointed to each of the thirteen provinces. The presence of these officials, whose appointment appears to have been inspired in some cases by the desire of the Government-General to relegate them to posts of relative obscurity in the hinterland, failed, however, to curb the authority exercised by the local princely families over their former fiefs, and particularist tendencies were further encouraged by long-standing rivalry between the northern and southern provinces: a rivalry based on the impatience and resentment felt by the more cosmopolitan and commercially-minded southerners at the arrogance and feudal ways of their isolated kinsmen in the north.[31]

---

communications between the coast of Annam and the Mekong, was never completed.

[31] Jacob Egli in *Combat*, 28, 29, and 31 July 1949.

# V

# Opposition to French Rule

AFTER the capture of the Emperor Ham Nghi in 1888 armed resistance was confined to the mountainous frontier region in the north where recruits were drawn from landless peasants and from the remnants of the Chinese armed bands who had been operating in the Red river delta. In 1891 control of this troubled area was handed over to the military authorities, who were invested with full civil and military powers and entrusted with the task of pacification.

The methods employed to complete this difficult task are said to have been worked out between the Governor-General, de Lanessan, and Colonels Pennequin and Gallieni:[1] they were based on the collection of intelligence concerning tensions, jealousies, and feuds among the rebel leaders, and also of more general information which would enable an assessment to be made of the factors serving to bolster morale. This was then exploited to disrupt and demoralize the enemy, while military action was limited to establishing military garrisons at communications and supply centres with orders to restrict punitive action to the minimum and to neglect no opportunity to acquire the confidence of the local population. When local security conditions improved the population were entrusted with the organization of their own defences, and the garrisons then moved forward to the edge of the pacified area.

This method, which was later to be employed with success in Madagascar and Morocco, was well suited to the pacification of wide areas or difficult terrain with the small forces available for military operations in colonial territory, and it avoided the devastation that followed in the train of military columns operating in hostile territory; but the exploitation of local rivalries tended to undermine the authority of the central Government in whose name the operations were officially carried out, while the habit of contracting alliances with local feudatories in order to gain some immediate advantage was to hinder the political evolution of the Protectorate.

[1] H. Brunschwig, La Colonisation française (1949), pp. 182-7.

The pacification of the mountainous region was facilitated in 1894 by an agreement with the Chinese Government on the policing of the frontiers, so that with one exception, the armed bands had been dispersed by 1897.[2] After this open opposition to French rule was mainly confined to recurrent disturbances provoked by the demands of the tax collectors in the poor and over-populated provinces of Annam or in the recently reclaimed and still unpoliced Transbassac area of Cochin-China.

In 1905, however, the Japanese naval victory at Port Arthur, by revealing that an Asian nation with Western technical equipment could defeat a European power, aroused a fervent hope that national independence might be regained in Vietnam. The proposal that Vietnamese should equip themselves with the necessary scientific and technical knowledge to enable them to take over those functions in the Protectorate which had hitherto constituted a French preserve was put forward by two distinguished members of the 'scholar' class, named Phan Boi Chau and Phan Chau Trinh. Whereas Chau proposed that foreign, and preferably Japanese, aid should be enlisted, Trinh believed that France could be brought to realize the wisdom of encouraging such a development, and recommended that French assistance should be sought in order to prepare Vietnam technically and industrially for independence.

In pursuance of his plan Chau went to Japan, where he was soon joined by a number of young Vietnamese including a prince, Cuong De, who was a claimant to the throne of Annam.[3] After his expulsion from Japan in 1910 Chau settled in Canton, where in 1913 he founded a political group, the Viet Nam Quang Phuc Hoi (Association for the Restoration of Vietnam), by recruiting members from among the local Vietnamese community. During the next four years this group was responsible for a number of isolated disturbances and outrages in Tongking and Cochin-China. Meanwhile Phan Chau Trinh, who had presented a memorandum to the Governor-General in 1906

[2] The armed band which remained in existence was under the command of a guerrilla leader named De Tham. De Tham, with whom the French authorities found it expedient on two occasions to arrange a truce, continued to operate from bases in a mountainous area to the east of Thai Nguyen—the Yen Tre—until 1913.

[3] Cuong De was descended from Gia Long's eldest son, Prince Canh, who, as a child of four, had accompanied Pigneau de Behaine to France in 1784. On Canh's death the succession to the throne had been vested in Gia Long's fourth son, the Emperor Minh Mang.

courageously reproaching the French administration with exploiting the population, kept up his agitation in favour of reforms and sponsored the formation of study groups. Both these nationalist leaders were to serve terms of imprisonment in French jails and to end their days under French police supervision, but by their example and by the moral influence they exercised they were able to indicate to the rising generation the practical steps to take in order to regain their independence.

## THE NATIONALIST MOVEMENT

During the war years (1914–18), the Vietnamese official class also provided leaders for an abortive rising in Annam, which was designed to take place in May 1916. The plans for this rising were laid by a group of 'scholars' and junior mandarins, who had been encouraged to take action by the withdrawal of a number of military units for service in France. The conspirators recruited a band of armed supporters and also succeeded in suborning a detachment of Vietnamese troops billeted in Hué, while one of their number disguised as a fisherman managed to contact the young Emperor Duy Tan, without arousing the suspicions of his entourage, and persuaded him to support the rising. But the French authorities got wind of these goings on and disarmed the troops implicated two days before the rising was due to take place. Duy Tan, in a desperate attempt to retrieve the situation, escaped from the palace, but he proved unable to rally any supporters and was captured three days later in a pagoda on the outskirts of Hué. The collapse of the conspiracy was followed by stern repressive measures, those implicated being either executed or sent to penal settlements, while Duy Tan himself, together with his father, the ex-Emperor Thanh Thai, was exiled to the island of Réunion in the Indian Ocean.

The throne was then given to Prince Buu Dao, a son of the Emperor Dong Khanh. The new Emperor, who took the reign-name of Khai Dinh, found that he could do little to help his subjects. He tried nevertheless to persuade the French authorities to abandon coercive methods of government and to adopt a policy directed to securing the co-operation of the Vietnamese in the administration of the Protectorate. With this end in view, Khai Dinh went to France in 1922, ostensibly to visit the Colonial Exhibition at Marseilles but in fact to persuade the French Government to adopt this policy; and although his *démarche* was unsuccessful, he profited from his stay in Paris to entrust his only child, the nine-year-old Prince Vinh Thuy, to the care of a former French Resident at Hué, Eugène Charles, with instructions to give the boy a modern education, and to bring him up at the same time to respect Confucian values so that he should be well equipped to direct national destinies during a period of transition.

The decision to educate Vinh Thuy in France, and away from the decadent court, where the dignitaries consoled themselves for the loss of effective authority by nurturing implacable hatreds and conducting devious intrigues against their colleagues, was probably well inspired. But the selection of a senior colonial official, possessed of an imposing presence, to supervise the education of the sensitive, intelligent, and rather shy heir of the Nguyen dynasty, is open to question. Nevertheless Vinh Thuy was to spend the next ten years in this middle-class household, and although he paid a brief visit to Hué after the death of his father in 1925 to be enthroned under the reign-name of Bao Dai, it was not until 1932 that he finally returned to Annam, where he was greeted with enthusiasm by the population, who flocked to welcome him on his journey from Tourane in the belief that he would persuade the French to install a less oppressive régime.

Bao Dai attempted to fulfil these expectations and immediately proclaimed his desire to reign as a constitutional monarch. He also announced his intention of reforming the mandarinate and the administration of justice and reorganizing public education. This declaration was followed, in May 1933, by his personal assumption of responsibility for the conduct of national affairs, while the elderly ministers who had discharged the functions of government during his minority were replaced by younger men.

The collaborators whom he chose to assist him included Ngo Dinh Diem,[4] the Governor of Phan Thiet province, who had acquired a reputation for patriotism and integrity: Diem was given the portfolio of the Ministry of the Interior and appointed head of the Secretariat attached to a commission composed of Vietnamese and French officials charged with the task of

[4] See below, p. 469

elaborating the proposed reforms. But after some months of fruitless discussions it became apparent that the conservative element at the court, in alliance with the French representatives on the Commission, was sufficiently powerful and well informed to frustrate the young Emperor's generous intentions. Bao Dai, who was aware that his entourage were engaged in some cases in betraying his confidence to the French authorities, accepted defeat and resigned himself to the ineffectual role of a protected sovereign.

After the formation of the Popular Front Government in 1939, however, Bao Dai made another fruitless attempt to persuade the French to relax their administrative stranglehold and went to Paris to urge that relations between the French authorities and the court of Annam should at least conform to the terms of the treaty of 1884, which had been persistently ignored by the Government-General, but during his visit he discovered that the archives of the Ministry for the Colonies, which was responsible for carrying out its provisions, contained no copy of this basic document.[5]

## POLITICAL REFORMS

The reforms which Bao Dai attempted in vain to carry out had first been proposed in a series of essays and newspaper articles by Pham Quynh, a talented Tongkingese mandarin and journalist: they were principally designed to renovate existing institutions and included the reorganization of the mandarinate, the appointment of ministers responsible to the Emperor, and the election of a Consultative Assembly.

The last of these proposals had already been partially put into effect by the setting up of a regional Consultative Assembly in Tongking, and in 1925 a similar body was elected in Annam by a restricted number of enfranchised citizens, but the Assembly's charter confined its debates within narrow limits and denied it the right to formulate recommendations of a political nature. In spite of this interdiction, however, two of its members, who had previously attracted some attention by their agitation in favour of reforms, tried to found a political party, the 'Vietnamese People's Progressive Party', with a platform based on Pham Quynh's proposals. But their efforts were

[5] *Le Monde*, 23 Feb. 1946.

frustrated by the French authorities, who merely shelved the application for the requisite official permission.

Meanwhile similar proposals were being canvassed in Cochin-China, where the Vietnamese moneyed class were able to make their wishes known in the Colonial Council, to which they elected 10 out of the 24 members. In 1923 a wealthy Vietnamese named Bui Quang Chieu, who had acquired French citizenship, successfully formed a party, the 'Constitutionalist Party', to press for constitutional government. This party attracted popular support two years later by presenting the Governor-General with a list of further demands, including freedom of the press, the right to hold meetings and to form associations, increased representation in the Colonial Council, and the opening of the administrative service to Vietnamese. Finally, in 1926, Bui Quang Chieu left Saigon amid scenes of great enthusiasm to present these demands to the French Government. However, he was coldly received in Paris; and when he returned empty-handed the representatives of the Constitutionalist Party in the Colonial Council lost their zeal for reform and contented themselves with the personal advantage derived from membership of this body.

The success achieved by the French authorities in blocking or disrupting all attempts by the Vietnamese to reform their archaic system of government and to obtain some relaxation of the restrictions on their liberties appears to have been largely due to the adoption of tactics based on the fomenting of regional and personal rivalries and on the suborning of individual nationalists, who were in no position to resist the threats and blandishments of the French Security Service. Moreover the authorities were ably seconded in their endeavours by the reactionary French community in Cochin-China, which sent a deputy to the French National Assembly and could count on the assistance of powerful financial groups with interests in Indochina to oppose any attempt to modify the existing régime. This community, which was made up of officials, representatives of French business interests, those engaged in trade or industry on their own account, and settlers, had few social contacts with the local population, whom they met for the most part in the capacity of domestic servants or clerks. They were therefore inclined to justify their privileges, large salaries, or handsome profits by proclaiming their conviction that the

Vietnamese were incapable of conducting their affairs without French assistance.

After the failure of these overt attempts to obtain concessions, political agitation assumed a conspiratorial form, and such organized activities as the Vietnamese were allowed to engage in, whether of a religious, educational, sporting, or even commercial nature, tended to serve as a platform for the propagation of political ideas and, on occasion, as cover for subversive action.

This tendency was demonstrated by the founding of a clandestine political group, the Viet Nam Quoc Dan Dang (VNQDD—National Party of Vietnam), following discussions between journalists and school-teachers co-operating, at the beginning of 1927, in the production of a series of booklets on current events on behalf of a small publishing firm in Hanoi. Although the publishing business was soon closed down the VNQDD, which had adopted the methods, organization, and political programme of the Kuomintang, continued to enrol recruits, so that the membership rose to 1,500 by the beginning of 1929. But the party's activities, which included blackmail, assassination, and the manufacture of bombs, soon attracted the attention of the French authorities, and after the arrest and interrogation of some of its members the French Security Service discovered the revolutionary aims and extensive ramifications of the organization. Further arrests were delayed, however, until the investigations had been completed. The VNQDD leaders for their part, who were aware of the danger in which they stood, decided, after a tardy attempt to reorganize the party on more secure lines, to promote an armed rising.

In February 1930, after a report that Vietnamese troops at Lao Kay were ready to mutiny and march on Hanoi, the VNQDD leaders ordered their supporters to make preparations for a general rising, which was to take place on the night of the 9–10th. Although this order is reported to have been countermanded, four companies of troops at Yen Bay, who were not informed of the change of plan, mutinied and killed their officers; isolated affrays also took place at Can Thao and

Hung Hoa, some villages revolted in Hai Duong province, and bomb outrages were perpetrated in Hanoi. The repression was so drastic that the surviving VNQDD leaders fled to Yunnan after an abortive attempt to reconstitute the Central Committee.

## THE INDOCHINESE COMMUNIST PARTY

The collapse of the VNQDD left the Indochinese Communist Party in the forefront of the struggle for national independence. This party had been formed in the previous January at a conference in Hong Kong which had been attended by representatives of three regional Communist groups. Its founder was a Comintern agent known as Nguyen Ai Quoc.[6]

Nguyen Ai Quoc, who was born in 1890 in North Annam, where his father occupied a minor post in the local administrative service, had signed on as a galley boy on board a French merchant ship in 1911, and in that capacity he is reported to have visited ports in Europe, Africa, and America. During the winter of 1913 he abandoned his seafaring life and came ashore in London, where he found a job as a dishwasher at the Carlton Hotel, graduating in due course to the cake-baking section of the kitchens. Some five years later he moved to Paris, sharing lodgings with the 'scholar' and reformer Phan Chau Trinh, whom he helped in his precarious job as photographer's assistant and retoucher. He is described at this period of his life as an industrious and earnest young man, who appeared obsessed by the wrongs of colonized peoples. He formed no close personal ties, was fastidious in his choice of words, and found solace in his loneliness and an outlet for his sentimentality in the company of children.

In spite of the correctness of his demeanour and the austerity of his tastes, he was to reveal in the Paris of the Versailles Conference remarkable abilities as a political agitator, in which capacity he was soon active among the Vietnamese community,[7] forming an Association of Vietnamese Patriots on whose behalf

[6] Quoc's real name appears to have been either Nguyen Van Thanh or Nguyen Van Cung (Le Thanh Khoi, p. 44). The variation Nguyen Tat Thanh has also been suggested (*Figaro*, 28–29 May 1948).

[7] During the 1914–18 war more than 43,000 Indochinese troops and a labour corps of 49,000 had been sent to Europe (E. J. Hammer, *The Struggle for Indo-China* (1954), p. 60).

he presented a memorandum to the representatives of the great powers at Versailles. This memorandum, which was based on Point Six of President Wilson's Fourteen-Point programme invoking the interests of colonized peoples, omitted all reference to national independence and merely demanded that a stop should be put to the abuses caused by the arbitrary exercise of power in Indochina and that the Vietnamese should be accorded certain basic liberties, including protection from arbitrary arrest and imprisonment.[8] Although the demands were unheeded, his courageous initiative attracted the sympathetic attention of left-wing journalists, who arranged for the memorandum to be published in the socialist newspaper *Le Populaire*. The editor of this newspaper also accepted further articles from the author, who then adopted the pen-name of Nguyen Ai Quoc, or 'Nguyen the Patriot'.

His journalistic activities brought Quoc to the notice of socialist circles in Paris, with the result that he became an affiliated member of the French Socialist Party (SFIO) and was able, in the capacity of delegate for the French Colonies, to attend the historic party convention at Tours in 1920, which was to result in a majority vote in favour of the party's adherence to the Third International: a vote which led to the foundation of the French Communist Party. Quoc, who had voted with the majority, was appointed a member of the 17th Ward in the Communist Federation of the Seine; and in the following year he founded a League of Communist Countries, editing on its behalf a weekly newspaper *Le Paria*. In 1923 he was delegated by the French Communist Party to attend a Congress of the International Peasant Council (Krestintern), and left clandestinely for Moscow where he remained throughout the following year. In January 1925 he appeared in Canton in the guise of an interpreter attached to the press section of the Soviet Mission—the Borodin Mission—which was engaged at that time in the task of reorganizing the Kuomintang Party and armies. Quoc's duties with the Mission left him ample leisure both to maintain liaison on behalf of the Comintern with a Communist-controlled organization, the Pan-Pacific Confederation of Trades Unions, and to found, in collaboration with other Asian Communists, an ephemeral League of Oppressed Peoples. He was also able to contact the Vietnamese

[8] Devillers, p. 57 n.

political refugees in Canton, who had already provided Phan Boi Chau with support. In June 1925 Quoc selected six of these Vietnamese as founder members of an Association of Vietnamese Revolutionary Youth (Viet Nam Thanh Nien Cach Mang Dong Chi Hoi), which was to be the precursor of the Indochinese Communist Party, and personally assumed the task of indoctrinating and instructing them in Communist techniques. At the same time he arranged for suitable candidates to be admitted to the Military Academy at Whampoa, where officer cadets for the Kuomintang armies were being trained by Chinese instructors under the supervision of a group of Russian military advisers.[9]

By the end of the year the first Vietnamese to be trained and indoctrinated were reinfiltrated into Indochina with instructions to form Communist cells and to recruit and dispatch suitable candidates to Canton for training as Communist agents.[10] When the rupture of the uneasy coalition between the Kuomintang and the Chinese Communist Party in March 1927, compelled the Borodin Mission to return to Moscow, Quoc, in spite of the modest nature of his official functions, was considered of sufficient importance to accompany the party. Before he left he was able to make arrangements for his directing role in the formation of the Association of Revolutionary Youth to be assumed by a Central Committee, and this Committee obtained permission from the francophobic Kuomintang authorities for the Association to continue its activities on the understanding that these were directed exclusively against French Indochina. However, this permission was withdrawn at the end of 1928, and the Committee was then compelled to shift its headquarters first to Kweilin and later to Hong Kong.

The removal of Quoc's restraining influence enabled the effervescent and disputatious representatives of the Vietnamese Association of Revolutionary Youth to give free rein to their anarchic tendencies, and at the Association's first Convention in May 1929 the three delegates from Vietnam refused to obey

---

[9] The Comintern directives which Quoc expounded had been laid down in 1920. These were that Communist parties in Asian colonial territories should confine themselves to attacks on feudal and religious institutions and seek to ally themselves with the bourgeoisie in the struggle for national independence and, concurrently with these overt activities, install a clandestine organization (Le Thanh Khoi, pp. 440–1).

[10] Ibid. p. 443.

the Comintern's directives or to recognize the authority of the Central Committee. Moreover on their return to Vietnam these delegates proceeded to found a dissident Indochinese Communist Party, whose authority was recognized in Tongking and North Annam: an action which was promptly followed in Cochin-China, where a nationalist political group affiliated to Phan Boi Chau's Association for the Restoration of Vietnam also assumed the label 'Communist'. Faced with this defiance of their authority, the Central Committee in Hong Kong decided to reveal its Communist affiliations and changed the name of the Association to that of the Annamite Communist Party.

At this time of crisis and confusion a report was received that Quoc was in Siam, and the Central Committee decided to send him an urgent appeal for assistance. The appeal proved successful, and in January 1930 Quoc met representatives of the Communist splinter groups in Hong Kong, where he succeeded in persuading them to recognize the authority of the Central Committee. As a *quid pro quo*, however, the delegates were able to obtain his consent to the adoption of the name Vietnam Communist Party by the reunited association,[11] and it was agreed that the Central Committee should transfer its headquarters to Haiphong.[12]

The decision to set up the headquarters of the Central Committee in Tongking, where its members would be exposed to the pressure of the party hotheads and to the danger of arrest, must have filled Quoc—who remained in Hong Kong—with misgivings, for he was aware that the cadres might tend in their juvenile eagerness for action to neglect security precautions. The situation in Vietnam also appeared to favour bold initiatives since the world-wide economic depression was now adversely affecting the Indochinese economy and the failure of two successive paddy crops had led to the expropriation of many smallholders. The Communist cadres thus proceeded to exploit agrarian discontent in the provinces of North Annam, where famine conditions and unabated fiscal demands had produced an explosive situation, and mass demonstrations were organized which took the form of marches on local administra-

[11] The name Vietnam Communist Party was changed to Indochinese Communist Party in October 1930.

[12] In April 1931 the Indochinese Communist Party was officially recognized by the Central Executive Committee of the Third International as a national section of the Comintern.

tive centres for the ostensible purpose of acquainting the authorities with the plight of the rural population. These demonstrations, which led to tax rolls being burnt and public buildings sacked, culminated, on 12 September 1930, in a march by 6,000 peasants on the town of Vinh, and the setting up of 'Soviets' in two adjacent districts. Meanwhile the disturbances in the provinces of Ha Tinh and Nghe An were supported by strikes throughout the country and by minor disturbances in Central Annam and Cochin-China.

The French authorities reacted with vigour, employing European troops and aircraft to quell the risings; and public order was restored, at the cost of some 10,000 civilian casualties, by the end of the year.[13] In the ensuing repression many arrests were made, with the result that in 1932 the number of political prisoners confined in Indochinese jails, penal settlements, and 'special camps' was estimated at 10,000.[14] Moreover the French Security Service, aware that the discontent in North Annam had been exploited by Communist agitators, devoted particular attention to disrupting the party's organization, and succeeded in arresting the members of the Regional Committee for Tongking and some members of the Central Committee in April 1931.

The Indochinese Communist Party was also deprived of its link with the Comintern by the arrest of Nguyen Ai Quoc in June 1931, following the seizure of incriminating letters in the possession of one Hilaire Noulens, the head of the Comintern's Far Eastern Bureau in Shanghai, which revealed that Quoc was working on behalf of this Bureau as Comintern liaison agent for South East Asia.[15] Although he was acquitted of the charge that his activities constituted a threat to the security of Hong Kong, the court nevertheless ordered that he should be deported from the colony on board a French ship: an order that delivered him into the hands of the French authorities in Indochina. However, after the counsel for the defence had contested this decision and successfully appealed on his client's behalf to the Privy Council, Quoc left the colony and disappeared.

---

[13] Le Thanh Khoi, p. 445.
[14] Chesneaux, p. 215.
[15] R. Magnenoz, *De Confucius à Lénine* (1951), pp. 113–14.

## THE NATIONALIST MOVEMENT IN COCHIN-CHINA

After the suppression of the Communist-led risings in North Annam the centre of agitation shifted to Cochin-China, which in virtue of its colonial status enjoyed a more liberal régime than the protected territories of Annam and Tongking. During 1932 the two protagonists who were to lead the opposition to French rule arrived in Saigon; and these men, Tran Van Giau and Ta Thu Thau, who had just completed their studies—the former in Moscow and the latter at a French university—represented in their persons the IIIrd and IVth International respectively.

Thau, who returned at the beginning of the year, lost no time in forming a clandestine group of Trotskyist supporters which was promptly suppressed by the French Security Services, but at the beginning of 1933 it was reconstituted ostensibly as an organization for the education of the Vietnamese working man. Meanwhile Giau, who appeared in Saigon in October 1932, was reorganizing the Communist Party's Regional Committee, which had been broken up in the previous year.

At the beginning of 1933 in association with Ta Thu Thau, Giau founded a French-language newspaper, *La Lutte*, which soon acquired considerable influence in the political life of the colony, and in May 1933 two candidates—a 'Stalinist' and a 'Trotskyist' respectively—were, with the support of *La Lutte* and in spite of official disapproval, elected to the Saigon Municipal Council. During the next two years the Indochinese Communist Party, which remained an illegal organization, re-emerged in Annam in the guise of rural friendly societies, and in Tongking under the cover of an Indochinese Democratic Front. Liaison was then established between the reconstituted Regional Committees, while arrangements were made in 1935 for a party convention to be held at Macao, at which a Central Committee was elected. In the following year, complying with Comintern instructions, the Communist Party temporarily abandoned the class struggle and the campaign against French imperialism and attempted to form a united front against the Fascist danger.

The concession by the French Government in that year of freedom of speech and association to the populations of the French colonies enabled the Communist Party to pursue its activities overtly in Cochin-China. These activities assumed the form of agitation for the convention of an Indochinese Congress and for improvements in labour conditions. In June 1936 the Central Committee decided that the Communist Party should become a legally constituted political organiza-tion, but in accordance with Comintern instructions the clan-destine networks were maintained.

Meanwhile the Trotskyist faction had become increasingly restive at the use to which *La Lutte* was being put to promote the 'united front' policy, and although the uneasy alliance was maintained until the Saigon municipal elections in 1937, when one Trotskyist and two Stalinists were elected, Ta Thu Thau and Tran Van Giau then agreed to dissolve their partnership. The newspaper, however, remained under Thau's control. The Trotskyists provided further evidence of the influence which they had acquired over the Saigon working class and in Cochin-Chinese nationalist circles when in April 1939 Ta Thu Thau and two of his lieutenants were elected to seats on the Colonial Council, which represented a stronghold of the established order.[16]

The outbreak of war in Europe, which was followed by the legal dissolution of the Communist Party in France, enabled the French Security Service to carry out mass arrests of Communists in Cochin-China. These resulted in the destruction of the Trotskyist organization, but the Stalinists, with their clandestine networks intact, were able to survive. However, the advantage which they had gained by their foresight was thrown away by the hasty action of the Regional Committee, which now decided to exploit the situation in order to stir up a revolt among the discontented and gullible peasantry in the Mekong delta. The rising, which was organized by the clandestine action sections set up by Tran Van Giau, took place on 22 November 1940 in the border provinces of the Plaine des Joncs, whence it spread to the Transbassac, but the French, employing troops, police, and aircraft against the insurgents, crushed the movement in the space of two weeks. The internal security re-established by such methods was to remain practically untroubled until the Japanese *coup de force* of 9 March 1945.

[16] The Trotskyist success in Cochin-China is ascribed to Ta Thu Thau's energy and disinterest and also to the Trotskyists' rejection of Moscow's opportunist policy (Devillers, p. 69).

## THE CAO DAI SECT

The suppression of the Yen Bay mutiny in 1930 had left the leadership in the struggle for national independence to the Indochinese Communist Party, who in the absence of an urban proletariat were to base their action on an impoverished and indebted rural population. But in spite of their skill in exploiting agrarian unrest, Communist economic theories did not appeal to the bulk of the rural population, who remained attached to their traditional way of life, and they aroused the opposition of the middle class. Thus in Cochin-China Communist claims to leadership were disputed by a number of ephemeral political groups and, later, by two religious sects—the Cao Dai and the Hoa Hao—which were to acquire political and para-military importance.

The Cao Dai sect was the first-born of these religious movements. This sect originated in psychic experiments by a group of Vietnamese clerks in Saigon–Cholon in 1925, who in the course of their experiments established communications by table-turning, with a ouija board, and finally by the use of a 'beaked wicker basket', with great spirits, including a sage of the Tang dynasty and another guiding spirit particularly distinguished by his 'high level of moral and philosophic teachings'.[17] This spirit, who had at first refused to reveal his identity, finally announced that he was no less a personage than 'Cao Dai himself, the Supreme Being, the All Powerful, Sovereign Master of the Universe', who had assumed the name of Cao Dai in order to preach a new religion.

After this revelation Cao Dai appears to have instructed the manipulators of the 'beaked basket' to approach on his behalf one Le Van Trung, a former member of the Colonial Council and contractor to the Government, whose shady financial reputation, addiction to opium, and indulgence in the pleasures of the flesh did not appear to warrant such a mark of attention on the part of the deity. However, Trung, who had 'gotten the most out of life to the point that, at the moment that the young men were sent to him, he had nearly ruined all his fortune',[18] was quick to appreciate the interest of such an important con-

[17] G. Gobron, *History and Philosophy of Caodaism*, trs. by Pham-Xuan-Thai (1950), p. 21.
[18] Ibid. p. 25.

tact, and he resolved from that day forth to lead an exemplary life, abandoning without the slightest inconvenience the smoking of opium, the consumption of alcohol, and the eating of meat. This spectacular conversion gave rise to much speculation in Saigon–Cholon and aroused the interest of a rich widow, Mme Monnier, who provided funds for the purchase of land near Tay Ninh which became the site of the Caodaist 'Holy See'.

Meanwhile the cult of Cao Dai began to attract adepts in Saigon–Cholon and also in the countryside, where teams of missionaries under Trung's directions made many converts.[19] Besides directing these missionary activities Trung also provided on a generous scale for the administration of the new sect by creating, on the advice of an adept named Pham Cong Tac, an imposing hierarchy modelled on that of the Roman Catholic Church. Trung, in his capacity as the eldest of the children of God and possessor of the spiritual power, became the Cao Dai 'Pope', and a consistory of cardinals invested with legislative powers was established to assist him. The edicts of this consistory were carried out by an executive branch composed of 36 archbishops, 72 bishops, and 3,000 priests. In addition to this consistory, a college of women dignitaries presided over by Mme Monnier was founded.

Meanwhile Trung and Pham Cong Tac pressed forward vigorously with the construction of a spacious temple at the 'Holy See'. This building, which was to serve as a model for many minor Cao Dai oratories throughout Cochin-China, was built on the lines of a church, with a nave, aisles, and an apse, the entrance being flanked by twin towers. But if the plan was that of a church, the sugary filigree-like decoration, the upturned eaves of the three-tiered roof, and the stucco dragons in pastel shades entwining the pillars in the nave conformed to the traditional décor of a pagoda.[20]

[19] The success on the Cao Dai missionaries has been ascribed to the fact that the rural population whose religious beliefs are based on an amalgam of Animism and Genii worship, overlaid by Buddhist, Confucian, and Taoist customs and beliefs, were attracted both by the supernatural and marvellous elements of Cao Daism and also by the few demands made upon the adept, who was required merely to prostrate himself once a day before the altar of Cao Dai, and to obey the injunction 'not to kill, to avoid cupidity, luxury, gaiety and sin in words' (ibid. p. 35).

[20] The Cao Dai temple at Tay Ninh, with its occidental plan and oriental overlay, was an appropriate setting for the religious services of a sect claiming to

# 88 FRENCH INDOCHINA

Trung's last years were saddened by the intrigues of his principal lieutenant, Pham Cong Tac, who controlled the 'College of Mediums', and also a powerful secret society, the Pham Mon. Moreover Trung had laid himself open to his lieutenant's insidious attacks as his moral regeneration had not been accompanied by any marked improvement in the dubious financial methods with which he had been accustomed to conduct his business before his election to the Cao Dai papacy. In consequence the complaints of the adepts about his unscrupulous misuse and even embezzlement of funds had become a source of grief to Trung and of embarrassment to the sect when he was 'disincarnated' in 1934.[21]

Trung's death gave rise to a struggle for the succession, which ended in the following year, after a number of schisms and the setting up of at least one 'Anti-Pope', to the advantage of Pham Cong Tac, who proceeded to place the sect, now numbering some 300,000 adepts, on a sound administrative and financial basis. After the outbreak of the Second World War, however, the French authorities, who had hitherto refrained from interfering with Cao Dai activities, were aroused to action by the intrigues of the sect's leaders with Japanese agents. In June 1940 the temple at Tay Ninh and Cao Dai oratories throughout Cochin-China were closed, while Pham Cong Tac himself, together with five of his advisers, were exiled to Madagascar. These measures were completed by shutting down the Cao Dai centre in Phnom Penh in the autumn of 1942. But the Japanese political police—the Kempeitai—who were then attempting to unite the elements of a nationalist opposition, established contact with Tran Quang Vinh, who had been the head of this Cao Dai centre, and encouraged him to form a committee to co-ordinate the sect's activities throughout Cochin-China. These activities assumed a para-military form towards the end of 1943, when groups of Cao Dai adepts began to be trained and armed to act as Japanese auxiliaries.

### THE HOA HAO SECT

Meanwhile in West Cochin-China, where the Cao Dai sect

represent the synthesis of mankind's main religions, except for Mohammedanism, which was rejected on the grounds that it was 'coarse'.
[21] A. M. Savani, *Visages et images du Sud Viet-Nam* (1955), pp. 76–77.

had many adepts, a rival religious movement was acquiring thousands of supporters among the primitive peasants of this rich and recently developed area. The founder of the movement, Huynh Phu So, was the son of a notable in the village of Hoa Hao, which is situated near the Cambodian border in the province of Chau Doc. So had been afflicted in his youth with a strange languor; and his father, hoping to cure this distressing ailment, had committed him to the care of a Buddhist priest who lived as a recluse in a pagoda at Tra Son in the Seven Mountains. During this period of seclusion So was instructed in Buddhist doctrine and also appears to have acquired some knowledge of magic. After the death of his mentor So, who had grown into a handsome young man of emaciated appearance with strange hypnotic eyes, returned to his native village, where he resumed the listless existence to which his continuing state of languor condemned him; but in 1939, during a stormy night, as lightning struck the great banyan tree in the centre of the village, he arose in a state of great excitement, and after prostrating himself before the family altar proceeded to expound the lofty tenets of Buddhist philosophy, ending his oration by declaring to those who had gathered around him that he was the apostle of a famous Buddhist monk who had lived in Cochin-China in the reign of Minh Mang and had been entrusted with the mission of preaching a 'reformed' Buddhism. Reports of this strange event, which had been followed by So's return to health, spread throughout West Cochin-China, where the simplicity of the doctrine which he expounded led to many conversions among the rural population, who were subjugated by 'the Master's' compelling personality. Moreover So, who possessed the gift of prophecy, increased the awe in which he was held by predicting that a series of catastrophic events was about to overwhelm Cochin-China, including an impending defeat of the French, a Japanese occupation, and the arrival of the Americans.

The French Security Service, alarmed by the activities and prophecies of this 'mad' bonze, arranged towards the end of 1940 for him to be confined in a psychiatric hospital in Cholon, but following his conversion of the doctor in whose care he had been placed, he was transferred to Bac Lieu. 'The Master's' presence in Bac Lieu, however, continued to cause unrest in the Transbassac and it was finally decided to transfer him to

Laos. At this juncture the Japanese, who were now installed in Indochina, intervened and arranged for him to be abducted and taken under their wing in Saigon. Nevertheless the Kempeitai, who may have hoped to exploit the popular enthusiasm aroused by Huynh Phu So, were soon compelled to recognize that the Hoa Hao sect did not possess leaders of sufficient mental calibre to play a leading part in a nationalist régime and lost interest in their protégé.

# VI

# The Japanese Occupation

AFTER the fall of Nanking at the end of 1937 and the loss of Hankow and Canton in the following year, the Chinese Government was driven to take refuge at Chungking on the upper reaches of the Yangtze, where it became dependent for imports on the Yunnan railway, on a route across Sinkiang and, following its completion in March 1939, on the Burma Road. The Yunnan railway represented the most important of these links which the Chinese Government still possessed with the outside world. In consequence traffic between Haiphong and Kunming soon reached considerable proportions. The use to which the railway was being put did not escape the attention of the Japanese, who soon brought pressure to bear upon the French Government to stop this traffic, but although the French agreed to ban the entry of war material into the port of Haiphong, other supplies for the Chinese Government, and in particular consignments of trucks and oil fuel, continued to be accepted and forwarded to Kunming.

Finally, in June 1940, the Japanese profited from the German invasion of France to present the French authorities in Indochina with an ultimatum, to which a time-limit was attached, which demanded the closure of Haiphong to all Chinese imports and also the acceptance of a Japanese Control Commission to supervise the enforcement of the ban.

The ultimatum embarrassed the Governor-General, General Catroux, who was unable to contact the French Government, which had been disorganized by the evacuation of the ministries to Bordeaux. Catroux was aware, however, that the forces available for the defence of Indochina against Japanese attack were inadequate for that purpose and that the Anglo-French talks which had taken place in June 1939 had revealed that no reinforcements could be expected from Malaya.[1] Moreover,

[1] Although 50,000 troops were stationed in Indochina, most of these belonged to Annamite, Cambodian, and Laotian militia units employed on security and garrison duties. Front-line troops consisted merely of some units of Colonial Infantry and Foreign Legionaries. The French navy was represented in Far Eastern waters by the cruiser *Lamotte Picquet*, which had been launched in 1926, by four

although the country had been equipped with airfields and a naval base, the absence of industrial equipment made Indochina dependent either on accumulated stocks of war material or on the continued arrival of such supplies from France. But existing stocks of war material were totally inadequate in the event of an invasion, while the ability of the French Government to make good deficiencies was now open to question.

When he had completed this bleak assessment of his resources, and had made every effort to get American or British help, Catroux had no alternative but to accept the Japanese demands. However, this decision was to result in his replacement, since when communications had been re-established with France the Minister for Colonies disapproved of his action. When Catroux refused to accept the official reprimand, maintaining bluntly that his action had been justified, his attitude aroused misgivings in Bordeaux and on Admiral Darlan's recommendation the Government decided to replace him by Vice-Admiral Decoux, the Commander-in-Chief of French naval forces in the Far East.

Decoux, who took over his functions on 20 July, was soon faced with further Japanese demands, which were presented on 2 August by the Chief of Staff of the Japanese 'Army of Canton', and included the concession of transit facilities across Tongking for Japanese troops, war material, and supplies, and the authorization to use local airfields. However, Decoux refused to be inveigled into discussions, objecting that he possessed no authority to make such concessions. The French Government approved his attitude and agreed to negotiate with the Japanese Government through its Embassy in Tokyo, these negotiations resulting, on 30 August, in the conclusion of an agreement[2] by the terms of which the Japanese Government formally recognized French sovereignty over Indochina and undertook to respect its territorial integrity. In return the French undertook to accept Japan's 'pre-eminent' position in the Far East and to

---

sloops, of which two were of recent construction, and by some river gunboats; while the air force possessed 15 Morane fighter planes, some obsolete bombers, and an assortment of reconnaissance aircraft.

[2] The French Ambassador in Washington elicited at this stage an unofficial statement from the American Under-Secretary to the effect that the State Department appreciated the difficulties with which the French Government were faced and did not consider that it would be justified in reproaching France if certain military facilities were to be accorded Japan.

grant certain military facilities in Tongking which would help the Japanese to terminate the 'China incident'. It was also agreed that a military convention should be negotiated without delay in Hanoi between the French and Japanese military authorities.[3]

These military discussions, which opened in Hanoi on 5 September, set the pattern for subsequent negotiations, during which the Japanese were able to extend their control pacifically over the whole Indochinese peninsula since, whereas admirable tenacity was displayed in resisting those Japanese demands which were considered exorbitant, important concessions were nevertheless made on the basis of the French assessment of the least that the Japanese would be prepared to accept. On 22 September, a military agreement[4] was signed giving Japan the right to use three airfields in Tongking and to station 6,000 troops there, to send not more than 25,000 troops at a time through Indochina, and to evacuate through Haiphong a Japanese division which had got into difficulties near the Tongking frontier. This last clause was subject to the conclusion of a further special convention. But that night this errant division, impatient at the protracted nature of the negotiations, crossed the frontier and advanced on Lang Son. Here after confused fighting the surrender of the main defence position on the 25th opened the road to Hanoi. However, further advance was halted by the personal intervention of the Japanese Emperor, who was patently anxious to prevent an extension of the conflict, and when the French prisoners had been released the division was allowed to proceed peacefully to Haiphong, where it embarked without further incident.[5]

Meanwhile a further incident had occurred at Haiphong, on the night of 25–26 September, when the military force which had arrived to assume guard duties at the three Japanese-controlled airfields started to disembark clandestinely in the vicinity of the port. Fortunately French liaison officers were able to allay the suspicions which appear to have prompted this action, with the result that the remainder of the Japanese troops disembarked pacifically the next day.

[3] Jean Decoux, À la barre de l'Indochine (1949), p. 100. Text of the agreement in IMTFE, 3 Oct. 1946, pp. 6936–9.
[4] Text in IMTFE, 3 Oct. 1946, pp. 6949–54.
[5] Decoux, pp. 114–20.

## SIAMESE AGGRESSION

Japan was not the only country to exploit the French defeat in Europe. Siam began to raise ancient claims to the Cambodian provinces of Battambang and Siem Reap and to Lao territory on the right bank of the river Mekong, comprising part of the principality of Bassac and the province of Pak Lay, which contained the tombs of the royal house of Luang Prabang and the royal teak forests. After the rejection of tentative Siamese demands for the cession of these territories by the Governor-General and by the Vichy Government a press and radio campaign was organized from Bangkok against the French Protectorate, while a series of incidents and provocations were engineered along the course of the river Mekong; these resulted by December 1940 in the creation of a state of undeclared war involving exchanges of artillery fire across the river and reciprocal bombing of Laotian and Siamese market towns.

At the beginning of January 1941 a Siamese force advanced into Cambodian territory and established a bridge-head around the frontier town of Poipet. On the 16th four French battalions went into action against this bridge-head, but the Siamese, who had been forewarned, counter-attacked and during the ensuing engagement compelled the French to withdraw. The failure of this operation combined with the surrender of the garrison at Lang Son undermined Decoux's confidence in his military advisers and served to confirm his belief in the superior capacities of naval officers, a belief which was reinforced by a successful engagement on 17 January in the Gulf of Siam between a French and Siamese naval force, during which about half the Siamese fleet was either sunk or severely damaged without loss to the French.

At this stage in the undeclared war the Japanese Government decided to stop the fighting and offered to mediate. The offer was backed up by the arrival of a powerful Japanese fleet which proceeded to cruise off the mouths of the river Mekong. On 3 January 1941 the contending forces yielded to this cogent argument and agreed to an armistice. The ensuing negotiations were laborious, but on 9 May a treaty was signed in Tokyo whereby the French surrendered the disputed territories on the right bank of the river Mekong, together with the province of

Battambang and Cambodian territory between the Dangrek hills and the 15th parallel of latitude.[6]

During the next seven months Japan extorted further concessions, both from the Vichy Government and from the Government-General, which enabled Japanese military control to be established over Indochina. On 29 July an agreement was signed by the Japanese Ambassador, and by Darlan, on behalf of the Vichy Government, recognizing that the defence of Indochina was henceforth a joint Franco-Japanese commitment and removing all restrictions on the number of Japanese troops which might be stationed in Indochinese territory. In addition to this concession, strategic roads and railways, together with port facilities at Tourane, Cam Ranh Bay, and Saigon, and seven airfields in south Indochina[7] were made available for the use of the Japanese armed forces. These facilities were exploited without loss of time in order to build up a forward base in Indochina for their plans for expansion in South East Asia.

In spite of evidence that military preparations for an offensive were proceeding on a vast scale, the French authorities appear to have been unconscious of the imminent danger with which they were faced, and on the night of 7–8 December Japanese troops were able to infiltrate into Hanoi without attracting the attention of the French garrison. On the morning of 8 December the head of the Japanese Military Mission called on Decoux to inform him of the Japanese attack on the American fleet in Pearl Harbour. Having imparted this interesting piece of news, the Japanese general asked for assurances that Decoux would do nothing to hinder the activities of Japanese forces. If Decoux refused, the Japanese would take over Indochina. After asking for a short delay in order to consult his advisers, Decoux agreed to discuss the implications of the situation with the Japanese.

The discussions, which continued throughout the following night, proved stormy, and although an agreement was reached on 9 December reaffirming French sovereignty over and administrative responsibility for Indochina, the maintenance of the *status quo* was purchased by an undertaking that the French

[6] Text in *Contemporary Japan*, June 1941, pp. 840–2. In October 1946 Siam agreed to return these territories to Cambodia and Laos respectively.

[7] These included the airfield at Saigon, from which Japanese bomber aircraft were shortly to take off to sink the battleships *Prince of Wales* and *Repulse* off the Malayan coast.

authorities would offer no opposition to Japan's aggressive designs in South East Asia, and would place Indochina's economic resources at the disposal of Japan. This agreement, which brought about the inclusion of Indochina within the 'co-prosperity sphere', enabled the Japanese to continue to use the services of French administrators, technicians, and soldiers in Indochina, an arrangement which freed trained Japanese personnel for service in other areas, but the advantages that the French derived from the arrangement were likewise considerable, since their nationals, numbering some 40,000, were spared the ordeal of internment under the terrible conditions prevailing in Japanese prison camps. However, Decoux's subsequent claim that the French flag, which might be more properly termed an Admiral's pennant, was the only Allied flag to fly freely not only over Indochina but in all the Far East[8] until the Japanese *coup de force* of 9 March 1945, ignored the fact that this concession was purchased by a degree of co-operation in, and subservience to, Japanese designs sufficient to deter the Tokyo Government from assuming direct administrative responsibility for Indochina.[9]

## DECOUX AS KING-MAKER

As contacts between Indochina and France were confined during the next three years to telegraphic communications, the Governor-General's position became similar to that occupied by the head of a satellite state. Decoux, the head of this state, has been described as by nature suspicious, masterful, and secretive; his conduct was inspired by unswerving loyalty to the Vichy Government.[10] Moreover his inability to appreciate the wider issues at stake in the conflict, his sterile and petty conception of French prestige, and his lack of compassion for the fate of the European communities in Malaya and Indonesia fitted him well for the role which he was called on to play.

[8] Decoux, p. 164.

[9] The services which the Japanese obtained from the French included, in addition to the provision of rice and minerals, the dispatch in January 1942 of French naval technicians to Borneo to repair oil installations sabotaged at the time of the Japanese invasion, and the surrender of more than 50,000 tons of shipping immobilized in Indochinese ports (G. Sabattier, *Le Destin de l'Indochine* (1952), p. 59).

[10] Gen. Mordant, *Au Service de la France en Indochine* (1950), p. 29.

The Admiral's autocratic temperament and purblind insensitivity were likewise apparent in his dealings with the sovereigns of the three Indochinese states. Although he sought to enhance their prestige by outward signs of deference and by making more liberal provision for their financial needs, this was done with the avowed intention of exploiting more effectively the respect in which they were held by their subjects,[11] and no encouragement was given them to play a more active part in the administration of their respective kingdoms. Nevertheless Decoux's subsequent discovery that these sovereigns were dissatisfied with their futile, if decorative role and resented the summary fashion with which their representations were dismissed, seems to have caused him pained and incredulous surprise.[12]

Decoux's inability to divine the feelings and to gauge the personalities of the Indochinese rulers is shown in his decision to intervene in the choice of a successor to the Cambodian throne, an action which was subsequently to lead to French discomfiture. For on the death of King Monivong in 1941, it was generally assumed that his eldest son, Prince Monireth, would be selected by the Council of the royal family to succeed him. But Monireth, who had served with the French Foreign Legion, was a man of blunt speech and decided opinions and Decoux viewed the prospect of his accession with misgivings. French influence was therefore brought to bear to secure the election of his nephew, Norodom Sihanouk, since this prince, who was then a boarder at the Lycée Chasseloup-Laubat in Saigon, possessed a capacity for short-lived enthusiasm and an artless candour which appeared to qualify him for the position of a protected monarch.[13]

The role of king-maker appears to have flattered the vanity of

[11] Decoux, p. 270.
[12] Ibid. p. 274.
[13] The ostensible reason for giving the throne to Norodom Sihanouk was a desire to make amends to the elder branch of the royal family since, on King Norodom's death in 1904, the French Resident had induced the Family Council of the royal family to set aside the claims of the deceased monarch's sons and elect his brother, Sisowath, who had assisted the French to pacify the country. On Sisowath's death in 1927, the claims of the elder branch were again passed over, and Sisowath's son, Monivong, had succeeded to the throne. Norodom Sihanouk was, however, descended from both these rival branches. Whereas his father, Prince Suramarit, was Norodom's grandson, his mother, Princess Kossaman, was a daughter of King Monivong.

the childless Governor-General, and he continued to take an avuncular interest in the youthful monarch, who for his part appeared to fulfil Decoux's expectations. But in spite of the political apathy shown by the Cambodian people, the tide of nationalism then lapping around the frontiers of the kingdom had led a group of young men, including a number of Buddhist monks, to engage in activities directed to securing national independence. The leader of this group was a Cambodian of mixed descent with the Vietnamese name of Son Ngoc Thanh, who was a member of the teaching staff of the School of Advanced Pali Studies in Phnom Penh. In 1936 Thanh had founded a Cambodian-language newspaper which by adopting a critical attitude towards the protectorate served as a rallying point for those discontented with French rule, and in 1942 he was sufficiently emboldened by the arrival of Japanese troops in Indochina to organize a demonstration by bonzes against the arrest of one of their number. This demonstration, which took place in front of the French Residency, got out of hand, but the Cambodian guards were prevented by religious scruples from effectively resisting their saffron-robed assailants and contented themselves with firing their rifles in the air. Finally, the French police dispersed the rioters; Thanh, who was threatened with arrest, escaped to Bangkok where the Japanese took him under their protection and sent him to Tokyo.

## THE ECONOMIC EFFECTS OF OCCUPATION

If Decoux's conception of his duty was inadequate and his treatment of the Indochinese sovereigns lacking in tact, the tenacity with which he sought, during recurrent and arduous negotations, to reduce the Japanese demands and to preserve the façade of French sovereignty is deserving some tribute. The energetic and successful measures taken to remedy the critical economic situation must also be ascribed to his credit.[14] Since more than half of Indochina's import and export trade had been conducted either with France or with French Overseas Territories, its interruption compelled the Government-General

[14] In 1938 Indochinese exports included 1,016,282 tons of rice, 58,023 tons of rubber, 548,010 tons of maize, and 1,578,038 tons of coal; imports were made up of petrol, fuel, and lubicating oils, textiles, pharmaceutical products, motor vehicles, and industrial equipment (*Annuaire des États Associés, 1953*, p. 32).

to seek other channels through which Indochina's essential requirements could be met and the economic asphyxiation of the country prevented, but after the elimination of the United States as a trading partner Japan represented the only customer for Indochinese products. Indications had already been afforded, moreover, of the Japanese intention to secure a 'preeminent' economic position in the Indochinese market: in July 1940 an official request had been made that Japanese traders should be accorded privileges similar to those enjoyed by French commercial interests, and in October a Japanese economic mission had arrived in Tongking in order to negotiate an economic agreement.

In May of the following year a pact and an economic agreement were signed which constituted the basis for future economic co-operation between the French and Japanese authorities. The pact provided that for a period of five years Japanese nationals should enjoy privileges similar to those enjoyed by the French, including the right to reside, travel, engage in commerce and industry, and to open schools, hospitals, and places of worship. The economic agreement was clearly designed to subordinate the Indochinese economy to Japanese requirements since by its terms the bulk of the rice surplus, together with the total production of manganese, tungsten, antimony, tin, and chrome, were reserved for export to Japan, payment for these purchases being made through an exchange clearing system which allowed for the settlement of balances in excess of 5 million yen either in gold or in a free currency. Provision was also made for periodic conferences to examine outstanding economic questions. However, the execution of this agreement was hampered by the shortage of shipping, which prevented the Japanese from transporting the agricultural products and minerals which had been acquired.[15]

The decline in exports was accompanied by a drastic reduction in imports, which fell in 1944 to 2 per cent. of their prewar tonnage. The sudden stoppage of imports and in particular the inability to replenish stocks of oil fuel and machine parts seemed likely to have a disastrous effect upon the internal economy, and constituted a definite threat to the tenuous

---

[15] Indochinese exports amounted in 1941 to 60 per cent. of the total tonnage exported in 1939; by 1944 exports had declined to 14 per cent. of the pre-war figure.

communications system which assured the cohesion of an area that had not been endowed by nature with geographical unity. However, the ingenuity of French and Vietnamese technicians was to prove equal to the challenge, with the result that the anticipated breakdown in communications was staved off and basic requirements of the European and Vietnamese communities continued to be met. The petrol shortage was overcome by restrictions on the use of motor vehicles, by the conversion of some of these vehicles to burn an alternate fuel, and by the intensive production of rice alcohol which was adapted for use as motor spirit. A substitute for oil fuel was also perfected, composed of a mixture of fish, coconut, and peanut oils. The shortage of textiles, hitherto almost entirely imported from France, presented another serious problem which was only partially resolved by an increase in the local production of cotton, by the employment of exotic fibres, and by the revival of the traditional hand-weaving industry which had fallen into decay following the importation of European machine-made textiles. Methods were also evolved to manufacture paper, soap, and some pharmaceutical products, with the result that by 1943 the local production of quinine became sufficient to meet local requirements.

In addition to the encouragement of technical research destined to remedy these shortages, the Government-General also undertook an ambitious programme of public works calculated to offset the damage to French prestige occasioned by the presence of Japanese troops on Indochinese soil. The programme included the reclamation of wide areas of agricultural land in Tongking, in North Annam, and in the Transbassac area of Cochin-China, and work on the communications system, including the completion of a road, which followed the course of the river Mekong, and linked Luang Prabang with Saigon, a distance of some 1,000 miles. Roads were also constructed giving access to the Moi plateaux from Saigon and to the river Mekong from the coast of Annam; the hill-station of Dalat, which had been selected as the future seat of the Federal Government, was laid out in a fitting style.

Such impressive achievements were accompanied by improvements in educational facilities designed to combat the influence of the schools which the Japanese, in virtue of the agreement of 6 May 1941, had been authorized to open and to ensure the availability of suitably qualified Vietnamese to replace officials who had hitherto been recruited in France. These improved facilities resulted in a large increase in the number of children attending village schools; and a science faculty was founded at Hanoi University, where the construction of hostels was also undertaken to house students from all parts of the country. The execution of this considerable programme was facilitated by the fact that during the war years French government approval was no longer required for the expenditure involved in the execution of these projects.

## THE FRENCH RESISTANCE MOVEMENT

The eclipse of French power in Indochina was not immediately apparent to the native population since the French Administrative Service continued to function throughout the country and French troops continued to discharge their traditional garrison duties. Moreover the Japanese, who were stationed principally at strategic points, were seldom to be seen in the towns; and they had incurred some popular odium at an early date by the arrogance of their demeanour and by their reluctance to pay for goods and services. Indeed the elegant Vietnamese are reported to have been discreetly and ironically amused by the pompous behaviour and squat appearance of these protagonists of a 'New Order' in Asia.

The French for their part soon became accustomed to their precarious and isolated position; the mode of life of this privileged minority was scarcely affected by the absence of wine and certain foodstuffs or by the paucity of textiles and luxury goods. Moreover, after initial reluctance to credit the extent of the national disaster, they found much to admire in the programme of the 'National Revolution' sponsored by the Vichy Government since they were instinctively attracted by the authoritarian principles and traditional values incarnated in the person of Marshal Pétain. Although Jews, Free Masons, and declared supporters of General de Gaulle were to suffer some persecution at the hands of the Federal Security Services, the community as a whole adapted themselves to their altered circumstances without undue repining.

However, some French civilians, belonging for the most part to that enterprising section of the community who were employed on the plantations, felt reluctant to remain inactive in a war which was likely to prove decisive for their country's future and attempted at an early date to establish wireless contact with American intelligence agencies in South China; these attempts proved successful, and during 1941 some networks were set up in Cochin-China, Annam, and Tongking which provided the Allies with intelligence on Japanese troop and shipping movements. In 1942 Free French emissaries started to contact French officers in command of posts on the Chinese frontier, with the result that by the beginning of 1944 regular wireless contacts had been established between the French Military Statistical Bureau in Hanoi, which was responsible for collecting and collating military intelligence, and the Free French Military Mission which had arrived in Chungking in October of the previous year. The existence of this wireless link was subsequently divulged by the head of the Statistical Bureau to General Mordant, the Senior General commanding French troops in Indochina, who availed himself of its existence to request instructions from the Free French Committee in Algiers on the action that should be taken in the event of an attempt by the Japanese forces to disarm the French garrisons. Meanwhile the presence of a French Military Mission in Chungking had also prompted Decoux, who was anxious to discourage any project that might be under consideration for an Allied landing in Tongking, to send his Diplomatic Counsellor to the Chinese frontier with instructions to convey to an emissary of the Free French Military Mission his appreciation of the local situation.[16]

In April 1944 a reply was received to Mordant's request for instructions which provided the basis for a plan designed to co-ordinate resistance activities throughout the country. Instructions were then drafted and issued to commanding officers laying down the course of action to be taken and the demolition work to be carried out in the event of a Japanese attack. Mordant, who had reached the age of retirement, asked in July 1944 to be relieved of his command, a request which was granted without demur by Decoux, whose relations with the Senior General were not cordial, but in the following

[16] Raids by American aircraft on Indochinese railways, ports, and coastal shipping, which had begun in the previous year, appeared to point to the possibility of a landing.

September, Mordant, then living in Hanoi, was appointed by the French Provisional Government Delegate-General for Indochina and invested with full military and political powers.

This appointment was to lead to some confusion, for, following the German invasion of unoccupied France, Decoux had himself officially assumed full responsibility for the conduct of Indochinese affairs. The anomalous position in which he had been placed by Mordant's appointment was finally explained to him by Mordant's successor, General Aymé. After registering a vigorous protest against a decision which was calculated to increase the difficulty and danger of the French position, Decoux was compelled to agree to the creation of a Council for Indochina composed of men who enjoyed the confidence of the leaders of the new French régime.

Mordant's appointment to the post of Delegate-General under the nominal authority of Decoux was, however, to introduce an additional element of danger into the local situation at a time when a Japanese attack was imminent since although Mordant, as Delegate-General of the French Provisional Government, was in receipt of instructions from General de Gaulle himself, from the Ministry of National Defence, and from the head of the French Section of Force 136,[17] he remained somewhat hazy in his conception of the potentialities and limitations of clandestine resistance and proved incapable of imposing his authority over the various underground groups which had been formed, without his knowledge, during the Japanese occupation. The reluctance of these groups to place themselves under his orders was due both to the clannish particularism which had long constituted a facet of French colonial life, and to the fact that Mordant was known to have rallied to the Free French somewhat late in the day and at the instigation of officers under his command. Moreover the assumption by the military authorities of responsibility for clandestine activities, which was accompanied by an almost total disregard for normal security precautions, gave rise to well-founded misgivings. For example, French agents who had arrived secretly from Calcutta were allowed to circulate freely in Saigon, and consignments of sub-machine guns and wireless transmitting sets, which had arrived in similar fashion, were for the most part collected, inventoried, and placed along with other stores in military

[17] Force 136 was an intelligence organization with headquarters in Calcutta.

depots, where they were seized on 9 March 1945 by the Japanese.[18] The danger presented by this rigid conception of the potentialities of clandestine resistance was further increased by a natural tendency on the part of a leisured colonial society to indulge in verbal indiscretions, which were frequently committed in the hearing of the domestic staff. Such reckless behaviour was to leave the Japanese in no doubt about what was going on.

## THE JAPANESE *COUP DE FORCE*

The reoccupation of the Philippine Islands in October 1944 by an American force under the command of General MacArthur made the sea-borne invasion of Indochina a feasible operation. The Japanese Military Command was aware that in such an eventuality French forces would be prepared to assist the invaders, thanks to their knowledge of French activities in Indochina and to the fact that French broadcasters continually stressed the intention of the Provisional Government to reconquer Indochina by force of arms. This lack of caution on the part of the local French community and the French Government, together with reports of increased air activities over Indochinese territory, provided the Japanese General Staff with arguments to convince the Tokyo Government that it had become necessary to take over administrative control. Accordingly at the beginning of 1945 a Japanese infantry division which had been operating in South China crossed the frontier on the pretext that reinforcements were required in order to meet the threat of invasion.

The arrival of this division enabled the Japanese Command to increase troop concentrations in Annam and to establish additional garrisons in Tongking and Laos. These military dispositions were made in such a manner that by the middle of February Japanese units were everywhere stationed in the vicinity of the French garrisons, and in some cases they were astride the roads which the French would be using in the event of an enforced retreat to the mountainous regions. These dispositions constituted a potential source of grave embarrassment since in January 1945 Mordant's plan of action had been approved by the French Ministry of National Defence. This

[18] Paul Mus, *Le Viet-Nam chez lui* (1946), pp. 5–6.

plan entailed the gradual withdrawal of all the main military units from the towns and their deployment in areas where a line of retreat was open to the mountainous regions, whence raids could be carried out, in the event of an attempt to suppress French sovereignty, against communications and military objectives in Japanese-occupied territory.

During the months of January and February 1945 the initial steps in the implementation of this plan were taken, French troops being withdrawn from the eastern section of Tongking and redeployed in the triangle formed by the Clear and Black rivers, where they were centred on a vast military camp at Tong under the command of General Alessandri. But although the general circumstances indicated danger, both the Delegate-General and Aymé discounted, on 8 March, a report from an agent in the pay of the Security Service that the Japanese were planning to attack between 8 and 10 March.[19] Fortunately General Sabattier, commanding the French troops in Tongking, formed a different opinion and acting on his own initiative declared a practice 'State of Alert' and left Hanoi to rejoin his operational headquarters. This action enabled the troops at Tong (in Tongking) to withdraw, after the Japanese *coup de force*, across the Black and Red rivers to the mountainous region whence, in the absence of effective air support, they were compelled to continue a gallant fighting retreat to the Chinese frontier.

Meanwhile in Saigon the Japanese Ambassador, who had asked to be received by the Governor-General on the afternoon of 9 March, presented Decoux with an ultimatum demanding that French military, naval, and air forces, together with the police, should be placed under Japanese command and that the Administrative Service and the banks should become directly subject to Japanese control, two hours being accorded for the acceptance of these demands. Aware of the unacceptable nature of the ultimatum the Japanese had in the meantime completed preparations to occupy military and administrative establishments throughout Indochina.

In Saigon–Cholon, although the Japanese attack surprised the French garrison in their barracks, resistance continued throughout the night. At Thu Dau Mot and Cape St. Jacques

[19] Their disbelief was ascribed to the absence of confirmation from military intelligence networks.

the Japanese encountered similar opposition, while in the Transbassac military and naval units based on Can Tho retired to the mangrove swamps around Ca Mau and kept up their resistance, in spite of discouraging natural conditions, for a further ten days.

Meanwhile in Cambodia, although the small French garrisons were able in some cases to take to the maquis, they were soon rounded up. Farther to the north the garrisons at Qui Nhon, Dong Ha, and Quang Ngai repulsed enemy attacks throughout the night, and at Hué, where some precautions had been taken, French troops managed to inflict relatively heavy casualties upon the enemy. But even in Tongking, where the army possessed a military fief in the frontier regions, resistance was soon overcome; in Hanoi, after Sabattier's 'State of Alert' had been cancelled on Aymé's orders, a surprise attack was launched on the citadel during the evening, and although the garrison put up a spirited resistance, the exhaustion of their ammunition compelled them to surrender on the following day. At Lang Son the forts, with their defences weakened by treachery, fell to the Japanese on the afternoon of 10 March.

Thus within the short space of twenty-four hours all French resistance had been overcome with the exception of the force under the command of Alessandri which was retreating towards Son La; in addition, some scattered parties of survivors had been able to take refuge in swamps in the Transbassac or in the forests of Central Annam and Laos. Moreover the military collapse had been accompanied by that of the resistance organization since the 'Action Sections' attached to this organization failed to carry out any of the prescribed demolitions, the failure being ascribed to the absence of liaison between the various resistance groups and also to a lack of co-ordination within the Sections themselves, which prevented them from reacting quickly enough to the emergency.

### BAO DAI AS PUPPET EMPEROR

The *coup de force* of 9 March also surprised the Vietnamese. Bao Dai, who had spent the day hunting near Quang Tri in company with the Senior Resident, was detained by the Japanese on his return to Hué in the early hours of the morning, and guarded until dawn in the gardens of the imperial city.[20] In the afternoon, when the resistance of the French garrison had been overcome, the Japanese Ambassador informed him that the *coup de force* had been designed to restore Vietnamese independence. In return for this service, however, the Ambassador demanded that Vietnam should agree to co-operate with Japan in 'Greater East Asia'.

The Emperor, who had at first supposed that the Japanese intended to demand his abdication, summoned a meeting of his ministers, at which it was agreed without a single dissenting voice that a favourable reply should be given to this demand. This decision amounted to recognition that the sovereign's duty to his people required that he should make every effort before the impending Japanese defeat to unify and consolidate the country in order to make good subsequent claims to national independence. Loyalty to the French connexion or to an Allied cause which the French Government-General had themselves abandoned obviously represented a secondary consideration in the choice which Bao Dai was called upon to make.

The national independence which had been restored was nevertheless mortgaged by the presence of Japanese troops, but in spite of this limitation Bao Dai sought to form a Government which would command a measure of popular support, and on 17 April he appointed Professor Tran Trong Kim, whose reputation was based on his academic attainments and on his ardent patriotism, to the premiership. The Government tried at first to obtain from the Japanese the powers which would enable them to unify and administer the country, but their efforts met with scant success. In March, however, Bao Dai had been allowed to affirm his authority over Tongking by the appointment of a Viceroy and in July the French concessions in Hanoi, Haiphong, and Tourane were officially abolished. Finally, on 8 August the Japanese authorities agreed to transfer the administration of Cochin-China to the Vietnamese Government. The Government also sought to acquire popular support by exempting the poorest section of the community from the payment of the onerous poll-tax, and a general amnesty was proclaimed for political prisoners, numbering 10,000, who were detained in penal settlements.[21]

[20] *Le Monde*, 23 Feb. 1946.
[21] G. de Chézal, *Parachuté en Indochine* (1947), p. 49.

During the months preceding the Japanese surrender the country slowly drifted into a state of anarchy, the process of administrative disintegration being hastened by the dislocation of internal communications caused by the Allied air attacks on the railway system and coastal shipping and by the state of disrepute into which the mandarinate had fallen under the Protectorate. The inability of the Imperial Government to substitute its authority for that of the French administration was demonstrated by the refusal of the rural population to pay taxes; and the bourgeoisie, in the heady atmosphere that precedes revolution, were able to indulge unchecked their political pretensions and childish vanity in an orgy of demonstrations, processions, and public meetings, which contributed only towards the paralysis of the administrative machine. Meanwhile, following the failure of the rice crop in November 1944, famine conditions were prevalent in North Annam and Tongking and resulted during the ensuing months in a heavy death-roll among the rural population in these areas.

# Part III

# THE STRUGGLE WITH THE VIET MINH

# VII

## Refugee Activities and Events following the Japanese Surrender

THE French troops who succeeded in reaching China after the Japanese attack of 9 March 1945 numbered some 6,000,[1] and after the sick and wounded had been evacuated an effective force of some 2,140 Europeans, and 3,223 Indochinese troops remained under the command of Sabattier. These troops were officially placed at the disposal of the Chinese Generalissimo Marshal Chiang Kai-shek, the Allied Commander in the Chinese theatre of war, but as most military questions were dealt with by the Marshal's American Chief of Staff, General Albert C. Wedemeyer, who was concurrently in command of locally based American forces, the French troops were in fact at the disposal of the American General.

Wedemeyer appears, however, to have viewed the arrival of the fugitives with some dismay; although he was prompt to arrange for a generous measure of medical aid and assistance to be provided for the numerous sick and wounded who had accompanied the French troops in their arduous fighting retreat, he displayed marked reluctance to rearm and re-equip the valid survivors. This was perhaps due to recognition that in his capacity as Chiang Kai-shek's Chief of Staff he was unable to authorize an action which would have been contrary to the wishes of the Chinese Government, who intended to exploit the collapse of French rule in Indochina. Nevertheless, Wedemeyer was anxious to avail himself of the extensive intelligence networks which the French were thought to be operating and proposed to Sabattier that the French should co-operate in this field with local representatives of the American military intelligence organization, the Office of Strategic Services (OSS).

However, Sabattier was unable to comply with this request because resistance activities in Indochina were the responsibility of another military intelligence organization, the Direction

[1] Sabattier, p. 231.

Générale des Études et Recherches (DGER), which was independent of his authority.[2] This organization had set up an advance base at Kunming under the cover of a military mission which was known as Mission 5. The head of this Mission, Jean Sainteny, showed little enthusiasm for Wedemeyer's proposal, giving as an excuse Mission 5's dependence on a regional headquarters in Calcutta, an attitude which, in view of the Mission's reliance on British and American supplies and logistic support, was perhaps unwise.[3]

## HO CHI MINH'S PROVISIONAL GOVERNMENT

After the Japanese occupation intelligence on the situation in Indochina became a priority requirement of the Chungking Government. In consequence the Governor of Kwangsi Province, General Chang Fa-k'uai, finding that he was unable to obtain information on the situation in Tongking through other channels, was compelled in last resort to turn to the Indochinese Communist leaders who had sought refuge in his province at the end of 1939.[4] These leaders had met in May 1941 under the chairmanship of Nguyen Ai Quoc, who emerged on this occasion from the obscurity in which he had elected to shroud his activities for a number of years. The meeting, which was held in the small town of Chingsi, had been attended by members of the Central Committee of the Indochinese Communist Party, by delegates from certain Communist associations, and by representatives of some nationalist 'splinter' groups, and it had resulted in the foundation of the Viet Nam Doc Lap Dong Minh Hoi (League for the Independence of Vietnam), which was later to become known colloquially as the Viet Minh.

The political platform adopted by this League subordinated the class struggle to the achievement of national independence, which was to be obtained with Chinese and American assistance; the régime which the Viet Minh proposed to install was to be based on universal suffrage, decentralization, and a measure of agrarian reform. After adopting this programme

[2] Sabattier, p. 224.
[3] Jean Roger, alias Jean Sainteny, who was a hero of the French Resistance, belonged to that enterprising band of Free Frenchmen destined to hold positions of trust and responsibility following the collapse of the Vichy régime.
[4] Devillers, p. 72.

the delegates approved the initiative of the Communist leaders in promoting the formation of guerrilla bands to operate against the French in the province of Cao Bang, a task which had been entrusted to one Vo Nguyen Giap, a schoolmaster from Hanoi.[5]

The choice of Giap for this dangerous mission proved a good one and the methods to which he resorted, including the implanting of agents and the setting up of intelligence networks, soon enabled him to extend his influence over a wide area. These networks and agents provided Quoc with the sort of intelligence on the situation in Tongking which Chang Fa-k'uai needed.

Faced with increasingly peremptory demands from Chungking, Chang Fa-k'uai had tried at first to obtain the required information by enlisting the services of adherents of the Vietnamese nationalist groups who had been living, in some cases for years, in South China, and at his instigation in October 1942 a Congress of these political groups was held in Liuchow,[6] which led to the formation of a political league, the Viet Nam Cach Menh Dong Minh Hoi (League of Vietnamese Revolutionary Parties) or, in abbreviated form, the Dong Minh Hoi. But in spite of the provision of a subsidy to pay for the setting up of intelligence networks across the border, it soon became apparent that the nationalist groups forming the Dong Minh Hoi were split by personal rivalries, and in spite of their pretensions to the contrary possessed no organization and few supporters in Tongking. When their inability to provide the required information had become apparent, Chang Fa-k'uai received a message from Quoc offering to place at his disposal the clandestine organization which Quoc's party possessed in Indochina. The message was conveyed from the prison where Quoc, who had had the misfortune to incur the displeasure of the Chinese authorities by his attempts to suborn supporters of the nationalist groups, had been confined under conditions of considerable discomfort for about a year.

Chang Fa-k'uai, who had been responsible in 1927 for the expulsion of the Chinese Communists from Canton, appears to have been aware of Quoc's past activities on behalf of the

---

[5] See below, p. 433.

[6] Although members of the Indochinese Communist Party were expressly debarred from attending, delegates of the Communist-controlled Viet Minh League were able to take part in the discussions.

Borodin Mission. He therefore suggested that in order to make the offer palatable to the Chungking Government Quoc would be well advised to change his name. Quoc promptly complied with this suggestion and assumed that of 'Ho Chi Minh', or 'He who enlightens', an alias which in view of the task that he was proposing to undertake appeared both appropriate and auspicious. Chang Fa-k'uai then informed the Chungking authorities that an Annamite revolutionary of great capacity, one Ho Chi Minh, had offered to organize intelligence networks and to stir up unrest in Tongking on behalf of the Chinese Government.[7] The Chungking authorities, whose files contained no reference to such a personality, welcomed this proposal, whereupon Ho Chi Minh, alias Nguyen Ai Quoc, was set at liberty and joined the Dong Minh Hoi.

The advantages which the Communist Viet Minh were to derive from this arrangement were considerable, for a portion of the subsidy paid to the Dong Minh Hoi, together with training facilities at a camp near Liuchow, were now available to them and they were able to recruit with impunity supporters among the nationalist groups. The Chinese authorities for their part, in return for their financial aid and technical assistance, were provided with a flow of reports on the situation in Tongking, which compensated perhaps by their profusion for the fact that the intelligence provided was, in most cases, trivial and on occasion, inaccurate.[8]

During the summer of 1943 the Viet Minh bands, which had been based at first in the mountainous region around Cao Bang, extended their activities southwards into the provinces of Bac Kan and Thai Nguyen. The French authorities reacted to these infiltrations by increasing the number and frequency of patrols, with the result that the Viet Minh, who were not prepared at this stage to risk engagements with French troops, were forced to withdraw. Meanwhile the representatives of the nationalist groups in China, who had recognized the need for union by adhering to the Dong Minh Hoi, tempered this recognition by their inability to agree on the election of an executive committee,[9] but although in the absence of such a committee the Dong Minh Hoi was condemned to a nominal

[7] Devillers, p. 105.
[8] Ibid. p. 106.
[9] P. Célerier, *Menaces sur le Viet-Nam* (1956), p. 21.

existence, the Viet Minh were able to exploit their adherence to the Dong Minh Hoi to carry out their operations in its name.

The prospect of Japanese defeat was to induce the Chinese authorities, however, to make a further attempt to forge an effective instrument which could be used to install a puppet Government in Hanoi. In March 1944, therefore, a second Congress was held in Liuchow, at which the proceedings were expedited by Chang Fa-k'uai's presence in the town. At this Congress the representatives of the nationalist groups reaffirmed their adhesion to the Dong Minh Hoi; a Provisional Government was also formed in which Ho Chi Minh, as representative of the Dong Minh Hoi, obtained a portfolio, and a proclamation was issued announcing the Government's intention to eradicate Japanese and French Fascism and to regain national independence with Chinese assistance.

However, the Provisional Government was to prove as illusory a creation as the Dong Minh Hoi; the nationalist delegates representing the VNQDD hastened back to Yunnan, where they were soon congenially engaged in internecine disputes,[10] while many of the nationalist exiles, in preparation for the day when they would return under Chinese protection to Tongking, either enlisted in the Kuomintang armies or in Vietnamese 'Free' companies. Nevertheless the formation of a Provisional Government enabled the Viet Minh in Tongking to pursue their activities under cover of its authority, and in the course of the following winter, with the arrival of about 200 volunteers from China, they were able to resume their activities in the mountainous region. In October 1944 Ho Chi Minh himself staged a sprightly entry on to the stage of world history when, with an escort of Chu Van Tan's guerrillas, he crossed the frontier and established his headquarters in Thai Nguyen province in order to 'intensify the struggle'. After the arrival of these reinforcements Viet Minh bands, which were now equipped with Thompson sub-machine guns, modern rifles, grenades, and adequate supplies of ammunition, started to infiltrate into the provinces of Bac Kan, Tuyen Quang, Bac Giang (later renamed Pha Lang Thuong), and into the three military territories of Lang Son, Cao Bang, and Ha Giang, where they attacked isolated posts and massacred

[10] Devillers, p. 109.

9

village notables, even showing some readiness to engage French patrols.[11]

The Japanese *coup de force* of 9 March 1945 facilitated these activities by leaving the Viet Minh undisturbed to consolidate their bases and to increase the range of their activities, since the Japanese contented themselves with occupying the provincial towns while their military patrols were generally confined to maintaining communications between their garrisons. This short interregnum was also exploited by the Viet Minh to train and arm their partisans with Allied assistance,[12] but although they were patently anxious to impress their countrymen with the consideration in which they were held by the Allies, they displayed marked reluctance to incur casualties or to invite reprisals by attacking the Japanese and confined their contribution towards the victory to an attack on the hill station of Tam Dao, which was garrisoned by forty men.

By the early summer the Viet Minh had succeeded in extending their zone of influence to the fringes of the Red river delta, and in July the towns of Bac Kan and Tuyen Quang fell into their hands. Meanwhile, their emissaries and agents who, as the summer advanced, were allowed greater liberty of action by the Japanese police, exploited this tacit connivance to contact the Viceroy in Hanoi, Phan Ke Toai, and certain members of Bao Dai's entourage.

In spite of their energy and enterprise, the Japanese surrender found the Viet Minh unprepared for the emergency. However, some measures had been taken, including the transformation of their guerrilla units into a National Liberation Army, while on 7 August a Congress is alleged to have been held at which Ho Chi Minh was elected to the presidency of a National Liberation Committee. When rumours of an imminent Japanese sur-

---

[11] Devillers, pp. 112–13.

[12] The initial contact between the Viet Minh leaders and American and French intelligence officers appears to have been arranged through the good offices of a Canadian, Laurie Gordon, who had established himself in Yunnan, where he enjoyed the status of a free-lance intelligence agent. Gordon, who had formerly been employed in Tongking by the American oil company Texaco, had been able, following the arrival of Japanese troops in Indochina, to set up a local intelligence organization with which he continued to remain in wireless contact at his base in Yunnan until the Japanese *coup de force*. He was later instrumental in arranging for a team of military instructors, composed of Americans and volunteers from Mission 5, to be dropped in July 1945 at Viet Minh headquarters near Thai Nguyen (Jean Sainteny, *Histoire d'une paix manquée* (1953), pp. 58–59).

render started to spread during the early days of August, Viet Minh agents and partisans were ordered to infiltrate towards Hanoi, where on 16 August the Japanese, taking official cognisance of the Imperial rescript which announced Japan's surrender, handed over administrative authority to Phan Ke Toai who, in a futile attempt to stem the rising tide of revolution, hurriedly summoned the regional Consultative Assembly.

Meanwhile Viet Minh agents and partisans began to arrive in the town. They were accompanied by Vo Nguyen Giap, the brilliant student of Marxism and revolutionary technique, who in the course of the following days displayed a ruthless purpose which, with the passive approval of the Japanese, resulted in the seizure of administrative control by the Viet Minh. The situation was favourable for resolute and rapid action since the supporters of the nationalist parties, surprised by the turn of events, were still in China, and the French troops remained disarmed and consigned to their encampments.

On 17 August, during a public meeting in front of the municipal theatre, Viet Minh emissaries suddenly appeared on the balcony and replaced the Imperial Standard by a red flag inset with a yellow star.[13] This symbolic gesture was the signal for similar flags to appear throughout the town where the demonstration quickly assumed the proportions of a popular rising. On the following day the Viet Minh managed to contact the Viceroy, Phan Ke Toai, who was relieved to learn that their interest in his person was confined to the desire that he should formally divest himself of his authority in favour of a Provisional Committee. Viet Minh stalwarts then proceeded to occupy administrative buildings and, after brief parley with the Japanese, seized the locally stored armaments of the Indochinese Guard.[14]

THE UNITED NATIONAL FRONT IN COCHIN-CHINA

While these events were taking place in Hanoi the revolution was following a different pattern in Cochin-China. Here the Communist organization had been disrupted by French repressive measures, while the national groups enjoyed Japanese support. Representatives of the Vietnamese Independence

[13] Devillers, p. 136.
[14] Ibid. p. 137.

Party, the Group of Intellectuals, the Civil Servants' Union, the Trotskyist group, the Advance Guard of Youth, the Cao Dai, and the Hoa Hao met in Saigon on 14 August and, with the Japanese approval, formed a United National Front.[15] An Executive Committee was then elected which was entrusted with the functions of government. The United National Front, however, reflecting the irresolution and divided opinions of its members, proved incapable of controlling the situation, while incidents involving the Advance Guard of Youth, which had been infiltrated by Communist elements, appeared to herald an attempt by the Viet Minh representative, Tran Van Giau, to seize power. But after this preliminary attempt at intimidation had failed, Giau was compelled, in view of the weakness of his position, to rely on bluff and in last resort on his powers of persuasion in order to achieve his ends.

After an intensive propaganda campaign designed to portray the Viet Minh in the guise of a powerful resistance movement which had acquired Allied recognition and support in return for important services rendered, Giau met the representatives of the United National Front. At this meeting Giau appealed to the nationalists, who were now suffering some qualms about their past reliance on Japanese support, exhorting them to hand over political power to the Viet Minh, who would be best able to secure national unity and independence. Unaware of the origin and composition of the Viet Minh League, the members of the United National Front proved receptive to these arguments and agreed to adhere to a political organization possessing such impressive credentials. The conclusion of this alliance was marked on 25 August by a grandiose public demonstration assuming the form of a march-past in which almost every organized body in Cochin-China took part. The Trotskyist group, however, with a foreknowledge born of experience, refused to participate, proclaiming by their absence their insuperable mistrust of Giau's intentions. On the same day a Provisional Executive Committee for South Vietnam or, in Viet Minh parlance, the Nambo, was set up. This Committee was composed of nine members, of whom six were Communists.[16]

[15] The Advance Guard of Youth, which was to provide the Viet Minh with a nucleus of shock troops, had been formed, on Decoux's instructions, in order to encourage sport and outdoor pursuits among the studious Vietnamese.

[16] Devillers, p. 142.

## BAO DAI'S ABDICATION

These revolutionary events in Hanoi and Saigon had been preceded on 7 August by the resignation of the Tran Trong Kim Government. Although he accepted the Government's resignation, Bao Dai instructed the ministers nevertheless to remain in Hué to deal with routine administrative business and to assist him with their advice, but the absence of a central Government during the critical days when the Viet Minh were establishing their claim to rule the country symbolized the final collapse of the imperial régime.[17]

After the Japanese surrender Bao Dai remained for some days without news of events in North and South Vietnam, but reports finally reached him that whereas the Viet Minh, who were believed to enjoy Allied support, controlled Hanoi, the Cochin-Chinese nationalist groups had set up a Government in Saigon. On receiving this information Bao Dai decided to abdicate,[18] and an emissary was dispatched to Hanoi, with the request that the Viet Minh authorities should send representatives to Hué empowered to accept his abdication.

This decision appears to have been based on the realization that he was unable to control or even to influence the course of events and also on the fear that the turbulent nationalist groups in the south might be tempted to oppose by force of arms the Viet Minh claim to represent the country. Bao Dai hoped therefore that, by handing over his authority to the Viet Minh, who seemed best able to negotiate with the Allies, he would manage to dissuade the Cochin-Chinese from advancing a claim to autonomy which could be exploited by the French to re-establish their authority.

On the arrival of the Viet Minh representatives, the Emperor's abdication was proclaimed on 23 August, from the Belvedere of the Five Phoenixes surmounting the triple gateway

[17] Hué, which had originally been selected by the geomancers on account of the propitious configuration of its site, was singularly ill-adapted to be the seat of a central Government exercising its authority over the widely separated deltas where the bulk of the Vietnamese race were settled. For the capital of the Nguyen dynasty, hemmed in between the enveloping spurs of the Annam chain and the sea, depended for its communications with Hanoi and Saigon on the Trans-Indochinese Railway and the Mandarin Road, and these had been subjected for many months to damaging air attacks.

[18] Meanwhile Bao Dai's ministers, fearful, apparently, of being involved in the fall of a discredited dynasty, had decamped.

of the imperial city through whose central portal General de Courcy had insisted on riding with an escort of Zouaves ninety years before. In his message to the Vietnamese people Bao Dai exhorted all political parties and classes to support the Democratic Republican Government in Hanoi and, after expressing regret that he should have been unable to render any appreciable service to the nation, concluded: 'As for myself, during the twenty years of my reign I have tasted much of bitterness. Now I feel happy to become a free citizen of an independent country.'[19]

A week later Bao Dai, who had reassumed his personal name of Vinh Thuy, left to take up an appointment as Supreme Counsellor to the Viet Minh Government. Thus by 23 August 1945 the Viet Minh had succeeded in establishing their authority, by sheer audacity, sense of strategy, and exaggerated claims to Allied support, over Tongking, Annam, and Cochin-China.

At the end of this momentous month Ho Chi Minh, who had appeared in Hanoi on the 28th, dissolved the National Liberation Committee and formed a Provisional Government in which the portfolios of the interior, national defence, finance, propaganda, education and youth were all held by Communists. The formation of this Government was followed on 2 September by an official proclamation announcing the independence of Vietnam and the advent of the Democratic Republic. On this historic occasion Ho, borrowing the opening paragraph of the American Declaration of Independence, brazenly proclaimed before a vast concourse of people in Hanoi: 'All men are created equal. They are endowed by their Creator with certain inalienable rights; among these are Life, Liberty and the pursuit of happiness.'[20] After this introductory homage to principles which his Government was prepared to flout, he proceeded with demagogic exaggeration to enumerate the accumulated grievances against the French Protectorate, declaring that the French:

In the province of politics . . . deprived our people of every liberty.
They have enforced inhuman laws; to ruin our unity and national consciousness, they have carried out three different policies in the North, the Centre and the South of Vietnam.

[19] Quoted Cole, p. 19,
[20] Ibid. pp. 19–21.

They have founded more prisons than schools. They have merci-lessly slain our patriots; they have deluged areas with innocent blood. They have fettered public opinion; they have promoted illiteracy. To weaken our race they have forced us to use their manu-factured opium and alcohol.

In the province of economics, they have stripped our fellow-citizens of everything they possessed, impoverishing the individual and devastating the land.

They have robbed us of our rice fields, our mines, our forests, our raw materials. They have monopolized the printing of bank-notes, the import and export trade; they have invented numbers of un-lawful taxes, reducing our people, especially our countryfolk, to a state of extreme poverty.

They have stood in the way of our businessmen and stifled their undertakings; they have exploited our working class in a most savage way.

In concluding his harangue, Ho announced that Vietnam would henceforth have no further dealings with France, that the treaties signed by France on Vietnam's behalf were null and void, and that the privileges which the French had arrogated to themselves were abolished.

Meanwhile throughout the whole of Vietnam the revolution gathered momentum. 'People's Committees' sprang up every-where usurping the traditional authority of the mandarins and notables, while armed gangs proceeded, in the name of the Democratic Republic, to imprison and liquidate 'reactionary' elements.

# VIII

## The Reoccupation of Indochina

THE principles that were to govern future relations between metropolitan France and the Empire were laid down at a Conference convened by the French Committee for National Liberation (CFLN) at Brazzaville in French Equatorial Africa in January 1944. The Conference was presided over by René Pleven in his capacity as Commissioner for Colonies and was attended by eighteen Governors-General or Governors of French West and Equatorial Africa, Cameroons, Somaliland, Madagascar, etc., by the Residents-General of Morocco and Tunisia, as observers, and by a delegation from the Representative Assembly of Algiers, General de Gaulle himself being present at the opening session.

Although de Gaulle and Pleven are reported to have arrived with the intention of sponsoring bold readjustments in the relations between France and the colonies and, in particular, with that of encouraging the political evolution of France's African possessions, the resistance encountered from representatives of the colonial Administrative Services, the French community, and French commercial interests deterred them from attempting to carry out these generous intentions. In consequence the recommendations adopted were of a cautious and conservative nature which, though possibly suitable to the primitive social conditions in Africa, were manifestly inadequate to satisfy the demands of the more evolved and politically conscious Indochinese.

The Conference recommended that colonial representation in France should be greatly increased and that representative Assemblies should be set up in the colonies composed of European and native delegates elected by universal suffrage. It was also recognized that the time had come to increase local recruitment for executive posts in the Administrative Services, to encourage industrial development in colonial territories, and to abandon the recourse to impressed labour. The preamble of the political recommendations laid down that 'the aims of the work of civilization which France is accomplishing in her possessions exclude any idea of autonomy and any possibility of development outside the French Empire bloc. The attainment of "self-government" in the colonies, even in the most distant future, must be excluded'.[1]

The affirmation of this basic principle, which was thus elevated to the status of a dogma, was to place a disastrous mortgage on Franco-Vietnamese relations since the Vietnamese, proud of a national identity which had been forged in the course of a long and troubled history, were not prepared to merge their country in a French-controlled federation of states. In France, however, where an Action Committee for the Liberation of Indochina was set up in September 1944, under the chairmanship of Pleven, the Vietnamese reaction to the French proposals had not been foreseen as the absence of information from this distant possession made the changes that had taken place during the years of isolation difficult to assess.

The Committee for National Liberation, undaunted by their ignorance of local conditions, began to draw up a project of constitutional reform in February 1944; which was incorporated in a Declaration by the Provisional Government promulgated on 24 March 1945.[2] The Declaration provided for the federation of the five territories composing Indochina, the powers vested in this Federation being exercised by a Council of State, the members of which were to be nominated by, and responsible to, the Governor-General. Provision was also made for the creation of a Federal Assembly, composed of representatives of local French interests and of the populations of the five territories. The functions of this Assembly were restricted, however, to voting the budget and to the discussion of measures submitted for their approval by the Council of State. Finally, the Declaration guaranteed the democratic rights of Indochinese nationals and granted a measure of local economic autonomy.

These provisions and concessions, which were principally designed to limit intervention by the ministries in Paris in Indochinese affairs and to reinforce the authority of the Governor-General, were manifestly insufficient to provide an acceptable basis for future negotiations. The Declaration was

[1] *La Conférence Africaine Française, Brazzaville, 30 janvier 1944–8 février 1944* (Algiers, Commissariat aux Colonies, 1944), p. 35.
[2] *J.O.* 25 Mar. 1945, pp. 1607–8 (Cole, pp. 5–7).

thus bound to handicap French representatives in their initial contacts with the Viet Minh leaders. Moreover these contacts were to take place under unusual circumstances, since after the Japanese capitulation on 7 August, orders were received at French headquarters in Calcutta to drop into Indochina the skeleton teams of administrators, soldiers, and agents, who had been assembled for that purpose.[3] These teams, which included French Commissioners for Tongking and Cochin-China respectively, were, however, captured and detained on their arrival, since during the relatively short space of time that had elapsed since the eclipse of French power, popular sentiment in Vietnam had undergone a profound and dramatic change.

This change had been brought about by the brief taste of freedom, by Japanese propaganda, and by the skill with which the Viet Minh had exploited the popular desire for independence. In consequence, whereas the French Commissioner-designate for Tongking, following the death by poison of one of his party, was able to take refuge with Chinese troops advancing on Hanoi, his colleague in Cochin-China, Jean Cédile, after some unpleasant misadventures in the paddy-fields near Tay Ninh, was taken to Saigon and placed under house-arrest by the Japanese. But if the official representatives of the French Provisional Government were unable to carry out their mission, unofficial emissaries of the French Intelligence Service were to prove more successful in their attempt to impose the French presence upon the authorities in Tongking.

### THE CHINESE IN NORTH INDOCHINA

When news of the Japanese surrender reached Kunming on 15 August the head of Mission 5, who had no official instructions for such an eventuality, received a message from Paris instructing him to take such action as he considered appropriate. He decided to go in person to Hanoi, and tried to persuade the local representatives of the American OSS to provide the necessary transport. Agreement was finally reached that the French should be accompanied by a party of representatives of the OSS under the command of Major Patti, who was responsible locally for the collation of intelligence on Indochina, and

[3] Devillers, p. 150.

after some delay the party, consisting of seven American and five French agents, left for Hanoi. Their unheralded arrival at the airport of Gia Lam without credentials of any sort caused the Japanese some perplexity. After a palaver, however, Sainteny succeeded in persuading them that he had been sent to ascertain the conditions and requirements of French prisoners, and Patti had been entrusted with the arrangements for an impending visit by an Allied Commission who would be empowered to receive the formal surrender of the locally based Japanese troops. But the arrival of the party in the town raised such a stir that a hostile crowd collected outside the hotel to which they had been driven. The Japanese then insisted that, as their presence was endangering the safety of the other guests, the French party must move elsewhere and in order to persuade them to do so they agreed to Sainteny's demand that the Governor-General's residence should be placed at their disposal; here the French agents were to live in semi-captivity for several weeks.[4]

The representatives of the OSS, however, who had been left at large, were soon the object of most flattering attentions designed to enlist American support for the Viet Minh. Indeed, so persuasive did the Viet Minh prove that Patti is reported to have adopted their cause with a zeal which shocked and offended the captive French community.

Meanwhile Sainteny, who had been making unsuccessful efforts to persuade the French Government to substantiate his claims to be its official representative in Tongking, was compelled to move out of the Governor-General's palace on 9 September in order to make room for General Lu Han, the Commander of the Chinese armies which were to occupy Indochina to the north of the 16th parallel, in virtue of a decision reached at the Potsdam Conference.[5] These armies had crossed the frontier at the end of August, and were now

[4] Sainteny, p. 73.
[5] The fate of Pierre Messmer, the French Commissioner-designate for Tongking, was still unknown. Decoux (p. 345) believed that de Gaulle preferred a Chinese rather than an American occupation because the French mistrusted American intentions; they were aware of Roosevelt's opinion that Indochina should not 'go back to France' but should be administered by international trusteeship. In Roosevelt's view 'the case of Indo-China is perfectly clear. France has milked it for one hundred years. The people of Indo-China are entitled to something better than that' (*Memoirs of Cordell Hull* (New York, 1948), ii. 1597).

advancing on Hanoi down the Red river valley and also from Lang Son.[6]

The Chinese troops, with their strange accoutrement and clutter of camp-followers, caused consternation among the population, but it was soon noted that, although they were patently intent on exploiting to the full the possibilities of profit that the occupation of Tongking offered, they were relatively well disciplined and reasonably well behaved. The economic exploitation of Tongking had also been facilitated by the introduction of Chinese currency as legal tender at an advantageous rate of exchange. Besides the opportunity afforded by this exchange-rate to make extensive local purchases, the Chinese armies were in the fortunate position of having much to sell since on his arrival in Tongking Lu Han had laid claim to all weapons, war-material, stocks, chattels, and real estate in the possession of the Japanese without consideration for the manner in which such property might have been acquired. The seizure, and subsequent liquidation of this loot resulted in the monthly payment of dividends to officers serving on the General's staff, while the Chinese soldiers, stimulated by this example, were able to supplement their pay by the sale of the furniture, fixtures, plumbing, and even the tiles of the properties in which they were billeted.[7]

The Viet Minh for their part exploited the rapacity of the Chinese forces to maintain the political advantage which they had acquired.[8] Moreover Lu Han himself had been quick to appreciate that any attempt to shake the grip which the Viet Minh had secured on the administration might lead to chaos and civil war. He therefore advised the Vietnamese nationalists who had arrived in the baggage-train of the Chinese armies to negotiate with the Viet Minh for a share in the government.

During these negotiations Ho Chi Minh revealed an extra-

[6] Along their route the Chinese dissolved the Viet Minh's 'People's Committees' in the towns and villages and replaced them by committees composed either of the VNQDD party members accompanying the Yunnanese troops or of Viet Nam Quang Phuc Hoi supporters who were with the armies approaching from Lang Son.

[7] Célerier, p. 76.

[8] A 'gold week' having been organized to provide funds for the purchase of arms, the Viet Minh had at their disposal a stock of this precious metal with which to buy Chinese connivance in their seizure of power. Thus Ho Chi Minh was able to present Lu Han, on his arrival, with an opium smoker's set in solid gold (Devillers, p. 193).

ordinary ability both to elude a settlement and to avoid a rupture with the Chinese authorities. Thus although agreements with the nationalist groups were announced on 23 October, on 19 November, and on 24 December, the Viet Minh were able nevertheless to thwart all attempts to form a coalition Government. These tactics dismayed the nationalists, whose exasperation was further increased by the fact that general elections were to take place on 23 December, for they were aware that their exclusion from the Government would deprive them of all means of influencing the results and lead to their discomfiture at the polls.

Meanwhile, the Viet Minh, who were continuing to play for time, provided Lu Han with a further excuse for tolerating this unsatisfactory state of affairs by officially dissolving the Indochinese Communist Party, which was replaced by an Association for Marxist Studies on 11 November. Finally, on 19 December the Viet Minh, yielding to Chinese pressure, agreed to postpone the elections until 6 January, and three days later, Ho Chi Minh officially recognized that the nationalist groups had been handicapped in the election campaign by undertaking to reserve a block of 70 out of the 350 seats in the Assembly for their representatives. The elections, which were held in Tongking, Annam and, clandestinely, in some parts of Cochin-China, were attended by many irregularities and by some evidence of a readiness to fabricate returns; nevertheless the results, which gave the Viet Minh a clear majority in the Assembly, were probably fairly indicative of the state of public opinion at that time.

This victory had been obtained despite the deplorable administrative record of the Provisional Government, for after their seizure of power the Viet Minh had proceeded to sacrifice most of the remaining financial resources of the state by abolishing the monopolies and the poll-tax from which 50 per cent. of public revenue had been derived; for good measure, and with the middle-class vote in mind, they had also done away with the tax on smallholdings and that levied on traders and professional men. These demagogic measures had, however, deprived the Government of the means to pay the civil servants, who were either dismissed or reduced to accepting meagre remuneration in kind.

Meanwhile the famine which had ravaged the overpopulated

provinces of North Annam and South-West Tongking in the spring again threatened to assume catastrophic proportions since the Japanese *coup de force* in March had led to the imprisonment of the French engineers responsible for the maintenance of the dykes in the Red river delta. Following heavy rains in the course of the summer the rivers in spate had broken through the weakened defences and inundated one-third of the ricefields in Tongking; floods were succeeded by drought, so that half the December paddy crop was lost. Moreover the classic measure for averting famine which consisted in shipping part of the Cochin-Chinese rice surplus to the north, could not now be applied since rail and road communications with the distant Mekong delta had been interrupted by air attack and sabotage, while coastal shipping had been either destroyed or else requisitioned by the Japanese.

When the gravity of the situation became apparent, the Hanoi Government had set up on 15 November a committee to deal with this emergency who took steps to encourage the cultivation of soya beans, manioc, sweet potatoes, and maize, but this tardy measure was insufficient to avert catastrophe, and between November 1945 and June of the following year famine claimed more than half a million victims in the stricken villages of Tongking and North Annam.

### THE BRITISH IN SOUTH INDOCHINA

The task of getting together a French Expeditionary Force for service in the Far East had begun in May 1945, but progress had been slow and this force was still in an embryonic state at the time of the Japanese surrender. When the news of the surrender was received in Paris, the decision was immediately taken to detach for service in Indochina the Massu group, which formed part of the 2nd Armoured Division, and the 9th Colonial Infantry Division; and on 17 August General Leclerc, who had been appointed to command French military forces in Indochina, left Paris ostensibly to take up his command. On his arrival at Karachi he accepted an invitation from Admiral Mountbatten to visit him at the headquarters of the South East Asia Command in Kandy, where he was given assurances that equipment, ammunition, and stores would be made available to the French from stocks in Ceylon and also that logistic support would be provided. However, it was estimated that at least two months must elapse before French troops could be assembled and transported to Indochina.

Meanwhile, in accordance with the agreement reached at the Potsdam Conference that South East Asia Command should provide troops to reoccupy Indochinese territory to the south of the 16th parallel, Major-General Douglas Gracey, commanding the 20th Indian Division, had been appointed to lead a force of British and Indian troops to Indochina with orders to disarm the Japanese and to obtain the release of prisoners of war. He was also instructed that his responsibilities included the maintenance of law and order with the face-saving proviso that unnecessary intervention in the local political situation should be avoided.[9] Advance parties of Gracey's force began to arrive in Saigon during the first week of September, where a Communist-dominated Provisional Executive Committee had been set up on 25 August. The formation of this Committee had been followed by a further deterioration in local security conditions, since prisoners who had been released from the Cochin-Chinese penal settlements were abroad in the town and, armed with weapons acquired from the Japanese, were engaged in pillaging the population.

On 2 September Tran Van Giau, acting on instructions from Hanoi,[10] organized a public demonstration on an impressive scale, to display the unshakeable and disciplined determination of the Vietnamese to defend their newly-won independence against any attempt to reimpose French tutelage. The march-past, however, degenerated into disorders in the course of which five Europeans were killed and property was damaged. Although these excesses were condemned officially by the Executive Committee, Giau realized that in the existing state of public excitement any contacts that he might have with the French or British authorities would be misconstrued as 'treason', while the British and French for their part would blame the Viet Minh for any further incidents. He agreed therefore to the reconstitution of the Committee on the basis of nine nationalist to four Communist members, and he himself resigned the chairmanship in favour of a Communist sympathizer named Pham Van Bach.

[9] *The Times*, 25 Oct. 1945.
[10] Devillers, p. 154.

Meanwhile Jean Cédile, the French Commissioner for Cochin-China, had been able on 27 August to contact Giau and some members of the Committee. At this meeting Cédile put forward the proposal that the Declaration of 24 March should serve as a basis for negotiations, but this was rejected out of hand by Giau and his colleagues, who pointed out that it was patently inadequate to meet a situation in which the Vietnamese were already in effective possession of their independence. After the failure of this attempt to find a basis for negotiations, relations between the French and the Vietnamese slowly worsened, and several incidents occurred involving arrests of Vietnamese and Eurasians who were known to be well disposed towards the French.

Gracey, who arrived in Saigon towards the middle of September, thus found himself faced with a situation of great complexity.[11] He was aware, however, that the British troops were to be withdrawn as soon as a French force could be assembled, and in view of the explosive situation and the nature of his instructions the rapid arrival of this force must have seemed to him eminently desirable. During the week that followed his arrival the situation in Saigon went from bad to worse and the Japanese showed a marked reluctance to carry out their security duties. Faced with the mounting danger of an armed rising Gracey, who disposed at that time of 1,800 officers and men, yielded to French pressure and agreed, with some reluctance, to authorize the distribution of weapons to 1,400 French prisoners of war belonging to the 11th Colonial Infantry Regiment, who were confined to their barracks in Saigon.

This decision was to have momentous consequences. For exasperated by the behaviour of the Vietnamese and by the contempt with which they were being treated by a small detachment of Free French troops who had just disembarked, the French soldiers proceeded to behave in a provocative manner towards the local population, with the result that incidents occurred. These incidents provided the French with a pretext to reassert their authority, and on the night of 23–24 September public buildings in Saigon were seized, practically without

---

[11] Available information on the situation in Vietnam was summarized in *The Times* on 14 September as follows: 'There seem to be only two parties of any significance [in Vietnam] at the moment, the Viet-min and the Communists. The Viet-min, which is the stronger, is especially active in the north.'

resistance, by troops of the 11th Colonial Infantry Regiment, who expelled in the process the Executive Committee from its headquarters in the town hall. This action was greeted with an explosion of relief by the French community who, acting on the fallacious assumption that their troubles were now at an end, proceeded to lay hands on and to ill-treat Vietnamese in the French quarter of the town. These unfortunate incidents aroused the indignation of British and American journalists present in Saigon, and gravely embarrassed Gracey, who sought to minimize their gravity by disarming the French troops, who were again confined to barracks, but as a result of the night's work public buildings in Saigon remained in French hands.

The Vietnamese reacted with tardy but hysterical violence, and on the 24th a number of incidents occurred in the port area in which Europeans were either abducted or assassinated and the central market was set on fire by an armed band. On the 25th a hideous massacre was perpetrated on a housing estate—the Cité Heraud—where 450 French and Eurasians were either kidnapped or murdered in bestial fashion by an infuriated mob. At this stage Giau, who had hitherto exercised a restraining influence in the deliberations of the Executive Committee, assumed the direction of resistance; yielding to the natural violence of his temperament he decreed a general insurrection, a general strike, and the evacuation of Saigon–Cholon which was to be blockaded and reduced to ashes. These bombastic instructions were followed by the ruthless implementation of a scorched-earth policy throughout the rich Cochin-Chinese provinces.

Although this drastic and suicidal policy was supported at first by all classes of the population, French administrators, planters, and businessmen who were living under the protection of Allied bayonets in Saigon were slow to realize the depth and passion of a popular movement inspired by ardent patriotism, weariness of European tutelage, and a desire for social justice; and these representatives of a vanished régime continued to proclaim their obstinate and ill-founded belief that with firmness and the application of force the crisis could be surmounted and the French re-established in their former privileges: a belief that was based in many cases on long acquaintance with certain facets of the fluid national character.

In August 1946, however, the representative of the influential French newspaper *Le Monde*, who had penetrated in the wake of Leclerc's troops into these devastated provinces, questioned this tendency to compare the present situation with past outbreaks of religious fanaticism and agrarian unrest which had been endemic under French rule.

The battlefield of Cochin-China [he wrote] has been terribly devastated. West Cochin-China, in particular, is in a state of appalling misery. The Viet Minh have carried out their 'scorched-earth' policy there. In defiance of the most elementary interests of the local population, the leaders of the Viet Minh bands or combat groups have coldly and methodically carried out destruction on an unbelievable scale. In most of the towns in the delta and the Transbassac all public buildings have been burnt down and private homes burnt or demolished, while the population has been forcibly constrained to flee before the French advance. The roads have been cut in many places, the bridges destroyed, and the crops burnt. Entire provinces in the south will need reconstruction.

Drawing the lesson from this state of affairs, he concluded:

It is altogether impossible to overestimate the strength and extent of the nationalist movement which has aroused all classes of the Cochin-Chinese population. . . . The participation, or at least the consent of the population, deeply moved by the ideal of independence and by the promise of social revolution, has been necessary for such destruction to be carried out from one end of the country to the other without opposition.[12]

Nevertheless the day when a French journalist could assess the extent of the devastation in the Cochin-Chinese provinces was still distant. Meanwhile in blockaded Saigon, from which a part of the population had fled, Allied troops continued to be involved in daily affrays with Viet Minh guerrilla fighters, and on 24 September an American officer, Colonel A. P. Dewey, who was a nephew of the Governor of New York State and the head of the Mission sent by the OSS to south Indochina, was ambushed and killed. The assassination threatened for a time to cloud Franco-American relations,[13] some credence having been attached to Viet Minh-inspired rumours that the French, who were outraged by the attitude and intrigues of

[12] Devillers in *Le Monde*, 2 Aug. 1946.
[13] Hammer, p. 118.

representatives of the OSS, had connived at the murder. For Dewey was known to have favoured the claim of the Provisional Executive Committee to represent the Government of Vietnam and to have disapproved of the reckless manner in which the French had regained administrative control in Saigon,[14] and even the cry of 'I am American' with which he had tried to deter his assailants appeared to represent a claim to benefit from some invidious if unspecified apartheid. Indeed the suspicions aroused by certain American activities [15] caused the French to welcome with relief and gratitude the British readiness to accept their assessment of the situation and to assist them in their attempt to regain control over south Indochina. French satisfaction at this co-operative attitude was expressed by the London correspondent of the newspaper *Figaro*, who wrote on 2 October:

> It is realized with increasing clarity in London that the troubles in Indochina are the work of the Japanese, and that the 'separatist' Annamite government has in no way the importance that is attributed to it by certain American correspondents, who would appear to be ill-informed about the real situation, of which they possess only a distorted picture.

### THE RETURN OF THE FRENCH

Meanwhile the equipping of French troops for service in Indochina had been proceeding with dispatch, and on 3 October, commando units of the 5th Colonial Infantry Regiment, representing the advance guard of the Expeditionary Force, landed in Saigon, their arrival being followed two days later by that of Leclerc himself. Leclerc embarked without delay upon the pacification of the Cochin-Chinese countryside. His task was made easier by an agreement that the British force should maintain public security in Saigon and clear a triangle of territory to the north, which would then be used as a concentration area for the Japanese troops. This arrangement freed French troops for a series of operations which were conducted with audacity, speed, and decision and led to French control being rapidly re-established over the towns and principal roads in Cochin-China.

[14] *NYHT*, 26 Sept. 1945.
[15] *Le Monde*, 6 Oct. 1945.

On 5 October British and French troops proceeded to clear the Viet Minh out of the Saigon–Cholon suburbs, and on the 23rd a British force, which included an Indian contingent, set out in the face of stiff opposition to occupy the towns of Thu Dau Mot and Bien Hoa.

The arrival of the Massu group enabled Leclerc to launch an operation to occupy My Tho, forty-five miles from Saigon, and on 25 October a commando force captured the town at dawn, after a surprise landing on the water-front. The force then moved north to Vinh Long, and on the 29th occupied Can Tho.

## THE CAMBODIAN *MODUS VIVENDI*

During the same month a party of French and British officers, accompanied by an armed escort, was sent by air to Phnom Penh to arrest the Cambodian Prime Minister on the grounds that 'his activities threatened the security of Allied forces and he was working against Cambodian interests',[16] and he was brought back to Saigon. The Prime Minister thus ignominiously abducted was none other than Son Ngoc Thanh, the former member of the teaching staff at the School of Higher Pali Studies, who had placed himself under Japanese protection in 1942. He had been brought back to Cambodia by the Japanese when King Norodom Sihanouk, on Japanese inspiration, proclaimed his country's independence in March 1944. The French civilians were then interned, and Thanh was appointed Minister of Foreign Affairs. Aspiring to play the leading part in the liberation of his country, Thanh next staged a revolutionary uprising and arrested his colleagues in the Government, assuming the premiership himself. He then attempted to strengthen his position by holding a referendum on the question of national independence, which resulted in an overwhelming vote in favour of independence. Nevertheless Thanh's past reliance on Japanese support disqualified him from negotiating a settlement with the Allies, while his use of revolutionary tactics to acquire political power had alienated and alarmed the court and responsible Cambodians generally: consequently an emissary was clandestinely sent to Leclerc in Saigon, where plans were made for his arrest and removal.

The loss of their leader did not deter Thanh's supporters

[16] *NYT*, 22 Oct. 1945.

from continuing the struggle, and they fled to the provinces of Battambang, Sisophon, and Siem Reap, which were still under Siamese control. Here the Siamese helped the fugitives, who called themselves Khmer Issaraks, or 'Free Cambodians', to form armed bands and allowed them to set up a Committee to co-ordinate their activities in Bangkok. During the next two years, however, more than half of these Khmer Issaraks laid down their arms, while the remainder, numbering some 2,500, took to brigandage and in some cases came to an understanding with the Viet Minh, who were to establish themselves in the coastal area and in inaccessible frontier regions to the north and east.

Meanwhile a *modus vivendi*[17] was signed in Phnom Penh on 7 January 1946 whereby Cambodia acquired the status of an autonomous state within the French Union, but autonomy was restricted by the appointment of French advisers and by the fact that the approval of the French Commissioner was required for the promulgation of laws, regulations, proclamations, circulars, and general instructions, as well as for decisions reserved because of their importance for the signature of the king. The French authorities also remained responsible for internal security and for Cambodia's foreign relations, while the direction of a number of important services, including certain categories of public works, some judicial matters, the treasury, customs, mines, and railways, was vested in the Federal authorities. In spite of these grave limitations and restrictions, the *modus vivendi* at least gave the Government some say in local administration and enabled Cambodian officials to occupy responsible posts from which they had hitherto been excluded. Moreover the disappointment caused by the limited nature of the French concessions must have been lessened to some extent by the knowledge that the country had no trained personnel capable of directing the services which remained under foreign control.[18]

[17] R. Lévy, *L'Indochine et ses traités, 1946* (Paris, 1947), pp. 41–46.

[18] Although the French authorities had neglected to provide the necessary facilities, and had appropriated only 8 per cent. of the Cambodian budget for educational purposes in pre-war years, the Cambodians themselves, in marked contrast to the Vietnamese, had shown little interest in higher education. Thus although a senior high school, the Lycée Descartes, had been opened in 1935, only four pupils from this establishment had succeeded in obtaining their school-leaving certificate by 1939 (M. F. Herz, *A Short History of Cambodia* [1958], pp. 66–67).

## VIET MINH RELATIONS WITH THE SECTS

The rapid and successful conclusion of these operations in the delta was followed, at the beginning of November 1945, by the dispatch of an armoured column in the direction of Tay Ninh, which led to the capitulation of the Cao Dai 'Holy See'. When road communications with Phnom Penh had been re-established, the column moved northwards and, after driving the Viet Minh from the rubber plantations around Loc Ninh, occupied the township of Ban Me Thuot in the uplands of Annam on 1 December. While this operation was proceeding the large French community at Nha Trang on the coast of South Annam was relieved by a seaborne force, and towards the end of the year the arrival of further reinforcements, including units of the 9th Colonial Infantry Division, enabled French control to be extended to the towns in the Transbassac and to the area south of Saigon–Cholon.

On 24 February 1946, after the reoccupation of the town of Ca Mau at the extremity of the Indochinese peninsula, Leclerc announced in a special order of the day, 'the total re-establishment of peace and order' throughout Cochin-China and South Annam.[19] This fallacious claim is surprising on the part of a general who was not given to brazen misstatements, but Leclerc was unable to foresee that the 'pacification' represented no more than a passing phase in the protracted hostilities. For the Viet Minh, who had launched their partisans armed in some cases with rifles acquired from the Japanese but mostly with swords, pikes, and sharpened bamboo poles against the French armoured vehicles in their triumphant sweep across the great plains of Cochin-China and into the foothills of Annam, were now to move their headquarters into trackless, unhealthy, and sparsely populated regions, and to adopt methods of warfare which were more appropriate to the disparity in armament. Moreover the outbreak of hostilities in Tongking soon compelled the French Command to shift units to the north which were required to combat Viet Minh tactics in Cochin-China, and to entrust Vietnamese militia troops of doubtful military value with the maintenance of security.

This change in tactics was to be carried out, however, by another Viet Minh commander since the scorched-earth policy

[19] *Figaro*, 6 Feb. 1946.

and the violent methods by which Tran Van Giau had attempted to establish his control over the movement for national independence had alienated the Cochin-Chinese nationalists and led to clashes with the Cao Dai and Hoa Hao adepts.[20] An initial affray with the Hoa Hao had taken place on 8 September 1945, when a force of some 15,000 adepts armed with knives and appropriate agricultural implements had attempted to occupy the town of Can Tho, which had been selected by the 'Master', Huynh Phu So, to be the capital of a Hoa Hao kingdom in the Transbassac. The attack had been repulsed with great slaughter by a detachment of the Viet Minh-controlled Advance Guard of Youth, with the assistance of the Japanese garrison. Although an uneasy truce was then patched up, a subsequent Viet Minh attempt to arrest So had again driven the sect into opposition, and after the reoccupation by French forces of the Transbassac towards the end of the year the sanguinary Hoa Hao had exacted a fearful vengeance on local Viet Minh sympathizers and their dependants for the discomfiture which they had suffered at Can Tho.

Meanwhile Viet Minh relations with the Cao Dai sect had also become strained. Although the Cao Dai had been ready at first to accept Viet Minh leadership, Giau's subsequent attempts to take over command of the sect's militia force had led to disagreements which culminated in Tran Quang Vinh's forcible detention in the Viet Minh camp.

Giau's ruthless methods were also to lead to the defection of another group. This group, who lacked the religious pretensions of the Hoa Hao and Cao Dai sects, had first attracted public attention at the ceremonial marches-past of August and September 1945, where they had been represented by a delegation bearing a voluminous green banner on which the legend 'Binh Xuyen Bandits' was inscribed as the social justification for their presence.[21] These bandits formerly operated on a smaller scale from the swamps to the south of Cholon, where

---

[20] Giau's methods had already been demonstrated in Saigon prior to the French attack when he had engineered the mass arrest and execution of the Trotskyist leaders. Giau had also successfully brought pressure to bear on the Viet Minh Central Committee in Hanoi to agree to the execution of Ta Thu Thau, the Cochin-Chinese Trotskyist leader who had been captured, after the Japanese capitulation in Quang Ngai province, on his return from a visit to Tongking (Hammer, p. 110).

[21] Lucien Bodard in *Figaro*, 14 Oct. 1948.

their principal hideouts had been located in the administrative district of Binh Xuyen. Their activities were principally confined at that time to the organization of vice rackets and to the exaction of protection money from wealthy Chinese, but the deterioration in public security following the Japanese *coup de force* had presented them with a unique opportunity to extend the scope of their activities, while the release of prisoners from the Cochin-Chinese penal establishments brought them many recruits.

The Binh Xuyen leaders, however, infected by the contagious patriotism which swept Vietnam after the abolition of the French Protectorate, had placed their men, armament, and wealth derived by blackmail of the Overseas Chinese community at the disposal of the Provisional Executive Committee. Their services had been accepted, and one of their leaders named Le Van Vien,[22] alias Bay Vien, was placed in charge of municipal affairs. Le Van Vien was able to turn his local connexions to good account and raised a substantial sum for the Committee's war chest. Giau thereupon, impressed by this demonstration of revolutionary efficiency, presented him with a long list of Vietnamese whose continued existence was considered to constitute a threat to the cause of national independence, but Le Van Vien, shocked at this revelation of the sanguinary methods by which the Communists were proposing to consolidate their hold on political power, refused to carry out these assassinations. When the Executive Committee was compelled to evacuate Saigon–Cholon the Binh Xuyen bandits retired to their former operational zone to the south and southeast of the twin towns, but Le Van Vien, who was aware that he had forfeited Giau's confidence, continued to maintain a wary vigilance and refused to allow his 1,300 relatively well armed men to be incorporated with the Viet Minh forces.

Thus as a result of Giau's ruthless methods, at the beginning of 1946 the Executive Committee had only a few bands of militant Communists and some units of the Advance Guard of Youth under their direct control. The Viet Minh leaders in Hanoi, whose means of communication with the south were slow and unsatisfactory, appear nevertheless to have realized that their representative in Cochin-China had become a con-

[22] See below, p. 429.

troversial figure, and recalled him to Hanoi in January 1946, when Giau's functions as Viet Minh Military Commander were taken over by Nguyen Binh, a Tongkingese who had first attracted the attention of the Cochin-Chinese police in 1929 by his activities on behalf of the VNQDD: activities which had earned him a six years' prison sentence at the penal settlement on the island of Poulo Condore. After serving this sentence all trace of his whereabouts had been lost until he returned, in November 1945, to assume command of the Viet Minh military zone to the north-east of Saigon.

After his appointment as Military Commander for Cochin-China, or, in Viet Minh parlance, the Nambo, Binh adapted Viet Minh tactics to the altered situation by forming a Security Service and 'Suicide Squads', with which he sought to inspire terror and to increase Viet Minh prestige by the assassination of 'traitors' and by isolated attacks on selected targets.

## ADMIRAL D'ARGENLIEU

During the months in which French troops under the command of Leclerc were overcoming Viet Minh resistance, the struggle to reaffirm French sovereignty was pursued on the political and diplomatic planes by the French High Commissioner, Vice-Admiral Thierry d'Argenlieu, who had been appointed to this post on 13 August 1945.[23] The news that another Admiral had been appointed to the highest office in Indochina was received with some dismay, for although he is reported to have embarked on his mission with the same liberal intentions which had inspired de Gaulle and Pleven on their arrival at Brazzaville, d'Argenlieu was to display a rigidity of mind and a preference for authoritarian methods which rendered him peculiarly open to the arguments marshalled by the reactionary elements in the colony against any ill-considered

[23] After serving in the navy during the First World War, d'Argenlieu had retired in 1920 with the rank of lieutenant to enter the Carmelite Order, and in 1932 he was chosen as provincial of this order. On the outbreak of war in 1939 he had returned, however, to his former profession with the rank of lieutenant-commander. He was captured after the fall of France but escaped and joined the Free French in London, where he was appointed successively High Commissioner for the Pacific, Commander-in-Chief of Free French naval forces based on Britain, Assistant Chief of the Free French General Staff, and in 1945 Vice-President of the Board of Admiralty and Inspector of Naval Forces.

project that might be calculated to weaken French paramountcy.[24]

After his appointment, d'Argenlieu went to the French possession of Chandernagor near Calcutta, where he set up a temporary headquarters and started to recruit the staff which would be required to assist him in his duties as President of the Federal Government. In early October he paid a visit to Chungking, where he succeeded in obtaining certain assurances of a general nature in regard to Chinese intentions. He then returned to Chandernagor, and after completing his preparations he left for Saigon on the last day of the month.

After his installation in the Palais Norodom, d'Argenlieu contented himself at first with organizing the Federal Services; in view of the subsequent failure of the Federal Government to exercise any authority this led to the recruitment of a plethora of officials with ill-defined responsibilities. He also selected a staff of advisers with past experience of Indochina, under whose influence he adopted a policy reported to have been based on the confident assertion of the French Security Service that Vietnamese personal, political, and regional rivalries could be exploited to French advantage, and on a belief current among French colonial administrators that the rural population was uncontaminated by the virus of nationalism.

This assessment of the internal situation induced d'Argenlieu to revert to the traditional French policy of fomenting dissensions by encouraging separatist tendencies in Cochin-China,[25] and this outmoded policy was to exert a disastrous influence on the negotiations for the peaceful settlement of Franco-Vietnamese differences.

D'Argenlieu indicated the policy which he proposed to pursue by a Federal order on 4 February 1946 announcing the creation of a provisional Advisory Council for Cochin-China which would be charged with the task of apprising the French Commissioner of the wishes of the local population, with the preparation of elections, and with the drafting of a constitution. The Council was to be composed of four French and eight Vietnamese members, designated for these functions by the High Commissioner on the recommendation of the French Commissioner, who would himself preside *ex-officio* over the

[24] Devillers, pp. 169–70.
[25] Paul Mus, *Sociologie d'une guerre* (1952), p. 187.

deliberations. It was, however, noted by ironic observers that when the Council met on 12 February seven out of the eight Vietnamese members were naturalized French citizens.[26] However, the French authorities were now free to adopt such measures as they pleased since Gracey, having completed the tasks assigned to him, had left Saigon on 28 January.

[25] Devillers, p. 175.

# IX

# Negotiations

AFTER the resistance in the south had been broken Leclerc was free to turn his attention to the reoccupation of Tongking and North Annam. But the nature of the opposition encountered by the expeditionary corps had convinced him that the Viet Minh enjoyed a widespread popular support, and he thus recognized that the safety of the large French community in the north required that the reoccupation of this area must be preceded by an agreement with the Viet Minh authorities. This contention was questioned by d'Argenlieu and his advisers, who considered that negotiations with and concessions to such a Government would prejudice the future of the Indochinese Federation and of the French Union itself.[1] Leclerc is also reported to have foreseen that if the French were to fight their way back to Hanoi the Viet Minh authorities would establish themselves in the mountainous region where, with popular support and a minimum of Chinese assistance, they would be able to maintain themselves for many years.

If, however, the High Commissioner and the general commanding the Expeditionary Corps were in disagreement about the policy that should be adopted towards the Hanoi Government, they both recognized the necessity of negotiating the withdrawal of the Chinese forces from Tongking. Accordingly at the beginning of January 1946 Leclerc sent an emissary to Chungking with instructions to arrange with the Chinese Government for the evacuation of their troops, but when the Chinese insisted that the matter should form part of a general settlement, these negotiations had subsequently to be extended to include the discussion of other matters at issue between the two Governments.[2]

Meanwhile in Tongking the Viet Minh leaders, who had inaugurated their rule by a bitter onslaught on the administrative record of the Protectorate and who continued to criticize French activities in Cochin-China, were slowly coming to the

[1] Devillers, pp. 211–12.
[2] See below, p. 144.

realization that some measure of outside aid and assistance was required. However, the Chungking Government, with their representatives present in Hanoi, would be unlikely to furnish such assistance, while the State Department, which had now asserted some measure of control over the policy-framing proclivities of the OSS, were engaged through their local representatives in discouraging Viet Minh illusions concerning American readiness to provide political support in exchange for economic concessions. It thus appeared a logical step on the part of a Government which enjoyed no international recognition to explore the possibility of obtaining such aid and assistance from the French, who after re-establishing their control over Cochin-China were now actively engaged in making preparations for a return to the north either by force of arms or following a negotiated settlement. But whereas the Viet Minh leaders were inclined to consider that a revival of the past association with France in a modified form might present certain practical advantages, including an opportunity to liquidate the francophobic nationalist groups, the population of Tongking, who had been inflamed by months of anti-French propaganda, were not prepared for such a political *volte face*. In consequence although an initial meeting between Ho Chi Minh and French official representatives took place towards the end of September 1945, it was agreed that in order to avoid arousing public disquiet subsequent meetings should be held in secret.[3]

While these negotiations were going on in Hanoi and Chungking, the news of de Gaulle's resignation from the premiership on 20 January 1946 was received by the High Commissioner and his staff in Saigon with a dismay which was apparently partly caused by the fear that French policy might no longer be based on the provisions contained in the Declaration of 24 March 1945.[4] Leclerc, with his plans for the dispatch of a French force to Tongking far advanced, then decided to send General Valluy, commanding the 9th Colonial Infantry Division, to Paris in order to explain his plan for the re-occupation of strategic centres in Tongking and to urge the French Government to expedite the negotiations in progress with the Chinese Government, the need for haste being due to

[3] Sainteny, p. 171.
[4] Devillers, p. 212.

the fact that the landing of French troops in Tongking was dependent on the spring tides in the early days of March, which would allow the transports and the cruiser *Émile Bertin* to enter the port of Haiphong, the approaches to which had been allowed to silt up during the Japanese occupation. On 13 February d'Argenlieu also left for France, with the intention of defending his policy and of finding out the implications of the recent political changes. During his absence Leclerc assumed the functions of High Commissioner.

### FRANCE, CHINA, AND THE VIET MINH

Meanwhile the Viet Minh leaders, who were aware that negotiations were in progress between the French and Chinese Governments, appear to have finally recognized the necessity of coming to an agreement with the French, and on 16 February the secret discussions between Ho Chi Minh and Sainteny, hitherto impeded by the Viet Minh insistence on a formal recognition of national independence, took a more hopeful turn when Ho Chi Minh announced that he would be prepared to negotiate a settlement on the basis of a French acknowledgement of national independence within the limits imposed by Vietnam's adherence to the French Union.[5] The importance of this concession was recognized by Leclerc, who recommended to d'Argenlieu that the French Government should be asked to authorize the conclusion of an agreement along these lines.[6]

While the negotiations in Hanoi had thus entered a more constructive phase, the discussions in Chungking were continuing to make good progress, with the result that a treaty for the relinquishment by France of extraterritorial and related rights in China and an agreement regarding Sino-Indochinese relations were signed on 28 February 1946. By the terms of the treaty France agreed to transfer to China the French concessions in Shanghai, Tientsin, Hankow, and Canton.[7] Under the agreement Chinese nationals were to continue to enjoy the

---

[5] Sainteny had been appointed French Commissioner for North Indochina in October of the previous year.

[6] Sainteny, pp. 175–6.

[7] Yin Ching Chen, ed., *Treaties and Agreements between the Republic of China and Other Powers, 1929–1954* (Washington, 1957), pp. 259–65; *J.O.* 19 May 1946. The leased territory of Kwang Chou Wan had been returned under a Sino-French convention signed at Chungking on 18 August 1945 (ibid. pp. 235–7).

rights and privileges they had traditionally held in Indochina, Haiphong was to be made a special zone for the free transit of goods on the way from or to China, Chinese goods were to be transported by rail through Tongking duty free, and the section of the Yunnan railway which ran through Chinese territory was to be transferred to China.[8] In return for these concessions the Chinese Government, in an exchange of notes of the same date, undertook to hand over to the French Command the entire responsibility for guarding Japanese prisoners, maintaining order and security, and protecting Chinese nationals in the territory of the Indochinese Union to the north of the 16th parallel, the relief of the Chinese troops to begin between 1 and 5 March and to be completed at the latest on 31 March. It was, however, stipulated that the Chinese and French military staffs should come to an agreement 'within the scope of the conversations now taking place at Chungking' with respect to the procedure for carrying out this operation.[9]

By 1 March these talks were so far advanced that the French military delegation was able to inform Leclerc that the Chinese had agreed to the dispatch of a French force. Next day, however, the Chinese representatives refused to sign the agreement on the pretext that, after mature reflection, they had reached the conclusion that General MacArthur alone was empowered to authorize the proposed landing of a French force in Tongking. In view of the fact that the ships carrying the French troops were already on their way to Haiphong, this refusal had serious consequences.

Meanwhile the negotiations in Hanoi were complicated by Viet Minh reluctance to reveal that they were in fact taking place. This reluctance was due to the fact that the nationalist parties would exploit such an announcement in order to stir up public disorder on the pretext that the cause of national independence was being betrayed. The Viet Minh consequently considered it essential to implicate the nationalist leaders in the settlement. This manoeuvre was facilitated by the Chinese military authorities, who had realized that their interests would best be served by supporting the existing régime in Tongking, and the nationalist leaders finally yielded to Chinese pressure and agreed to join a Government of 'Union and Resistance' on

8 Ibid. pp. 267–9.
9 Ibid. pp. 258–9.

24 February. When the political opposition had been thus neutralized, the Viet Minh were able to reveal, in an official communiqué on the 26th, that negotiations were in progress for a settlement with the French.

The constitutional position of the Hanoi Government was further strengthened by the opening of the National Assembly on 2 March. During a short morning session the Assembly proceeded to deal with a number of important matters, and after voting the investiture of the new Government it elected a Consultative Council under the presidency of the ex-Emperor Bao Dai, a National Resistance Committee under the presidency of Vo Nguyen Giap, a Permanent Committee, which was to function when the National Assembly was not in session and, finally, a Committee charged with the task of drafting a constitution. On the completion of this business the Assembly adjourned, and those members who were not required for further service, either in the Government or on the various committees, were dismissed and instructed to return immediately to their respective constituencies 'where important business awaited them'.

While the Viet Minh were thus engaged in running up a constitutional façade for their Democratic Republic, the negotiations between Ho Chi Minh and Sainteny had reached an impasse following the French Government's refusal to grant 'independence' or to agree to the unity of the three ky—Tongking, Annam, and Cochin-China—which had formerly constituted the Empire of Annam.[10] On 5 March it appeared, therefore, to the anxious French representatives in Hanoi that the arrival of the French fleet in Haiphong, which was scheduled to take place on the following morning, would be opposed both by the Chinese troops, who had received no orders to permit a French landing, and by the Viet Minh. However, to avoid an armed clash, the general commanding the Chinese forces in Tongking agreed during the evening to instruct the division in Haiphong not to oppose the French entry into the port, but these instructions were rejected by the local Chinese Commander on the grounds that he had not been

[10] The refusal to concede national unity was based on the constitutional obligation to obtain the consent of the population of the colony of Cochin-China and the subsequent ratification by the French National Assembly of such a change in territorial status.

informed in a 'sufficiently official' manner of the signing of a
Franco-Chinese agreement,[11] and he ordered fire to be opened
at point-blank range on the advancing armada. The French
replied, scoring a direct hit on 600 tons of ammunition awaiting
shipment to Manchuria, and in the ensuing confusion a cease-
fire was arranged between the contending parties.

Ho Chi Minh in the meantime had finally resigned himself,
with manifest reluctance, to the necessity of accepting the
French conditions, and on 6 March a preliminary agreement[12]
was signed by the French delegates and the representatives of
the Hanoi Government. By its terms the French Government
recognized the Republic of Vietnam as a 'Free State having its
own government, parliament, army, and treasury, belonging to
the Indo-Chinese Federation and to the French Union'. The
French Government also undertook to hold a referendum to
ascertain the wishes of the local population in regard to national
reunification, and bound itself to carry out these wishes. The
Hanoi Government undertook to accept amicably the French
troops who were to relieve the Chinese forces in accordance with
the terms of the Chungking agreement. The signatories also
agreed to a suspension of hostilities, to the maintenance of their
troops on their respective positions, and to create a favourable
atmosphere for frank and friendly negotiations which would
bear especially on the diplomatic relations of Vietnam with
foreign states, the future status of the Indochinese Federation
and of French economic and cultural interests in Vietnam. The
agreement was completed by a military convention fixing the
strength and composition of the French units which were to be
stationed in Vietnam north of the 16th parallel. This convention also contained an undertaking that French units would
be withdrawn and replaced by Vietnamese troops progressively
over a period of five years.

Although fighting between the French troops landing in
Haiphong and Viet Minh units had been prevented by this
agreement, the news of its signing was received with anger and
dismay in Hanoi, where the population had not been prepared
for such an eventuality, and to rally public support for this
change of policy the Viet Minh leaders were compelled to
reveal with unusual frankness the motives that had dictated

[11] Sainteny, p. 179.
[12] Text in *Notes Documentaires et Études*, No. 548 (Cole, pp. 40–41).

their action. On 7 March, in the course of a harangue to a vast crowd in front of the municipal theatre, Giap declared that the Government's decision had been influenced by the international situation, which was unfavourable to the cause of independence, and by the realization that resistance offered little prospect of victory and would have brought in its train untold devastation and suffering. Finally, he revealed that the Government intended to create conditions which would enable the struggle for complete independence to be resumed with success, a task which would be facilitated by the agreement's recognition of the Republic's right to manage its internal affairs. Ho Chi Minh, who spoke last, argued that the agreement would enable the Republic to emerge from its moral isolation and to obtain international recognition, and he suggested that the return of a specified number of French troops for a limited period was a small price to pay for the independence which the Republic might well be in a position to acquire in five years' time by negotiation. 'I, Ho Chi Minh', protested the crafty Communist leader in a final burst of eloquence nicely calculated to appeal to the sentimental Vietnamese, 'I have always taken you along the path that leads to liberty. I have fought all my life in the cause of national independence. You know that I would rather die than betray our country. I swear to you that I have not betrayed you.' [13]

While the Viet Minh leaders were engaged in this explanation the French Expeditionary Corps were concluding negotiations with the local Chinese Commander to land their stores and equipment in the damaged port of Haiphong. The quality and quantity of this equipment gave Giap, who was afforded an opportunity to observe these off-loading activities, some cause for reflection. On 9 March Giap also met Leclerc and, with a flash of insensate pride, is reported to have expressed the pleasure he felt in his capacity as the acknowledged leader of the Vietnamese armed resistance in meeting the great leader of the French resistance movement. Leclerc, however, who possessed the professional soldier's disbelief in the effectiveness of improvised armies, failed to rise to this historic occasion and treated his flamboyant and strangely accoutred visitor with some reserve.[14]

[13] Devillers, p. 231.
[14] Sainteny, p. 189.

In the meantime the Chinese military authorities were still trying to prevent French units from moving on from the port area by legalistic quibbles, but on 16 March, after the signing of the Chungking agreements in February, permission was given for a French column to enter Hanoi, where the French population gave it an enthusiastic welcome.

On the day before this Bao Dai, who had been discharging his functions of Supreme Councillor with unobtrusive discretion, was sent on a 'goodwill' mission to China. The decision to banish the ex-Emperor at this stage was possibly due to a fear that he might assume the leadership of that section of the population whose allegiance was given neither to the Chinese Kuomintang nor to the Third International.[15] Bao Dai for his part must have greeted with relief the chance to escape from Hanoi,[16] as in addition to the delicacy and danger of his position his patience had been sorely tried by Ho's sentimental effusions, which were peculiarly embarrassing to a man of reserved temperament trained to maintain the hieratic impassiveness required of a Confucian ruler. Bao Dai's exile seemed to mark the final eclipse of a dynasty which had ruled the empire for 140 eventful years.[17]

The return of French troops to Hanoi did not deter the Chinese and Viet Minh authorities from disputing the implementation of the recently signed agreements with an oriental capacity for chicanery, while no move was made for several weeks to repatriate the Chinese forces. Finally, towards the end of May, one of the Chinese armies started to withdraw in the direction of Kwangsi, and this was followed by other troop movements towards the frontier. By 15 June Chinese forces in Tongking were represented by a division waiting to embark at Haiphong, though many members of the Chinese commissariat services and government departments still remained and were actively engaged in the sale or transportation of booty.

[15] The failure to arrange for his assassination may be ascribed to the influence of Ho Chi Minh, who in spite of years spent as an itinerant Communist revolutionary had retained some vestiges of the traditional Vietnamese respect for the established hierarchy.

[16] His wife, the Empress Nam Phuong, and his children had found a precarious refuge with the Redemptionist Fathers in Hué.

[17] The ex-Emperor Duy Tan, whose legendary attempt to lead a national uprising against French rule in 1916 and subsequent service with the Free French forces represented complementary claims to represent the Vietnamese nationalists, had been the victim of an aeroplane accident in January 1946.

## THE LAO ISSARA

Although the Chinese troops had almost completed their evacuation of Tongking by the middle of June, one division, the 93rd independent Infantry Division, remained in northwest Indochina until the end of the month, their presence being ascribed to their desire to complete the seizure of the opium crop from the Meo tribal groups before evacuating the area. This aroused resentment but no surprise, as these troops, after rounding up the French parties parachuted into the region, had devoted themselves exclusively to pillage.[18] Whereas their return to the north was to be delayed for some months by these tactics, the French were soon able to reoccupy the territory to the south of the 16th parallel, where the local ruler, Prince Boun Oum of Champassak, and the population were well disposed towards them. Thus although a company of Colonial Infantry arrived in Pakse at the beginning of October, any farther advance up the Mekong valley was held up by the presence of Chinese troops to the north, who threatened to resist such a move by force of arms.

Meanwhile the leaders of a Lao resistance movement were able to profit from the interregnum to set up a Government in Vientiane. For although Sisavang Vong, the King of Luang Prabang, appreciated the need of French protection in the absence of adequate economic resources and sufficient trained personnel to make good a claim to independence, these views were not shared by a small, but active minority of his subjects, calling themselves 'Free Lao' or 'Lao Issara', and including most of the *élite*, who were determined to have done with the protectorate. Moreover this group was able to enlist the support of a Lao prince named Phetsarath, who held the dual office of Viceroy and Prime Minister and ranked, in virtue of his functions, second to the king himself.[19]

Phetsarath, who was in Vientiane at the time of the Japanese

[18] The Japanese troops and officials whom the 93rd Division had been sent to round up and disarm had moved south to the British-occupied zone before the division's arrival (Katay Sasorith, *Le Laos* (1953), p. 50).

[19] The office of Viceroy or Maha Oupahat had been vested for three generations in the family of Oun Keo, a brother of Anourouth, the last king of Vientiane, Oun Keo's grandson, Boun Khong, the father of Phetsarath, having been confirmed in his rights by Pavie in 1895 (P. le Boulanger, *Histoire du Laos français* (1931), p. 202 n.).

capitulation, showed his hand on 1 September 1945, when he issued an official proclamation, without consulting the king, which reaffirmed the abrogation of the French Protectorate and the independence of the Lao provinces; and he followed this up a fortnight later with a second announcing the union of the southern with the northern provinces. But Phetsarath had reckoned without the king, and on 17 September Sisavang Vong informed him that the Protectorate remained in force: an announcement which embarrassed the Viceroy and angered his supporters, who set up a Defence Committee in Vientiane. After some weeks of stalemate, the king attempted to assert his authority and dismissed Phetsarath from both his offices on 10 October; the Defence Committee, with Chinese connivance, then voted a provisional constitution, formed a provisional People's Assembly, and nominated a Government, completing this constitutional upheaval ten days later by deposing Sisavang Vong, who had refused to ratify these revolutionary proceedings. However, the Lao Issara then realized that the French would refuse to recognize a Government established by such methods, and they attempted to substantiate their claims to represent the legal Government by negotiating for Sisavang Vong's return to the throne in the role of a constitutional monarch. Although the king's assent to this arrangement was finally extorted on 20 April 1946, this proved too late to save the Lao Issara Government from being driven out of Vientiane by French troops.

The French had had to await the conclusion of the Chungking agreement of 28 February before beginning their advance on Vientiane. Finally, on 17 March, a force concentrated to the south of Savannakhet occupied that town without opposition and then moved on Thakhek, which fell on the 21st. Here the French halted to clear the western sector of the road, *Route Coloniale* 12, to Vinh, which represented the principal line of communications between the Viet Minh and the Lao Issara and Vietnamese armed bands in the Mekong valley; this operation was completed in the face of stiff resistance by the 25th, when the advance on Vientiane was resumed. During this advance the French were hindered by demolitions and harassed by armed bands, while the Vietnamese installed in the area, fearful of being singled out for reprisals, fled in thousands across the Mekong and took refuge in Siam, a course of action also adopted by the Lao Issara Government before the French occupied Vientiane on the 25th. The French then set out for Luang Prabang, which they entered on 13 May, finally completing their reoccupation of Lao territory at the end of the rainy season.

Meanwhile a *modus vivendi*[20] had been signed on 27 August, implicitly recognizing the unity and autonomy of the Lao provinces; and in March 1947 elections were held to a Constituent Assembly, which completed its task with French assistance on 10 May, when a constitution was promulgated. The preamble to this constitution[21] proclaimed the unity of the Lao provinces under the sceptre of H. M. Sisavang Vong, who was styled 'King of Laos', and declared the status of the kingdom to be that of an independent state within the French Union. Elections to a National Assembly followed in November; and at the opening ceremony the king handed a letter to the French High Commissioner formally confirming the Constituent Assembly's decision in regard to the kingdom's status and announcing the Government's readiness to negotiate agreements to put it into effect. But these negotiations were to be delayed until July 1949 by events in Vietnam.

### COCHIN-CHINESE AUTONOMY

Meanwhile the Franco-Viet Minh agreement of 6 March 1946 had been completed by a further agreement on 3 April fixing the location and strength of the respective garrison forces in Tongking and North Annam. This agreement also contained provisions for the setting up of Joint Committees responsible for the maintenance of liaison between the French and Viet Minh commands. Nevertheless, relations between the French and Viet Minh authorities remained strained. Impressed though they were by the quality and quantity of French military equipment the Viet Minh continued by press campaigns and radio attacks, by strikes, by interference with French food supplies, and with the recruitment of labour, to demonstrate the degree of freedom which they now enjoyed and the fact that the presence of the French Expeditionary Corps in Tongking was unwelcome.

[20] Text in Lévy, pp. 55–60.
[21] Text in Cole, p. 57.

On 24 March d'Argenlieu, yielding to Leclerc's insistence, agreed to meet Ho Chi Minh on board the cruiser *Émile Bertin* in the Bay of Along (Bay of the Dragon), a site of great natural beauty near Haiphong. The meeting between the French High Commissioner and the Viet Minh Prime Minister, whose visit coincided with an impressive review of French naval vessels, revealed the existence of some difference of opinion in regard to the venue of the conference which was to be convened in accordance with the 6 March agreement. Whereas Ho insisted that the negotiations should take place in Paris, where he hoped to find a more liberal approach to the Vietnamese problem than had been displayed by the French authorities in Saigon, d'Argenlieu, who was anxious to insulate the Viet Minh leaders from contact with French political circles, proposed that the conference should be held at Dalat in South Annam; and he sought to instil a greater sense of reality into Ho Chi Minh, whose pretensions appeared to him excessive, by assuring him that 'one did not go to Paris like that; one had, at least, to be invited'.[22] In the communiqué issued after this meeting it was announced that agreement had been reached for the dispatch of a parliamentary mission to Paris and for a preparatory conference to be held at Dalat during the first fortnight in April; this conference was to be followed by official negotiations in Paris.

An invitation to send a delegation to Paris was received by the Hanoi Government on 11 April; Ho Chi Minh in his capacity as *de facto* head of a state was also invited to visit France, an invitation accompanied by the proviso that while he was the official guest of the Republic he would be expected to conduct himself with a fitting reserve.[23]

Meanwhile in Cochin-China in the course of a session on 12 March the provisional Advisory Council had expressed grave disquiet at the news of the agreement of 6 March, but Cédile was able to assure the Councillors that it represented no more than a regional arrangement between the authorities in Hanoi and the French Commissioner for Tongking and North Annam, and in no way concerned Cochin-China, which enjoyed the legal status of a colony, a fact implicitly admitted by the omission to consult the Councillors.

[22] Devillers, pp. 249–50.
[23] *Le Monde,* 12 Apr. 1946.

I wish to declare [concluded Cédile], that the French Government intends to set up in Cochin-China, as in all the other countries forming the Indochinese Federation, a régime that will enjoy a freedom equivalent to that at present enjoyed in Cambodia, and similar to that envisaged for Tongking. Cochin-China will, in her turn, soon have her government, her parliament, her army and finances, and will enjoy the same rights and advantages as the other countries which form part of the Federation.[24]

On 14 March, support for this contention was forthcoming when Marius Moutet, Minister for French Overseas Territories, confirmed in Paris that Cochin-China would be granted the constitution of a 'Free State'.

Emboldened by this official encouragement, the members of the Advisory Council proceeded on 26 March to discuss the formation of a provisional autonomous government, and proposed in the course of a secret session that Nguyen Van Thinh, a doctor of medicine and a wealthy landowner, should be given the office of Prime Minister.[25] During the last days of the month the movement in favour of Cochin-Chinese autonomy was given a semblance of popular support by carefully arranged public demonstrations, but in spite of some local hostility towards the Tongkingese the population, who were conscious of their ethnic identity with the inhabitants of North and Central Vietnam, for the most part refused to support a movement considered to represent a French manoeuvre designed to split the nation in its struggle for independence.

## THE DALAT CONFERENCE

On 17 April d'Argenlieu presided over the opening session of the Conference at Dalat. The French delegation included technicians from France and colonial administrators attached to the High Commissioner's office; the Vietnamese delegation was led by Nguyen Tuong Tam, leader of the VNQDD nationalist party. It was soon apparent that a wide divergence of views separated the two delegations, for although by the 6 March agreement the Hanoi Government had conceded that Vietnam should form part of the Indochinese Federation and the French Union, the Vietnamese delegation was not

[24] Devillers, p. 244.
[25] Combat, 2 Mar. 1946.

prepared to agree that membership of these organizations should entail any surrender of sovereignty. The delegation was willing that Vietnam should adhere to a French Union on condition that it represented an association of sovereign and independent states possessing their own armed forces and diplomatic service; and in return for technical and financial assistance was prepared to grant France economic advantages, commercial priority, and diplomatic pre-eminence. Its attitude towards membership of an Indochinese Federation was similarly conditioned by the refusal to agree to Vietnam forming part of a federation in which no recognition was accorded to Vietnamese predominance in numbers, wealth, and energy, or in which the administrative services attached to the High Commissioner's office constituted either a super-Government or assumed the role of indispensable intermediary between the Vietnamese and French Governments. Indeed the only kind of federation to which the delegation in its capacity as representatives of the Hanoi Government would have been prepared to adhere was an organization that was principally designed to co-ordinate the economic activities of its members, and in which the role of the French High Commissioner was confined to the exercise of his diplomatic functions.

In addition to these basic differences in regard to Vietnam's future relations with the Indochinese Federation and with France, the atmosphere was soon envenomed by French military activities in Cochin-China, where local Commanders, basing their action on the colonial status of the area, were neglecting to observe the armistice.

On 11 May, the work of the Conference was formally concluded. The results achieved were summarized by Nguyen Tuong Tam on his return to Hanoi as a general agreement on the fact that the Conference had failed to reach agreement on any item on the agenda.[26]

In spite of this the Hanoi Government continued with its preparations to send a delegation to the official and definite negotiations which were to take place in Paris, since Viet Minh leaders now had good reason to believe that their demands would be sympathetically received by the French Government. This optimism was based on the report of the Vietnamese deputies who had visited Paris at the end of April: not only had

[26] Célerier, p. 108.

these deputies been most courteously received, but they had had occasion to note that in the draft constitution which had been adopted on 19 April by the French Constituent Assembly provision had been made for a French Union 'based on consent'.[27] Moreover Ho Chi Minh, who had formerly been a member of the 17th Ward in the Communist Federation of the Seine, seems to have felt some confidence that he would be able to revive his former contacts with the French Communist leaders and use their influence to further the cause of Vietnamese independence.

Faced with the Viet Minh determination that the negotiations should take place outside the sphere of his authority, d'Argenlieu profited from French political preoccupations to advance the cause of an autonomous Cochin-China, and after the opening of the Dalat Conference he authorized the visit of a Cochin-Chinese political delegation to Paris in order to explain the local situation to French deputies and also, incidentally, to counter-balance the success of the 'goodwill' mission from Tongking. On 18 May he paid a visit to Hanoi, where he again recommended that the forthcoming conference should be held in Indochina and warned the Viet Minh leaders that 'he might soon find it impossible to maintain his opposition to Cochin-Chinese aspirations for autonomy'.[28] On his return to Saigon, therefore, d'Argenlieu allowed preparations for the declaration of an autonomous régime in the south to go forward. These were to result, on 26 May, in a vote by the Cochin-Chinese provincial Councillors of a motion supporting the Advisory Council's proposal for the constitution of a Provisional Government which would be charged with the task of establishing a republican régime. The official reply to this motion was delayed, however, for some days, and finally on 30 May d'Argenlieu, acting on his own responsibility, recognized the Republic of Cochin-China 'as a free state having its own government, parliament, army and finances, and forming part of the Indochinese Federation and the French Union'.[29]

The official proclamation[30] of an autonomous Republic of

[27] 'Union librement consentie'. The draft constitution was rejected by the referendum of 5 May.
[28] Devillers, p. 267.
[29] Ibid., p. 270.
[30] Text in *Notes Documentaires et Études*, No. 554, pp. 7–8 (Cole, pp. 9–11).

Cochin-China took place two days later, when a list was published of the ministers who were to form the Provisional Government under the presidency of Thinh. These ministers were appointed by, and remained responsible to, the President, who was to render account of his stewardship to the Advisory Council, which was to approve the budget but was not to take action on expenditure appertaining to the government.[31] As the internal and external security of the Cochin-Chinese state remained a French responsibility, while French approval was still required for the appointment of provincial administrators and even the heads of the technical services, the powers entrusted to the Cochin-Chinese Government, in spite of its authoritarian structure, were extremely limited.

Although his official recognition of the Cochin-Chinese Republic had been made dependent on the subsequent ratification of his action by the competent constitutional body of the French Union, and subject to the result of the referendum which had been provided for in the agreement of 6 March, d'Argenlieu's rash initiative placed the French Government in a position of grave embarrassment. Whereas the proclamation of an autonomous Cochin-Chinese Republic had diminished the prospect of an agreement with the Viet Minh, without prior ratification by the French Assembly the French Government was unable to recognize the authority of a republic over territory which still retained the status of a colony. However, in spite of its grave implication, d'Argenlieu's action attracted little attention in France, but on 3 June the Communist newspaper *L'Humanité* asked, with well-founded anxiety: 'What is afoot in Saigon? We have had frequent occasion to draw attention to the activities of a handful of Cochin-Chinese autonomists who represent no one but themselves.'

### THE FONTAINEBLEAU CONFERENCE

On 31 May Ho Chi Minh, accompanied by the Viet Minh delegation, left for France. Their departure proved ill-timed since, following the rejection of a referendum on the draft constitution, a 'caretaker' Government had been installed in France, where general elections were to be held on 2 June. However, the Viet Minh delegation, who had spent long years

[31] Hammer, p. 169.

in the claustral atmosphere of a French colony or in remote Chinese provinces, were eager to visit the 'new' France which had emerged from the war, and to study the chequerboard of international affairs from the vantage-ground of Paris. Moreover their suspicions of d'Argenlieu's intentions provided an added incentive for them to hasten their departure. These suspicions were to be confirmed in the course of their journey when news was received of the proclamation of an autonomous republic in Cochin-China. Although Ho is reported tactfully to have ascribed this action to a 'misunderstanding', it was considered by the other members of the delegation to constitute a breach of the 6 March agreement and to represent a deliberate attempt to prejudice the outcome of the negotiations.[32]

Ho was greeted by Sainteny, who had been charged with the administrative arrangements for his official visit to Paris and also with the delicate task of advising him on his official and unofficial contacts. Sainteny had further been instructed to explain to the delegation that the opening of the Conference would have to be postponed, and to tell them that accommodation had been reserved for them at Biarritz where they were to be welcomed by the sub-prefect of the department and the deputy-mayor on 12 June.[33] Although most of the delegation soon left 'like a flock of sparrows'[34] for Paris, Ho remained a fortnight in Biarritz, where he indulged in the customary pursuits of a holiday maker. After the elections had taken place, and Georges Bidault had succeeded in forming a Government, he too left for Paris.

The President of the Democratic Republic of Vietnam, who had disappeared from his Paris haunts twenty-three years earlier to attend the Krestintern Congress in Moscow, is reported to have betrayed some alarm as he approached the French capital; an alarm which may perhaps have been inspired by the change that had taken place in his fortunes since the days when he occupied his modest lodging there. However, Ho, whose political affiliations were tactfully described on this occasion as 'socialist', soon adapted himself to the role of head of an Associate State who was paying an official visit to France, and his receptions at the Hôtel Royal-Monceau were well

[32] Devillers, p. 271.
[33] L'Humanité, 13 June 1946.
[34] Sainteny, p. 202.

attended by left-wing politicians, by journalists, and by representatives of French financial and commercial interests, with the result that he was soon in contact with those circles whose support he had hoped to recruit for the Viet Minh cause. The Parisians for their part are reported to have given a friendly welcome to the little 'man of superior attainments' with his wispy beard and inseparable topee, who was soon a familiar figure in the capital.

The preliminary arrangements for the Conference gave rise to controversy, for whereas the Viet Minh wished it to take place in Paris—both for reasons of prestige and also because of the facilities for social contacts which the capital provided— the French Government, with similar considerations in mind, proposed that it should take place at the palace of Fontainebleau, where a discreet surveillance of the delegates would present fewer difficulties. The fact that all available accommodation in Paris would be required to house the delegates to the Peace Conference, which was due to open on 29 July, provided a decisive argument in favour of Fontainebleau. The choice of a suitable personage to lead the French delegation was also attended by some difficulty since although d'Argenlieu had proposed that he should himself be in the chair, the Viet Minh, who had been further exasperated by the French occupation, on the Admiral's orders, of the provinces of Pleiku and Kontum, objected to this proposal. Finally, as Ho Chi Minh had decided not to participate directly in the work of the Conference, the French agreed to appoint a less controversial figure, selecting for this task Max André, a former director of the Franco-Chinese Bank who had led the French delegation at the Dalat Conference, while an old associate of Ho's, Pham Van Dong,[35] was appointed head of the Viet Minh delegation.

The aspect of this austere personage, whose rare and wintry smile seemed out of place on a countenance otherwise set in lines of bleak and permanent disapproval, was not of a nature to inspire confidence in the outcome of the negotiations, and when the Conference opened on 6 July Dong's reply to the Chairman's address of welcome served to confirm these misgivings.

[35] See below, p. 431.

It is with great distress that I say [he informed the delegates] that certain clauses of the armistice of 6 March have not been observed by the French authorities in Vietnam and that hostilities, instead of ceasing immediately, are still continuing and French troops, instead of remaining in their positions, have done their utmost to gain territory. . . . We wish to protest with all the force of which a people of 20 million men are capable, staking everything on the legitimate defence of our country, against mutilation, against the creation of a free state of Cochin-China and the recognition of its provisional Government by the French authorities in Saigon.[36]

This official protest was followed by the revelation that the Viet Minh had in no way modified the proposals put forward at the Dalat Conference. Moreover the insistence with which they now demanded that the Hanoi Government should enjoy effective economic autonomy, including the right to nationalize local enterprises and to open the Vietnamese market to international trade, alienated and alarmed French commercial and financial interests.[37] In consequence, although the French Government was anxious to end a state of war which was proving costly and a drain on military strength, its ability to do so was circumscribed by the fact that a decision to grant the political and economic concessions demanded would have been contrary to the tradition that had hitherto guided French expansion overseas. The French delegates therefore replied evasively to Viet Minh demands that a date should be fixed for the referendum in Cochin-China, for without the guarantees which they considered essential for the safeguard of French interests they were naturally unwilling to surrender the pledge that Cochin-China represented in French hands.

In the meantime the Viet Minh delegates, by their reliance on advice by left-wing politicians, proceeded to reduce the negotiations at Fontainebleau to the level of a domestic political dispute since the zeal with which French Communists, whose knowledge of colonial problems was slight, had espoused the Viet Minh cause alienated the sympathy of other French political parties. Moreover while the Viet Minh delegates were arousing resentment by their tactless behaviour, Ho himself failed to maintain the attitude of prudent reserve recommended

[36] Conférence Franco-Vietnamienne, *Discours de M. Pham-Van-Dong . . . prononcé à l'ouverture de la séance inaugurale à Fontainebleau le 6 juillet 1946.*
[37] Jean Clementin in *Combat,* 16 Feb. 1950.

by Marius Moutet, and caused some official uneasiness by his readiness to meet individuals whose loyalty to France and to the French Union appeared open to question. Thus on the day on which the Fontainebleau Conference opened he received a delegation from a parliamentary group led by the Algerian political leader, Ferhat Abbas, and the communiqué issued after this meeting, to the effect that 'the analogy existing between the problems facing Algeria and Vietnam was notably the subject of an exchange of views',[38] was not calculated to allay these misgivings.

At this stage in the proceedings d'Argenlieu, whose recognition of an autonomous Cochin-Chinese republic was patently designed in Vietnamese opinion to amputate their country of its richest province, proceeded to wreck the lingering hopes of a settlement by convening a second Dalat Conference, which met on 1 August. He invited to it delegates from Cochin-China, Laos, and Cambodia and observers from South Annam and the mountainous region of the south, but no representatives of the Viet Minh. The news of this, and in particular the report that representatives from Cochin-China had been summoned to attend, provoked an immediate reaction at Fontainebleau, where Pham Van Dong lodged an energetic protest and demanded to be informed of the reasons for d'Argenlieu's action. On 1 August, dissatisfied with the French reply, the Viet Minh delegation proposed that further sessions should be suspended until more information was available concerning the purpose of the Dalat Conference, which appeared to represent a manoeuvre directed against the Hanoi Government.[39] After some days' delay, André informed the delegates that the Conference at Dalat had been convened merely for the purpose of ascertaining the view and opinions of the Indochinese populations in regard to the proposed Federation: a matter which concerned not only Vietnam but all the peoples of Indochina.

On 14 August, the Inter-Ministerial Committee for Indochina made an effort to prevent a breakdown of the Conference by proposing that an attempt should be made to reach a restricted agreement,[40] but although the delegations were to

[38] *Le Monde*, 8 July 1946.
[39] Ibid 2 Aug 1946.
[40] Devillers, p. 302.

agree, on the night of 9–10 September, upon the terms of a *modus vivendi* covering certain economic and financial aspects of the negotiations, this was later repudiated by Pham Van Dong who again raised the question of the Cochin-Chinese referendum. This incident ended a Conference which had served principally to show that no basis for negotiations existed, and on 13 September the Viet Minh delegation left for Toulon, where they embarked on board a passenger ship for Haiphong.

Ho Chi Minh, however, who had arranged a special passage for himself on board a sloop which was delayed some days by engine trouble, remained behind in a state of perplexity and indecision. For although Pham Van Dong and the other delegates had been content to return to Tongking conscious of their moral rectitude and of the fact that they had yielded nothing in the course of the acrimonious discussions which had been a feature of the Conference, Ho, with a keener sense of political realities and of his responsibilities towards the Vietnamese people, was clearly perturbed at the prospect of returning without any means of restraining the Viet Minh hotheads from a resort to force. On the 14th, therefore, he had further discussions with Moutet and also with Bidault, the French Prime Minister. Finally, acting possibly on the personal assurance of Maurice Thorez, Secretary-General of the French Communist Party, that the general elections in November would result in a Communist-led Government being installed in France, Ho resolved to stake his political future on this forecast by assuming personal responsibility for the concessions which the delegation had not been prepared to make; and on the night of 14–15 September, he signed in haste and secrecy a *modus vivendi* on behalf of the Hanoi Government.

By the terms of this agreement[41] the Government of the Democratic Republic undertook to facilitate the resumption of French economic and cultural activities, to accept the Indochinese piastre as the currency unit, and to join an Indochinese customs' union. In return for these concessions the French Government agreed to co-operate with the Hanoi Government in bringing about a cessation of all acts of hostility and violence in Cochin-China and South Annam, and to introduce a régime in those regions which would be based on 'democratic liberties,

[41] Text in Cole, pp. 43–45.

including the liberty of opinion, education, commerce and circulation'. But in spite of the prospect of an armistice and of the introduction of a more liberal régime in Cochin-China and South Annam, the fact that the *modus vivendi* included no formal recognition of Vietnamese 'independence' and also failed to fix a date for the referendum made its terms extremely unpalatable to the population in Tongking, where the news of Ho's initiative caused perplexity and disssatisfaction.[42]

## DR. THINH'S SUICIDE

The failure of the Fontainebleau Conference, which was scarcely palliated by Ho Chi Minh's action in signing the *modus vivendi*, may probably be ascribed to the fact that whereas the Viet Minh leaders had forfeited their ability to make concessions by the demagogic methods and extravagant promises which had enabled them to seize power, the French Government for its part was in no position to put through a policy involving the ultimate evacuation of Cochin-China and the surrender of French economic interests to a Communist-dominated Government composed for the most part of men who had suffered personally from the repressive methods employed to maintain the French Protectorate. Such a policy would have represented an act of imaginative statecraft surpassing the capacity of the harassed leaders of the French Fourth Republic. But if the refusal to surrender their economic interests or to abandon their supporters can scarcely occasion surprise, the subsequent failure of French Governments to produce an acceptable alternative policy was to influence in disastrous fashion the outcome of the impending struggle, and to strengthen the Communist hold over the movement for independence. This failure must be ascribed at least in part to the refusal of French administrators, financiers, and settlers to envisage a solution entailing the surrender of effective administrative control.

The methods by which French administrative control could be maintained were elaborated during the ensuing months in Cochin-China, where Nguyen Van Thinh had been installed as Prime Minister of a Provisional Government. These consisted in ostensibly surrendering all administrative functions

[42] *Le Monde,* 21 Sept. 1946.

to an autonomous government which was then prevented from exercising them effectively. Accordingly Cochin-Chinese had to be found who would be sufficiently pliable to play the part assigned to them,[43] since although the ministers in Thinh's Government were soon apparently engaged in directing government departments, these departments were in fact controlled by members of the French Colonial Service occupying secretarial positions on their staff; and the dependence of the Cochin-Chinese Government on subsidies from the Federal treasury represented a further check on their freedom of action.

Thinh, whose sincerity and good intentions were generally acknowledged, was thus faced with the dual task of combating the French colonial administration and of conducting the business of government in an autonomous state which remained both legally and effectively a French colony. Moreover, he was soon attacked in the Council of Cochin-China[44] by the representatives of French interests, who accused the Government of a preference for conciliatory methods and blamed the Prime Minister in particular for his failure to display the energy and ruthless sense of purpose required to arrest the deterioration in public security which had followed Nguyen Binh's resort to terrorist tactics. But whereas Thinh was thus accused of incompetence and lack of energy by French administrators and settlers, his dependence on French support was in itself sufficient to alienate popular support from his Government.

The French authorities soon decided that Thinh possessed neither the necessary prestige nor the personality for his impossible task, while his reluctance, based on irrefutable moral objections, to approve a French-inspired proposal to reopen the gambling establishments in Cholon served to increase their exasperation. The selection of a more accommodating figurehead was therefore under active consideration when Thinh was found hanged by a length of copper wire from the hasp of his bedroom window; a medical textbook open at the appropriate page was considered to constitute proof of suicidal intent. Thinh's demise occasioned some remorse on the part of erstwhile critical friends, who accorded him a splendid funeral,

[43] André Fontain in *Le Populaire*, 28 Jan. 1947.
[44] The Advisory Council had now assumed the name of Council of Cochin-China, and had increased its membership from 14 to 42 by decree.

and on 15 November, Colonel Nguyen Van Xuan,[45] the Deputy Prime Minister, was appointed Prime Minister *per interim*.

---

[45] Xuan had achieved the rare distinction of serving as a cadet at the French Military Academy of Artillery and Engineering, and had returned to Indochina in the course of the war. After the Japanese *coup de force* of 9 March 1945 he had preferred captivity with his brother officers in the citadel at Hanoi to service under a puppet Vietnamese Government (*Figaro*, 8 June 1948). The possession of these credentials was considered to outweigh any objections that might be raised to his appointment on the score that he was a French citizen and spoke no Vietnamese and displayed an ignorance of the business of government, which d'Argenlieu's successor was later to describe as 'total' (*L'Humanité*, 5 June 1948).

# X

# The Outbreak of Hostilities

BEFORE he left for France on 31 May 1946 Ho Chi Minh had announced the formation of a 'popular national front', or Hoi Lien-Hiep Quoc-Dan Viet Nam, which was to be known under the shortened name of the Lien Viet Front. This Front, which had been provided with the uncontroversial political platform of 'independence and democracy', included within its ranks representatives of every section of the population without distinction of class, religion, or race; it was designed, in conjunction with the Communist-dominated professional associations, to close the net in which the population were to be enmeshed and subjected to surveillance, indoctrination, and exploitation by their Communist masters.

Having revealed his solicitude for the population by the creation of the Lien Viet Front, Ho then took the necessary steps to ensure that the business of government would not suffer in the absence of those ministers who would be accompanying the Viet Minh delegation to France, appointing Huynh Thuc Khang,[1] the Minister of the Interior, president *per interim*, while the direction of Khang's important ministry was entrusted to Vo Nguyen Giap, who continued to hold the office of president of the High Council for National Defence.[2]

The temporary redistribution of ministerial portfolios invested Giap during Ho's absence with the principal responsibility for the conduct of affairs. This energetic and ruthless young man had, however, formed the opinion at the abortive Dalat Conference, that national unity and independence would not be conceded round a conference table.[3] He was thus anxious to exploit the truce in order to build up Viet Minh military strength and also, with French connivance, to crush the francophobic nationalist parties. In pursuit of this second objective he dispatched Viet Minh units in the wake of the

[1] Khang had formerly been the headmaster of the Thang Long school in Hanoi, where Giap himself had been employed until 1939 as a member of the staff.

[2] The National Resistance Committee had been renamed by a decree of 5 April 1946 the High Council for National Defence.

[3] Devillers, p. 266.

Chinese forces with orders to expel the Dong Minh Hoi armed groups from the towns of Phu Lang Thuong and Lang Son.

During the months of June and July these units were able to complete their occupation of the Dong Minh Hoi-held areas in North Tongking and to start the task of driving the VNQDD partisans from the Red river valley, an operation which was completed in November by the occupation of the frontier town of Lao Kay. Meanwhile those members of the nationalist parties who had remained in Hanoi helped Giap to carry out his plan by their refusal to desist from acts of aggression against French soldiers and civilians. Consequently French approval was easily obtained for the Viet Minh to carry out a series of raids on VNQDD centres in the town, which put a stop to further activities by that party.

While these measures were being taken to suppress the nationalist opposition, the build-up of the Viet Minh forces continued. The methods which were adopted conformed to Mao Tse-tung's directions in regard to the strategy to be followed by a semi-colonial and semi-feudal country at war with an imperialist power: directions which assumed the need to prepare for a long war. Giap therefore proceeded to make arrangements for bases to be set up in the wild mountainous provinces of Bac Kan, Ha Giang, Tuyen Quang, and Thai Nguyen—an area to be known as 'the Viet Bac'—to which regular units could retire in the event of hostilities, and where further units could be trained in preparation for the day when Viet Minh regular troops could engage the well-equipped French Expeditionary Corps on equal terms.

In June the Viet Minh forces in Tongking and North Annam numbered about 31,000, their armament being composed for the most part of weapons originally supplied for the use of the Indochinese Guard, and mortars, rifles, and sub-machine guns purchased or otherwise acquired from the Japanese and Chinese. Further supplies of weapons and equipment were thus urgently needed. But although stocks of war material had fallen into the hands of traffickers in neighbouring countries, the extent to which the Viet Minh were able to avail themselves of these supplies was limited by their lack of money, and so the Hanoi Government, which had already reimposed many of the taxes levied under the Protectorate, now sought to raise more revenue not only to pay for the business of government but also for the clandestine purchase of war material.

In the disrupted state of the Vietnamese economy the collection of duties on imported goods offered an obvious means of increasing public revenue: customs officials were therefore recruited and installed in Haiphong, but their presence there proved to be a source of irritation to the French and gave rise to a number of incidents involving members of the local Chinese community since the Chinese, acting on the assumption that the Chungking treaty had been ratified by the Hanoi Government, refused to pay the duties demanded by the Viet Minh. This attitude involved the French authorities in Haiphong in frequent interventions on behalf of Chinese merchants who were being detained by the Viet Minh following their refusal to pay the sums demanded. On 29 August 1946, after an incident of this kind, French troops expelled the Viet Minh from the customs house. This incident was settled by the personal intervention of Giap, who agreed to leave the French in temporary occupation of the building but rejected the French proposal that customs control in Haiphong should be a joint Franco-Viet Minh responsibility.

However, notwithstanding Giap's patent desire to prevent a deterioration in the situation, incidents involving French troops and Viet Minh militia guards persisted: they included a Viet Minh attack in July on a French patrol near Lang Son and a further attack in the same month upon a convoy near Bac Ninh. In this tense and troubled atmosphere the news of the signature of the *modus vivendi* agreement of 14 September was received with bewilderment and disappointment, a reception which aroused French misgivings concerning Ho's ability to impose its acceptance upon his followers. These misgivings were increased by the enthusiastic welcome given to Pham Van Dong and the Viet Minh delegation on their return to Hanoi on 3 October, but in spite of these French fears 'Uncle Ho' when he landed on the 20th was greeted with rapturous affection by the population.

After Ho's return to Hanoi the Constituent Assembly was convened for it to approve the conduct of the Government and to complete the construction of the régime's constitutional façade. On the eve of this meeting Giap proceeded to arrest those surviving representatives of the nationalist parties who were thought to possess the courage or temerity to mar, with misplaced criticism, the unanimity of the official proceedings. On 31 October, when the Constituent Assembly met, Ho Chi Minh, after an able defence of his conduct of affairs, resigned, but was promptly invited by the Assembly to form a new Government. The list of ministers which he presented to the Assembly on 3 November revealed that the portfolios previously held by the nationalist leaders had all been entrusted to Viet Minh stalwarts, Giap himself being officially appointed Minister of National Defence.

On 9 November the Assembly adopted a draft constitution,[4] which had been drawn up by the committee appointed for that purpose. The constitution omitted all reference to the French Union, and affirmed the untrammelled sovereignty and unity of the Vietnamese state. It also provided for the enfranchisement of women, and granted freedom of speech, assembly, and religious belief, but was chiefly remarkable for the wide powers conferred upon the Assembly's Standing Committee. This Committee, which was composed of fifteen members, was authorized to approve legislation, supervise government activities and, in consultation with the cabinet, to decide even upon the gravest issues including war and peace: it therefore occasioned no surprise when six members of the recently dissolved Indochinese Communist Party and two Communist sympathizers were elected to membership of this very powerful body. On 14 November, following a decision to dispense the Government from any obligation to put the provisions of the constitution into effect, the Assembly was prorogued.

THE START OF HOSTILITIES

After the breakdown of the Fontainebleau Conference in September 1946 the relations between the French authorities and the Hanoi Government deteriorated still further. This was caused by Viet Minh persistence in eluding French proposals to proceed with the formation of the joint Franco-Vietnamese force under French command which, in conformity with the provisions of the military agreement of 3 April, was to be responsible for public security in Tongking and North Annam.

[4] Text in Vietnam News Agency, *Vietnam, a New Stage in Her History* (Bangkok, 1947), pp. 11–22 (Cole, pp. 30–39).

The suspicions to which these prevarications gave rise were reinforced, moreover, by Viet Minh attempts to substitute their own currency unit for the Indochinese piastre and to enforce customs' control in Haiphong in violation of the terms of the *modus vivendi*. With the intention of curbing these pretensions General Morlière, the acting Commissioner for Tongking, issued on 10 September a notice setting out the measures which the French authorities proposed to take—as from 15 October—to establish temporary control over imports and exports. Although this prior notice of French intentions aroused no immediate reaction, the attempt to enforce customs control drew an official protest from the Hanoi Government.[5]

By the beginning of November French control over the entry of goods into Haiphong had given rise to a number of incidents, and on the 20th the attempted seizure of a junk with a contraband cargo led to the capture of the whole French party by Viet Minh militia guards, or *Tu Ve*. An attempt to secure the release of the prisoners by force led to the erection of barricades in the centre of the town. Their appearance was countered by the expulsion of the Viet Minh militia guards from the defence posts they were occupying in the French quarter. On the next day representatives of the liaison committee[6] arrived from Hanoi with instructions to settle the incident on the basis of a cease-fire and the reoccupation by French and Viet Minh troops of their original positions, but the French Commander refused to order the withdrawal of his troops, objecting that they were still under fire. At length, after further discussions, agreement was reached for a cease-fire without a French withdrawal.

Despite this agreement General Valluy, who had assumed command of the French Expeditionary Corps on 18 July, intervened at this stage with a demand that Viet Minh military and para-military forces should evacuate Haiphong forthwith: this demand had been preceded by a personal message to the local French commander, Colonel Debès, uging him to exploit the incident in order to improve the position of the French forces.[7]

<hr/>

[5] On 8 November the Constituent Assembly also formally condemned the French action (Célerier, p. 150).

[6] Set up to supervise the execution of the agreement of 5 April 1944. See above, p. 152.

[7] Devillers, p. 336. The reason for Valluy's action, which seemed designed to provoke a resumption of the fighting, is reported to have been that, in the event of a Viet Minh attempt to expel the French from Tongking, the undisputed

On the 22nd Debès's resolve was steeled by the receipt of a further signal from Valluy informing him that all the means at the disposal of the French should be used to secure complete control of Haiphong and to bring the Viet Minh military command to a more reasonable frame of mind.[8] The next morning, acting on these instructions, Debès delivered an ultimatum to the local Viet Minh authorities demanding the evacuation of their forces from the Chinese quarter and from the eastern suburbs of the town, two hours being accorded for the completion of this operation. When this ultimatum had expired French troops went into action and proceeded to occupy the Chinese quarter. Meanwhile the guns of the cruiser *Suffren* had opened fire on the Vietnamese sector of the town, inflicting heavy casualties upon the population, who tried to escape to open country.[9] Fighting continued sporadically for several days, but by the 28th Haiphong and the adjacent airfield of Cat Bi were in French hands.

The Hanoi Government was surprised by this ruthless French action; and as it was unprepared for an immediate outbreak of hostilities it tried to gain time by seeking to reach a settlement which would not involve too damaging a loss of prestige, but on the 27th Morlière disappointed these hopes when he acquainted Giap with the French demands, which included not only the total evacuation of Haiphong by Vietnamese military and paramilitary units but also the occupation by French troops of a fairly extensive zone around the town, together with control of road communications between French garrisons throughout Tongking.[10] On the receipt of these demands the Viet Minh ordered civilians to leave the towns and began to move office equipment and files to the base areas in the Viet Bac. These precautionary measures were accompanied by the withdrawal of Viet Minh regular units from Hanoi, where their security duties were taken over by militia troops, or *Tu Ve*. The withdrawal of these units was followed by increasing evidence of Viet Minh preparations for armed resistance.

possession of the port of Haiphong would be essential for the reinforcement and supply of the Expeditionary Corps (Jean Clementin in *Combat*, 10 Feb. 1950).
[8] Devillers, p. 336, quoting Institut Franco-Suisse d'Études Coloniales, *France et Viet-Nam . . . d'après les documents officiels* (Geneva, 1947), p. 42.
[9] The casualties caused by this naval bombardment were later estimated at a minimum of 6,000 killed (Chesneaux, p. 256).
[10] *Le Monde*, 3–4 Dec. 1946.

Meanwhile the deterioration of the situation in Central Annam caused the French Command to send a battalion of Foreign Legion troops to Tourane with orders to occupy the local airfield, which was an important staging point for aircraft on flights between North and South Vietnam. This action represented a violation of the 3 April agreement and evoked, as might be expected, an official protest from the Hanoi Government. At this critical juncture Sainteny, who had reluctantly consented to return to Tongking with full civil and military powers and the rank of colonial governor, arrived in Saigon and proceeded to Hanoi on 2 December. The local situation appeared to justify his forebodings, for the indisciplined *Tu Ve* troops were provoking recurrent affrays which had led to a marked deterioration in security conditions. By the 19th the aggressive behaviour of the *Tu Ve* units, together with the persistent attempts which were being made to hamper French movements by the erection of barricades, led Morlière to demand that the *Tu Ve* troops should be disarmed and that responsibility for assuring freedom of movement in Hanoi should be handed over to the French military police. These demands, which appear to have been mistakenly regarded as an ultimatum, led to the decision that a surprise attack should be launched upon the French positions during the following night. Meanwhile, in order to lull suspicion, the Viet Minh leaders continued to provide evidence of their pacific intentions, and that morning Ho Chi Minh wrote a friendly letter to Sainteny in which he expressed concern at the existing state of tension and recommended that Sainteny should, in co-operation with Giam, his recently appointed Under-Secretary of State for Foreign Affairs, find some means of restoring public confidence,[11] while Giap for his part recommended that Morlière should cancel the order confining French troops to their quarters, urging that a display of confidence would serve to dissipate the existing alarm.

At six o'clock in the evening a Eurasian agent employed by the French reported that the Viet Minh were about to launch a general attack on the French positions. On receipt of this information, the troops, who had been given leave to go into the town, were hastily recalled and preparations made to meet the danger. Two hours later sabotage at the Hanoi power

[11] Devillers, p. 354.

station gave the signal for a general assault by Viet Minh militia troops on French posts and French-occupied houses, but as a result of the precautions which had been taken, casualties among the French forces and the civilian population were relatively light.[12] Sainteny himself, however, was wounded when the armoured car in which he was trying to reach military headquarters in the citadel was blown up on a mine detonated from the Vietnamese Mayor's house.[13] Next day French armoured vehicles counter-attacked and occupied Ho Chi Minh's official residence, from which Ho, who was reported to be ailing, had decamped in haste.

The rising in Hanoi, which was followed by similar unsuccessful assaults on French garrisons throughout Tongking and North Annam, was greeted almost with relief by a large section of the French press, who welcomed the clarification of a situation which had hitherto appeared obscure: a sentiment echoed by Moutet, the Minister for French Overseas Territories, who declared: 'Before a resumption of negotiations can be envisaged, a military decision is necessary. I regret the necessity, but you cannot commit with impunity acts of madness, such as those committed by the Viet Minh.'[14] But in spite of the general indignation aroused by this proof of Viet Minh perfidy the implications of a resort to force continued to be stressed:

It is inconceivable that we should imagine [wrote the Assistant Secretary-General of the Socialist Party in a press article which appeared towards the end of the month] that the problems of our future relations with Vietnam can be settled by force. Such a solution would impose terrible sacrifices in human lives upon our people. Moreover on the economic and social plane it would compromise national recovery and depress the living conditions of the working class, which are already difficult enough. Finally, it would have grave repercussions upon our future relations not only with the Annamite people, but also with the other peoples of the French Union, not to mention possible developments on the international plane.[15]

[12] French casualties amounted to 43 killed and 200 French nationals were abducted.
[13] Pierre Voisin in *Figaro*, 21 Jan. 1947.
[14] *Le Monde*, 5–6 Jan. 1947.
[15] Yves Dechezelles in *Le Populaire*, 26–27 Jan. 1947.

### BOLLAERT AS HIGH COMMISSIONER

Although the expulsion of the Viet Minh rearguard from Hanoi was delayed for several weeks,[16] the French forces proceeded without delay to re-establish contact with their garrisons in Tongking and Annam. The first and most important of these operations, which was completed in the early days of January, was the reopening of the road between Hanoi and Haiphong. On 7 February the beleaguered garrison of Hué was relieved by a force from Tourane, and Nam Dinh with its important cotton mills was reached by an armoured column on 11 March. By the middle of March the French had re-established their control over the principal towns in Tongking and Annam, with the exception of Qui Nhon and Vinh, but in spite of the success of these operations, it was observed with misgivings that the Viet Minh, in conformity with Chinese Communist tactics, had in no instance committed their regular units to battle, and that their control over the countryside remained unimpaired. Indeed even in Cochin-China, where Viet Minh guerrilla bands and assassination squads had resumed their activities on a considerable scale, only those localities where French troops were garrisoned were able to enjoy relative security.[17] The Expeditionary Corps was therefore faced with the prospect of prolonged and exhausting operations against elusive guerrilla bands inexpugnably entrenched in swamps, mountains, or forests throughout the length of Vietnam.

The persistence of Viet Minh resistance made a negotiated settlement at some time or other inevitable, but the odium which the Viet Minh had incurred by their surprise attack on 19 December 1946 prevented any immediate attempt being made to reopen the discussions. In consequence, although Ho proposed a cease-fire in a broadcast appeal to Léon Blum, the French Prime Minister, on 29 December and an attempt was made in early January 1947 to submit a memorandum to Marius Moutet when he visited Hanoi, both these initiatives were ignored.

[16] The French were hampered in their attempts to expel this Viet Minh rearguard by the fact that these troops had taken refuge in a quarter of the town which was inhabited for the most part by Chinese.

[17] Voisin in *Figaro*, 22 Jan. 1947.

Meanwhile d'Argenlieu revealed on 2 January the plan by which the French authorities were hoping to escape from the impasse.[18] This plan, which he divulged in an interview to a press correspondent, was based on the formation of a coalition of anti-Communist personages and groups with which a settlement could be negotiated. The figurehead chosen to lead this coalition was none other than the ex-Emperor Bao Dai who, since his expulsion from Tongking in March 1946, had been living in penurious exile in Hong Kong, but the emissary whom d'Argenlieu dispatched to contact him was received evasively since Bao Dai suspected that he had been cast for the role of pawn in an intrigue principally designed to intimidate the Viet Minh. Moreover the probable composition of the nationalist coalition which he would be required to lead was of a nature to daunt the most stout-hearted of Gia Long's descendants, for though it would include some men of integrity, culture, and intelligence, many dubious appetites and interests would also be represented in its ranks.

The prospects of such a coalition were improved, however, by the fact that many Vietnamese who had been inspired by patriotism to join the Viet Minh were now dismayed to discover that their desire for national independence was being exploited in order to impose upon the country an alien Communist régime, which was likely to prove more destructive of the national heritage than had been the case with the short-lived French Protectorate. Moreover additional encouragement could be drawn from the fact that the rural population, who had at first given the Viet Minh their wholehearted support, were becoming resentful of the Viet Minh officials, whose capricious tyranny was unrestrained by traditional customs, and whose demands upon the village economy took small account of the labour that the fulfilment of their increasing requirements represented for the community. Nevertheless it was recognized that the success of any attempt to break the Communist grip upon the countryside must depend on the readiness of the French Government to concede to the new interlocutors the independence and unity the Viet Minh had failed to obtain at the Fontainebleau Conference.

D'Argenlieu himself did not supervise the attempt to find a nationalist solution to the Vietnamese imbroglio since he had,

[18] Devillers, pp. 363-4.

finally, exhausted the patience of the French Government by his bold initiatives. His recognition of an autonomous Government of Cochin-China and his convocation of a Federal conference at Dalat were held in French left-wing circles to have been responsible for the outbreak of hostilities, and his inability to bring order out of the administrative chaos prevailing in Saigon laid him open to criticism by all shades of political opinion. The occasion for his removal was the promulgation on 4 February of a Federal decree, without the authorization of the French Government, which dispensed with previous reservations and accorded to Cochin-China unconditionally the status of a 'free state' associated with France within the framework of the Indochinese Federation and the French Union.[19] On 20 February, therefore, d'Argenlieu was recalled to France, where his services were appropriately recognized, in view of the part he had played in promoting a military solution of Franco-Viet Minh differences, by the award of the Médaille Militaire.

The choice of his successor was delayed by grave differences of opinion within the French Government in regard to policy in Indochina. The Communists and a section of the Socialist Party continued to urge the reopening of negotiations with the Viet Minh, but the representatives of the Popular Republican Party (MRP)—the third party in this uneasy coalition— refused to consider such an eventuality and insisted that negotiations must in future be conducted with representative nationalists. Finally, on 5 March, Émile Bollaert was appointed High Commissioner for France in Indochina, for the limited period of six months, an appointment probably to be ascribed to the administrative ability he had shown as Prefect of Lyons, and, later, as Commissioner for the Lower Rhine.

This aspect of his mission was stressed in his instructions, which specifically charged him with the reorganization of the local administrative services, the integration of the Indochinese states with the French Union, and, lastly, with the mission of conducting an exploratory approach to representative Vietnamese nationalists; the French Government's desire to reassert its authority in this distant theatre of war was revealed by an injunction that the High Commissioner must 'enforce,

[19] *Le Populaire*, 5 Feb. 1947.

at all levels of the military hierarchy, scrupulous discipline and obedience to government directives'.[20]

Accordingly on 28 March Bollaert left for Saigon. There towards the end of the following month he received an official communication from Hoang Minh Giam, the Viet Minh Minister of Foreign Affairs.[21] This opened with a reference to the resolution carried by the national congress of the French Socialist Party on 21 March, to the effect that no occasion should be neglected which might lead to a reopening of negotiations to settle Franco-Viet Minh differences. This proposal was embarrassing both to Bollaert, who had become convinced of the need for a nationalist solution, and also to the French Command who were engaged in planning, for the end of the rainy season, a series of operations designed to destroy the enemy bases in the Viet Bac. However, the expulsion, on 4 May, from the Ramadier Government of the Communist ministers who were the principal advocates for the resumption of negotiations enabled the French authorities in Indochina to adopt a firm and discouraging attitude towards this Viet Minh approach,[22] and an emissary was dispatched to Tongking with instructions to acquaint Ho Chi Minh with the French conditions for an armistice. These conditions were based on the guarantees that Valluy considered essential to the safety of the French garrisons, and included the surrender of half the weapons estimated to be in Viet Minh possession, the restitution of hostages, prisoners, and deserters, and the arrangement of facilities for French troops to move freely throughout the Viet Minh zone: the Viet Minh troops, however, were to be consigned to areas allocated to them by the French Command.[23]

After some days of arduous travel, the emissary was able on 12 May to acquaint Ho Chi Minh in person at Viet Minh headquarters in the Viet Bac with the French reply, but in spite of their desire for an armistice the Viet Minh found the conditions unacceptable and even dishonourable.[24] The

[20] Chesneaux, p. 267, quoting a statement by Jean Letourneau, Minister for French Overseas Territories, in the National Assembly on 27 January 1950.
[21] He had been appointed Minister of Foreign Affairs after a ministerial reshuffle in March.
[22] The five Communist ministers were expelled following their refusal to support the Government's economic policy.
[23] Speech by P. Coste-Floret, J.O. 1 Mar. 1949.
[24] Devillers, pp. 389–90.

rejection of the French terms enabled Bollaert to proceed without more ado with his plan to encourage the formation of an anti-Viet Minh front, while the French Command continued with their preparations for a campaign designed to bring the Expeditionary Corps decisive victory. In furtherance of this plan Bollaert, in a speech in Hanoi on 13 May, questioned the right of any one group to speak on behalf of all Vietnamese, and on 5 July at Nha Trang he further clarified his objection to Viet Minh pretensions when he assured his audience that France would never deliver the Vietnamese people into the hands of a minority whose conduct was inspired by totalitarian principles.

Meanwhile in Annam and Tongking, with French encouragement, the scattered elements of a nationalist opposition to the Viet Minh began to come together. The movement had already been given momentum on 12 April when a provisional Administrative Committee had been set up in Hué. This Committee was provided with an executive arm in the form of a security force and entrusted with the administration of the provinces of Quang Tri and Quang Nam, and in Hanoi on 19 May a similar committee was set up which was entrusted with the administrative responsibility for liberated areas in Tongking. Finally, in the course of a ceremony on 24 May, at which the former residence of the French Governor was formally presented to the Cochin-Chinese Government, the use of the words 'Vietnamese nation' to describe the ultimate recipients of this gift encouraged a belief among nationalists, who were inclined to attach an exaggerated importance to such nuances, that the French would be prepared to concede national unity to a government from which the Viet Minh leaders had been excluded.

# XI

# Bollaert's Mission and the Return of
# Bao Dai

DURING the years 1946 and 1947 the Crown Colony of Hong
Kong provided a refuge for many fugitives from Tongking,
including Bao Dai who, after his hurried departure from Hanoi,
had established himself there to await the outcome of events.
The ex-Emperor, whose life had been spent under French
tutelage, was now able to indulge in this rich and garish city
a taste for informal amusements from which he had hitherto
been debarred, but he continued to follow the course of events
in Vietnam with anxious attention. He was therefore aware
that after the expulsion of the Viet Minh from Hanoi the
proposal had been made that some other intermediary should
be found with whom to negotiate a settlement, and that certain
colonial administrators had proposed him for this role. As he
suspected, however, that the French might be tempted to use
him merely as a pawn in some intrigue designed to bring the
Viet Minh to a more reasonable frame of mind, he remained
evasive and aloof when French emissaries first tried to contact
him at the beginning of 1947.

He informed Bollaert's political adviser, Paul Mus, who came
to visit him in May, that he would ask as much of France as Ho
Chi Minh, possibly more,[1] and in July he declared in an interview to the representative of a Saigon newspaper: 'I am neither
for the Viet Minh nor against them: I belong to no party.
Peace will return rapidly when the French realize that the
spirit of our people today is no longer what it was ten years
ago.'[2] Finally, at the beginning of August, Bao Dai announced
that he would be prepared to negotiate with the French on the
basis of national unity and independence.[3]

Meanwhile Bollaert had returned to France at the beginning

---

[1] Hammer, p. 210.
[2] Devillers, p. 399.
[3] Ibid. p. 403.

of June to acquaint the French Government with his findings.[4] On his return to Saigon he declared at a press conference on 22 July, that the French Government wanted a truce without victors or vanquished, and intended that it should be followed by negotiations at which all Vietnamese parties and groups would be represented. In pursuit of this goal he left for Hanoi, in company with his principal advisers, intending to announce a cease-fire on 15 August, to be followed by negotiations based on recognition of Vietnam's 'independence within the French Union' and on the integration of Viet Minh military forces with those of the Expeditionary Corps. This speech was postponed, however, by his sudden recall to Paris for further consultations with the Government.[5]

As a result Bollaert's terms were watered down, the offer of an armistice being withdrawn and 'freedom within the French Union' substituted for 'independence'. On 10 September, when Bollaert was finally able to make his eagerly awaited speech at Ha Dong,[6] his offer represented little advance on former proposals. Although the French Government declared that it would no longer oppose the popular demand for the reunion of the three ky—Tongking, Annam, and Cochin-China—and no reference was made to a Federal Government, 'freedom within the French Union' was still to deprive the Vietnamese of control over defence and foreign policy, and a French High Commissioner was to supervise the common services and to arbitrate differences between the three states. The French Government also reserved the right to provide the ethnic minorities inhabiting the upland regions of North and South Vietnam with a special status. When he had outlined these proposals, which were either to be accepted as a whole or rejected outright, Bollaert appealed to all the religious communities and social groups in the country to select as their

---

[4] In marked contrast to his predecessors, Bollaert was to display throughout his tenure of office a patent anxiety that his policy should in fact reflect the fluctuating intentions of the French Government.

[5] Bollaert's recall is reported to have been engineered by Valluy, the Commander-in-Chief of the Expeditionary Corps, who had almost completed preparations for an offensive in Tongking designed to inflict a decisive defeat upon the Viet Minh (P. Naville, *La Guerre du Viet-Nam* (1949), pp. 175–8). Valluy's assurance that a military solution now lay within the French grasp, appears to have induced the MRP representatives in the Government, who were opposed to renewed negotiations with the Viet Minh, to insist on a reconsideration of French policy.

[6] Text in *L'Année Politique, 1947*, pp. 360–2 (Cole, p. 62).

representatives those who would be best qualified to bring negotiations for a settlement to a satisfactory conclusion; however, he expressed some reserve in regard to the qualifications for this task of certain unspecified Viet Minh leaders who had been implicated in the Hanoi rising of December 1946.

By their failure to concede 'independence' the proposals caused general disappointment, and both the Viet Minh and the nationalist groups in the French zone promptly rejected them. In Hong Kong, however, where Bao Dai had invited 'leaders of all existing parties, whatever might be their political opinions, to come and inform him about the situation so that he should decide on the steps that should be taken in order to obtain an honourable and lasting peace', the twenty-four delegates who had responded to this appeal tempered their rejection of the offer by an invitation to Bao Dai to seek, 'in co-operation with France, a solution to Franco-Vietnamese problems based on equality and justice'.[7]

Bao Dai proved attentive to this appeal since he is reported to have discounted the possibility that independence could be won by force of arms,[8] and he feared that the control which the Communists had established over the resistance movement would both justify the French Government in its refusal to negotiate a settlement and deprive the Vietnamese of American support in their struggle.[9]

Moreover, his decision to intervene was fortified by his disapproval of Communist methods and of the Communist-inspired terror which had cost countless lives, including those of many servants of the dynasty, while his remaining scruples may have been removed by reports that the Viet Minh had deprived him of Vietnamese nationality and condemned him to death.[10] Accordingly on 18 September Bao Dai issued a proclamation in which, after announcing his readiness to

---

[7] Devillers, pp. 408–10. The delegation is reported to have been composed of authentic nationalists and of Vietnamese whose first loyalty lay with France, the proportion having been decided by the French authorities who were responsible for issuing the exit visas.

[8] The collapse of the Kuomintang régime could not have been foreseen in 1947.

[9] William Bullitt, wartime Ambassador to France and an influential member of the Republican Party, who was received by Bao Dai towards the end of the month, is reported to have confirmed these apprehensions by assuring him that American support for Vietnamese claims would be provided more readily if they were not put forward by a Communist-dominated Government (Devillers, p. 411 n.).

[10] *Le Monde*, 30 Dec. 1947.

examine with the French authorities the proposals that had been made at Ha Dong, he proceeded to outline his conception of the mission that he had undertaken in the following words:

I desire first of all to obtain for you independence and unity and, in conformity with your wishes, to reach an agreement based on reciprocal guarantees, so that I may be in a position to inform you that the ideal for which you have striven in fierce resistance has been attained.

Then I will lend you the full weight of my authority to arbitrate in the dispute that has set you one against the other.[11]

The heir of the Nguyen dynasty appeared well suited to discharge this complex task since he was endowed with intelligence of a high order and possessed a lofty conception of the national destiny. He was also to show capacity for conducting intricate political negotiations and a shrewd ability to divine the intentions of, and on occasion to outwit, both his European and Asian opponents. Nevertheless, these qualities were in some measure vitiated by his desire to confine himself to the role of arbitrator and mediator and by a natural diffidence and indolence which made him chary of public appearances and averse to the well-publicized gesture.

### THE JOINT DECLARATION

While a nationalist opposition to Viet Minh pretensions was thus slowly taking shape, the situation in Cochin-China remained confused. On 6 December 1946 Dr. Le Van Hoach had been elected by the Council of Cochin-China to succeed Thinh as head of the Government, but this appointment had caused the acting Prime Minister, Xuan, grave displeasure, and after the installation of his successor he had left for France, where he was soon engaged in political intrigue in Paris.

The choice of Hoach seems to have been partially due to the influential position which he occupied at the Cao Dai 'Holy See', where he was political adviser to the Superior, Pham Cong Tac, who had been brought back from exile in August. His return had been followed by an official announcement of the sect's decision to support the Saigon Government, and in November the Cao Dai militia force, which had been operating

[11] *L'Année Politique, 1947*, p. 310.

under Viet Minh command, rejoined the adepts at the 'Holy See'. After a retaliatory Viet Minh raid on Tay Ninh in January 1947 an agreement was signed between the French authorities and the Superior officially authorizing the sect to maintain a militia force of 1,470 partisans and to garrison sixteen defence posts in the province.[12]

The Cao Dai decision to support the Government was followed in March 1947 by the return to the French-controlled zone of the Hoa Hao 'Generalissimo', the fierce moustacheoed Tran Van Soai (alias Nam Lua), who was accompanied by 2,000 armed followers and his formidable wife.[13] This important personage proceeded to set up his headquarters at Cai Von, which was the terminal of the ferry across the river Bassac to Can Tho and a focal point for barges carrying the paddy to Saigon–Cholon. During the following month, the Hoa Hao 'Master', Huynh Phu So, was murdered by the Viet Minh near Long Xuyen, his body, in view of its potential magic properties, being sawn in two and the sections buried in separate localities in order to minimize the risk of subsequent resurrection. Although his fate was kept secret from the adepts, who were merely informed that he had withdrawn for a while, the assassination aroused fierce resentment and led to an agreement, on 18 May 1947, between the French military Command and Tran Van Soai, whereby the latter undertook, in return for supplies of arms and a brevet conferring on him the non-existent rank of a 'one-star' general, to expel the Viet Minh from areas inhabited by the Hoa Hao and to collaborate with the local authorities.[14]

[12] This limitation on numbers was soon circumvented by the formation of a 'Papal Guard', a 'Battalion of Honour', and a battalion of 'shock troops', while numerous militia units were unofficially recruited for the defence of the scattered Cao Dai communities.

[13] Mme Tran Van Soai commanded a force of black-garbed amazons who compensated for their physical inferiority by their ferocity to prisoners. A square-set, middle-aged woman of obvious determination, Mme Soai was alleged to keep a tight control over the sect's finances and to arrange on occasion for the elimination of the 'Generalissimo's' rivals.

[14] Soai's authority over the sect's militia forces was disputed by Nguyen Giac Ngo, who controlled the region of Cho Moi in the province of Long Xuyen. Soai's principal lieutenants, including Lam Thanh Nguyen (alias Hai Ngoan) whose fief was centred around Chau Doc, Le Quang Vinh (alias Ba Cut), who was to set up his headquarters at Thot Not, and Ba Ga Mo, likewise maintained pretensions to semi-independence in their relations with the Hoa Hao headquarters at Cai Von. But in spite of their insubordinate attitude, Soai was able to maintain the bulk of the Hoa Hao militia forces under his direct command.

The decision of the Cao Dai and Hoa Hao sects to oppose the Viet Minh did not lead, however, to any general improvement in public security. In consequence the Government was soon under attack in the Council, where Hoach was accused by the French representatives of pusillanimity and lack of energy and on 2 August was asked to reconstitute his Government. Aware that Xuan was intriguing against him in Paris, Hoach decided to put a stop to this by inviting his rival to join the new Government in the capacity of Deputy Prime Minister. Xuan, who had just been promoted to the rank of Brigadier General in the French army, returned to Saigon elated by his promotion and proceeded to bring about Hoach's downfall.

Xuan carried out his objective on 29 September and three days later was himself invested with the task of forming the new Government, but the choice of Xuan for the premiership displeased Bao Dai, who had reason to doubt the strength of Xuan's attachment either to his person or to the cause of national unity. He therefore asked Bollaert, in conformity with the undertaking that he had given at Ha Dong, to replace the Cochin-Chinese Provisional Government by an Administrative Committee similar in constitution to the committees which had been set up in Annam and Tongking.[15] Xuan then succeeded in allaying these misgivings by re-naming his Government the 'Provisional Government of South Vietnam'.

Meanwhile Bollaert had been encouraged to open official negotiations by a change of Government in France, which had led to the appointment of an MRP deputy, Paul Coste-Floret, to the Ministry of French Overseas Territories. Bollaert's arguments, and particularly his readiness to employ the word 'independence', convinced Bao Dai that the time had come to act, and he agreed to meet the High Commissioner in the Bay of Along on 6 December.[16]

The ex-Emperor, who arrived by flying boat accompanied by his cousin Prince Vinh Can, was received by Bollaert on board the flagship *Duguay-Trouin*, which had now replaced the cruiser *Émile Bertin* on the Far East station. During the ensuing discussions a large measure of agreement seems to have been reached on the questions at issue, with the result that a joint Declaration was drafted recognizing Vietnam's right to inde-

15 *Le Monde*, 7 Oct. 1947.
16 Devillers, p. 418.

pendence and to bring about its unity freely. The Declaration was accompanied, however, by a secret protocol, imposing important restrictions on independence, particularly in the diplomatic and military spheres.

Overjoyed at the concession of 'independence' and apparently acting on the assurance that the protocol represented no more than the minutes of the discussions, Bao Dai was persuaded to initial both these documents: an action which had embarrassing consequences since on his return to Hong Kong he found that whereas his advisers were prepared to approve the joint Declaration, they unanimously rejected the restrictions contained in the protocol.[17] Moreover their arguments appear to have convinced Bao Dai that his good faith had been abused; and anticipating that the High Commissioner would now attempt to exploit his initial advantage in order to impose a settlement on these unsatisfactory terms, he decided to leave for Europe, where he hoped to recover his freedom of action. He left Hong Kong on 26 December and after a brief visit to London installed himself in Geneva.

Bollaert, who had himself returned to Paris, was quick to divine the motive which had prompted Bao Dai's sudden journey and, determined to maintain his control over the negotiations, he too travelled to Geneva, where his insistence was rewarded by further conversations which took place between 7–13 January 1948. These discussions merely served to confirm that the negotiations had reached an impasse. While Bollaert refused to consider any amendments to the protocol, Bao Dai insisted that he had not been empowered to sign a binding agreement and that the proposed concessions were insufficient to rally nationalist support. The discussions were concluded by a non-committal communiqué to the effect that a further meeting would take place in the Bay of Along on 13 February. Bollaert then returned to Saigon, and Bao Dai rejoined his family, who were then living in Cannes.

In France Bao Dai was soon in a position to assess the attitude of French political parties towards the question of Vietnamese independence. During visits to Paris he had discussions with the Prime Minister, Robert Schuman, and with Coste-Floret.[18]

[17] Bao Dai's advisers were either personal friends or fugitives from the Viet Minh, whom the hazards of exile had assembled in Hong Kong.
[18] Célerier, p. 220.

His inquiries revealed that Bollaert's policy was only supported by a narrow majority in the National Assembly, and that the Communists, the majority of the Socialist Party, and some Radical Socialists and MRP deputies were opposed to negotiations which would exclude the Viet Minh. Moreover a political movement—Le Rassemblement du Peuple Français—which had been launched with notable success by de Gaulle in April 1947 was reported to be opposed to any alienation of French sovereignty in Indochina in favour of the Vietnamese nationalists. The revelation of these political divisions confirmed Bao Dai in his opinion that any agreement would have to be ratified by the French National Assembly if the danger of its subsequent repudiation was to be avoided.

Meanwhile Bao Dai's prolonged stay in France, together with reports of his political activities in Paris, was proving a source of considerable irritation to Bollaert, who had been expressly empowered by the Government to conduct the negotiations for a settlement. Finally, after the confirmation of Bollaert's mandate on 21 February for a further period of six months, Bao Dai resigned himself to the necessity of reopening the negotiations and returned to Hong Kong towards the middle of March.

### THE ALONG BAY AGREEMENT

During the early months of 1948 the Vietnamese nationalists were in a state of political effervescence, and a coalition—the Vietnamese National Rally—was formed under the leadership of Le Van Hoach, uniting the political groups and politico-religious sects in the French-occupied zone on the basis of a programme limited to providing Bao Dai with support in the forthcoming negotiations. On 22 February a Congress met in Saigon, which was attended by adherents of the National Rally and by representatives of the Provisional Government and of the Administrative Committees of Central and North Vietnam, but the proceedings revealed the existence of important divergences of opinion in regard to the question of setting up a central Provisional Government, and a decision on this question was deferred until Bao Dai's views could be ascertained.

Bao Dai's return to Hong Kong was thus to be the signal for

another influx of Vietnamese, whose representative capacity was in some cases open to question, and on 26 March a proclamation was read before a gathering of these personalities in which Bao Dai expressed himself in favour of the formation of a central Government on the grounds that, as the 'existing revolutionary Government'—the Viet Minh Government—'was handicapped by the international situation and ill fitted to engage in negotiations, the formation of a government which reflected more nearly the political situation in the world was both a logical and a necessary step'.[19] Its mission was to be limited, however, to that of bringing about the country's military, administrative, and economic reunification.

In conformity with this decision Cochin-Chinese political leaders were summoned on 24 April to Hong Kong, where a procedure was agreed on for the formation of a central Provisional Government under the leadership of Xuan, the Prime Minister of the Provisional Government of South Vietnam.[20] Accordingly on his return to Saigon Xuan summoned a meeting of representatives from North, Central, and South Vietnam, at which the decision to set up such a government was formally endorsed. On 27 May Xuan presented the members of this Government to Bao Dai in Hong Kong, and on their behalf he undertook to implement the directives and to obey the instructions of the exiled monarch.

The French Government now displayed some reluctance to approve the reunification of the three *ky* unconditionally, and limited their recognition to taking 'official cognizance' of the constitution of a central Provisional Government. For his part Bollaert had agreed to raise no objection to this step on condition that Bao Dai both recognized the Government himself and undertook to countersign the protocol, which the High Commissioner still adamantly refused to amend. His persistence was rewarded on 5 June, when an agreement was signed by Xuan on board the cruiser *Duguay-Trouin* in the Bay of Along in the presence of Bao Dai, who countersigned it.

[19] *Bull. d'Information de la France d'Outre Mer*, No. 15, June 1948.
[20] Xuan was chosen following Ngo Dinh Diem's refusal to accept this task. Diem, who had been described by a nonplussed journalist in the previous year as a man 'who considered himself predestined for an important role in the government of his country' (*L'Aube*, 10 Apr.1947), declined to accept the premiership on the grounds that the equivalent of 'dominion status' was the essential prerequisite for his acceptance (David Schoenbrun in *Collier's*, 30 Sept. 1955).

This agreement is reported to have reproduced the joint Declaration and the protocol, which had been drafted six months previously. While the terms of the protocol still remained secret, the joint Declaration[21] recognized Vietnam's 'independence' within the French Union and its right to bring about its unity freely. The Declaration also contained an undertaking on the part of the Vietnamese Government to respect the rights and interests of French nationals, to ensure respect for democratic principles by constitutional means, and to accord priority to French nationals in the recruitment of the advisers and technicians for the economic organization of the country. It also made provision for a series of subsidiary agreements covering cultural, diplomatic, military, economic, financial, and technical relations between the two countries.

The news of the signing of the agreement was well received in Vietnam. In spite of important and unpublished restrictions, the formal recognition of independence and the acknowledgement of Vietnam's right to bring about its national unity represented real concessions, which placed the future relations between the two countries on a new and more hopeful footing. Bao Dai, however, was aware that formal ratification of the agreement by the French National Assembly would be required for the proposed change in the status of Cochin-China, and he decided to return to France to await this ratification and the completion of the impending negotiations there.

### REACTIONS IN INDOCHINA

Although the publication of the joint Declaration had been well received, the Vietnamese were accustomed to treat declarations of intention with wary scepticism, and fears were expressed that the French authorities would seek to nullify the concessions which had been made.

In the Viet Minh zone, however, the news that France had conceded national independence and unity to Bao Dai is reported to have aroused a fervent hope that the country would be spared an interminable war with its attendant suffering. The Viet Minh leaders, who were aware that the prompt and generous implementation of the terms of the agreement would be likely to cause widespread discontent and defections, thus

[21] Text in *J.O.* 14 Mar. 1953, p. 2406 (Cole, p. 72).

awaited Bao Dai's return with some misgivings. But the chronic weakness of successive French Governments delayed the ratification of the agreement, and the occasion that this afforded representatives of the French community entrenched in the Council of Cochin-China to block the efforts of the Xuan Government to establish its authority, strengthened nationalist suspicions that the French merely intended to exploit their anti-Communist sentiments for the purpose of perpetuating their rule.

These suspicions were increased by Coste-Floret, who made a statement in the National Assembly on 8 June to allay misgivings aroused by the insinuations being made in the Council of Cochin-China and the French-language press in Saigon. This statement described the agreement merely as a step towards the pacification of the country and gave the Assembly to understand that no major concessions had been made either in the diplomatic or in the military sphere.[22] The malaise was aggravated by the patent reluctance of the French Government to submit the Bay of Along agreement for ratification to the National Assembly, for the Vietnamese, who were unaware of the precarious nature of French parliamentary majorities, tended to believe that French politics were dominated by the Indochinese problem.

Meanwhile the Administrative Committees for North and Central Vietnam were replaced by governors responsible to the central Government, but all attempts to persuade the Council of Cochin-China to vote its own dissolution were rebuffed and merely provoked that body into electing a Cochin-Chinese, Tra Van Huu,[23] to the vacant office of Prime Minister. The effect of the Council's refusal to accept the loss of regional autonomy was increased, moreover, by the reluctance of the Federal Services and the Administrative Section of the Expeditionary Corps to hand over the areas under their control to officials of the central Government, a reluctance based on their fear that the dubious capacity of these officials might endanger the lives of French troops and civilians. Consequently during the ensuing months the central Provisional Government appeared to achieve nothing more substantial than the distinction of adding to the existing administrative confusion. It can

[22] *J.O., Débats Parlementaires*, 1948, p. 3290 (quoted Devillers, pp. 434–5).
[23] See below, p. 432.

occasion no surprise that under these discouraging conditions the initial enthusiasm which had inspired it should have cooled, or that, in the morally depressing atmosphere of Saigon, public rumour should soon have accused individual members of Xuan's cabinet of indulging in peculation and malpractices. The population for their part were quick to draw shrewd and unflattering conclusions from the spectacle of an impotent central Government dependent on French bayonets and subsidies, and to compare the moral standards of the nationalist ministers unfavourably with the austere disinterest of the Viet Minh agents, with whom they were also in contact.

### THE ÉLYSÉE AGREEMENT

In July the resignation of the Schuman Government was followed by the formation of a French Government under the premiership of André Marie, a Radical Socialist deputy. Marie shared, however, his predecessor's reluctance to allow the controversial subject of French policy in Indochina to be raised in the National Assembly, and although he was compelled to fix a day for a debate on this subject Marie, aware that his Government would be unlikely to survive the ensuing division, managed to persuade the deputies to agree to a postponement of the debate and to approve a declaration endorsing the Government's policy in general terms. This declaration, which omitted all reference either to Bao Dai or to Ho Chi Minh, recognized that the existing régime in Cochin-China did not meet the requirements of the situation and expressed agreement with the proposal that the population should be allowed to decide freely on the status of the territory 'within the framework of the French Union'.[24]

Although this parliamentary stratagem, which amounted to a tacit refusal to ratify the Bay of Along agreement, successfully prolonged the life of the Marie Government by nine days, it caused grave disappointment to the Vietnamese, who were justifiably concerned at an apparent refusal of the French Government to honour the terms of an agreement which had been negotiated on its behalf.

On 2 September Bollaert announced that he would refuse to accept any further prolongation of his mandate, which was due

[24] Devillers, p. 439.

to expire on the 30th of the month. During the remaining weeks he brought pressure to bear upon the Federal Services to divest themselves, in favour of the central Government, of responsibility for the collection of taxes, while steps were taken to hasten the hand-over of the three provinces in South Annam which remained under French military control. Bollaert's departure marked the end of that phase of the protracted struggle during which the French had retained the military and political initiative.[25]

On 20 October it was announced that Léon Pignon had been appointed to succeed Bollaert.[26] The decision to appoint a senior official in the Colonial Service to a post of such importance is reported to have been due both to the Government's inability to choose between candidates enjoying the support of rival political parties and to the fear that a political appointment might encourage extraneous attempts to influence French policy.[27] Although this appointment caused disappointment in Saigon where Pignon was considered to lack prestige, it was welcomed by Bao Dai, who was aware that the newly appointed High Commissioner had resolutely and consistently opposed the resumption of negotiations with the Viet Minh: a course of action which continued to be recommended by the French Socialist Party.[28] This reinforcement of his position was particularly appreciated by Bao Dai at this juncture, since during the months that had followed the signing of the Bay of Along agreement the unity of the nationalist groups and the politico-religious sects had been subjected to considerable stress.

This was due to the existence of separatist tendencies in Cochin-China and to the desire for autonomy in Annam and

[25] On 3 December Bollaert, addressing the National Congress of the Radical Socialist Party, admitted that his attempts to find a solution to the political impasse in Vietnam had been temporarily thwarted by the hesitant policy of the Government, which had undermined Vietnamese confidence in French intentions (Célerier, p. 238).

[26] Pignon, who was a member of the Colonial Service, had first been posted to Indochina in 1932. During the war he had rallied to the Free French Forces and was Secretary of the Brazzaville Conference. In September 1945 he returned to Tongking, and after serving on the staff of Sainteny and d'Argenlieu he had been appointed French Commissioner in Cambodia, whence he had been transferred early in 1948 to the Political Section of the Ministry of French Overseas Territories (The Times, 21 Oct. 1948).

[27] Célerier, pp. 239–40.

[28] Frédéric-Dupont, Mission de la France en Asie (1956), pp. 50–54.

Tongking, where the regional governors had been invested with unusually wide powers. Moreover the habit which the Cao Dai and Hoa Hao militia forces were developing of deserting the French-controlled zone, under energetic and unscrupulous guerrilla leaders, together with the intrigues and pretensions of nationalist personalities who professed allegiance to Bao Dai but refused to support Xuan's Government, threatened, in the absence of an agreed political programme and an arbitrator, to reveal the incapacity of the nationalists to dispute Viet Minh claims to leadership.[29] Faced with the danger that the movement which he had sponsored would be discredited before he could assume responsibility for its direction, Bao Dai appears at this stage to have realized that his return to Vietnam could no longer be delayed.

The French Government, alarmed at the mounting cost of the war and anxious to encourage Vietnamese military and financial participation in the struggle, was now alive to the fact that a national state under the authority of Bao Dai would be able to claim international recognition, and in due course American aid, against the Communist threat to its frontiers and internal security. These considerations proved sufficiently cogent to induce both parties to seek some means of surmounting the difficulties which had hitherto prevented the ratification and implementation of the agreement. On 16 January 1949, therefore, Bao Dai received Pignon at Cannes; and later in the month they met again in Paris, where it was finally decided that the statement of principles contained in the Declaration of 5 June 1948 should be confirmed and determined in a personal letter which Vincent Auriol, President of the French Republic, acting in his capacity as President of the French Union, should address to Bao Dai.

In this letter, which was known as the Élysée Agreement of 8 March 1949,[30] President Auriol undertook, in the name of the Government, that France would raise no *de jure* or *de facto* obstacles to the inclusion of Cochin-China within the frontiers

---

[29] At the end of 1948 the Hoa Hao leaders, Nguyen Giac Ngo, Lam Thanh Nguyen, and Le Quang Vinh, together with their armed followers, had deserted the French-controlled zone, and in February 1949 the Cao Dai military commander, Nguyen Van Thanh, following the rejection of a proposal to create a neutral zone around Tay Ninh, instructed the Cao Dai militia forces to oppose any attempt by the French or by the Viet Minh to occupy their defence posts.

[30] *Notes Documentaires et Études*, No. 1147, 20 June 1949 (Cole, pp. 72–79).

of Vietnam provided that the people of Cochin-China were first consulted. An undertaking was also given to sponsor the constitutional procedure which would allow this change of status to be brought about. This undertaking was, however, accompanied by a claim to have incurred special obligation towards the non-Vietnamese peoples whose historical home was situated in Vietnamese territory, and although France was prepared to recognize the traditional dependence of these people on the Crown of Annam, their evolution was to be safeguarded by special statutes which would be the subject of further discussions between the French Government and Bao Dai.[31] The concession of independence was also qualified by the retention of defence and foreign relations in French hands, a stipulation which had contributed to the failure of the Fontainebleau Conference. Moreover, although the Vietnamese Government was to be granted internal sovereignty, French nationals were to be tried by French law and citizens of the French Union and of states enjoying privileged judicial status were to be tried before mixed tribunals. Vietnam's economic and financial independence was similarly restricted by the proviso that businesses and property belonging to citizens of the French Union would not be subject to expropriation without the prior consent of the French Government, while the national currency was both to be included within the French monetary zone and to be common to the three Associate States, with which Vietnam would be expected to form a customs union.

Since Bao Dai's return had been made conditional on the inclusion of Cochin-China within the frontiers of Vietnam, immediate steps were now taken to comply with the procedure which would enable this to take place. However, the French constitution provided that a change in territorial status must be preceded by the expression of a desire for such a change by the territorial Assembly of the region in question, which should then submit its request to the French National Assembly. As the Council of Cochin-China did not constitute such a body, it was decided to create a territorial Assembly for the express and

[31] The area affected by this provision comprised the potentially fertile but un-developed upland regions. French solicitude for the welfare of these non-Vietnamese peoples was thus ascribed by many nationalists to the influence of French financial interests, and in particular to the machinations of the Bank of Indochina.

exclusive purpose of informing the French National Assembly of Cochin-China's desire for union with Annam and Tongking.

The procedure adopted was for the provincial Administrative Councils to designate forty-eight Vietnamese delegates, while sixteen French delegates were chosen from among the members of the Council of Cochin-China and the French Chamber of Commerce and Agriculture.[32] On 19 April this territorial Assembly held its opening session, and although the French delegates attempted to impose certain conditions, the motion in favour of a change of status was carried on the 25th, with six dissenting votes and two abstentions. When he heard that the motion had been carried, Bao Dai left France for Dalat, where he proposed to set up his headquarters. His unheralded arrival, and the absence of any public demonstrations in his favour caused some disappointment among his supporters, but the sovereign, who had returned without the concessions which would have served to rally the Vietnamese around him, was uncertain of the welcome that he would receive.

The delicate position in which he was placed was analysed, some weeks later, by the representative of the newspaper *Combat*.

It has been easy for Bao Dai until now [declared this journalist] to play 'hide and seek' with those who are at the head of French affairs and to profit from their hatred of Ho Chi Minh in order to obtain personal advantages and large subsidies and, in addition— thanks to the heroic tenacity of the resistance—important political concessions for Vietnam. . . . Bao Dai's efforts are, however, doomed to failure, because he enjoys no personal prestige and possesses no authority in the country. Personally, he has neither the taste, nor the desire for power—particularly under present circumstances. . . . He does not possess the instincts of a despot or of a conqueror, or of a martyr. I believe, however, that, in spite of his failings, he is intelligent and patriotic, and that these qualities will prevent him from becoming a party to French intrigues. In the final analysis, his position is closer to that of Ho Chi Minh than to that of Coste-Floret. . . .

His entourage, moreover, have no moral prestige or political authority, and none of the administrative or technical abilities which are required to reorganize the country.

Bao Dai has at his disposal no effective means of action.[33]

[32] *Le Populaire*, 1 Apr. 1949.
[33] *Combat*, 19, 20, and 22 May 1948.

This description of the monarch's hapless and friendless state, if based partially on captious nationalist criticism, revealed nevertheless the weakness of his position, for the success of his attempt to free the country from both French and Communist domination depended in the last resort on the readiness of the nationalists themselves to accept his leadership. But in spite of the danger with which they were threatened the nationalists remained tragically divided by regional and personal rivalries. Moreover many of the personages who now performed the pilgrimage to Dalat failed signally to inspire confidence either in the unity or in the prospects of the nationalist cause; they included that 'astute scoundrel' the Cao Dai 'Pope', Pham Cong Tac; the Hoa Hao 'Generalissimo', Tran Van Soai; 'Colonel' Le Van Vien, the leader of the Binh Xuyen bandits, who had rallied to the Xuan Government in June 1948, and other colourful personalities who had established their precarious dominion over ill-defined areas of Cochin-China.[34]

Among the various groups who offered their allegiance to Bao Dai the nationalists from Annam and Tongking, belonging in many cases to families which had traditionally staffed the administrative service of the Empire, probably represented the most mature and stable element. In Tongking a section of these nationalists had formed in 1943, under Japanese patronage, a small political group, the Dai Viet Quoc Dan Hoi, or Dai Viet (National Party of Greater Vietnam), which had subsequently supported the Tran Trong Kim Government. After the Viet Minh seizure of power in August 1945 this group had been officially dissolved, but with the assistance of the Chinese-sponsored nationalist parties was able to survive this difficult transition period. After the eviction of the Viet Minh from Hanoi and the flight of the nationalist parties to China the Dai Viet found themselves the only surviving political group of any consequence in the French-occupied zone in Tongking, and they profited from this position to recruit supporters in the local Administrative, Police, and Security Services. When one of the ablest of their leaders, Nguyen Huu Tri, was confirmed by Bao Dai in his functions as Governor of North Vietnam the Dai Viet seemed likely to establish their control over nationalist activities in Tongking, but whereas the Dai Viet were prepared to offer their allegiance to Bao Dai, the important Roman

[34] Ibid. 20 May 1949.

14

Catholic minority, numbering some 1,700,000, or more than 6 per cent. of the total population, held back.

Their attitude was due to the knowledge that they were partly responsible for the advent of French rule and represented, in the eyes of their countrymen, the 'claws' which, in the words of the Regent Ton That Thuyet, had enabled the French crab to progress and occupy the land. In August 1945, therefore, the three native-born Apostolic Vicars, conscious of the latent dislike and suspicion with which Roman Catholics were regarded, had associated themselves officially with the movement for national independence and encouraged Roman Catholics to show their patriotism by participating actively in the struggle. Moreover on 23 September, Mgr. Tong, Apostolic Vicar of Hanoi, had addressed an appeal to Rome on behalf of himself and his colleagues in which he implored the Papal benediction on, and prayers for, the cause of Vietnamese independence,[35] and in November the Apostolic Vicars had published a joint pastoral letter in which they exhorted their co-religionists to support the new régime. This desire on the part of the Vietnamese hierarchy that Roman Catholics should redeem their unfortunate reputation deprived the nationalist cause of the support of an important minority who were in the last resort irreconcilably opposed to the Communists.[36]

Ho Chi Minh, realizing the important asset that Roman Catholic support would represent for the Hanoi Government, had attempted to ensure that a conciliatory attitude should be adopted towards the Christian communities; and after Bao Dai's exile in March 1946 he had appointed Mgr. Le Huu Tu, the Apostolic Vicar of Phat Diem, to the office of Supreme Adviser, but this gesture was nullified by the action of the militant Communists, who profited from the disturbed conditions to interfere in the administration of the communities and to prevent the celebration of the mass. In consequence the Vicariates of Phat Diem and Bui Chu, which were adjacent and compact areas on the coast near the borders of Annam, were compelled to look to their own defence. Militia forces were formed which, under the white and yellow flag of the Vatican

[35] Devillers, pp. 185–7.

[36] It was only in December 1951 that the Church, through the Apostolic Delegate, Mgr. Dooley, forbade Vietnamese Roman Catholics to adhere to the Communist Party, to co-operate with it, or to commit any act that might facilitate its accession to power (*Le Monde*, 17 Dec. 1951).

City, were able for three years to keep the Viet Minh at bay and to maintain a precarious neutrality.[37] It was only towards the end of 1949, following a Viet Minh attack on the area, that the Apostolic Vicars of Phat Diem and Bui Chu abandoned their pretensions to neutrality and proffered their allegiance to Bao Dai.

The existence of these anarchic tendencies among his followers and the absence of popular support offer some explanation of the misunderstandings that were to arise between the French authorities and the head of the Vietnamese state, due to the differing conceptions of the role which Bao Dai now agreed to assume, and whereas the French were to demand from their ally effective co-operation and, in particular, a readiness to act as general factotum and recruiting officer for the French Union forces, Bao Dai for his part considered that his principal tasks were the healing of national divisions and the restoration of national unity.[38]

Meanwhile, as he waited for continued Viet Minh resistance and the materialization of American aid to enable him to win effective independence from the French by slow but inevitable stages, Bao Dai contented himself with the evasive tactics which had proved partially successful during the protracted negotiations preceding the Élysée Agreement. However, if the French failed to lure him from his retreat in the upland region of Annam, where he indulged a natural propensity to inaction and a taste for big-game hunting, they were at least able to insist on his co-operation in promulgating some unpopular decrees and to subject his activities and contacts to surveillance.

### THE RETURN OF THE LAO ISSARA EXILES

The conclusion of the Élysée Agreement of 8 March 1949 enabled a similar agreement to be drawn up with the Lao Government. This agreement, known as the General Franco–

[37] The region of Phat Diem was created through the initiative of a Vietnamese priest, Father Six, who had obtained from the Emperor Tu Duc a grant of all the land in that area which he could win from the sea. Father Six, with the assistance of the local Christian communities, proceeded to construct a series of dykes parallel to the sea, which were designed to capture the alluvium in the Gulf of Tongking. In the space of thirty years he was able, by slowly pushing this system of dykes seaward, to reclaim an area of eight miles, which became some of the most fertile rice-producing land in the world (Lyautey, pp. 377–8).

[38] J. de Coquet in *Figaro*, 18 May 1949.

Laotian Convention of 19 July 1949,[39] recognized Laos as an independent state within the French Union, established the restrictions on sovereignty and the reciprocal obligations attached to this status, and laid down the principles to be observed in drawing up the supplementary agreements with France and the Associate States of Vietnam and Cambodia.

The signing of this convention led the Free Lao, or 'Lao Issara' ministers, who had been living in Bangkok since the summer of 1946, to dissolve the exiled Government on 24 October of the same year: a decision officially based on the wish, now that the principal aims of the resistance movement had been achieved, to free their supporters, who represented a large proportion of the *élite*, for the task of building up an independent state. But the ministers may also have been influenced to take this decision by the bitter internal disputes which were threatening to disrupt the Government. For Prince Phetsarath, who had only agreed to assume the effective leadership of the Lao Issara movement in December 1946, after receiving the assurance that he would have the last word in the event of a difference of opinion with the ministers, had proceeded to exploit this advantage to pursue an ultra-nationalist policy despite the ministers' protests, and after acrimonious discussions the Government finally dispensed with his services on 19 October 1949. Besides their conflict with Phetsarath, the ministers were also at loggerheads among themselves; in May Phetsarath's younger brother, Prince Souphannouvong,[40] had so scandalized his colleagues by his readiness to approve the use of Lao territory by Viet Minh armed bands that he was expelled from the Government.

In November the 'Lao Issara' episode was brought to a satisfactory conclusion when a French plane brought the exiles—except Phetsarath and Souphannouvong—back to Vientiane, and the task of reabsorbing them was completed so rapidly that in May 1953 four out of the seven ministers in the Royal Government, including the Prime Minister himself, were former members of the Lao Issara resistance movement.[41]

Phetsarath himself remained behind in Bangkok, proudly

[39] *Notes et Études Documentaires*, 14 Mar. 1950, No. 1295, p. 15.
[40] See below, p. 431.
[41] U.S. State Department release of a note from the Lao Government, 6 May 1953.

insisting on his reinstatement in the office of viceroy, or at least on the Crown Prince, Savang Vatthana, coming in person to invite him to return. His exile was shared for some months by his brother, who had set up a Liberation Committee there with the support of a handful of dissident Lao Issara supporters in October. But Souphannouvong, accompanied by his supporters, soon moved to North Vietnam, where his presence provided the Viet Minh with a convenient cloak for their aggressive designs against the neighbouring kingdom. Indeed the presence of this 'Lao Liberation Committee' on Vietnamese soil inspired a subsequent claim that a 'Laotian National Assembly' had met in August 1949 and proclaimed a 'democratic republic':[42] a preposterous falsehood designed to mislead the outside world, where information about the internal affairs of this inaccessible kingdom was not readily available.

[42] Denis Warner in *Daily Telegraph*, 18 Nov. 1950.

# XII

## The Pau Conference and the Retreat
## to the Red River Delta

In May 1949 the French National Assembly, in spite of opposition from Communist and right-wing deputies, adopted a bill approving the union of Cochin-China with the Associate State of Vietnam and thus enabled the instruments of the Élysée Agreement to be exchanged, on 14 June, between Bao Dai and Pignon, the French High Commissioner. On this occasion Bao Dai, after explaining that his retention of the imperial style was due solely to the consideration that it would provide him with international status, repeated his solemn promise that the Vietnamese people 'who had fought heroically for their national independence' would themselves be asked to decide the form of the future government.[1]

Following Xuan's resignation Bao Dai proceeded to constitute a new Government in order to negotiate the subsidiary agreements for the transfer of such administrative services and institutions as remained under French control. This Government was presided over by Bao Dai himself and Xuan was appointed Deputy Prime Minister; the portfolios of Foreign Affairs and the Interior were given to Nguyen Phan Long, a Tongkingese journalist who was known to hold the opinion that American support would enable Vietnam to acquire full independence.

Meanwhile, in the absence of a National Assembly, the creation was announced of consultative bodies who would be empowered to tender their advice to the head of the state. These bodies were to include a Privy Council, composed of nominated representatives of religious organizations and minority groups, and a Censors' Council, comprising three nominated representatives from each province.[2] While the administrative division of Vietnam into three regions was maintained, the dependence of the regional governors on the central

[1] *Le Monde*, 15 June 1949. The less controversial title of 'Head of the State' was finally adopted.
[2] Ibid. 5 July 1949.

Government was ensured by the retention of certain discretionary powers and by their nomination being vested in the head of the state.

Negotiations for the subsidiary agreements were, however, retarded until September, the delay being ascribed to a visit by the Minister for French Overseas Territories, Coste-Floret, and the frequent absences of Bao Dai himself from Saigon, where, due to the refusal of the French authorities to hand over the High Commissioner's palace, he was incongruously and inadequately housed in a secondary residence which had been that of the French Governor of Cochin-China.

During the summer months Bao Dai paid an official visit to Hué and also to Hanoi. In both these cities he was agreeably surprised by the warmth of his reception,[3] but although he and Pignon remained personally on friendly terms, the relations between the nationalist Government and the French authorities were uneasy.[4] The delicate nature of these relations was revealed in August when Nguyen Phan Long, who may possibly have been emboldened by a State Department comment on the 8 March agreements,[5] declared to an American press representative that 'H.M. Bao Dai's Government desire the Franco-Vietnamese agreements of 8 March to be interpreted in their most liberal sense, which would practically make Vietnam an independent nation enjoying a status equivalent to that of Australia in the British Commonwealth'.[6] This expression of dissatisfaction with the French concessions provoked a tart warning from the French-controlled Radio Saigon to the effect that the Vietnamese Government would be well advised to consider the danger that might result from too hasty an action and from ill-considered attempts to raise the price of co-operation.[7]

[3] Frédéric-Dupont, pp. 5–9.
[4] Bao Dai had appointed as his principal private secretary his cousin, Prince Buu Loc, who was personally indebted to the High Commissioner for assistance in re-establishing his fortunes which had suffered a setback following his services on the staff of a broadcasting station in German-occupied France (C. Bourdet, in *Combat*, 24 Jan. 1950). The descendants of Gia Long were estimated by the end of the French Protectorate to number about 10,000. The existence of this clan of often querulous and in some cases disloyal relatives who were frequently in poor circumstances represented a considerable burden for the Emperor.
[5] *DSB*, 18 July 1949, p. 75.
[6] *Le Monde*, 12 Aug. 1949.
[7] Ibid. 29 Aug. 1949.

Finally, on 1 September, the delegates who had been nominated to sit on the Joint Committees for negotiating the agreements on the transfer of powers met in the Saigon town hall. The tone of the discussions recalled, however, the disagreements which had been a feature of the abortive conferences with the Viet Minh leaders and reports of these dissensions encouraged the French community, who remained opposed to a policy of concessions, to vociferous expression of the belief that it was very dangerous 'to trust the nationalists who, even if they were anti-Communist, were nevertheless obsessed by a secret desire to boot the French into the sea'.[8] Nevertheless the negotiations made slow progress, and at the beginning of December Pignon was able to announce that the principal agreements would be drawn up at the end of the year.

On 30 December twenty-seven complementary agreements were signed, under which future relations between the two states were settled in the judicial, police, and security spheres, while separate conventions dealt with the transfer of press and information, social services, education, sport, public works, and public health. Arrangements were also made for the control of domestic trade, fisheries, mines, agriculture, woods and forests to be vested in the Vietnamese Administrative Service, while a military convention established the function of the Vietnamese army and the future allocations of bases and garrisons. In view of the troubled state of the country, however, a separate provisional agreement allowed for some delay in the implementation of the military agreement.

Although national unity and a large measure of internal autonomy had been conceded, the Vietnamese still remained dissatisfied, objecting that independence was subject to grave limitations, particularly so far as trade and the administration of justice was concerned. Moreover during the month marking the conclusion of these negotiations the war, which had hitherto been represented as a domestic dispute of concern only to the French Union, became an international issue when in the beginning of December some 26,000 Kuomintang troops, escaping from their Communist pursuers, crossed the border from Kwangsi province into Tongking.

In anticipation of such an event the French Government had

[8] J-H. Guérif in *Le Monde*, 17 Sept. 1949.

already agreed to the dispatch of reinforcements and military equipment from France, and at the same time a unit of King Cobra aircraft had been detached for service in Indochina.[9] But the arrival of these Chinese troops, who were followed in January 1950 by some 5,000 fugitives from General Li Mi's disbanded Yunnanese armies, caused great uneasiness to the French authorities, though fortunately the subsequent evacuation of these fugitives to South Vietnam, where they were interned on Phu Quoc island in the Gulf of Siam, proceeded without occasioning the expected incursions into Indochinese territory of Communist troops.[10]

Nevertheless the arrival of the Chinese Communist troops at the frontier transformed the struggle in which the Expeditionary Corps was engaged from an attempt to impose an unpalatable political settlement upon a recalcitrant subject people to a holding action at a distant and exposed section of the line where the western powers were resolved to halt further Communist expansion. In consequence the American Government[11] was encouraged to review its policy towards a country now directly exposed to an external threat of aggression and, in virtue of this threat, entitled under the provisions of the Mutual Defence Assistance Act of 1949 to receive American military aid.

On 14 December the possibility was already mooted in the French press that credits amounting to $75 million, which had been voted to provide military aid for the 'general region of China', might be earmarked for Indochina on the very wide interpretation that this vague geographical designation included the whole of South East Asia.[12] The grant of military aid, however, remained conditional on the ratification by the French Assembly of the Élysée Agreement of 8 March 1949, since this ratification was required before Vietnam could claim international recognition as an Associate State within the French Union. But even at the end of the year the French Government, already preoccupied with its attempts to persuade

---

[9] Paul Ramadier in *Bourse Égyptienne*, 18 Nov. 1950.

[10] Although some of these Kuomintang troops were to volunteer for work on Cambodian rubber plantations and in the coal mines at Hon Gay, the majority remained the victims of melancholia on Phu Quoc island until their repatriation in May–June 1953 to Formosa.

[11] After the embarrassment caused by Patti's intrigues with the Viet Minh the Americans had avoided any further attempts to intervene in Indochinese affairs.

[12] *Le Monde*, 14 Dec. 1949.

a recalcitrant Assembly to vote the budget, was still hesitating to take this necessary step.

The Viet Minh, however, who were not hampered by dependence on such exigencies, lost no time, after the arrival of Chinese Communist troops at the frontiers, in seizing the diplomatic initiative. On 14 January 1950 President Ho Chi Minh issued a statement in which, after proclaiming that the Government of the Democratic Republic of Vietnam triumphantly declared to the Governments of the world that it was the only lawful Government and represented a unified Vietnamese people, he expressed readiness to establish diplomatic relations with any country that was prepared to respect equality of rights and the territorial and national sovereignty of Vietnam.[13] The Government of the People's Republic of China was the first to acknowledge this *démarche* and on the 18th agreed to exchange Ambassadors. On the 30th the Soviet Union followed suit and in February the satellite states of Poland, North Korea, Rumania, and Hungary also accorded diplomatic recognition to the Democratic Republic of Vietnam.

The advantage gained by the Democratic Republic was, however, of short duration since on 29 January the French Assembly finally ratified the agreements that had been signed the previous year with Vietnam, Cambodia, and Laos. The Department of State, which had been awaiting the news of this ratification with much impatience, instructed the American Consul-General in Saigon on 7 February to inform the heads of the Governments concerned that diplomatic recognition had been accorded their respective states as 'independent states within the French Union'.[14] The Foreign Office, however, with greater circumspection, announced on the same day that the British Government recognized the states as 'Associate States within the French Union'.[15]

After this prompt sign of friendly interest, the kind and amount of military and economic aid which might now be expected became a subject of lively speculation in Vietnam, where the Government of Bao Dai had been dissolved. This dissolution had been greeted with relief by the outgoing ministers who had found difficulty in dealing with the routine

---

[13] *Soviet News*, 1 Feb. 1950 (Cole, pp. 95–96).
[14] *DSB*, 20 Feb. 1950, p. 291.
[15] Foreign Office Press Release, 7 Feb. 1950.

work of government under the rather nonchalant premiership of the head of the state whose representative duties had involved frequent absences from Saigon. The new Government, from which Xuan had been excluded, was presided over by Nguyen Phan Long, whose belief in the reality of American support remained unimpaired and who decided to take advantage of the imminent arrival of an American economic mission to make a bold claim on behalf of his Government to receive economic and even military aid direct. In pursuit of this chimera the Prime Minister informed an American press representative on 14 January that he would undertake to defeat the Viet Minh in six months, provided enough aid was forthcoming. His estimate was that the sum of about $146 million would be required for economic rehabilitation and for the formation of a national army.[16]

But the Prime Minister's pretensions were bluntly opposed by Lieut.-General Marcel Carpentier,[17] who said:

I will never agree to equipment being given directly to the Viet Namese. If this should be done, I would resign within twenty-four hours. The Viet Namese have no generals, no colonels, no military organization that could effectively utilize the equipment. It would be wasted, and in China the United States has had enough of that.[18]

Meanwhile, although the American Government in February had asked to be informed of French requirements regarding stores and equipment,[19] a report was current in Paris that the provision of aid was to be conditional on a formal undertaking by the French Government to grant complete independence to the Associate States.[20] Jean Letourneau, Minister for French Overseas Territories, however, clearly expressed the French refusal to entertain such a proposition in an interview on 9 April, when he said:

In our view the solution of the problem is not a political one. That question has been settled by the agreements of 8 March [1949] and by the transfer of powers that followed. . . . What has been

[16] *NYT*, 15 Feb. 1950.
[17] Carpentier had succeeded Blaizot in September 1949 as General Commanding French Forces in the Far East.
[18] *NYT*, 9 Mar. 1950.
[19] *Le Monde*, 24 Feb. 1950.
[20] Ibid. 27 Apr. 1950.

created by these agreements . . . are sovereign and independent states within the French Union. There are no longer any powers in the hands of the French administration in any of the three states of Indochina.[21]

The French point of view was finally accepted by the United States on 8 May, when Dean Acheson, the American Secretary of State, after an exchange of views with the French Foreign Minister in Paris, issued a statement in which he recognized that the problem of meeting the threat to the security of Vietnam, Cambodia, and Laos, was primarily the responsibility of France and of the governments and peoples of Indochina, and announced, in the name of the United States Government, that he considered the situation to be such as to warrant the provision of economic aid and military equipment to the Associate States and to France.[22] The decision was estimated by a disillusioned French minority to have prolonged the war by 'one or two years' although the length of this new lease might be curtailed if the American Senators were to decide at a later date to launch their electors' milliards on a more privileged sector of the anti-Communist front.[23]

But while a section of the French press viewed with misgivings the prospect of dependence on American aid for the future prosecution of the war, the readers of the *New York Herald Tribune* were already aware of the nature of the dilemma in which the American Government had been placed by this decision.

Everyone knows [Mr. Walter Lippmann had written on 4 April] that the great majority of the people of Indo-China are bitterly opposed to the continuation of French rule, and that they could be united behind a government only if that government were clearly and certainly destined to make Indo-China as independent as Indonesia, the Philippines, India, Pakistan, and Ceylon. But if Bao-Dai or anyone else were promised independence, it is equally certain that the French army could not be induced to continue the war. The French officers and troops and the French assembly may be willing to fight for the preservation of French interests in this rich colony. They cannot be counted upon to fight a dangerous, dirty, inconclusive war which is to end in the abandonment of the French

[21] *Le Monde*, 17 Apr. 1950.
[22] *DSB*, 12 June 1950, pp. 977–8.
[23] *Combat*, 15 May 1950.

interests in Asia. . . . Put bluntly but truthfully, the French army can be counted on to go on defending Southeast Asia only if the Congress of the United States will pledge itself to subsidize heavily—in terms of several hundred million dollars a year and for many years to come—a French colonial war to subdue not only the Communists but the nationalists as well.[24]

On 24 May Auriol, in his capacity as President of the French Union, was handed a letter by the American Ambassador announcing the intention of his Government to establish an economic aid mission in Saigon which would maintain liaison with the Governments of the Associate States and with the French High Commissioner.[25] In spite of this prompt action the modesty of the sum that was initially made available, amounting to $23½ million for the fiscal year ending 30 June 1951,[26] caused some disappointment. At the end of June seven Dakota aircraft, representing the first instalment of American military aid for French Union forces, were ceremonially handed over to the French authorities in Saigon. The aircraft were followed by shipments of war material which started to arrive during August, and during that month a Military Assistance Advisory Group (MAAG) was sent to supervise the distribution of supplies. Meanwhile the American Consulate had been raised to a Legation in February and provided with a large staff.[27]

An agreement on defence and mutual assistance was signed by the American Minister, Donald Heath, and by the representatives of France and the Associate States on 23 December.[28] This agreement laid down the conditions under which American aid would be apportioned, and established the principle that all materials provided would be handed over to the French Command, while direct relations between the Associate States and MAAG were to be expressly precluded. The signing of this agreement marked a dramatic change in the American attitude towards a war of which their disapproval had hitherto been indicated by the refusal of the United States Government to allow the re-export of American war material from France to

[24] *NYHT*, 4 Apr. 1950.
[25] *The Times*, 28 May 1950.
[26] *Le Monde*, 2 June 1950.
[27] *Straits Times*, 19 July 1950.
[28] U.S. Dept. of State, *U.S. Treaties and Other International Agreements*, No. 2447.

Indochina, so that propellers of American manufacture had to be removed from Spitfire aircraft which were being shipped to the Far East.[29]

This agreement also represented a decisive defeat for the claims advanced by Nguyen Phan Long, whose tenure of the premiership, contrary to his expectations, had been brief. The dismissal of his Government in May had surprised only Long himself, for he had consistently ignored political realities and had antagonized the French by a bid which was both naïve and premature for American support, while he had failed, in spite of his conciliatory attitude towards the Viet Minh, to win any increased support for the régime. His tenure of office had served, however, to demonstrate that future Prime Ministers must be chosen for some time to come only from that small group of Vietnamese whose credentials presented adequate guarantees of their loyalty towards the French connexion, although in the eyes of the sceptical and uncompromising nationalists the possession of such credentials was sufficient to disqualify the holders from occupying any official position at all. Thus the choice of such personalities to lead successive Governments was soon to be advanced as proof of the unreality of Vietnamese independence.

The continued reliance of the central Government on the bayonets of the French Expeditionary Corps was effectively demonstrated in March, when a demonstration was staged against the visit of two American destroyers to Saigon. There a large crowd bearing Viet Minh flags and portraits of Ho Chi Minh, on finding the road to the waterfront blocked set fire to the market and a number of buses, under the quizzical gaze of the municipal police who refused to intervene. In view of the inability of the Vietnamese authorities to quell the riot, French Union troops were used to restore order, and in the absence of the fire brigade, which had refused to answer the call of duty, the stallholders themselves succeeded in extinguishing the blaze.

On 6 May the formation of the new Government was announced under the premiership of Tran Van Huu, who was a former Prime Minister and Governor of South Vietnam.[30] The new Prime Minister immediately announced that he

[29] L. M. Chassin, *Aviation Indochine* (1954), pp. 67, 75.
[30] See above, p. 189.

would abandon the equivocal attitude towards the Viet Minh that had hitherto been maintained by some of the supporters of 'the Bao Dai solution', and would combat the terrorist outrages which had become almost an accepted part of life in the French-occupied zone. He was supported in this task by the Minister of the Interior, Nguyen Van Tam,[31] who proceeded to organize a national Security Service with which to combat the clandestine activities of the Viet Minh. Tam, who had solid ground for his hatred of the Viet Minh, undertook his important task with considerable energy. The Security Service which he proceeded to organize succeeded in disrupting the Viet Minh clandestine organization in Saigon–Cholon and by the adoption of Viet Minh methods, including occasional resort to torture, brought about a marked improvement in conditions throughout Cochin-China.[32]

<h2 style="text-align:center">THE PAU AGREEMENTS</h2>

The Élysée Agreement had been completed by the signature of other agreements, involving an exchange of letters with the King of Laos on 19 July, and with the King of Cambodia on 8 November. In these letters provision had been made for the calling of a conference between the Associate States, at which common interests were to be discussed and arrangements made for the future exercise of those functions hitherto discharged by the Federal Government, including posts and telegraphs, immigration control, foreign trade, customs, currency, and development plans. This conference had originally been proposed for January 1950, but the delegates met finally at Pau on 27 June.

It was preceded by a meeting at the Élysée, at which matters were discussed relating to the French Union and the delegates were informed of the French Government's intention to set up

[31] See below, p. 430.
[32] Torture had been employed by the French in their efforts to combat the Viet Minh, particularly when information was urgently required from recalcitrant prisoners. The methods were reported to include the administration of electric shocks by means of wires attached to terminal parts of the body, more energetic methods, such as that of the 'aeroplane', which entailed hoisting the victim to the ceiling by the thumbs previously attached behind the back, being occasionally employed. The creation of a Vietnamese Security Service enabled the French to abandon the use of such methods to the Vietnamese, who incurred the resultant odium.

a ministry which would be specifically charged with maintaining relations with the Associate States. The portfolio of this ministry was to be entrusted to Jean Letourneau, the Minister for French Overseas Territories.

By the end of July the discussions at Pau, although they were described as amicable, had achieved but little. This seems to have been due to a tendency on the part of the delegates to take a strongly nationalist line,[33] an attitude that was probably due to the recognition that compromise would be mistaken for weakness by their respective Governments. Moreover the impending abolition of French internal control in Indochina had aroused misgivings among the Cambodians and Laotians in regard to Vietnamese intentions, which the brief period of the Protectorate had lulled but not removed. While the Laotian delegates—representing a land-locked country possessed of ill-defined and disputed frontiers, which included only a minority of inhabitants of Lao race—sought to base their claims on the advantages that Vietnam would be likely to derive from continued economic union with its hinterland, the Cambodians—who had inherited, together with the imperial traditions of the vanished Khmer Empire, a fear of the prolific and industrious Vietnamese who had evicted them in the course of the seventeenth and eighteenth centuries from the delta of the river Mekong—tenaciously insisted on parity of representation with Vietnam on the joint Economic and Financial Committees. Moreover the examination of the French residuary estate that was to be divided among the Associate heirs revealed that all the nascent industries, and almost all of Indochina's economic equipment, were in Vietnam, so that Laos and Cambodia remained necessarily tributary to their disquieting neighbour and also dependent on the port of Saigon for their foreign trade. In order to neutralize the strength of the Vietnamese position, both the Cambodian and the Laotian delegations tended to display separatist tendencies suggesting that they might be forced, should the Vietnamese Government prove obdurate, to co-operate economically with Siam.[34] In these difficult circumstances French mediators not unnaturally encountered considerable difficulty in obtaining agreement even in such limited fields as the apportionment of customs'

[33] *Observer*, 23 July 1950.
[34] *Le Monde*, 25 Nov. 1950.

receipts and measures designed to ensure freedom of navigation on the river Mekong.[35]

The inability of the delegates to reach any satisfactory solution to the economic problems with which they were now confronted cannot have been altogether displeasing to the delegates of the late protecting power, but the French were themselves embarrassed by the presence, in an unofficial capacity, of representatives of the same French business interests which had previously contacted Ho Chi Minh at the Hôtel Royal Monceau during the Fontainebleau Conference. These representatives had now installed themselves in the vicinity, and made no secret of their desire to ensure the inclusion in the agreement of formal guarantees to protect French commercial interests and, in particular, to obtain the acceptance of a quota system which would establish the proportion of imports to be handled by French and Vietnamese business houses, for with far-sighted acumen they foresaw that the Vietnamese, who had no commercial representatives abroad, only modest capital resources, and a dubious reputation for commercial honesty, might be tempted at some later date to remedy these deficiencies by legislation designed to wrest from their French competitors the import trade which they were unable to capture by competitive means.[36]

A further source of embarrassment to the French delegates was the ambiguity that had been allowed to subsist in regard to the exact nature of the French Union. This had enabled the French Government to maintain that the Union, under French paramountcy, was a group of states associated with France, but the Indochinese delegates, basing their contention on a different interpretation of the relevant section of the French constitution, lost no opportunity of advancing the claim that the French Union was in fact an association of free and equal peoples.

Meanwhile in the face of these recurrent disagreements the work of the conference continued to make slow progress. After six weeks of arduous discussion provisional agreement was reached on the future administration of the 'autonomous' port of Saigon, which Vietnam undertook to keep open, together with facilities for access, to Cambodia and Laos. The

[35] *The Times*, 10 Oct. 1950.
[36] Bruno Rajan, in *Le Monde*, 12 Aug. 1950.

responsibility for operating the port was to be vested in a board on which the Associate States and France, together with locally employed technicians and labour, were to enjoy equal representation. Further protracted negotiations resulted in a decision to set up a consultative committee for the river Mekong. This body would be charged with the task of submitting recommendations at meetings of a quadripartite conference, which would be responsible for ensuring freedom of navigation on the river itself and in the approaches to the Mekong and to the port of Saigon. A decision to form a customs union was also reached, and the apportionment of the total revenues from customs duties was provisionally fixed at 71 per cent. for Vietnam, 22 per cent. for Cambodia, and 7 per cent. for Laos.

When the Pau Conference had been in session for three months the Viet Minh threat to Cao Bang, a strategically important town in North Tongking, led to the tardy withdrawal of the garrison, which was overwhelmed in the course of its retreat, together with the military column that had been sent to cover the evacuation. This event, which effectively demonstrated the futility of the chicanery and suspicions that had hitherto been a feature of the discussions, caused the Chairman, Albert Sarraut, who had held the office of Governor-General from 1911 to 1919, to profit from the news of the disaster to confront the delegates with their responsibilities. After pointing out that the Conference, which had been convened in order to discuss economic problems, had placed too much stress on political implications, with the result that the negotiations had tended to revolve around irrelevant conceptions of national sovereignty, Sarraut, indicating the lessons to be drawn from events in Tongking, addressed the delegates as follows:

The grave events that have just occurred at Cao-Bang show that there at least no futile quibbles are involved. In these circumstances, are we then here in Pau to go on calmly scratching out clauses under the pretext of protecting sovereign rights, which are threatened by none of us, behind paper ramparts; ramparts which would be rapidly devoured by the conflagration resulting from the enemy offensive if we were not so closely united?[37]

This admonition and reminder, combined with the general lassitude and the approach of winter in the Pyrenees, induced a

[37] *Le Monde*, 15–16 Oct. 1950.

more conciliatory frame of mind, and the discussions made better progress.

In the remaining agreements the principle adopted was to invest the three Governments within their national frontiers with the functions that had hitherto been discharged by the Federal administration. The co-ordination, within the framework of the customs union, of measures that the Governments might subsequently adopt was assured by the creation of Study Committees, which were composed of the representatives of the Associate States and France, and by the periodic convention of quadripartite inter-governmental conferences. Agreement on the outstanding financial items on the agenda was reached on the basis of the recognition of the fiscal autonomy of the three states, and these were required to consult with one another, and with France, when measures were contemplated which were likely to affect any one of the other Associate States, or France and the French Union. It was also decided to retain the piastre as the unit of currency for the whole of Indochina, while the privilege of issuing this currency was to be vested in an institute, the activities of which were to be directed by a board composed of representatives of the three states and France. On 29 November the Conference finally completed its labours.

In spite of the laborious efforts that had preceded their conclusion, the agreements failed to satisfy the signatories. While the Associate States were inclined to resent the restrictions imposed on their financial and administrative autonomy, the French regarded with some dismay the facilities that had now been afforded the Indochinese Governments to interfere with their economic interests. Moreover the creation of the quadripartite committees provided a cumbersome and complex alternative to the Federal Government, while the reluctance of the Associate States to compromise whenever their recently acquired 'independence' was considered to be threatened aroused forebodings. Nevertheless, in view of the need that the Associate States had of one another and of France, these agreements, by providing the Indochinese Governments with the appurtenances of sovereignty and by imposing restrictions on their use, probably provided the most realistic solution to a quandary which arose chiefly from a need to reconcile an emotional demand for independence with the practical requirements for long-term technical, economic, and military assistance, since in addition to their inability to protect their frontiers or to combat the prevailing insecurity within their territories, the Associate States also lacked the technicians and the trained administrators required to conduct the normal business of government.

This lack of trained personnel may be ascribed partly to the tendency under the French Protectorate to restrict opportunity for higher education and to concentrate on the formation of junior civil servants and clerks, with the result that although the faculties of law and medicine at Hanoi University had provided Indochina with a limited number of barristers and doctors, and some Indochinese had been able to attend universities and technical colleges in France, there was a notable lack of senior civil servants and engineers;[38] in these circumstances the need for French advisers and technicians limited in a very practical sense the independence that had been accorded. The adherence of the Associate States to the French Union also entailed restrictions on sovereignty in the sphere of military defence and in the conduct of foreign and economic policies.

Hedged about, then, with these limitations, the Indochinese states became members of a French Union, the interests of which were to be the responsibility of three central organs: the Presidency, the High Council, and the Assembly. The office of President of the French Union was held *ex officio* by the President of the French Republic who represented the permanent interests of the Union, and he was assisted by a High Council, composed of delegates appointed by the French Government and by representatives from each of the Associate States.[39] The function of the Council was limited, however, to that of assisting the French Government 'with the general administration of the Union', while the Council was in turn assisted by an Assembly of the French Union.

[38] The Vietnamese who had qualified as civil and mining engineers could be counted on one hand, while no Vietnamese possessed any specialized knowledge of public finance. Vietnam also had no merchant marine captains, air pilots, or foreign-language professors (Danielle Hunebelle in *Le Monde*, 31 Oct. and 1, 2 & 3 Nov. 1951). The number of Laotians with university degrees was estimated at less than twenty (J. Egli in *Combat*, 28, 29 & 31 July 1949). Cambodia boasted one Cambodian-born Doctor of Medicine.

[39] The number of Associate States, in the absence of Tunisia and Morocco, which had failed to acquire this status, was limited to Vietnam, Cambodia, and Laos.

This Assembly had met for the first time in December 1947 at Versailles, and was attended by delegates who had been elected by local assemblies throughout the French Overseas Departments and Territories, and by delegates from the Associate States. An equal number of representatives from metropolitan France had been elected by the National Assembly and by the Council of the Republic. The Assembly of the French Union, which might have constituted in embryonic form a Parliament of Overseas Territories, was, however, reduced to impotence by the refusal of the French National Assembly to alienate the smallest fraction of its legislative powers. The Assembly was in consequence permitted merely to take cognizance of projects and proposals submitted for its consideration by the National Assembly, or the French Government, or the Governments of the Associate States, to deliberate upon draft resolutions presented by its members, and to forward proposals to the French Government or to the High Council.

The existence of these advisory and consultative bodies, which in spite of their high-sounding names were without any authority and served for the most part to provide agreeable sinecures for French Union personages, who welcomed an occasion to visit Paris without expense to themselves, was a subject of ironic comment among the Vietnamese, who pointed out the manifest inability of the National Assembly to provide anything more substantial than a façade for the generous conception of the French Union foreshadowed in the first Constituent Assembly of 1946, as 'France enriched, ennobled and expanded' which will 'tomorrow possess a hundred million citizens and free men'.[40] The general disillusionment with the state of the Union was voiced in October 1950 by the Vietnamese Prime Minister, Tran Van Huu, who declared that he had more confidence in the efficacy of American aid than in any assistance that might be forthcoming from the French Union.[41] He was compelled, however, to return to Saigon during the month by events in Tongking, where Viet Minh forces, in fulfilment of General Revers's prediction,[42] were

[40] Words of Pierre Cot, rapporteur of the Unified Constitution of the French Republic (quoted by Herbert Luthy in *The State of France*, pp. 219–20).
[41] *Le Monde*, 27 Oct. 1950.
[42] In May 1949 Revers, who was Chief of the French General Staff, had been

conducting a series of operations designed to hasten the evacuation of French garrisons from the frontier areas.

### THE CAO BANG DISASTER

The arrival of the Chinese Communist forces at the frontier had enabled the Viet Minh to make rapid progress in the build-up of their armed forces, and following the promulgation of a decree ordering the mobilization of all the national resources in manpower and material,[43] General Vo Nguyen Giap broadcast a declaration in February 1950 affirming that the period of guerrilla activities was over and the war of movement was beginning;[44] as an earnest of his intentions he began, before the rainy season, to deploy increasingly large numbers of troops, who were backed up by a more liberal use of supporting fire in attacks on French positions. That same month a post near Lao Kay garrisoned by a force of French-officered Nung and Thai militia had been captured following an assault by five Viet Minh battalions. On 25 May four Viet Minh battalions who were supported by a formidable concentration of gun and mortar fire forced the French garrison at Dong Khe to evacuate their post, which was a strategetically important position on *Route Coloniale* No. 4, a road which ensured communications between Cao Bang and Lang Son. Although Dong Khe was recaptured by parachute troops on the 27th, the increasingly aggressive tactics of the Viet Minh and the improvement in their armament and, in particular, their use of field-guns and anti-aircraft batteries in widely separated areas indicated that the balance of military power was passing from the French. Fortunately the advent of the rainy season, which lasts in Tongking from June to October, halted the operations and gave the Expeditionary Corps some respite.

During the next campaigning season, however, the persistent failure of the French Government either to dispatch adequate reinforcements or to insist on the implementation of that part of General Revers's report which recommended the withdrawal of French garrisons from the mountainous region of Tongking

---

sent to Indochina to report on the possible effect that the Communist victory in China would have on the military situation in Tongking. See also below, p. 407.

[43] *Le Monde*, 23 Feb. 1950.

[44] *Combat*, 28 Feb. 1950.

to the perimeter of the Red river delta was to involve the Expeditionary Corps in disaster. This failure has been ascribed to the fact that in Saigon, where political considerations often dictated the conduct of the war, Pignon, who was charged with local responsibility for military operations, was himself reluctant to approve the evacuation of the garrison from Cao Bang, where he placed undue reliance upon the loyalty of the local Tho tribal population.[45] Preference was therefore given during the 'dry' months of the winter of 1949–50 to the task, which had also been proposed in the Revers report, of pacifying the agriculturally productive regions of Tongking, and especially to the occupation of the southern part of the Red river delta, which included the towns of Thai Binh, Ninh Binh, and Phu Ly. The acceptance of this decision by the French military authorities must, however, occasion some surprise, for fairly complete coverage was available in regard to the substantial amount of military aid in the form of rifles, submachine guns, mortars, anti-aircraft guns, and technical assistance which the Vietnamese were now receiving from China.[46]

This tendency on the part of the French Command to underestimate the rate of progress in the build up of the Viet Minh forces has been ascribed to an impatience among senior officers with the nature of hostilities, which gave little scope for any large-scale or classic military operations, and also to the fact that the officers commanding the three services had previously served in the Indochinese theatre of war, and judging from their past experience they refused to credit the Viet Minh with the ability to overcome their logistic difficulties or to abandon their guerrilla tactics for classic warfare.[47]

After a decision by the French cabinet on 14 August to reduce the strength of the Expeditionary Corps by 9,000 men,[48] it became evident, however, that the evacuation of the garrisons from Cao Bang, and from the military posts along *Route Coloniale*

---

[45] Jacques Mordal, *Marine indochine* (1953), p. 181. The difficulties involved in the retention of an isolated and beleaguered garrison at Cao Bang may be gauged when it is recalled that the dispossessed Mac princes were able to maintain themselves with Chinese support in that inaccessible area from 1652 to 1677, in spite of repeated attempts by the rulers of Tongking to evict them.

[46] Jean Marchand, *Le Drame indochinois* (1949), pp. 120–1.

[47] Charles Fauvel in *Le Monde*, 20 Oct. 1950.

[48] Frédéric-Dupont, pp. 115–16. The reduction, which was made against military advice, was due to the refusal of the Assembly to consider the employment of National Service recruits in Indochina.

No. 4 could no longer be delayed. This operation was carried out under the most difficult conditions, for on 16 September the Viet Minh, who had succeeded in concentrating fourteen battalions in the vicinity, again attacked the post at Dong Khe which was defended by two companies of the Foreign Legion and some militia troops. This post, against which the Viet Minh had been able to mass batteries of howitzers,[49] fell on the 18th, and by its fall considerably reduced the prospects of evacuating the Cao Bang garrison.

On 3 October the Cao Bang garrison, consisting of 1,600 troops, set out, accompanied by some 1,000 partisans and 500 Vietnamese and Chinese civilians, to try and reach Lang Son, which lies eighty-five miles to the south. Before this a force of Moroccan troops numbering 3,500 had begun to advance from That Mhe, which is situated fifteen miles to the south of Dong Khe, to join up with the column from Cao Bang in order to assist in the withdrawal. The Viet Minh, who outnumbered the French Union troops by three to one, sought to prevent the success of this operation, and being favoured by the mountainous terrain and the defiles through which the road passed were able to disrupt the Cao Bang column, who were compelled to burn their trucks and abandon their equipment. Meanwhile the relief force, under repeated Viet Minh attacks, were themselves forced to take to the hills bordering the road. On the 6th the remnants of the Cao Bang garrison and the relief column met, but they were unable to face the sustained and fanatical fury of the Viet Minh attacks, and on the 7th, after desperate hand-to-hand fighting, they were overwhelmed.

This disaster, which constituted the greatest defeat in the history of French colonial warfare, led to the abandonment in rapid succession of the posts guarding the road, while on the night of the 17th–18th the important garrison town of Lang Son itself, which commands the main route to China, was evacuated in such haste that guns, mortars, automatic weapons, together with some 8,000 rifles and important stocks of food, ammunition, and sufficient uniforms subsequently to equip an entire Viet Minh division, were left for the enemy.[50]

The evacuation of Lang Son was followed by the withdrawal of the garrisons from the posts at Dinh La and An Chau to the

[49] Sabattier, p. 343.
[50] Marchand, *Drame indochinois*, p. 139.

south, which opened up the roads to the coast in the vicinity of Along Bay; and the evacuatioh of Lao Kay early in November left the Viet Minh in undisputed possession of the frontier zone from the coastal town of Mon Cay—which remained in French hands—to the frontier of Laos. The sombre communiqué in which the extent of the disaster was revealed contained the admission that 'for the first time we have had to do with an enemy perfectly armed and equipped, who have an excellent radio network and know how to co-ordinate their movements'.[51] The only consolation that the French can be said to have derived from their defeat was due to their air force, which raided Cao Bang on the night of 24–25 October and surprised the Viet Minh imprudently celebrating the 'liberation of the frontier area'. The raid abruptly terminated these festivities, and two battalions of Chinese Communist troops who had been invited to the fête retired in confusion, together with their casualties, to Chinese territory.[52]

Even the sanguine Giap appeared surprised by the rapidity, scope, and completeness of his success, but he adapted his plan of campaign to exploit this situation by bringing his troops rapidly to the borders of the delta and to the approaches of Mon Cay and Along Bay. Meanwhile Viet Minh broadcasts announced the triumphant return of Ho Chi Minh to Hanoi for the anniversary of the rising of 19 December 1946. The President of the Democratic Republic of Vietnam was to disappoint his audience, however, and to remain for many 'dry' and 'rainy' seasons in the limestone caves and huts of the northern redoubt.

The delay that was to occur in the Viet Minh reoccupation of their capital could not have been foreseen in the early days of December, for the French civil and military authorities, who had hitherto tended to underrate the capacity of the enemy, were now anticipating the withdrawal of the Expeditionary Corps from Tongking. Fortunately the arrival in November of General Juin, Chief of the French General Staff, served to check the growing panic. Nevertheless on 4 December Pignon officially instructed the authorities in Hanoi to ensure that the families of the French civil and military personnel serving in North Vietnam were ready to leave at short notice.[53] These

[51] Le Monde, 12 Oct. 1950.
[52] Chassin, p. 85.
[53] Le Monde, 6 Dec. 1950.

instructions aroused considerable alarm among the sorely tried French residents who proceeded hastily to dispose of their household effects at some loss to themselves.

In France the news of the fierce fighting which had preceded the destruction of the columns in the mountainous region of Tongking and the evacuation of Lang Son had aroused some public remorse at the shabby treatment which the Expeditionary Force had received, and in this improved moral climate the Prime Minister, René Pleven, was able to assemble essential reinforcements and to proceed with plans for the rapid formation of the national Indochinese armies which had hitherto consisted only of 'symbolic' battalions.

On 5 November Letourneau, Minister for the Associate States, and Pignon accompanied Bao Dai when the latter officially opened an inter-service training college at Dalat, where it was proposed to train officers at the rate of 150 a year for service with the infantry, artillery, and armoured units and signal corps of the future Vietnamese army.[54] The opening of this training college served also as a prelude to Franco-Vietnamese discussions on the training and equipping of the national army, of which Bao Dai was to assume supreme command. He was to be assisted by a High Military Committee composed of French and Vietnamese political and military advisers. It was agreed also that during 1951 four divisions should be formed, partly from recruits and partly from Vietnamese troops serving with the Expeditionary Corps, who would be transferred to the national army.[55] The Vietnamese Government for its part undertook to contribute 35 – 40 per cent. of the national revenues towards the expenses incurred by the creation of this army. These proposals were approved with commendable speed by the French National Assembly and on 8 December a Military Convention was signed in Saigon which provided for the constitution of the High Military Committee and incorporated the arrangements for the creation of four divisions. This Convention was completed by an agreement initialed on the 23rd between France, the United States, and Vietnam, which defined the respective responsibilities of

[54] *Le Populaire*, 3 Nov. 1950. The establishment of this school was overdue. Although a training programme had been initiated at the end of 1948, by November 1950 a modest total of 200 officer cadets had been accepted under the scheme at various French military training establishments (*NYT*, 20 Aug. 1950).
[55] *Le Monde*, 9 Nov. 1950.

the three states for the provision of the military equipment and financial assistance which would be needed.

Meanwhile the French Government sought to shift some of the responsibility for French reverses in Tongking on to the shoulders of the local authorities, and decided to recall both the High Commissioner and the general commanding the French forces in the Far East. The difficult succession was offered to General Jean de Lattre de Tassigny, the Commander-in-Chief of Western Union land forces. De Lattre, together with Generals Leclerc and Juin, was one of a triumvirate of French military commanders who had achieved fame in the Second World War when de Lattre had commanded the French First Army which had liberated eastern France from the shores of the Mediterranean to the Vosges, but in spite of his distinguished record he remained a controversial figure. Although he was endowed with personal courage, ardent patriotism, and had proved his ability to command military forces in the field, he also possessed histrionic gifts of a high order which included a legendary capacity for volcanic expressions of displeasure, partly offset, however, by considerable ability to charm. It was perhaps inevitable that his egocentric personality and forceful, and on occasion, overbearing manner, his frequent injustices, together with his disregard for normal civilities and his extravagant attachment to marks of attention and respect—particularly if these were considered to be due to his person— should have made him many enemies. But the devotion of a competent and carefully selected staff—his 'Brains Trust'— whose personal convenience was ruthlessly subordinated to his own, together with the admiration he aroused among the troops, must be held to constitute proof that he possessed the transcendent qualities which alone would excuse, if not altogether justify, the frequent excesses of his autocratic temperament. Both the qualities and the defects of this remarkable personality were now to find the occasion for their full development on a vast and complex stage.

The readiness of de Lattre, who held the highest military post in Western Europe, to assume command in the Indochinese theatre of war caused some surprise. He may have been influenced in this decision by his only child, Bernard, for the young de Lattre, who was serving as a lieutenant in Tongking, had suggested in letters home during the dark months of

October and November that his father's strong hand and incisive leadership were needed to check the demoralization
that was becoming apparent not only among the civilian
population in Hanoi but even in the ranks of the Expeditionary
Corps itself.[56] This appeal to a soldier who had always attached
supreme importance to morale may not have been made in
vain, since on 6 December General de Lattre's appointment as
Commander-in-Chief and High Commissioner was announced.
His dual appointment followed a government order defining the
powers of the Minister for the Associate States, who was to be
vested with authority over all military forces serving in Indochina and with the responsibility for the defence of Indochinese
territory.[57]

De Lattre, after consultations with the appropriate government departments and the selection of officers and officials to
serve on his military and civilian staff, arrived in Saigon on
17 December. His arrival was the occasion for a display of
temperament which clearly indicated his intention to instil new
fervour and fresh resolution into the officers and men serving
under his command. Although his stay in Saigon was brief it
was long enough to spread dismay among the numerically
important contingent of senior officers bureaucratically entrenched in the southern capital. Another stormy scene, which
was clearly calculated to reverberate throughout the messes
and garrisons of Indochina, marked his departure on the 19th
for Hanoi, where an impressive parade of French Union troops
had been staged in his honour. On completing his tour of
inspection de Lattre made a short speech to the assembled
officers, and addressing himself particularly to the 'captains
and lieutenants', assured them that the ground would no longer
shift under their feet and that henceforth they would be
*commanded*.[58] This energetic approach to the grave task awaiting
him proved an effective and legitimate means of restoring
morale and imposing discipline at a time when Viet Minh

[56] G. Salisbury-Jones, *So Full a Glory* (1954), p. 247.
[57] *The Times*, 6 Dec. 1950. Letourneau was to allow de Lattre considerable
latitude in the conduct of operations. The government order appears to have
been inspired by the desire to loosen the control that had hitherto been exercised
over French forces in Indochina from Paris, where the General Commanding French
Union troops had been compelled to give prior notification to the Ministry of
National Defence, even of his intention to change the location of a battalion
(Mordal, p. 186).
[58] *Le Monde*, 21 Dec. 1950.

forces were massing on the borders of the Red river delta in preparation for an attempt to win a decisive victory.

But after the immediate danger had been averted the Com-mander-in-Chief continued to insist that all local personages, together with an important contingent of troops, should be present whenever, on his frequent journeys, he was due to arrive at, or to leave from, an Indochinese airfield. This idiosyncracy resulted in much waste of time, while his frequent outbursts against those unfortunate subordinates whose decisions or actions failed to meet with his approval led to increasing reluctance, particularly on the part of his civilian staff, to take any initiative if there was a chance that the person responsible might thereby bring down upon his head an expression of de Lattre's displeasure.

# XIII

## 'Le Roi Jean'[1]

THE news of de Lattre's appointment to command the Expeditionary Corps was received with satisfaction by Giap, who regarded it as a compliment both to himself and the troops under his command, and he greeted his new opponent with the following salvo: 'The French are sending against the "People's" Army an adversary worthy of its steel. We will defeat him on his own ground.'[2]

Steps to give effect to this challenge were soon taken. Late in December 1950 the Viet Minh began a general harassing action against the French posts guarding the approaches to the delta and at the same time threatened the defences between Hon Gay and Mon Cay; by 22 December Viet Minh concentrations were reported near Tien Yen, although they were dispersed by a parachute battalion and the use of jellied petroleum, or 'Napalm', bombs.[3] After leaving the French for some weeks in uncertainty about their intentions, the Viet Minh next made an attack on the night of 13–14 January 1951 against a small post near Vinh Yen, thirty-seven miles north-west of Hanoi. This post fell to them on the morning of the 14th, and a mobile group which had been sent to its relief was also surrounded and assailed by the Viet Minh, who had taken up their position on the hills dominating the road.[4] In spite of heavy casualties the group was able to extricate itself from this trap, and regained its base at Vinh Yen, where the Viet Minh had installed themselves during the previous night on the heights to the north-west and east of the town.

De Lattre, who landed at the Vinh Yen airstrip during the day, concluded, in view of the numbers engaged, that the

[1] His autocratic manner earned de Lattre this nickname.

[2] Jean Lacouture in *Le Monde*, 5 Dec. 1952.

[3] Napalm bombs consist of wing-tanks filled with jellied petroleum which burst into flames on contact with the ground. They had been effectively employed earlier in the year by aircraft operating in Korea and were to be widely used in Indochina against Viet Minh troops and the enemy-occupied villages where the dwellings thatched with Nepa palm-leaves were peculiarly vulnerable.

[4] Mobile groups comprised infantry, artillery, a contingent of sappers, and a communications section. Their strength varied between 2,000 and 3,000 men.

attack must represent the beginning of an offensive directed against Hanoi itself. He therefore returned to his headquarters, where he ordered the mobilization of all available reserves and the diversion of civil and military aircraft to the task of transporting troops from Cochin-China to the battlefront. On the 15th the French launched from the south-west a counterattack led by a mobile group of North African troops with the object of driving the Viet Minh from the heights around Vinh Yen. By the afternoon of the 16th this counter-attack, well supported by aircraft using napalm bombs and machineguns against compact enemy formations, had achieved its objective. In the course of the following night, however, the Viet Minh, who had received reinforcements, recaptured two of the three hilltops they had been compelled to abandon, but the punishment which their massed formations had received obliged them to abandon the field of battle during the night of 17–18 January and to withdraw to their base areas in the Viet Bac. The battle, in which from 25 to 30 of their battalions had been engaged,[5] cost the Viet Minh some 6,000 casualties[6] and showed that without air and adequate artillery support Giap was unable to meet de Lattre 'on his own ground'.

The outcome of the fighting, combined with the stimulating presence of the Commander-in-Chief, did much to restore military and civilian morale; and now, in conformity with the recommendations in the Revers report, work on the construction of a defence line was begun. This work, which was pursued with great energy under the eye of de Lattre himself, who carried out frequent inspections and surprise visits, resulted in the space of six months in the completion of 600 concrete strong-points stretching from the Bay of Along to Vinh Yen and covering the main invasion route from China.[7] Meanwhile de Lattre was busy also in increasing the number of mobile groups. These, which together with the parachute units formed the main striking force, were used both to parry attack and also to carry out offensive operations in enemy-controlled territory.[8]

[5] The strength of a Viet Minh battalion was estimated at 1,000 men.

[6] Mordal, p. 191.

[7] By the end of the year 1,200 strong-points were completed, each of which was garrisoned by a section. The posts were constructed in groups of five or six, situated from one to two miles from each other, and sited so as to provide supporting fire in the event of an attack (Marchand, p. 168).

[8] Besides these operations by mobile groups and parachute units, Franco-

In March the General left for Paris in order to put his demands for reinforcements before the National Defence Committee. They included certain increases in the number of officers, n.c.o.'s, and technicians whose services would in the main be required to train the national armies.

While de Lattre was away in France concentrations of Viet Minh troops—estimated on 17 March at 20,000—were detected to the east of the Hanoi–Haiphong road in the wild hill country around Dong Trieu, where their presence constituted a threat to the adjacent coastal area, and even to Haiphong itself.[9] On the 23rd–24th a series of attacks was launched against a string of French posts on the eastern fringe of this area. These attacks, which were designed to entice French reserves into difficult country, failed in their purpose since the French Command, divining the enemy's intention, kept their reserves where they were, while the garrisons were able in most cases to elude their assailants and withdraw to the south. After some days the Viet Minh, perplexed at the failure of their plan, carried out an assault on one of the twin villages at Mao Khe, and there, in spite of spirited resistance, they compelled the garrison to take refuge in the other village. This village was also attacked in the course of the following night by a large force, but here, though the enemy succeeded in breaching the defences, they were compelled at daybreak to relinquish this foothold. On 5 April the Viet Minh, who had failed to achieve any of their objectives, accepted defeat and began to withdraw their forces from the area.

The operations around Dong Trieu, in which French aircraft and artillery were again used with decisive effect against an enemy attacking in close formation, had revealed certain weaknesses in the Viet Minh military organization, and in particular their inability to change their plans to meet an unexpected development, but the operations had shown also that the Viet Minh could now assemble and maintain a large force at considerable distance from their bases in the Viet Bac. The un-

Vietnamese commandos, who were partly recruited in Viet Minh prison camps, carried out raids of surprising audacity deep into the enemy zone, where their appearance nonplussed the Viet Minh who were liable to find themselves at a loss when faced with a situation for which no provision had been made in their well-thumbed textbooks on the conduct of guerrilla warfare.

[9] French reserves had been grouped near Vietri in anticipation of an attack on Hanoi from the north.

successful outcome of their operations, however, compelled the Viet Minh Command to reconsider the employment of tactics which were resulting in the decimation of their regular units. The result of these reflections was enshrined in an order of the day in which Giap blandly informed the troops whom he had exposed to such punishment that they would be well advised to recall that guerrilla warfare would be their chief means of action in a struggle which would be long and arduous.[10]

### VIET MINH CONGRESSES AND CONFERENCES

Meanwhile the Viet Minh leaders who had hitherto been engaged in ensuring the survival of the resistance movement were encouraged by Chinese Communist example to undertake the political reorganization of the areas under their control. On 16 March 1951 the Viet Minh transmitting station, 'The Voice of Viet-Nam', announced that a 'National Congress' had been held somewhere in North Vietnam between 11 and 19 February at which a decision had been reached to found a 'new political party'—the Vietnam Lao Dong (Workers) Party.[11] This party, which was described in its manifesto[12] as a 'vanguard army, a general staff, a powerful, clear-sighted, determined, pure and thoroughly revolutionary political party' all rolled into one, which had come into being solely in response 'to a longing on the part of the whole Vietnamese nation', was stated to include among its members, 'the most patriotic, the most ardent, the most revolutionary workers, peasants, and intellectual workers'. The delegates to the Congress were also assured through the mouth of its secretary-general, Truong Chinh, that the party, whose policy was based on 'Marxist-Leninist theory, democratic centralism, criticism and auto-criticism, would perpetuate the glorious historic career of the progressive revolutionary parties'.

The party whose nativity was heralded with such an explosion of Communist jargon represented in fact the official re-emergence of the Indochinese Communist Party which, after its official dissolution in November 1945, had successfully

[10] Camille Rougeron in Le Monde, 19 Apr. 1957.

[11] The avoidance of the use of the word 'Communist' was probably inspired by a desire to confuse non-Communist observers as to the real complexion of the new party.

[12] NCNA, 6 Apr. 1951 (Cole, pp. 106–10).

maintained an undisputed control over the movement for national independence through its party members, who had continued to occupy key positions in the administration and the army. The programme which had been expounded at the 'National Congress' clearly revealed by the authoritative tone of its pronouncements the dominant role that the party intended to assume in the direction of the state, for it contained directives in regard to agrarian reform, education, religion, and the treatment of ethnic minorities, and the need was stressed for a merger of the Viet Minh League with the Lien Viet and for increased assistance to the Cambodian and Laotian resistance movements.

The Viet Minh authorities, however, appeared to have been expecting the Lao Dong Party's recommendations, for delegates from the resistance movements and representatives of the Viet Minh League and the Lien Viet were already present in North Vietnam, where another 'National Congress' was inaugurated on 3 March. This Congress was alleged to have been attended by delegates from all parts of Vietnam and from Siam and Western Europe, including 'representatives from all circles of the people, among whom were white-haired old men who had walked many days with their sticks'. The opening session was attended by Ho Chi Minh himself, who was welcomed to the Congress by Pham Ba Truc, a renegade Catholic priest. In his reply to Truc's address of welcome Ho expressed his happiness at seeing 'the forest of the National United Bloc blossom and bear fruits with its roots deeply connected with the entire people in an "undying spring".' He then proceeded to direct the delegates on the action they should take and, having announced his requirements, he dedicated to the Congress the following distich inspired by the occasion:

> Union, union, broad union,
> Success, success, great success

'which all delegates pledged to bear in mind together with his teachings'.[13]

The decision to merge the Viet Minh League with the all-embracing and somewhat amorphous Lien Viet bloc was based on the fact that the more prominent members of the League, which had been formed in May 1941 in Kwangsi, had been

[13] Viet Minh News Service, *Viet-Nam Information* (Rangoon), Nos. 377 and 379.

co-opted into the ranks of the Lao Dong Party. The merger was therefore designed to eliminate the League's 'rump' by incorporating in the Lien Viet the members who had not been selected to join the Lao Dong Party, and as the Lien Viet possessed an inferior social cachet the 'noble action' of the Viet Minh League in agreeing to this merger was to be mentioned more than once during the proceedings. Under the firm direction of Ton Duc Thang, a veteran Communist agitator who was elected president of the Central Committee, the delegates decided in the course of the debates to create a Lien Viet Front with a political platform which would embody Truong Chinh's directives.

The Government of the Democratic Republic, having completed the reorganization of its internal political affairs, was now free to turn its attention to a measure which it was calculated would encourage unrest and civil war in neighbouring territories, namely the creation of a joint United Front of Vietnam, Cambodia, and Laos. The agents selected for this purpose were the disgruntled Lao quisling, Souphannouvong, and a Communist agent of Vietnamese-Cambodian descent named Sieu Heng.[14]

The credentials of Sieu Heng, the young leader of a phantom 'Cambodian Liberation Army', were also open to question, for he merely presided over 'the Central Office South', a body that had been invested temporarily by an imperialistically minded Viet Minh Government with jurisdiction over Cambodia, South Vietnam, and *Lien Khu* V (South-Central Vietnam). This office, after initially establishing its headquarters in South Vietnam, had moved later to south-west Cambodia, where the trackless and sparsely inhabited nature of the countryside afforded greater security from surprise attack. In spite of his grandiose title, Sieu Heng's chief function seems to have been that of ensuring liaison between the self-styled Khmer Issaraks and Viet Minh military units, which were either based on, or temporarily operating from, Cambodian soil.[15]

A Conference of the 'united fronts' of Vietnam, Laos, and Cambodia was held later in March. Undeterred by the fictitious nature of the Cambodian and Laotian representation Ton Duc Thang, who led the Vietnamese delegation, proceeded

[14] Denis Warner in *Daily Telegraph*, 18 Nov. 1950.
[15] Hunebelle in *Le Monde*, 31 Oct. and 1, 2 & 3 Nov. 1951.

to forge an instrument which would justify the continued use of neighbouring territory for the transit of military supplies and for attacks on French Union garrisons. The discussions were said to have been held 'in a most cordial atmosphere' and the Conference set up a People's Committee and issued a manifesto 'urging the peoples of the world to support the joint national united front'. When the Conference ended Ton Duc Thang marked the historic nature of the occasion by presenting to the puppet Cambodian and Laotian delegates 'American guns captured by Vietnamese troops from the French Army', while the delegates, with becoming modesty, offered their mentor 'cultural works showing that the Cambodia and Laotian peoples had a history and a culture of their own'.[16]

### DE LATTRE'S VISIT TO AMERICA

While these important conferences were taking place in the Viet Bac the French were preparing to pacify that small but thickly populated part of the Red river delta which lies between the Canal des Bambous and the sea. When this operation was finally launched towards the middle of April 1951 the Viet Minh, taking advantage of the French pre-occupations, were able to concentrate a force—estimated at forty battalions—to the south of the defence positions in South-West Tongking.[17] The measures taken by the French Command to check this offensive included the dispatch from the neighbouring town of Nam Dinh to the banks of the river Day of a recently formed battalion of Vietnamese troops in which Lieut. Bernard de Lattre commanded a company. During the night of 29th–30th the young de Lattre, who had installed himself with a platoon of his company on a limestone crag near the river, was killed by mortar fire. The death of his only child appeared temporarily to stun the Commander-in-Chief, who handed over the direction of the battle[18] and accompanied the body of his son, together with the bodies of two n.c.o.'s who had fallen in the same action, back to France, where funeral obsequies were held in the Chapel Saint Louis at the Invalides. This cruel personal loss aroused widespread sympathy for the

[16] *Viet-Nam Information*, No. 385.
[17] R. C. Romilly in *Combat*, 3 Oct. 1951.
[18] The battle resulted on 8 June in a Viet Minh withdrawal.

bereaved father, but it served also to focus public attention on the slow seepage of French lives that the war in Indochina entailed.

When de Lattre returned, the advent of the rains gave him the opportunity to devote more of his time and attention to the formation of the national armies and to the responsibilities which devolved upon him in his capacity of High Commissioner. As High Commissioner he was present at a prize-giving ceremony at a Saigon secondary school on 11 June, and there he profited from the occasion to make a noble and moving appeal to the pupils exhorting them to abandon their captious criticism and facile irony with which many Vietnamese sought to conceal their sense of frustration and perplexity. De Lattre then faced his audience with the choice either of joining the Viet Minh, saying, 'There are some among them who are fighting well in a bad cause',[19] or, if they loved their country, of actively participating in a war in which their future and that of their country were both at stake.

The nationalist ministers appear to have realized for their part that the time was come to abandon the mental reservations which had hitherto prevented them from co-operating wholeheartedly with the French. On 19 April the Prime Minister, Tran Van Huu, after a visit to the battlefield of Vinh Yen in the company of de Lattre, boldly proclaimed in the name of his Government that the struggle against the Viet Minh would be carried on without mercy, and the law against subversive activities rigorously enforced.[20] On 14 July an imposing military review, which was attended by Bao Dai in person, was held in Hanoi, and next day a general decree was signed authorizing the Government to mobilize all the means and resources of the state.[21] This general measure was followed on the 19th by the conscription of Vietnamese doctors of medicine up to the age of 55,[22] and on the 27th a further decree announced the call-up of a small contingent of conscripts for a short period of military training.[23] The decision to restrict the call-up to these groups was due to the lack of Vietnamese officers and n.c.o.'s qualified

[19] Jean de Lattre de Tassigny, *Appel à la jeunesse vietnamienne : discours prononcé à Saigon le 11 juillet 1951 . . . à la distribution des prix du Lycée Chasseloup-Lambert.*
[20] Salisbury-Jones, p. 264.
[21] *Manchester Guardian*, 16 July 1951.
[22] *Le Monde*, 19 July 1951.
[23] *New Statesman*, 30 July 1951.

to form the cadres of the battalions that were to be formed, and also to delays in the delivery of the military equipment from the United States, which were ascribed to the priority given to the Korean theatre of war.[24]

In view of the increasingly important role the United States was destined to play in Indochinese affairs, de Lattre indicated at this stage that he would welcome an invitation to visit Washington, where he counted on his powers of persuasion not only to combat American suspicions about French intentions but also to obtain certain increases in military supplies needed for the equipment of the national armies. His initiative was rewarded by an invitation from the Chiefs of Staff Committee to visit Washington in September. During his visit de Lattre, in a series of discussions, addresses, and press interviews, including an appearance before the television cameras, did much to persuade the American public not only that effective national independence had been given to the Associate States but also that France's role in Indochina was disinterested. Here his innate ability to handle press representatives stood him in good stead, while his spirited defence of French actions, together with his stumbling but game attempts to express himself in a foreign tongue, aroused interest in his cause and sympathy for his person. De Lattre's conferences with the service chiefs were successful: his requests for quicker deliveries of outstanding supplies were approved and it was agreed that allocations of aircraft and artillery, as well as ammunition, automatic weapons, amphibious vehicles, and napalm bombs should be increased.[25]

The discussions at the Pentagon were proceeding in an atmosphere of mutual comprehension when the inopportune arrival in Washington of the Vietnamese Prime Minister threatened to embarrass the French delegation who were conducting negotiations on behalf of, but without reference to, the wishes of the 'independent' Government that this particular Prime Minister represented. Tran Van Huu had been attending the San Francisco Conference, where he had been much elated by the consideration with which he had been treated, and seemed unaware that his presence was unwelcome to de Lattre, but after a meeting had been arranged between him and

[24] *Figaro*, 19–20 Jan. 1952.
[25] *Le Monde*, 25 Sept. 1951.

President Truman, Huu was persuaded to return to Vietnam, where the mobilization decrees were causing discontent and unrest, with the result that the young men in South Vietnam who had been called up for military training were tending to evade military service by enrolling in the militia forces of the politico-religious sects.

The attitude of the Cao Dai and Hoa Hao sects was a cause of disquiet at that time not only to the nationalist Government but also to the French military command, for both the Cao Dai and Hoa Hao leaders were prepared to accept deserters from the armed forces and were also opposing government attempts in the areas under their control to carry out a census, which was, of course, an essential preliminary to conscription. Relations between the sects and the central authorities had been deteriorating for some months, as had been revealed on 7 June, when the Cao Dai Chief of Staff, Trinh Minh The, together with 2,500 troops had deserted from the 'Holy See' near Tay Ninh and set up his headquarters in an area of swamp and jungle near the Cambodian frontier. His desertion was known, moreover, to have been connived at by the acting Commander-in-Chief of the Cao Dai forces, Nguyen Van Thanh.

Although precedents for The's action were not wanting, the young leader's powerful and disquieting personality lent particular significance to his defection since The had acquired, in the course of the prolonged and confused guerrilla fighting which had devastated Cochin-China, the respect and devotion of the men under his command, together with a reputation for military prowess. His rapid promotion from ferryman on one of Cochin-China's rivers to Chief of Staff of the Cao Dai militia forces had, however, awakened confused ambitions, which transcended the vulgar considerations of self-interest that prompted the actions of his feudal peers, and his hatred of graft and self-indulgence, capacity for ruthless action, and addiction to bouts of hysteria, contributed to the alarm and admiration with which he was regarded. In consequence The, in the absence of nationalist leaders of established reputation and requisite moral stature, had acquired a considerable following even among the Saigon bourgeoisie, who considered that he possessed the qualities and antique virtues which they were reluctantly compelled to admire in the Viet Minh. The creation of a nationalist maquis was therefore welcomed in these circles on the grounds that it might provide a refuge from French-inspired attempts to dragoon them into active participation in the war against the Viet Minh.

The French authorities, aware of the existence of this latent support for the Cao Dai leader, took energetic measures to deprive The and his dissident band of further assistance from the 'Holy See'. The, surprised by this prompt riposte to his desertion, reacted by instigating terrorist outrages in Saigon. The first of these was a dastardly affair: it was contrived by placing clockwork-controlled plastic charges in vehicles which were driven to two car parks in the centre of the town where they blew up and killed or injured some twenty civilians, including enterprising and vivacious children who gained a precarious livelihood by proffering their services as car park attendants. The second was perpetrated by priming bicycle frames with these charges. The bicycles were then wheeled into the courtyard of the Vietnamese security head-quarters, a legitimate target, where their explosion caused a panic but no casualties among the occupants of this sinister building.[26]

The stabilization of the military situation in Tongking had thus failed to produce an equivalent improvement in the moral climate of the nationalist zone, where the leaders of the Cochin-Chinese sects continued to intrigue and rebel against the Franco-Vietnamese authorities, and conscripts for national service were displaying scant enthusiasm for the soldier's lot. This unsatisfactory state of affairs had been revealed both by the defection of Colonel The, and by the assassination, in August 1951, of General Chanson, the French Commissioner for South Vietnam, by a person with ill-defined Cao Dai–Dai Viet affiliations. The nationalists for their part could justify their failure to co-operate by pointing to the illusory nature of their independence, which had effectively been demonstrated in May when the overwrought deputy head of the French Security Service in Dalat had shot out of hand, notwithstanding that Bao Dai himself was then in residence, fourteen men and six women whom he had seized at random, in reprisal for the

[26] The employment of this modern explosive and the ingenuity displayed in its use gave rise to inevitable rumours that The had acquired his 'know-how' from agents of the American Central Intelligence Bureau who, in their desire to promote a third force, had provided the Cao Dai Colonel with some technical assistance in addition to moral support.

murder of the French police commissioner by suspected Viet Minh agents.[27]

### THE ATTACK ON NGHIA LO

With the end of the rainy season the Viet Minh, who had earlier in 1951 carried out a raid into the northern part of the region between the Red and Black rivers, proceeded on 22 September to launch an operation against the southern part of this area with the object of capturing Nghia Lo. This town, fifty-three miles to the west of Yen Bay, is situated in a small and fertile plain at a point where several mountain tracks converge, and constitutes a strategic position of some importance. It was defended by a small garrison, composed of Thai militia troops, who occupied two defence posts, of which one was in Nghia Lo itself while the other was situated on a rocky eminence dominating the town. The Viet Minh, who had committed a division to the operation, launched a furious attack on the French positions on the night of 2–3 October, but in spite of the reckless bravery of the assailants, who returned again and again to the attack, the posts held until dawn, when the arrival of air support forced the Viet Minh to withdraw to the shelter of the surrounding hills. Although the attacks were renewed on the following night, the dropping of two parachute battalions to the north of Nghia Lo and of a third to the south finally compelled the enemy to abandon the operation, and on the 15th Viet Minh advance units recrossed the Red river on their way back to the division's base area near Yen Bay.

The operation, in which the Viet Minh with furious courage and regardless of casualties had launched wave after wave of assailants against isolated French posts, supported and supplied by the French air force, foreshadowed the future character of the war by revealing the ability of the Viet Minh to move their troops and also vast supply trains of coolies across the wild mountainous region between the Red river and the Mekong with relative impunity. The French for their part, faced with these insidious tactics and not being prepared to abandon the whole of north Indochina to the enemy, were to maintain

[27] *The Times*, 17 May 1951. It was later alleged, in mitigation of French responsibility for this atrocity, that the Vietnamese mayor of Dalat had been forewarned of Jumeau's sanguinary intention. But the mayor, underestimating the danger that threatened his compatriots, had merely advised the Frenchman, in view of his overwrought state, to take no immediate action.

isolated garrisons at strategic centres in this vast and rugged mountain area, which were permanently exposed to surprise attacks by marauding enemy forces.

The defence of Nghia Lo had been conducted in de Lattre's absence by his deputy, General Salan, an officer with a long record of service in Indochina. On 19 October de Lattre returned to Saigon, where he was accorded an impressive reception, but in spite of the success of his visit to the United States, the Commander-in-Chief, who had been warned in Paris of the probable nature of the disease from which he was then suffering, had returned in somewhat sombre mood. His temper reflected his physical condition and became increasingly uncertain, and he displayed marked reluctance to deal with arrears of work, mostly of an administrative nature, which had piled up during his absence, or to divert his attention from the military situation in Tongking. But the murder of Jean de Raymond, the French Commissioner in Cambodia, by a Vietnamese servant employed at the Residency on 29 October, gave his civilian advisers a chance to warn him that conditions in that kingdom were causing them concern.

### EVENTS IN CAMBODIA

The deterioration which had taken place in Cambodia both in the political sphere and in public security, could be partly ascribed to the promulgation of a constitution on 6 May 1947, modelled on that of the French Republic: it was fathered by Prince Yutevong, an idealistic and energetic member of the royal family, whose admiration for the French political system had led him to underrate the difficulty of transplanting such a system to a feudal kingdom where the throne represented the only stable institution. This constitution[28] granted Cambodians civil liberties and rights equivalent to those enjoyed by French citizens and established a National Assembly elected by universal suffrage, together with a second chamber, the Council of the Kingdom, the members of which were either designated or elected by the National Assembly and provincial or municipal councils, with powers limited to proposing amendments to, and delaying the enactment of, bills for a period of one month. By its provisions, the royal prerogatives were mainly restricted

[28] Extracts in Cole, pp. 52–57.

to designating the Prime Minister, presiding over cabinet meetings, ratifying legislation, and convoking the National Assembly. The king was also invested with supreme command over the armed forces and empowered to dissolve the National Assembly at the request of the ministers: a prerogative retained at the instance of the French advisers who had assisted in drafting the constitution.

Before his death in July 1947 Prince Yutevong was to prejudice Cambodia's political future still further by founding a political party and providing it with an efficient controlling organization on French lines. This 'Democratic Party' soon attracted to its ranks extremist elements, including disgruntled officials, members of the teaching profession, and Buddhist priests who, although deprived of the right to vote, exercised considerable political influence.

Some indication of the fractious temper of this pseudo-intelligentsia had been afforded in 1946, when a consultative assembly convened to examine the draft constitution had refused to confine its activities to the task in hand and proceeded, despite the protests of the Prime Minister, to discuss political matters. When the National Assembly first met in December 1947, after elections in which the Democratic Party won 54 out of the 74 seats, the irresponsible behaviour of the deputies exceeded the worst forebodings. They showed little interest in the routine business of government and confined themselves principally to intrigues designed to advance party interests and to sterile agitation for complete national independence.

Finally, on 18 September 1949, the king, who was then engaged in negotiating an agreement with the French Government and was aware that the deputies were unlikely to approve its terms, dissolved the Assembly at the request of the Prime Minister, Yem Sambaur, who was himself the leader of a dissident group of Democrat deputies. But this action placed Norodom Sihanouk in a difficult position, since although the constitution laid down that in the event of a dissolution general elections should be held within a maximum period of two months, he was aware that if they were held at that juncture another Democrat majority would be returned. He therefore decided to defer the elections for the time being and to retain Yem Sambaur's Government in office.

On 8 November 1949 a treaty[29] was signed under which Cambodia obtained independence on conditions similar to those accepted earlier in the year by Bao Dai in the Élysée Agreement of 8 March. But in the absence of a National Assembly some other way had to be found to implement its provisions, and it was finally decided to incorporate these provisions in a series of protocols. However, the French authorities in drafting these documents availed themselves of this opportunity to water down some of the concessions obtained under the treaty and Yem Sambaur refused to sign them.[30] This refusal angered the French, and French pressure, combined with accusations of corruption and the Government's failure to cope with the mounting unrest, led to Yem Sambaur's dismissal in May 1950.

During the next twelve months interim Governments were formed under the premiership first of the king and then of his uncle, Prince Monipong. But conditions failed to improve, exports fell off, and Cambodian politicians, who laid the blame for the situation squarely on the French authorities, continued to bicker among themselves. Finally, it was decided to face these politicians with their responsibilities, and to hold elections in September 1951. These elections again resulted in the return of 54 Democrat deputies and the king charged the Democrat leader, Huy Kanthoul, with the task of forming a Government. Shortly afterwards the new Prime Minister profited from Sihanouk's desire for better relations with the Assembly by asking him to arrange with the French authorities for the repatriation of Son Ngoc Thanh, who was regarded as something of a national hero. The French agreed to this and Thanh, who had been living for six years under police supervision in France, returned to Phnom Penh on the day after de Raymond's assassination, to be greeted with great enthusiasm by a large crowd estimated at more than 100,000.

### DE LATTRE'S DEATH

The popular demonstration in Phnom Penh, which seemed partly inspired by an urge to defy the French authorities, combined with the result of the Cambodian elections, added point to the warning which de Lattre had received from his advisers.

[29] *Notes et Études Documentaires*, 7 Dec. 1949, No. 1241.
[30] Herz, p. 81.

But he was to have little time to decide on appropriate action, for it had been arranged that he should return to Paris at the end of November, ostensibly in order to attend the inaugural meeting of the Council of the French Union but in fact for further medical consultations.[31] The intervening weeks were spent mostly in Hanoi, where he completed plans for an offensive designed to wrest the military initiative from the Viet Minh by the occupation of Hoa Binh, a provincial town on the Black river.

The decision to occupy Hoa Binh was based on the calculation that the presence of a French garrison in the town, which represented a vital communication centre for the Viet Minh, would cut the enemy off from the province of Thanh Hoa, which produced the rice surplus needed to feed their troops in the Viet Bac, while their zones to the south would at the same time be deprived of military supplies from the north. The French had failed, however, to take sufficient account of the nature of the terrain, which lent itself to the guerrilla tactics at which the Viet Minh excelled. While Hoa Binh itself is situated in a small plain dominated to the east, north, and south by heights which afford good natural cover, the road (*Route Coloniale* No. 6), which is the sole line of communication with the delta, is bordered along most of its length not only by hills and isolated crags that close in and overshadow it at certain points, but also by the jungle vegetation. Indeed, in view of the difficulties with which the Expeditionary Corps were shortly to contend, there is some grounds to suppose that the operation was designed to induce the recalcitrant National Assembly to vote the war credits—estimated for 1952 at 569 milliard francs[32]—and also to show the Americans that the Expeditionary Corps was prepared, and able on occasion, to abandon the defensive role to which it had been confining its activities since 1948, for the Government's Indochinese policy was now under increasingly heavy attack, both in the United States, where the conduct of military operations was criticized, and in France, where public uneasiness was growing at the cost and protracted nature of the war.

This uneasiness found expression in a debate which took place in the French National Assembly at the end of the year.

[31] Salisbury-Jones, p. 273.
[32] *Le Monde*, 18 Dec. 1952.

During this debate Pierre Mendès-France, a Radical Socialist deputy, basing his argument on technical and financial considerations, urged that attempts to internationalize the war should be abandoned in favour of a negotiated settlement with the Viet Minh. After a review of France's parlous economic state, which restricted freedom of action in the international sphere by reducing French Governments to humiliating dependence on American aid, he concluded his speech with the following assessment of the damage which was being caused to France's position in Europe by her commitments in Asia.

You will never succeed in organizing the national defences in Europe [he said] if you continue to send all your cadres to the East, to sacrifice every year, without any result, the equivalent of the number of officers leaving St. Cyr in a year and to spend annually 500 milliard francs, representing an additional 500 milliards of monetary inflation, which will bring in its train want, rising prices, and further social unrest which will not fail to be exploited by Communist propaganda. . . . By an incredible paradox, we have accorded priority to Asia at the very time when, in opposition to MacArthur's policy, in opposition to the policy of the old, isolationist Americans, the 'Europeans' from Churchill to Pleven last year, are upholding the thesis of the priority of Europe in the United States. . . .[33]

This speech was widely discussed and generally approved in France, but the cynical preparedness that it revealed to sacrifice the Vietnamese nationalists on grounds of expediency caused grave embarrassment to the French authorities in Indochina, where the Governments of the Associate States were just then being urged to increase their military and financial participation in the war. In France, however, even the MRP leaders, who had been mainly responsible for Indochinese policy, were compelled to take into account the increasing restiveness of the electorate and to express their readiness to envisage a negotiated settlement. This change of attitude was expressed in January 1952 by Robert Schuman, a former Prime Minister, who declared at a meeting of MRP supporters in the Department of the Haute Garonne that 'If an armistice can be concluded on honourable terms, France will not hesitate to make peace'[34]

[33] *L'Année Politique, 1951*, p. 401.
[34] *Le Monde*, 8 Jan. 1952.

On 10 November 1951, in order to close a gap in the defences and to delude the enemy in regard to French intentions, French forces reoccupied Cho Ben, a village thirty miles south-west of Hanoi which commanded access to the delta. Three days later a force composed of fifteen battalions accompanied by artillery units and armoured vehicles occupied Hoa Binh and a section of the Black river valley. This operation was completed by the 15th, when the shock formations withdrew, leaving the troops who had been detailed to hold the area to establish themselves in fortified positions. De Lattre meanwhile had assured Letourneau, the Minister of the Associate States, in a telegram which he sent to announce the successful conclusion of the operation, that the reoccupation of Hoa Binh represented more than a mere raid into enemy territory.[35]

On 20 November the General returned to France. Before his departure he contrived to show his constant preoccupation with the welfare of the troops, which constituted a likeable trait in his complex character, and also his ability to get the better of the hard-headed and tight-fisted representatives of French commercial and financial interests who were entrenched in Cochin-China. During a brief visit to Saigon he invited the leading representatives of these interests to attend a reception at the Palais Norodom. As the General had hitherto chosen to ignore the existence of this wealthy community, which had formerly enjoyed social precedence in the colony, the invitations caused both pleasure and some speculation among the recipients, but the motive behind this social volte-face was revealed when their host, satrap-fashion, informed his guests, many of whom were making exorbitant profits and exploiting to advantage the favourable exchange-rate, of his desire that they should subscribe the large sum of 25 million piastres for the Expeditionary Corps' Christmas celebrations. The General's guests, who had not hitherto given much thought to the welfare of the troops, and whose contribution to the war had been principally confined to the repatriation of profits and the transfer of capital, were taken aback by the means employed to present the demand and also by the amount which they were required to pay, but after hurried consultations they undertook to attempt to raise the required sum,[36] with the proviso that the

[35] Ibid. 16 Nov. 1951.
[36] A further precaution that was taken was to arrange, through political con-

levy should not be considered to constitute a precedent. Their alarm proved to be unnecessary since on 19 December de Lattre entered a Paris nursing home where after an operation he died on 11 January 1952.

On the day of his death he was raised to the dignity of Marshal of France: the news is reported to have been greeted by the dying man with the demand for an assurance that he was the only one to be thus honoured.

### THE EVACUATION OF HOA BINH

Generous tributes have been paid to de Lattre's achievements in Indochina. After his death the press, which he had consistently courted and skilfully exploited, contributed generously to a final apotheosis by tacitly ascribing even the grim necessity for an operation on the prostate gland to the hero's brief service in the Far East. The exact nature and importance of the contribution he made towards the prosecution of the war remains to be established, but the vital improvement in morale which followed his arrival in Saigon must certainly be ascribed entirely to de Lattre's credit. His refusal to countenance the evacuation of Tongking, his bold assumption of responsibilities which his predecessors had neither been entitled nor prepared to shoulder, combined with the salutary alarm which his presence inspired, all contributed to steel the wavering resolution of the Expeditionary Corps for the battles of Vinh Yen and Dong Trieu. Moreover the reputation he had acquired in Europe had served the French well, for the knowledge that he was opposed by a famous general appears to have incited Giap, who was anxious to prove that his own military talents were not merely confined to an ability to direct guerrilla activities, to expose Viet Minh regular troops in massed formations to punishment by French artillery and aircraft.

De Lattre, however, had introduced no radical changes in the conduct of the war, and by his refusal to envisage any attempt to reassert French control over land communications with China had tacitly admitted that a military victory at this stage was beyond the grasp of the Expeditionary Corps. He had contented himself, therefore, with increasing the number and

tacts in Paris, for the question of the General's arbitrary behaviour to be raised in the National Assembly.

effectiveness of the mobile groups, commandos, armoured and artillery units which were employed to raid enemy territory and to relieve hard-pressed garrisons. He had also strengthened the static defences of the Red river delta by the construction of a chain of fortifications that were destined to immobilize the equivalent of twenty battalions in defence duties and to prove ineffectual against Viet Minh infiltration.

De Lattre's failure to effect any basic change in strategy which would enable the French Union troops to recover their mobility makes it unlikely that the Expeditionary Corps was deprived of final victory by his death, but if his contribution in the military field was not decisive, his attempt to rally international support for a war which had hitherto lacked its impresario did meet with considerable success. It was fortunate indeed that at a time when Chinese Communist aid to the Viet Minh forces had shown the international implications of the struggle, the French cause should have had an advocate who could assure the American people with the accents of sincerity that France's action in Indochina was disinterested. Moreover, profiting from the changed character of the war, de Lattre was able during his brief proconsulate to give decisive impetus to the tardy formation of a Vietnamese army, first by persuading the Vietnamese to accept the principle of national conscription, and secondly by successfully negotiating in Washington for military aid to equip the national divisions that it was now proposing to raise and train.

However, these considerable achievements had been facilitated by a readiness in exchange for some immediate advantage to make promises and to give assurances which represented mortgages on the future. This reckless propensity was to place Salan, who succeeded de Lattre, in possession of an encumbered inheritance, and in spite of his predecessor's assurance to the contrary Salan was soon faced with the delicate and thankless task of withdrawing French Union troops from Hoa Binh since Giap, who had boasted after the fall of the frontier posts that French military activities would be confined henceforth to the Red river delta, now accepted the challenge which the French presence at Hoa Binh constituted to this claim. Two Viet Minh divisions, one based in North Annam and the other in the Viet Bac, had been dispatched to reinforce a third division near the Black river, while the remaining divisions, located to the north, east, and south-west of the delta, were instructed to profit from the absence of French operational troops in the Hoa Binh salient in order to infiltrate into the delta. Finally, on 10 December 1951, after preliminary skirmishes, the Viet Minh launched a night attack with a force of from four to five battalions on Tu Vu, the hinge of the line of posts established by the French to the north of Hoa Binh along the course of the Black river. This attack was carried out by successive waves of assailants, and although many foundered in the minefields or fell to machine-gun fire, a breach was finally blown in the defences, and after fierce hand-to-hand fighting the survivors of the garrison were driven to take refuge on an island in the middle of the stream. The arrival of aircraft, however, enabled the French to reoccupy the post next morning.[37]

The Viet Minh, displaying remarkable aggressive spirit, continued to keep up their pressure on the French posts along the Black river, with the result that Salan ordered the evacuation of this salient in order to devote his attention and reserves to the battle for Hoa Binh itself. The decision to evacuate the Black river posts proved a wise one, for Viet Minh pressure increased with the result that by the beginning of January 1952 communications between Hoa Binh and the delta were cut. In consequence the task of supplying the French garrison devolved upon the air force, who were able to use for this task a small airstrip, which was, however, both difficult to approach from the air and dominated by heights on which the Viet Minh had installed anti-aircraft guns and mortars.

On 1 January the Viet Minh attempted to complete the isolation of the Hoa Binh garrison by the capture of Xom Pheo, an important relay point along the road, but although the attack was repulsed with heavy loss, the position of the beleaguered garrison in Hoa Binh was precarious. Four days after this attack Salan decided to dispatch Mobile Group No. 1, which had played a major part in the victory at Vinh Yen, in an attempt to reopen communications with Hoa Binh by clearing Viet Minh guerrilla units and the jungle vegetation from the immediate vicinity of the road and then to assist in the evacuation of the garrison. This decision seems to have been hastened by the knowledge that Viet Minh regular troops who were not engaged in the Black river area were attacking defence

[37] Marchand, pp. 174-7.

posts in the delta where they had succeeded in establishing a corridor of hostile territory, stretching from Dong Trieu in the west to Phat Diem in the south. The French mobile group proceeded to carry out the first part of its arduous task in a methodical fashion, but the rate of advance was so slow that they did not reach Hoa Binh until 20 February. Two days later Salan ordered the garrison and the troops based on the strongpoints guarding the road to evacuate their positions. The evacuation seems to have surprised the Viet Minh, who did not believe that the French would be prepared to incur the resultant 'loss of face'. Their failure to divine the French intention caused them to react too slowly and too late, with the result that by the 25th the French column, composed of 20,000 troops and auxiliaries, were able to regain the shelter of their fortifications in the delta.

When the evacuation had been completed both the French and Viet Minh claimed that the operation had been a success. Whereas the French stressed that all major Viet Minh attacks had been repulsed with heavy loss to the enemy's elusive main striking force, which was estimated to have incurred heavy casualties,[38] and claimed that enemy plans to carry out a general attack on French defence positions along the Red river had been foiled, the Viet Minh pointed out, with some justification, that they had compelled the French to renounce their declared intention to maintain a garrison in Hoa Binh, and had demonstrated by their ability to force a withdrawal that the expulsion of French garrisons from the upland and mountainous regions of Tongking was final.[39] Moreover the Viet Minh had profited from the absence of the French units in order to infiltrate their regular troops into the delta, where most of the villages were now under their control.

Whether or not the operations around Hoa Binh had been to the mutual advantage of the contending parties, the course of the fighting had at least confirmed the accuracy of information which had been reaching the French Staff that, after the opening of armistice negotiations in Korea, the provision of Chinese military aid had been resumed on a substantial scale,

[38] Chassin, p. 124.
[39] According to statements made after the armistice by members of Giap's entourage, after their reoccupation of Hoa Binh the Viet Minh concluded that victory lay within their grasp (Henri Navarre, *Agonie de l'Indochine* (1956), p. 23 n.).

for the Viet Minh forces had shown that they were liberally equipped with light arms, machine-guns, mortars, anti-aircraft guns, and ammunition.[40] But if the improvement in Viet Minh armaments might have been foreseen, their ability to maintain, for a period of months, three divisions on operation service in an inhospitable region occasioned considerable surprise. This had been made possible by the heroic efforts of the entire civilian population in the Viet Minh zone which had been converted for the purposes of war into a vast labour camp. Indeed it was estimated in January 1952, by a French military spokesman in Hanoi, that the 'human supply trains' at the disposal of the divisions surrounding Hoa Binh comprised from 150,000 to 200,000 porters. These porters presented an easy target for aircraft attacks 'with machine-gun fire and napalm bombs as they trudged over the open plains',[41] while in the hill country they were exposed to the risk of malarial infection in a virulent form. The tragic lot of these civilians, of whom a large number were women, caused scant concern to the Viet Minh leaders, who occasionally recompensed some superhuman logistic exploit by the award of a 'Resistance Medal III Class'.

[40] R. Guillain in *Manchester Guardian*, 11 Feb. 1952.
[41] *NYHT*, 19 Jan. 1952.

# XIV

# From the Death of de Lattre to the Appointment of Navarre

THE news of de Lattre's death was received with dismay in Indochina, but gratitude for his services was tempered in some measure by recollection of the exacting and capricious manner in which he had exercised his authority. Moreover the civil servants and staff officers who had been accustomed, during his frequent absences, to deal with current affairs were able for some months to maintain the illusion of continuity and even, by the avoidance of bold initiatives, a precarious *status quo*. At the beginning of April 1952, the French Government announced that Jean Letourneau had agreed to assume the functions of High Commissioner and Minister for the Associate States, while General Raoul Salan was officially appointed Commander-in-Chief of Land, Sea, and Air Forces.[1] These appointments appeared to reveal a desire on the part of the Government to consolidate the achievements of an inflationary period in Indochinese affairs, and to reassert the pre-eminence of the civil authority.

Meanwhile the formation of a Vietnamese army had been making but slow progress since although the creation of such an army had been conceded in principle by the terms of the Élysée agreement, while the complementary agreements of 8 and 23 December 1950 respectively had provided for the formation of four divisions by the end of 1951, delays in the delivery of American equipment, combined with the reluctance of the French Command to surrender direct control over the Vietnamese units serving with the Expeditionary Corps, had prevented the implementation of this plan. In consequence, although thirty-six battalions of Vietnamese troops were in existence by January 1952, only one division had been formed, and that was assigned to the defence of the Crown Domains, while the remaining three divisions, without staff, artillery,

[1] *Le Monde*, 1 Apr. 1952.

engineers, and communications sections, consisted merely of a mosaic of infantry battalions.[2]

At the beginning of 1952, however, the French Ministry of National Defence, yielding to American pressure, decided to proceed without delay with the formation of two further Vietnamese divisions, using for that purpose stocks of clothing, equipment, and arms available in France,[3] and on 22 February the High Military Committee met in Saigon, to discuss the measures that should be taken to give effect to this decision. The measures decided upon included the appointment of Wing-Commander Nguyen Van Hinh[4] to the post of Chief of Staff of the Vietnamese army. Hinh, who was given the rank of Brigadier-General in that army, set up his headquarters, which included departments to handle the affairs of a future navy and air force, in Saigon.[5]

The task facing the General Staff was a considerable one. Although a large contingent of Vietnamese troops were serving with the Expeditionary Corps, Vietnamese officers were in short supply,[6] and although training facilities were adequate in the long run to remedy this deficiency, no short-term solution could be devised.[7] Moreover the recruitment of cadets of suitable calibre was hampered by the disaffection of the educated class. Consequently when young men with the necessary qualifications failed to come forward in sufficient numbers, the Vietnamese Government was compelled to conscript students who were attending courses at the university. Unfortunately the officers recruited by this method displayed in some cases more interest in the perquisites and privileges attaching to their rank than in the efficient discharge of their duties, an attitude which was combined on occasion with a townsman's disdain for the peasant soldiers whom they were appointed to command. The supercilious attitude of these scions of the bourgeoisie towards

[2] R. Guillain in *Le Monde*, 29 Jan. 1952; 'Gen. XX' in ibid. 15 Mar. 1952; Max Clos in *Combat*, 6 Mar. 1952.

[3] 'Gen. XX' in *Le Monde*, 15 Mar. 1952.

[4] See below, p. 430.

[5] A training school for air force personnel was opened in 1952 at Nha Trang, where a naval training school was also established in 1953 (*Combat*, 5 July 1952).

[6] Although 700 Vietnamese officers had been commissioned, only 80 were field officers, of whom four held the rank of colonel.

[7] Guillain in *Manchester Guardian*, 29 Jan. 1952. During 1952 50 Vietnamese officers were sent to France to attend courses at the Staff College and at naval, air, and communications training centres (*Combat*, 5 July 1952).

officers of the ill-armed and underpaid militia bodies was also a recurrent cause of friction and resentment, for many of the officers in the auxiliary forces, in spite of proven military capacity, were themselves debarred by lack of the requisite scholastic qualifications from access to the better-paid officer corps of the regular army.

In spite of the dearth of qualified and competent cadres, the ranks of the Vietnamese army were rapidly swollen during the following months by the transfer of locally raised units serving with the Expeditionary Corps, by the incorporation of militia troops, and by recruitment. These methods resulted by the end of the year in the creation of a Vietnamese army comprising fifty-four infantry and two parachute battalions, together with four artillery groups and some transport and maintenance units.[8] The cost of raising, paying, training, and arming these troops was apportioned between Vietnam, France, and the United States.[9]

The manner in which the Vietnamese financial contribution was assessed was to give rise, however, to some criticism, for a French parliamentary mission paying the customary annual visit to Indochina on behalf of the Budget Committee at the beginning of 1952 had been surprised and scandalized to discover that Vietnam had no budget. On 10 April, therefore, a member of the mission called the attention of the French National Assembly to this state of affairs, pointing out that in the absence of a budget both the use that the Vietnamese Government was making of funds advanced by the French treasury, and the proportion of the national revenue devoted to national defence, remained a matter for conjecture.[10] Letourneau, who was aware that criticism of this nature would have an adverse effect on the resolution of the National Assembly to prosecute the war, consequently presented Bao Dai with a list of proposals which included, in addition to the preparation of a budget, certain general measures designed to increase the national war effort.[11]

Although Bao Dai agreed on the expediency of the proposed

[8] *Annuaire des États Associés, 1953*, p. 69.
[9] The Vietnamese contribution to this common financial effort amounted in 1951 to 20 milliard francs, or an estimated 40 per cent. of the national revenue (ibid.).
[10] *Le Monde*, 11 Apr. 1952.
[11] *Figaro*, 24 Apr. 1952.

measures, neither the Prime Minister nor the cabinet, which continued to be composed principally of Huu's Cochin-Chinese friends, appeared to be capable of the incisive action that was now needed. Moreover the Prime Minister had acquired the conviction that he was both a statesman of international calibre and enjoyed considerable popular support in the country;[12] illusions which had led him to alienate French support by unconvincing attempts to assume the mantle of the patriot and to antagonize the head of the state by the private expression of the opinion that the expense involved in the maintenance of an imperial cabinet at Dalat represented an unjustifiable waste of public monies. This opinion was duly retailed to Bao Dai who, in spite of the eccentric location of his residence, was well informed about the sentiments of his ministers and despite such disparaging appraisement of his services intended to remain the architect of national independence and the arbitrator of nationalist differences. Moreover he was ably seconded in this determination by his principal private secretary,[13] Nguyen De,[14] who was generally credited in Saigon with a remarkable capacity for intrigue.

In June, therefore, Nguyen Van Tam was appointed to the premiership.[15] The new Prime Minister, who had acquired a reputation for energy and efficiency in the repression of terrorist activities, was to turn these qualities to good account. The cabinet was formed in the short space of three days. It included Le Thang, a representative of the Dai Viet Party from North Vietnam, and also Pham Van Giao, the monarchist Governor of Central Vietnam, who had acquired a legendary reputation for bold peculation and extravagant behaviour in his inaccessible fief.[16] The new Government then proceeded to elaborate without loss of time a number of measures, including a labour

---

[12] Even his colleagues in the cabinet were taken aback when Huu blandly assumed, on his return from the San Francisco Conference, that the civil servants detailed to greet him at the Saigon airfield and the schoolchildren who lined the route and waved flags in the rain had assembled spontaneously to do him honour.

[13] Prince Buu Loc, who had previously discharged these functions, was nominated Vietnamese High Commissioner in France in July 1952.

[14] See below, p. 430.

[15] Persistent and improbable rumours had been in circulation which may have originated in Dalat to the effect that Huu was plotting a coup d'état.

[16] Giao was responsible during the months of January and April 1949 alone for the financial transfers to France totalling 84 million francs (*L'Observateur*, 21 May 1953, p. 13).

code and a set of regulations which provided existing trade unions with legal status and also circumscribed their activities, and draft proposals for agrarian reform, while a decree was promulgated which set up a provisional national Consultative Council of twenty-one members, who were to be nominated for these duties by the head of the state.[17] The preparation of a budget was also taken in hand, and in August the Minister of Finance, who had managed at last to master the technical intricacies involved, produced the long awaited statement of the national finances. This budget instituted cuts in expenditure by government departments, and appropriated for defence purposes 58 per cent. of the national revenue, or some 30 milliard francs.[18]

In June Letourneau went to Washington to discuss increases in American aid. These discussions resulted in an agreement that American military and financial assistance should be increased to cover 40 per cent. of French expenditure in Indochina.[19] and the French undertook to use this additional aid to build up the national armies of the Associate States.[20]

Letourneau's visit also provided France with some moral satisfaction since in the final communiqué issued on 18 June the American Government temporarily overcame past suspicions of French intentions and explicitly recognized that

the struggle in which the forces of the French Union and the Associate States are engaged against the forces of Communist aggression in Indochina is an integral part of the world-wide resistance by the Free Nations to Communist attempts at conquest and subversion.[21]

In spite of the success of his mission, however, the Minister for the Associate States was still faced with the task of obtaining the approval of the National Assembly for expenditure estimated for the coming year at 589 milliard francs, or 8 per

---

[17] The debates and activities of the national Council, like those of the censors' council and the regional assemblies, were conducted with such discretion that these bodies appear to have been created solely in order to provide a contingent of representatives at official functions.

[18] Vietnamese were also doing their bit on the field of battle, and casualties among Vietnamese troops had accounted for 52 per cent. of the total French Union losses during the early part of the year (*Figaro*, 19 June 1952).

[19] *Combat*, 26 June 1952.

[20] *DSB*, 30 June 1952, p. 1010.

[21] Ibid.

cent. of the total French budget, a sum only partially offset by American aid, which was to be increased during 1953 from 200 milliard to 269 milliard francs.[22] But whereas the vote of the credits for 1952 had been facilitated by de Lattre's personal prestige and by the reoccupation of Hoa Binh, the inducement that was now to be offered to the recalcitrant deputies was the prospect that the Vietnamese army would shortly be in a position to assume some of the duties hitherto discharged by units of the Expeditionary Corps. Salan was therefore persuaded, in order to lend substance to this pretension, to accept a small reduction in the strength of the Expeditionary Corps, which was cut from 190,000 to 174,000.[23] Appropriate publicity was also given to the relief of a French Union battalion by a unit of the Vietnamese troops.[24]

The favourable evolution of the military situation was further stressed in November by the hand-over to Vietnamese militia units of security duties in the 'Old Provinces' of Cochin-China, which comprised territory to the south and west of Saigon–Cholon. The command of Vietnamese troops in these provinces was given to Colonel Jean Leroy,[25] a Eurasian who had previously held the post of administrator and military commander of Ben Tre province, which included an island of that name in the Mekong estuary. The decision to entrust Leroy with responsibility for military security in the 'Old Provinces' may have been inspired by the desire to remove an over-enterprising provincial administrator from his post and to incorporate the militia force under his command with the national army, but Hinh was aware that the type of warfare practised by Cao Dai 'Colonel' Trinh Minh The, Hoa Hao 'Colonel' Le Quang Vinh alias 'Ba Cut', and Leroy himself in their attempts to dispute with the Viet Minh—and on occasion with each other—the control of the Cochin-Chinese countryside conformed more closely to the national military traditions and represented a more effective means of combating the Viet Minh than the classic methods of warfare for which the Vietnamese troops were being trained and lavishly equipped.

The national army had inherited, together with the transport

[22] Report presented by Frédéric-Dupont to the Financial Committee for the military budget of the Associate States (*Le Monde*, 18 Dec. 1952).
[23] Navarre, pp. 26–27.
[24] Jean Lacouture in *Le Monde*, 12 Nov. 1952.
[25] See below, p. 429.

facilities designed to spare the French Union infantry undue fatigue, the inability of these heavily equipped troops to operate on foot, and in particular at night, against the enemy. In order to remedy this the Vietnamese General Staff towards the end of 1952 produced a plan for the creation of light battalions which would be entrusted with the task of combating Viet Minh regional troops and pacifying areas from which enemy regular units had been expelled.[26] By the beginning of 1953 this plan had been approved in principle by the French Government, and a meeting of the High Military Committee, attended by Letourneau and Juin, was held at Dalat in February at which the decision was reached to proceed without delay with the formation of these battalions, for which the Americans had undertaken to provide arms and equipment.

With the proviso that operational control should remain vested in the French Command the French representatives also agreed to recognize the autonomy of the Vietnamese army and to keep Bao Dai informed both of military plans and of the progress of operations.[27] Although the decision to proceed with the formation of these battalions was generally considered to represent the first step towards the formation of an effective national army,[28] Hinh's subsequent refusal to form these units from the partially trained militia troops, now numbering 120,000, entailed the enrolment of conscripts who were to be brought, in some instances under duress, to the training camps established for this purpose in North, Central, and South Vietnam.[29] These press-gang methods were, however, to have an adverse effect on the morale of these hastily trained units, and it was estimated that in Cochin-China by the end of 1953 an average of one out of the four companies composing a light

[26] This plan proposed the immediate mobilization of 40,000 conscripts who, after a brief course of training in guerrilla warfare, would be formed into light battalions each to have a strength of about 600 men and be officered exclusively by Vietnamese. Their armament would consist of sub-machine guns, rifles, grenade-throwers, and bazookas, while their action was to be supported in case of need by a force composed of fourteen companies equipped with mortars, 75 mm. guns, and machine-guns (Claude Guigues in *Indochine Sud-est Asiatique*, No. 23, Nov. 1953).

[27] *Annuaire des États Associés, 1953*, p. 72. The first intimation that Bao Dai had received of the French intention to evacuate Hoa Binh was the broadcast announcement that the operation had been completed (David Schoenbrun in *Colliers*, 30 Sept. 1955).

[28] Navarre, p. 58.

[29] Jean Leroy, *Un Homme dans la rizière* (1955), pp. 164–6.

battalion had deserted after six months' service, while the survivors were signally lacking in offensive spirit and adamant in their refusal to serve outside the region in which they had been conscripted.[30]

### THE VIET MINH OFFENSIVE IN NORTH VIETNAM

After the evacuation of Hoa Binh in February 1952 French Union troops in Tongking had been engaged during the rainy season in a series of operations designed to expel Viet Minh regular units from the delta, into which they had infiltrated in some thousands when the French forces were engaged in the Hoa Binh salient. These operations, in which aircraft, artillery, and armoured units were employed, had for their objective the pacification of a delimited area by the piecemeal destruction of Viet Minh hide-outs and the systematic elimination of Viet Minh agents: the pacification was preceded by a military occupation of the area, which was then surrounded and isolated from contact with neighbouring villages, while a team[31] of Vietnamese technicians and specialists, under the protection of militia troops, completed a security check of the population, appointed local administrators, provided essential relief, restored internal communications, and reopened markets.

Although the Viet Minh were able to keep most of their gains in the delta, and in particular to maintain their control over the countryside to the south of the Hanoi–Haiphong road where the Viet Minh Division 320 remained concealed in the Phu Ly–Thai Binh area, the pacification carried out by these laborious methods was to have a more durable effect than previous 'mopping-up' operations of a similar nature. These activities, however, were abandoned towards the end of the year, when available troops were withdrawn in order to meet a Viet Minh offensive which had developed against the French defence positions along the upper reaches of the Black river in North-West Tongking. For the Viet Minh Command had been engaged during the summer months in preparing their divisions for the winter campaigning season, a task facilitated by a

---

[30] Jean Leroy, *Un Homme dans la rizière* (1955), p. 166.

[31] The teams, which were named Mobile Administrative Groups for Operational Purposes (GAMO), had been formed at the instigation of Nguyen Huu Tri, Governor of North Vietnam.

generous provision of Chinese military aid, including ammunition, light arms, and anti-aircraft guns of various calibres, some
105 mm. guns, and a few trucks of Russian manufacture.[32]
In addition to war material, the Chinese authorities were also
providing facilities for training and re-equipping Viet Minh
units in camps located in the border provinces of Yunnan and
Kwangsi, while an increasing number of Chinese military
advisers, instructors, and members of the army medical corps
continued to arrive in Tongking, where they proceeded to
provide the Viet Minh with the benefit of experience acquired
in the course of the 'Chinese People's War of Liberation'.
Nevertheless, in spite of the efforts that were made to establish
Sino-Vietnamese relations on a basis of mutual cordiality and
confidence, the Viet Minh were quick to perceive that their
mentors, for all their tendency to pontificate, had little to teach
them in the conduct of guerrilla operations under local conditions.

By the beginning of October Viet Minh preparations for an
offensive were far advanced. Three divisions had been concentrated in the Phu Tho–Yen Bay area, and a fourth division
in Thanh Hoa province was preparing to take the offensive.
These troop dispositions led the French Command to suppose
that a major attack was impending on the delta, but on
14 October the divisions concentrated in North-West Tongking
crossed the Red river and, moving with speed across difficult
terrain, proceeded to carry out a series of attacks on French
posts in the region bounded by the Red and Black rivers. On
the night of 17–18 October one of these divisions delivered a
furious assault on the defence positions at Nghia Lo, which
had repulsed an attack in September of the previous year, and
succeeded on this occasion in overwhelming the garrison of
French-officered Thai troops. After the capture of Nghia Lo
the small French posts throughout the area, which had been
established merely to check guerrilla infiltrations and to exercise

---

[32] Deliveries of Chinese aid, consisting for the most part of arms of American
manufacture captured either from the Kuomintang armies or from American
forces in Korea, were estimated to have averaged some 3,000 tons a month since
the beginning of the year (Guigues in *Indochine Sud-est Asiatique*, No. 16, Mar.
1953). Consignments were brought to a railhead at the Chinese town of Ping-siang
near the frontier town of Lang Son, whence they were brought within Indochinese
territory to Cao Bang. These consignments were shifted by trucks and porters, in
spite of frequent air attacks, to the Viet Minh base around Thai Nguyen (R.
Guillain, *La Fin des illusions* (1954), p. 41).

general surveillance over the countryside, either fell to the Viet Minh or were abandoned in haste by their garrisons who withdrew by mountain paths to the Black river, where a line of watch towers and defence positions guarded the road (*Route Provinciale* 41) through the Thai-inhabited province of Son La to Lai Chau. On 23 October Viet Minh units reached the left bank of the Black river, where they halted to regroup and to await supplies which had been delayed by ceaseless air attacks on their extended lines of communication.

Meanwhile the French Command, who had been surprised both by the speed and the direction of the offensive, reacted to the emergency by instructing the retreating French Union troops to make either for Lai Chau, or for Na San some thirty miles to the south of Son La, where the existence of a landing ground would enable them to be reinforced and supplied or, if necessary, evacuated. Immediate steps were then taken to fortify the perimeter of these localities, civil aircraft being requisitioned to assist in the transport of the large amount of freight required for the purpose. These measures were accompanied by a decision to profit from the absence of the Viet Minh divisions from the Viet Bac in order to launch a reconnaissance in force in the direction of Yen Bay, a communications centre of great importance to the enemy.

On 3 November, a French force consisting of four mobile groups supported by armoured units and a naval detachment occupied Phu Tho, but although 250 tons of war material were captured and a number of arms workshops destroyed, the French failed to attain their objective. During the withdrawal a motorized and armoured brigade was ambushed by a Viet Minh regiment which had returned by forced marches from the north-west, and in the course of the ensuing engagement it suffered heavy casualties. Towards the middle of November the Viet Minh units on the left bank of the Black river were ready to launch the second phase of their offensive, and after overcoming French resistance to the north of Son La, they advanced on Dien Bien Phu, which they occupied towards the end of the month. While these operations were in progress the division from the Viet Minh-occupied province of Thanh Hoa had been coming up from the south, capturing in the course of their advance the defence posts at Balay and Moc Chau. On 23 November, advance units of this division approached Na San where they expected to encounter little resistance, but the delay had enabled the French to install a garrison of ten battalions there, and these were now entrenched behind barbed wire and minefields on the crests of the hills enclosing the airstrip. The Viet Minh, surprised by the strength of the French defences, thus failed to occupy the place.

On the night of 30 November–1 December, the Viet Minh again assailed the entrenched camp with a force of nine battalions, and concentrating their attack on two positions to the east and west of the perimeter respectively, breached the defences, but were compelled to relinquish this foothold next day. Although the attack was renewed, no further breach was made in the defences.

After the failure of this third and final attempt to capture Na San the Viet Minh, who were estimated to have suffered some 7,000 casualties, confined themselves to harassing action against the French positions designed to discourage any attempt by the garrison to raid their supply lines. The successful resistance at Na San was estimated by the French Command to have delayed the Viet Minh for three months in their advance to the river Mekong, but in spite of sorties by the garrison, on 20 and 29 December to Son La and eastwards to Kho Ngoi respectively, the French were unable to cut the enemy supply route across the Moc plateau, and after the Viet Minh attacks had been repulsed the entrenched camp served principally to immobilize a force of from ten to twelve French Union battalions whose requirements in arms, ammunition, food, and comforts represented a heavy commitment for the French air force.

Meanwhile the frugal and indefatigable Viet Minh troops, accompanied by hordes of porters, were able to range at will throughout the mountainous region where the forests and a canopy of morning cloud provided protection from air attack. The Viet Minh completed their incursion into North-West Tongking by crossing the Laotian frontier and overrunning the border posts in the province of Houa Phans, but with their supplies exhausted they postponed their attack on the provincial administrative centre of Sam Neua until the following campaigning season.

Although the bulk of their regular forces were engaged in the mountainous region, the Viet Minh were still able to occupy

French reserves elsewhere, and in Tongking, where the presence of two regular regiments and the Division 320 constituted a permanent threat to communications between Hanoi and Haiphong, the town of Phat Diem was attacked on 12 December. However, after some initial confusion, the Viet Minh, who seem to have been surprised by the speed and vigour of the French reaction, were repulsed with heavy casualties.

While enemy activities in the Red river delta were continuing to cause the French Command some uneasiness, unwelcome proof was afforded of the Viet Minh's ability to mount an offensive in Southern Annam, where the narrow coastal plains stretching south from Tourane to Cape Varella constituted the fifth Viet Minh military interzone, or *Lien Khu* V. The build-up of the armed forces in this region had hitherto been handicapped by the tenuous and precarious nature of communications with Viet Minh headquarters in the north. In January 1953, however, six regular Viet Minh battalions carried out an attack on posts guarding the approaches to An Khe, a township commanding an important approach to the upland regions, which stretch from the summit of the Annam chain to the river Mekong. Although some of these posts were either evacuated or captured, An Khe itself was saved by the dispatch of three parachute battalions: the timely arrival of these reinforcements also served to relieve pressure on Kontum and Pleiku, which were in danger of being overrun by Viet Minh raiding parties.

The French riposte followed on 29 January when a force of three naval commandos landed at Qui Nhon and proceeded to advance inland across the plain of Binh Dinh. This threat to their base area compelled the Viet Minh to withdraw the bulk of their forces from the upland region. When their objective had been achieved the French force re-embarked, evacuating with them 3,000 civilians, who seized this opportunity to escape from Viet Minh tyranny and from the destitution which was the lot of the population in *Lien Khu* V. But although they failed in their attempt to establish a permanent foothold in the upland region, the Viet Minh had been able nevertheless to leave behind them agents and partisans whose presence and activities maintained the local Bahnar tribal groups in a state of unrest.

## THE THREAT TO LUANG PRABANG

During the winter of 1952–3 reports continued to be received indicating that the Viet Minh were proposing to launch a spring offensive in the direction of the river Mekong. These reports revealed great activity among the Viet Minh regional troops, partisans, and agents, who had been implanted in North-West Tongking. Viet Minh agents were also engaged in reconnoitring Laotian territory, where they contacted local tribal groups whose services were used to locate military posts and to find out the strength of the garrisons. Reports were also received that representatives of the Viet Minh commissariat were purchasing available stocks of rice in this area, this rice then being concealed near the mountain tracks which Viet Minh units would shortly be using.

These clandestine activities were facilitated by the fact that Viet Minh agents and emissaries were not operating in *terra incognita*, for Viet Minh intervention in the internal affairs of Laos had begun in the spring of 1946, when their armed bands had assisted the Lao Issara in their resistance to the French reoccupation. After the flight of the Lao Issara leaders to Bangkok Viet Minh regional troops had kept up their pressure on the frontier posts, while their emissaries on their journeys to and from Siam had continued to pass through Laotian territory.

The Viet Minh had also exploited particularist tendencies and latent discontent with Lao rule among the ethnic minorities in order to stir up unrest in certain extraneous localities, including the region of Attopeu, where the Kha population had long resisted French attempts to establish their authority. Viet Minh armed bands were also active around Ma Ha Xay, astride one of the main supply routes from Siam to the Viet Minh-occupied provinces of North Annam, and in the region to the north of Vientiane, where their presence had effectively interrupted for some years road and river traffic between the administrative and royal capitals. These activities in Laotian territory were accompanied by preparations in Tongking, where toiling hordes of porters were engaged in building up stocks of food and ammunition at the limit of the assembly area from which the Viet Minh would shortly be launching their offensive.

Meanwhile French aircraft, in an attempt to delay this

18

offensive, were engaged in incessant raids on Viet Minh troop concentrations, in the Yen Bay–Phu Tho area and in Thanh Hoa province. Raids were also maintained on Viet Minh communications in an attempt to interrupt deliveries of Chinese military aid from Cao Bang and to halt the traffic between Hoa Binh and Moc Chau, which represented the advance base for the impending operations.

Besides these offensive activities the decision was also taken to fortify the perimeter of the airstrip on the Tran Ninh plateau in order to provide a refuge in case of need for the garrisons of outlying posts in the Laotian province of Xieng Khouang. This decision was implemented without loss of time by the dispatch of five battalions to this distant locality, together with essential equipment for the improvement of the airstrip itself.[33] Finally, in an ultimate attempt to thwart the Viet Minh plans, the French carried out a raid on Hoa Binh.

In spite of French efforts to deter the enemy, the Viet Minh divisions from the Viet Bac converged during the last days of March 1953 from their base areas upon Moc Chau, where four regiments were detached to contain the Na San garrison, and by the beginning of April Sam Neua was threatened by a force of fifteen battalions. On the 12th, therefore, Salan, realizing that the three battalions which formed the garrison would be unable to resist the impending assault, ordered them to withdraw to the entrenched camp on the Tran Ninh plateau, and although no time was lost in carrying out this order, the physical difficulties involved in this withdrawal proved considerable as the column, which had only twelve hours start of its agile pursuers, was compelled to follow a rough pony track across mountainous country. On the evening of the 13th Viet Minh advance units attacked the battalion of Laotian paratroops which formed the French rearguard. This attack was repulsed, but the column was again assailed on the 16th and forced to disperse at a point some fifty miles from the plateau. The break-up of the column was to lead to the loss of two-thirds of the French effectives, so that only 230 survivors finally managed to reach the entrenched camp.[34]

[33] Whereas Na San was at 45 minutes flying distance from the Hanoi airfields, the Tran Ninh plateau, which is at an altitude of 3,500 feet, was at one hour, 40 minutes flight from these airfields.

[34] Marchand, pp. 212–13.

While these events were taking place in the Laotian province of Houa Phans, five Viet Minh battalions at Dien Bien Phu set out and advanced on Luang Prabang from the north. In their advance they captured, in the face of stout resistance, the posts guarding the approaches to the valley of the river Nam Ou, and reached a point some thirty miles north of the royal capital where contact was established, on 28 April, with another Viet Minh column which was progressing down the river Nam Seng. This column formed part of the forces which had occupied Sam Neua. Faced with this threat to his capital, H.M. Sisavang Vong displayed a proud stubbornness and refused to leave Luang Prabang. The aged monarch's resolute attitude was to be rewarded since, although the French Command appears to have considered abandoning Luang Prabang without a struggle, the French Government, alarmed at the deplorable political effect of such an action, insisted that the royal capital should be defended.[35] Reinforcements were therefore dispatched to Luang Prabang, and the general mobilization of the population provided the labour force required to extend the small airfield and to prepare defences to the north.

By the 30th French aircraft under favourable weather conditions had transported three battalions of Foreign Legionaries and Moroccan troops, together with artillery, ammunition, barbed wire, and bulldozers, to the lovely but isolated capital. Meanwhile the popular will to resist, which had been increased by evidence of French ability to conjure out of thin air the means to oppose the Viet Minh bands, was further strengthened by the prophecy of a blind Buddhist monk, whose affliction had been recompensed by the gift of second sight. This venerable personage now foretold, with an admirable sense of the apropos, that the invaders would fail in their attempt to capture Luang Prabang, and that, although a second invasion would take place later, it would be followed by the withdrawal of the Viet Minh forces to the eastern side of the Annam chain. The credence attached to this prophecy proved to be justified; the Viet Minh columns, who had left behind them their porters, with their ammunition and food supplies, started to withdraw, abandoning much of the territory which they had overrun in the provinces of Luang Prabang and Xieng Khouang. But in spite of their failure either to capture the royal capital or to

[35] *Straits Times*, 8 May 1953.

reach the river Mekong, the Viet Minh left behind depots of rice and ammunition that clearly indicated their intention to return.

The prospect of a renewed offensive caused the French Command some perplexity, as no satisfactory strategy could be devised to oppose the infiltration of these lightly armed invaders, whose powers of resistance and mastery of guerrilla tactics had found a terrain which tried but did not exceed their capacities in the mountainous complex between the Mekong and the Red rivers. Through their command of the air[36] the French were able to establish, with a minimum of delay, entrenched camps around local airstrips which proved sufficiently well fortified either to discourage or to repulse an attack by troops who had arrived at the perimeter after forced marches across precipitous mountain country and whose artillery, ammunition, and rations had frequently failed to keep pace with their advance, but the control of the disputed territory remained with the Viet Minh, who were prepared to travel barefoot and lightly equipped through an area where the density of the population was estimated at five inhabitants to the square mile.

In their defence of North-West Indochina, however, in spite of the fact that they still remained principally confined to their camps and fortified positions, French Union troops were able to count on a measure of assistance from the local population, who regarded the Viet Minh as foreign invaders. In Laos this assistance was furnished principally by the commando groups of the National Guard, which had been formed in 1950 for the purpose of providing intelligence of enemy movement and harassing armed bands passing through Laotian territory. These groups, which were composed of about seventy men, were each recruited from a single village community and commanded by leaders who had been elected to this position by the other members of the group; these commandos were lightly armed and summarily equipped in the manner of Viet Minh guerrillas, while they received their orders from the provincial administrator, who transmitted his instructions through the village notables.[37] In the region between the Red and Black rivers the

---

[36] During the invasion of Laos in the spring of 1953 the French Command had at their disposal 345 operational aircraft (Chassin, p. 164 n.).

[37] R. C. Romilly in *Indochine Sud-est Asiatique*, No. 26, Feb. 1954.

role of the Laotian commando groups was assumed by Franco-Thai guerrilla fighters, who set up bases in inaccessible retreats from which they sallied forth to collect intelligence on the enemy and to raid Viet Minh-occupied centres.[38]

## THE NAVARRE PLAN

By May 1953 Salan, the Commander-in-Chief, General Chassin, commanding the French air force in Indochina, and General de Linarès, commanding the operational zone in Tongking, together with a number of senior officers, including Colonel Allard, the Chief of Staff, had all completed their tour of duty in this exacting theatre of war, the provision of relief for them having been deferred until the end of the campaigning season. On 8 May a French government communiqué announced that General Henri Navarre[39] had been appointed to succeed Salan as Commander-in-Chief of the armed forces in Indochina. Navarre, who was serving as Chief of Staff to Marshal Juin, Commander-in-Chief of the Land Forces of Western Europe, was an officer who had hitherto specialized in military intelligence, and his connexion with Indochina was alleged to have been limited to arranging for the discreet surveillance of Ho Chi Minh's contacts and activities during the Fontainebleau Conference. He was therefore an officer who was virtually unknown to the rank and file of the French army, while his somewhat colourless personality and natural reserve seemed unlikely to appeal either to the imagination or to the affections of the hard-bitten members of an Expeditionary Corps engaged in a desperate struggle in a distant and confused theatre of war. The Commander-in-Chief designate had, moreover, displayed understandable reluctance to accept the

[38] For more than a year the crack Viet Minh Regiment 148 was held in check by the followers of the Thai chieftain Cho Quan Lo (Chassin, p. 167 n.).

[39] From 1939 until the armistice in 1940 Navarre had been at the head of the German section of the military intelligence organization attached to the French General Staff. After the French surrender he had accompanied General Weygand to Algiers where he had been responsible for military intelligence and counter-espionage in French North Africa. In 1942, following his recall to France, he had joined the resistance movement and had been given the task of co-ordinating military espionage activities throughout the country. After the Allied landings he emerged from his concealment and in November 1944 had assumed command of an armoured regiment forming part of the French First Army, in which capacity he had occupied Karlsruhe and 'planted the regimental standard on the ruins of many German towns' (M. Olivier in *Indochine Sud-est Asiatique*, No. 26, Feb. 1954).

proffered appointment, a reluctance which had been increased
by the Prime Minister's private admission that in his opinion
the only solution to the Indochinese situation lay in the discovery of some 'honourable way out' of the imbroglio.[40]
Navarre was instructed, however, to leave for Indochina
within ten days and, after examining the military situation, to
return to Paris with a plan of action, but its scope was limited
by the stipulation that it must contain no demands for large-
scale reinforcements.[41]

Filled with forebodings in regard to his mission, Navarre
left for Saigon on 18 May. In Tongking, where de Lattre's
principal collaborators were preparing to return to France, he
found that an 'end-of-term' atmosphere prevailed. In consequence both Letourneau, who was shortly to be relieved of his
dual functions by the appointment of a resident Commissioner-
General, and Salan assured the newcomer that they considered
the situation, if not satisfactory at present, at least susceptible
of considerable improvement shortly.[42]

At the end of May Navarre officially assumed command of
the Expeditionary Corps and issued his first Order of the Day
in which he addressed himself to the French Union troops in
words which contrasted strangely with the vigorous self-
confidence that de Lattre had displayed upon a similar
occasion. 'I am counting,' declared the newly appointed
Commander-in-Chief, 'on the contacts that I shall have with
you, and particularly with those of you who are fighting in the
front line, speedily to remedy my inexperience.'[43] Navarre's
initial misgivings were increased by his examination of the
military situation, for while he had had occasion in Paris to note
the incapacity of the French Government to frame a policy
which constituted, in his opinion, an essential prerequisite for
the successful conduct of military operations, he found that in
Indochina the large number of troops employed for purely
defensive purposes had progressively deprived French Union
forces of their capacity for offensive action. In consequence,
whereas the Viet Minh had at their disposal seven regular
infantry divisions, which together with their independent regi-

[40] Navarre, p. 3.
[41] Ibid.
[42] Ibid. p. 61.
[43] *Le Monde*, 30 May 1953.

ments were now estimated to constitute an operational force with a strength equivalent to nine divisions,[44] the French Union forces were only able to muster seven mobile groups and eight parachute battalions, or the equivalent of three divisions.[45]

Navarre was also appalled to discover the extent of enemy infiltration, which was revealed by the fact that in the Red river delta, where more than 100,000 French Union troops, or the equivalent of five divisions, were immobilized in garrisoning 917 defence posts, the Viet Minh were estimated to control either completely or partially 5,000 out of the 7,000 villages in the deltaic plain.[46] But drawing some consolation from the strategic mobility of the French operational units and from the reserves of manpower in the Associate States, Navarre decided to appropriate a plan which had just been drafted by Salan, to support French requests for increased American aid.[47]

The plan, which was founded on the premise that during the next campaigning season a decisive engagement must be avoided, was designed to create an operational force more powerful than that of the Viet Minh and possessed of equivalent mobility. This objective was to be attained by increasing the armies of the Associate States with the object of entrusting them with the defence duties hitherto discharged by the Expeditionary Corps. It was recognized, however, that the relief of French units for operational purposes could not take place until the regions where they were employed in garrison duties had been pacified by the laborious methods employed with some success in Tongking.

The success of the plan depended on prompt and massive

[44] Navarre, p. 42.
[45] Ibid. p. 47. French Union forces in the spring of 1953 were made up as follows:
    (1) *Expeditionary Corps*:
        (a) Land forces: 175,000 regular troops, including 54,000 French, 30,000 North African, 1,8000 African, 20,000 Legionaries, 53,000 locally raised troops, and 55,000 auxiliary troops.
        (b) Naval contingent: 5,000.
        (c) Air force contingent: 10,000.
    (2) *Armies of the Associate States*:
        (a) Vietnamese army: 150,000 regular and 50,000 auxiliary troops.
        (b) Laotian army: 15,000.
        (c) Cambodian army: 10,000 (ibid. p. 46 n.2).
[46] Ibid. p. 46 n.1. The strength of the Viet Minh forces was estimated in May 1953 at approximately 125,000 regular, 75,000 regional, and 150,000 guerrilla troops (ibid. n.2.)
[47] Ibid. p. 74.

deliveries of American aid, which would be required to equip
the national armies, while large-scale reinforcements would
also be temporarily necessary to meet the Viet Minh offensive
which was likely to develop at the end of the rainy season. When
he had established the number and nature of these reinforcements, Navarre returned to Paris to place his findings and
requirements before the National Defence Committee; and
during most of the month of July he attended meetings at the
various ministries interested in and responsible for some aspect
of French activities in Indochina. He was also present at a
meeting of the Chiefs of Staff Committee, where objections
were raised to the scale of his demands on the grounds that their
satisfaction would have an adverse effect on the general
military situation in Europe and North Africa. However, in
view of the fact that failure to provide these reinforcements
might place the French in a position of inextricable difficulty,
the suggestion was mooted that an attempt should be made to
obtain an international guarantee of Laotian territorial
integrity, to lessen the responsibility of the French Command
for the security of that area.[48]

Navarre laid his requirements before the National Defence
Committee on 24 July.[49] During the ensuing debate the recommendation of the Chiefs of Staff Committee in regard to the
necessity of scaling down the demands for reinforcements was
adopted, while the proposal to increase the strength of the
national armies was approved, with the proviso that the cost of
the operation would have to be shouldered by the United
States Government. In spite of his insistence on the need for a
decision, Navarre was unable to obtain from this august
areopagus any firm directive in regard to the French obligation
to defend North Laos in the event of a Viet Minh attack.

After this meeting the persistent danger that secret information in regard to military operations in Indochina would be
divulged to the enemy was again demonstrated, for on his
return to Saigon Navarre's attention was drawn to an article
which appeared in the French weekly newspaper *France*

[48] Navarre, pp. 86–87.
[49] The National Defence Committee, which is presided over by the President of
the Republic, is composed of the Prime Minister, and the Ministers for Foreign
Affairs, the Interior, National Defence, French Overseas Territories, the Secretaries
of State for the three armed services, the Marshal of France, and the Chiefs of
Staff.

*Observateur* on 30 July, containing an exact account of the discussions which had taken place, including the Commander-in-Chief's admission that, although the Expeditionary Corps would be able to defend the Red river delta and Cochin-China during the impending campaigning season, the defence of other regions, and in particular of Laos, could not be envisaged with any degree of confidence. After considering the advisability of demanding an official inquiry into the origin of this embarrassing leakage, Navarre decided against this course of action on the grounds that such an inquiry would serve to confirm the accuracy of the information contained in the offending article.[50] This incident confirmed Navarre in his distrust of the press, while it demonstrated that perpetrators of such indiscretions were assured of relative immunity deriving from a fiction invented by the Ramadier Government in 1947 that a state of war did not exist in Indochina, where the Expeditionary Corps was officially engaged in large-scale police operations. As a result the French Communist Party was able to continue unabashed its exhortations to sabotage and mutiny, and the politicians and journalists who were opposed to the continued prosecution of the war were encouraged to maintain contacts with Viet Minh agents in Paris.

---

[50] Some of the persons involved in the leakage were to figure in the autumn of the following year in a scandal—'l'Affaire des Fuites'—that was occasioned by a further leakage of information on the matters discussed at meetings of this Committee (J-A. Faucher and J-L. Febvre, *L'Affaire des Fuites* (1955), p. 132).

# XV

# Towards the Crisis

In March 1953 Jean Letourneau accompanied the French Prime Minister, René Mayer, on the latter's visit to Washington. Letourneau, who was aware that the Americans were dissatisfied with the French conduct of military operations, had come prepared to silence American criticism by the production of a plan which had been hastily drawn up by Salan and was later to be adopted by Navarre. This plan contained proposals for the taking over by Vietnamese troops of the static defence duties hitherto discharged by the Expeditionary Corps, an arrangement which would free the latter for action against the regular Viet Minh units. The plan was approved by the Americans, who undertook to give prompt consideration to the manner in which the necessary financial assistance and military aid could best be provided.

This was the last occasion on which Jean Letourneau was to take part in such negotiations, for his position had been adversely affected by the findings of a parliamentary mission which visited Indochina to report on the expenditure of military credits early in 1953. Although the findings had been officially rejected on the grounds that the mission was not empowered to include strictures of a political nature in its report, the criticism it contained of conditions in Saigon, and in particular of Letourneau's stewardship, was to prove most damaging to his prestige. Moreover Paul Devinat, the Radical Socialist deputy leading the mission, had circulated a copy of this report privately among his political colleagues and arranged for extracts to be published in the columns of the weekly newspaper *Express*.

These published extracts, which criticized the attitude of French officials and even the conduct of the Expeditionary Corps, included the following summary of the mission's findings:

The practice of accumulating responsibilities has replaced the power that stems from prestige. The Minister who has become resident and discharges the functions of High Commissioner has also assumed responsibility for the conduct of military operations. In consequence, a veritable dictatorship has been established that recognizes no bounds to its authority and admits of no control: a dictatorship not of a man but of officials.

Moreover, the Minister's staff installed in the Palais Norodom, in their desire to deal with current problems with a lofty detachment, have forgotten that the essential part of their task is no longer to govern but to advise. For it is not now our business to draw up plans without recourse to constituted authority, but to adapt our daily conduct to the requirements of a subtle diplomacy: in Saigon our representatives have allowed themselves to become enmeshed in political intrigues.

Vietnamese ministers appear in the eyes of their countrymen to be French officials. The press is not free to criticize: letters are censored. This policy is fraught with dire consequences for those who are engaged in fighting the war. For an army which is waging war is entitled to show itself hard and exacting, but an army of occupation garrisoning innumerable small posts and enforcing security regulations that offer opportunities for making easy money is an army which is becoming demoralized and which, in the last resort, even if its presence is necessary, does our cause a disservice.[1]

Moreover, after eight years of *laissez-aller* and anarchy, the presence of a resident Cabinet Minister in Indochina has not led to the suppression of the daily scandals concerning the transfers of piastres, the settlement of war-damage claims, and the allocations of contracts which feature in the daily tittle-tattle of Saigon.[2]

Letourneau, who had been provided in January with a Secretary of State to act as his deputy in Paris, sought to anticipate the mission's censure, and proposed that he should be relieved of his dual functions. In compliance with this request the Government agreed to appoint a High Commissioner to each of the Associate States and to install a Commissioner-General in Saigon who would be responsible for the defence and security of Indochina and for French representation on the quadripartite committees which had been set up at the Pau Conference.[3] However, in spite of Letourneau's attempts to anticipate criticism, the adverse comments on his administration were to involve him in the loss of his portfolio in May.

Some days before his replacement the legend—which had

[1] *Combat*, 23–24 May 1953.
[2] *L'Humanité*, 22 May 1953.
[3] *Le Monde*, 23 Apr. 1953.

been persistently bolstered by Communist propaganda and spread by visiting political and military personalities who were frequently accompanied by their wives—to the effect that Saigon was a city of pleasure where entertainment was lavish, vice flourished, bribery was rife, and money which had been acquired by unavowable means was dissipated freely, provoked the exasperated and hard-pressed French Government into devaluing the Indochinese piastre from 17 to 10 French francs by a unilateral decision which constituted a flagrant breach of the Pau agreement.[4] The devaluation of 9 May, which was followed by the fall of the Mayer Government, adversely affected the moral climate both because of the grave offence that it gave to the Governments of the Associate States, who considered with some justification that their recently acquired national sovereignty had been flouted, and also because of its economic repercussions; these resulted in a rise in the cost of living and a fall in national revenue, of which a large percentage had been appropriated for the purposes of national defence. The devaluation also aroused the resentment of the Expeditionary Corps, whose rates of pay were adversely affected, and although an attempt was made to mitigate the resultant hardship by the retention of a proportion of service pay, which was reimbursed at the more favourable rate of exchange at the end of a tour of duty, this arrangement, which was a common practice in French prisons, caused additional irritation, while the extra returns now required were to lead in some cases to the withdrawal of n.c.o.'s from front-line positions to deal with this administrative chore.[5] Moreover, as the devaluation of the Indochinese piastre took place after French financial and commercial interests had completed the transfer of their capital and activities to other parts of the world,[6] Vietnamese nationalists, who were aware of the predominant role that the Bank of Indochina played in Indochinese affairs, concluded that the devaluation indicated a decision on the part of French moneyed interests, which had successfully recouped themselves for their losses, to withdraw their support

[4] Paul Reynaud, a former Prime Minister who had visited Indochina on a tour of the Far East earlier in the year, had also voiced moral indignation at the prosperous and carefree atmosphere of Saigon and at the modesty of the Vietnamese contribution towards the common war effort (*Figaro*, 1 Apr. 1953).

[5] Navarre, p. 101.

[6] *Le Populaire*, 9 June 1954.

from the official policy of obtaining a military solution to the Indochinese problem.

## NORODOM SIHANOUK'S CRUSADE FOR INDEPENDENCE

Letourneau's failure to retain his portfolio in the Laniel Government, which was finally constituted on 26 June, removed from the helm of Indochinese affairs an experienced minister who, conscious of the fragility of the parliamentary majority for the prosecution of the war, had consistently urged upon Bao Dai the necessity of checking unconsidered gestures by Vietnamese nationalists. These ebullient personalities were, however, now preparing to abandon their attitude of reserve and non-co-operation in order to demonstrate their dissatisfaction with the extent of French concessions.

An initial indication of the existence of this latent restiveness was provided in January when elections to communal and municipal councils had been held throughout nationalist-controlled territory. Although the restricted nature of the franchise, and the fact that polling took place in only one out of three villages in the nationalist zone,[7] might have been thought to have eliminated the possibility of electoral surprise, a list of candidates in Hanoi with a platform which ignored the municipal aspect of the elections and demanded 'a genuine unification of the country', elections to a National Assembly, and negotiations to end the war[8] won a sweeping victory. The subsequent meetings of the municipal council were to provide these nationalists with admirable opportunities to voice their grievances and apprehensions.

Meanwhile the cause of Vietnamese nationalism was to receive help from an unexpected quarter, for King Norodom Sihanouk of Cambodia had now been driven by his difficulties with the Democratic Party to assume personal responsibility for the Government, and to embark single-handed upon the complex task of securing national independence. The sequence of events which had led him to take this action stemmed from the formation of Huy Kanthoul's Government in September 1951 and Son Ngoc Thanh's return in the following month. Thanh, apparently intoxicated by his enthusiastic reception, lost no

[7] *Le Monde*, 24 Jan. 1953.
[8] Hammer, p. 290.

time in urging that independence must be won at any cost; and in order to propagate his views he founded a newspaper, the *Khmer Krauk* or 'Cambodian Awakening'. After the newspaper had been suppressed Thanh himself, accompanied by a handful of supporters, including Ea Sichau, the director of the Customs Service, joined forces in March of the following year with an Issarak band operating near the Siamese frontier to the north of the Great Lake; although his disappearance was at first ascribed to his capture by the Viet Minh, the appearance of tracts bearing his signature and incendiary broadcasts from a wireless transmitter installed across the border in Siamese territory soon dissipated this illusion.

Thanh's flight, in which prominent members of the Democratic Party were believed to have been implicated, increased Norodom Sihanouk's distrust of his ministers, and his suspicions regarding their loyalty were confirmed by their reluctance to sanction the measures which the situation demanded and by their readiness to arrest their political opponents. Finally, on 15 June 1952, he dismissed the Government, exiled Huy Kanthoul to France, and took over the functions of Prime Minister himself. In a message addressed to the ministers he had dismissed, the king reproached them with their demagogic behaviour and indifference towards the common weal, and specifically accused them of placing party interests before those of the nation and of treating the protests evoked by their arbitrary actions as attempts to betray democracy and subvert the constitution.[9]

At the same time he issued a proclamation in which he asked for emergency powers and undertook to obtain complete national independence within the space of three years, swearing 'before all the Tevadas and Most Real Powers' that at the end of this period he would submit to a public trial where his subjects would be called upon to decide whether he had fulfilled this undertaking. But the National Assembly were deaf to this appeal and refused either to endorse his action, or to divest themselves officially of the authority entrusted them by their electors: the deputies merely noted, therefore, that the king's action was based on the principle laid down in the constitution that all powers emanated from the throne and stressed their resentment by refusing to approve the Franco-

[9] Herz, pp. 106–7.

Cambodian treaty of 1949 or to vote the budget. These obstructionist tactics exasperated Norodom Sihanouk and he dissolved the Assembly on 13 January 1953.

A month later the king left Cambodia ostensibly for a holiday in Europe, but in fact to embark upon a 'crusade for independence'. After a short stay in Rome he moved to the south of France, where he addressed letters on 5 and 18 March respectively to the President of the French Republic, informing him that the sympathies of 80 per cent. of the Buddhist clergy and a large number of government officials and students in his kingdom were on the side of the Issaraks: a state of affairs which he ascribed to the fact that Cambodian independence was incomplete, particularly in the military, economic, and judical spheres. He announced his readiness to discuss appropriate measures to remedy this situation.

On 25 March he was invited to lunch with the French President, and after this meeting a communiqué was issued stating that agreement had been reached in principle on the course of action which should be adopted in order to satisfy Cambodian demands. But the Khmer monarch, who appeared reluctant to place undue reliance on post-prandial promises, installed himself at Fontainebleau, where he announced that he was ready to conduct the negotiations foreshadowed in the Élysée communiqué. However, after Letourneau had conveyed to him that his presence was a source of embarrassment to the French Government,[10] Norodom Sihanouk left Paris for Canada, ostensibly in order to convey his personal thanks to the Canadian Government for its courtesy in according diplomatic recognition to Cambodia.[11] On his arrival in Montreal, however, the king made a declaration to the press stating that his Government, which had undertaken the task of national restoration concurrently with the struggle against dissident elements and the Viet Minh, needed French assistance and also complete sovereignty in order to deprive the Communists of their pretensions to be fighting for national independence.[12] He then set off for New York, which may have constituted the ultimate goal of his journey, and here he declared to a representative of the *New York Times*, that unless

[10] *Le Monde*, 22 Apr. 1953.
[11] *Combat*, 11–12 Apr. 1953.
[12] *Le Monde*, 14 Apr. 1953.

the French gave his people more independence 'within the next few months' there was a real danger that they would rebel and join forces with the Viet Minh.[13]

Having delivered his message to the American people, Norodom Sihanouk left for Tokyo, where he announced that he would remain pending the outcome of the Franco-Cambodian negotiations, which had finally started at the end of April. In the middle of May he was persuaded to return to Cambodia, but shortly afterwards, while he was on a tour of inspection in the province of Battambang, he crossed the Siamese frontier and took refuge in Bangkok, where the arrival of a monarch whose ancestors had been vassals of the Siamese Crown caused Marshal Phibul's Government some embarrassment.

This unexpected change in the royal itinerary was, however, to provide another admirable opportunity to acquaint world opinion with French tergiversations and with the Cambodian demand for the equivalent of dominion status. An incendiary press communiqué issued by the royal entourage to the effect that 'Cambodians, disappointed and exasperated by the French refusal to accord real independence to their country have informed the King that the only way to obtain independence was to fight the French'[14] was of a tenor to arouse French misgivings and jubilation among Vietnamese nationalists. The coolness of his reception in Bangkok, where the king and his suite were provided with indifferent accommodation and requested not to indulge in political activities, led him, however, to return to Cambodia on 20 June, where he established his headquarters to the north of the Great Lake at Siem Reap to await the satisfactory conclusions of the negotiations with the French Government.

### THE SAIGON CONGRESS

While Norodom Sihanouk was attracting world attention to Cambodian demands, and also arousing his placid subjects to a realization of the state of political servitude in which they had been living, the French President was continuing the laborious negotiations which finally resulted in the formation of a new

[13] *NYT*, 19 Apr. 1953.
[14] *Figaro*, 18 June 1953.

Government under Joseph Laniel on 26 June. The formation of the Laniel Government had followed an unsuccessful attempt by Mendès-France, whose views on the need for a negotiated settlement with the Viet Minh were well known, to obtain the investiture of the National Assembly, but the measure of support which he had been able to command served to confirm Letourneau's assessment of the narrow parliamentary majority supporting French official policy in Indochina. Moreover this majority was being further undermined by Norodom Sihanouk's agitation, which was serving to foment and crystallize nationalist discontent throughout Indochina and to exasperate French public opinion. Letourneau had therefore warned Laniel, when the latter was Prime Minister designate, that a prompt gesture on the part of the French Government was urgently required to dissipate the existing malaise.[15]

This warning proved effective, and on 3 July, a Note[16] was handed to the High Commissioners of Vietnam, Cambodia, and Laos, in which the French Government made a 'solemn declaration' of its readiness to complete the independence and sovereignty of the Associate States by transferring to their Governments the various functions which had remained under French control, while the Governments were invited for their part to negotiate with the French the settlement of outstanding claims in the economic, financial, judicial, military, and political spheres.[17] On the same day the appointment was announced of a career diplomat and Ambassador to Tokyo, Maurice Dejean, to the post of Commissioner-General in Indochina.

The 'solemn declaration' of 3 July increased the effervescence among Vietnamese nationalists who foresaw that the impending negotiations would be conducted without reference to their wishes. Although he had repeatedly assured the Vietnamese people of his intentions to install a democratic régime, Bao Dai, who was aware of nationalist political inexperience and ignorance of the outside world, must have foreseen that the

[15] Laniel, p. 7.

[16] Text in *L'Année Politique, 1953*, pp. 578–9.

[17] The Prime Minister in the recently constituted French Government had assumed direct responsibility for the conduct of relations with the Associate States, being assisted in this task by a Deputy Prime Minister, Paul Reynaud, to whom authority was delegated to deal with Indochinese affairs, and by a Secretary of State, Marc Jacquet, whose secretariat formed part of the Prime Minister's office.

creation of a National Assembly of dubious representative character would serve principally as a forum for intemperate speeches which would both embarrass him in the negotiations and reinforce the position of those French political leaders who were prepared to negotiate a settlement with the Viet Minh at nationalist expense. But on this occasion the head of the state appears to have underestimated both the strength of feeling and even the capacity for action of his supporters, who had hitherto confined their criticism of his conduct of affairs to the privacy of their homes, for the nationalists, who had long been divided by personal and regional rivalries, were now seeking to demonstrate by some bold gesture that their wishes could no longer be ignored.

This desire for action was to provide Ngo Dinh Nhu,[18] who had been engaged in organizing a Roman Catholic trade union movement—the Vietnamese Federation of Christian Workers[19] —with the opportunity which he had been seeking, for in addition to the intellectual ability common to his family Nhu possessed a remarkable capacity for intrigue, together with some conception of the steps by which independence might be attained. These steps were to be preceded, in his opinion, by the formation of a front of national union to support the candidature of his brother, Ngo Dinh Diem, for the premiership. In consequence, following the publication of the French Government's 'solemn declaration' of 3 July, and when Bao Dai and Nguyen Van Tam had left for Paris for the negotiations, Ngo Dinh Nhu together with other nationalists in South Vietnam became actively engaged in an attempt to convene an unofficial national congress, to demonstrate the desire of the Vietnamese to have a voice in the direction of national affairs, and particularly in the conduct of the impending negotiations with the French Government. These activities met with considerable success since the project received the support of Mgr. Ngo Dinh Thuc, the Apostolic Vicar of Vinh Long, and Pham Cong Tac, the Cao Dai Superior, Tran Van Soai, the Hoa Hao 'Generalissimo', and General Le Van Vien, the leader of the Binh Xuyen resistance group, who was persuaded

---

[18] See below, p. 430.

[19] The Vietnamese Federation of Christian Workers, which was affiliated with the International Federation of Christian Workers, had a membership of 45,000 in July 1953 (*Annuaire des États Associés, 1953*, p. 105).

to offer his headquarters on the right bank of the canal giving access to the rice mills of Cholon—the Arroyo Chinois—as the venue for the proposed congress.[20]

Invitations were sent to personages throughout Vietnam to attend a national congress in support of 'National union and Peace'. This congress met in semi-clandestine fashion at the General's headquarters on 5 September.

Although Mgr. Thuc, who appears to have been seized with tardy apprehensions, failed to put in an appearance, while the Cao Dai Superior, who arrived late, was dissuaded by well-wishers from entering the hall, the opening session exceeded the expectations of the promoters. The discussions rapidly degenerated into a violent indictment both of the French authorities and, in spite of the vain objections of Le Van Vien, of the head of the state himself. Finally, in view of his inability to dominate the tumult, Le Van Vien, who had been elected to the chair, ordered his guards to clear the hall. The ensuing scandal was considerable, and although Vien and Soai joined with the Cao Dai Superior in sending a telegram to Bao Dai assuring him of their loyalty,[21] the press reports of this incident caused considerable irritation.

The publicity which this congress had received compelled Bao Dai to summon an official National Congress, in order to remove the impression of popular discontent and to reaffirm his own claim to represent Vietnamese nationalists in the forth-coming negotiations with the French Government. He sent Prince Buu Loc, Vietnamese High Commissioner in Paris, to Saigon to convene this congress and on 1 October a committee charged with the task of arranging the allocation of the seats at the congress met and in spite of the existence of divergences of opinion managed to settle this difficult problem.[22]

[20] Le Van Vien, who had been promoted to the rank of General in the previous year, had been authorized in February to form a fourth battalion of Binh Xuyen troops with which to ensure the security of the road from Saigon to the coast at Cap St. Jacques that had been repaired and reopened to traffic.

[21] *Le Monde*, 8 Sept. 1956.

[22] The allocation of the seats reveals the variegated nature of Vietnamese nationalism. The delegates included, in addition to 29 municipal councillors and 50 communal councillors, 8 representatives of professional associations, 25 representatives of political groups, 6 representatives of the commercial community, 3 representatives of the press, 3 representatives of cultural associations, 9 Binh Xuyen, 17 Cao Dai, 15 Hoa Hao, 15 Roman Catholics, 4 Buddhists, 1 'Militant' Buddhist, and 5 representatives of the ethnic minorities (*Combat*, 8 Oct. 1953).

The congress opened in the Saigon town hall on 12 October, and the delegates were officially charged with the specific tasks of making known to Bao Dai the desires of the Vietnamese people concerning future relations with France 'within the framework of the French Union', and of appointing advisers to assist him in the forthcoming negotiations. The congress, in spite of the narrow limits to which the discussions were supposed to be confined, had assembled in a state of suppressed excitement. The debates, however, proceeded without incident until the evening of the 16th, when under the influence of a group of energetic Tongkingese who were acquainted with Viet Minh propaganda methods, the congress threw discretion to the winds and unanimously approved, under the stress of intense feeling, a motion in favour of the 'total independence' of Vietnam.[23]

The news of this action created a sensation in Saigon, and pressure was immediately brought to bear upon the delegates to make them withdraw, or at least amend, a motion that threatened to bring Franco-Vietnamese relations into an impasse and to provide the peace party in France with an irrefutable argument in favour of negotiations with the Viet Minh. The debate was then resumed the next day, with the result that the motion was amended,[24] a refusal to participate in the French Union 'in its present form' being substituted for the demand for 'total independence' while, although complete confidence was expressed in Bao Dai to direct the forthcoming negotiations,

this confidence was mitigated by the provisos that the treaties resulting from these negotiations should be approved by a national assembly elected on the basis of universal suffrage, and that no discussions, propositions, or decisions concerning Viet-Nam should take place, or be taken in international conferences, without the agreement of the national government.[25]

### PROSPECTS FOR A NEGOTIATED SETTLEMENT

The irrational and emotional behaviour of the delegates at the Saigon congress added to the general bewilderment and

[23] *L'Année Politique, 1953*, p. 581.
[24] Ibid. p. 582.
[25] Haut-Commandant du Viet-Nam, Service de Presse et l'Information, *Bulletin*, 1 Nov. 1953, pp. 12–13.

irritation in France, where Laniel stigmatized their behaviour as 'deplorable', admitted the desirability of a negotiated settlement with Ho Chi Minh, and regretted that the Communist leader, who had declared on 2 September that only a complete victory could lead to peace, did not seem in a conciliatory mood.[26]

Meanwhile the conclusion of the protracted negotiations in Korea on 27 July had given rise to the belief in France that an armistice would follow in Indochina; a belief which had been reinforced by well-founded rumours[27] that after the conclusion of the Korean armistice the Government intended to negotiate a cease-fire. Indeed even Georges Bidault, the stubborn Minister for Foreign Affairs, was reported to have admitted before the Foreign Affairs Committee, on his return from the Washington Conference in July, that it was 'impossible to conceive that nothing would be done', after the Korean armistice, 'to seek, in the international sphere, with the support of our allies and, naturally, with our enemies, but not alone, ways and means of opening peace negotiations in Indochina'.[28] The signing of the armistice at Panmunjon thus encouraged the peace party in France to increase their efforts to prove, with scant regard for the effect that such an allegation might have on morale in the theatre of war, that the continuance of an 'anti-Communist crusade', which the powerful American army had found it expedient to abandon in Korea, was due to the existence of a conspiracy involving certain political groups, which were drawing the bulk of their funds from exchange manipulations, and also the French treasury, which depended on American financial aid towards the cost of the war in order to settle the national balance of payments with the dollar area.[29] But, if the existence of such a conspiracy may be discounted, the failure of the French Government to fulfil the popular expectation by concluding an armistice was probably due to divided councils within the French cabinet, to the refusal of the Viet Minh, who were confident of their ability to achieve further military successes during the impending campaign, to respond to French advances, and to the

---

[26] *L'Année Politique, 1953*, pp. 586–93.
[27] Laniel, p. 17.
[28] Quoted by Georges Remy in *Le Monde*, 24 July 1953.
[29] J. S. Servan-Schreiber, in ibid, 30 Apr. 1953 and Jean Fabiani in *Combat*, 23 Oct. 1953.

reluctance of France's allies to encourage her in such a course of action.[30]

This allied reluctance had been demonstrated at the Washington Conference of the Foreign Ministers in July. The Conference, at which a decision had been reached to invite the Russians to attend a four-power conference, had also included Franco-American discussions on the provisions of aid for Indochina. The result of these discussions[31] was announced by Laniel on 11 September, in a statement which revealed that, subject to the final approval of President Eisenhower, France would receive increased financial aid, to the tune of $385 million. The allocation of this sum, which was additional to the $400 million of American aid already appropriated for the fiscal year 1953-4, and to war material supplied either directly from the United States or by means of off-shore orders placed with French industry, was estimated to have increased the American financial contribution towards the cost of the war to a figure which covered 70 per cent. of the French expenditure.[32]

However, conditions were attached to the provision of this additional aid which were very unpalatable to national pride since the French Government officially undertook as a *quid pro quo* 'to make every effort to break up and destroy regular enemy forces in Indo-China',[33] to send out a specific number of reinforcements, and to complete the training of a stated number of Indochinese troops by the end of 1954. It also promised in confidence 'to take into consideration the opinions expressed by the American authorities in regard to the elaboration and execution of strategic plans'.[34]

These undertakings, together with the fact that the American Government had now assumed responsibility for financing and

[30] Late in 1952 the French Government had entrusted Prince Buu Hoi, a member of the Vietnamese royal house, with the secret, but fruitless, mission of contacting Viet Minh representatives in Rangoon on its behalf, in order to ascertain whether a basis existed for a negotiated settlement (Hammer, p. 310). Subsequent developments were to reveal, however, that such an approach should have been made through Peking, where the Chinese Government, on whose aid the Viet Minh depended, was anxious to establish their claims to paramountcy in Asia (Speech by Chen Yun, of the Chinese Politbureau, *NCNA*, 5 Mar. 1954).
[31] U.S.-French communiqué, 30 Sept. 1953, *DSB*, 12 Oct. 1953.
[32] *Financial Times*, 11 Sept. 1953.
[33] *NYHT*, 1 Oct. 1953.
[34] Navarre, p. 138 n. Navarre states that he was not informed of this undertaking and was left to discover its existence by chance shortly before he was relieved of his command.

equipping the armies of the Associate States, increased the delicacy of the relations between the French military authorities in Indochina and the Military Assistance Advisory Group (MAAG). In spite of the tactful behaviour of Donald Heath, the American Ambassador, and of General Thomas Trapnell, the head of the Advisory Group, American impatience at the defensive nature of French strategy and at the dilatory reluctance displayed to create autonomous native armies was met by French resentment of criticism, suspicions of American intentions, and exasperation at recurrent instances of a crude approach to complex problems. Moreover the importance of the American stake in the war also aroused misgivings among that section of French political opinion which believed that a negotiated settlement was inevitable. These misgivings were based on the recognition that by accepting aid which was provided on the express understanding that a renewed effort would be made to defeat the enemy, the French Government had forfeited their prerogative of initiating negotiations for a settlement.[35]

This disquiet in regard to the Government's Indochinese policy was revealed towards the end of October in the National Assembly when, in the course of the protracted debate in which Laniel had deplored the motion voted by the congress in Saigon, it was revealed that the majority of the deputies favoured a negotiated settlement and disagreed merely on the manner in which a settlement could best be achieved.[36] After this debate Marc Jacquet, Secretary of State, provided the Assembly with French Union casualty figures for the previous year. They showed that whereas the losses in dead and missing incurred by the contingent from metropolitan France amounted to 1,860, and those of the Foreign Legion and the African units totalled 4,049, 7,730 Vietnamese had been killed serving either with the Expeditionary Corps or with units of the national army.[37]

In view of the important contribution that the American taxpayer and the Vietnamese infantryman were making to the struggle, the motion finally voted in the National Assembly

[35] Servan-Schreiber in *Le Monde*, 30 Sept. 1953.
[36] *L'Année Politique, 1953*, pp. 586–93.
[37] *Manchester Guardian*, 28 Oct. 1953. The fact that Vietnamese troops had provided the bulk of the casualties occasioned surprise since official communiqués tended to stress the part that French units played in local operations.

displayed some lack of consideration for France's allies. The Assembly resolved that the armed forces of the Associate States should be expanded and should gradually replace French troops; that everything possible should be done to achieve peace in Asia by negotiation, and that the defence and independence of the Associate States should be realized within the French Union.[38] The motion also recommended that the free nations in those regions where their responsibilities were interdependent should be encouraged to share equitably in the common efforts and sacrifices.

The revelation afforded by this debate of a widespread desire for a negotiated settlement was exploited during the following month by the Viet Minh, whose regular units were then moving, for the third successive year, into north-west Indochina in preparation for a winter offensive. On 29 November the Stockholm newspaper *Expressen* published answers to a list of questions submitted by its managing editor to Ho Chi Minh through the good offices of the Viet Minh chargé d'affaires in Peking. The questions had been framed to establish whether the Viet Minh Government would be prepared to negotiate, and in that case what method could best be employed to reach a settlement; the replies revealed a readiness on the part of the Viet Minh Government to examine any proposals that the French might make and that the essential basis of an armistice was real French respect for the independence of Vietnam.[39]

In spite of the cautious wording of the replies, the *Expressen* 'scoop' aroused world-wide interest and apparently disposed of the French Prime Minister's contention that the Viet Minh were not prepared to consider a negotiated settlement.

## PRINCE BUU LOC'S GOVERNMENT

Vietnamese nationalists, whose suspicions of French intentions had already been aroused by the devaluation of the piastre, were quick to conclude from the publicity given to Ho Chi Minh's replies that the French were ready to withdraw the Expeditionary Corps and to leave them defenceless to their enemies. Their alarm was voiced by Ngo Dinh Nhu, the sponsor of the Movement for National Union and Peace, who declared

[38] *L'Année Politique, 1953,* p. 593.
[39] RIIA, *Documents, 1953,* p. 477.

bluntly to the Associated Press correspondent in Saigon that France was preparing to betray the Vietnamese.[40]

Meanwhile Nguyen Van Tam's prestige had suffered from his inability to control the proceedings at the official congress in Saigon. Moreover the energetic Prime Minister, whose assumption of office had been followed by the promulgation of a series of measures designed to hasten the formation of a national army and state, had now, like his predecessors, become involved in misunderstandings with the imperial cabinet at Dalat, and also with the French authorities. In addition, some coarseness of moral fibre had led Tam to transgress accepted canons of good taste both by allowing one of his daughters to accept wedding presents of inappropriate magnificence from the Chinese community in Cholon, and by the licence that he gave his mistress to exploit his official position in order to clinch profitable business deals. Thus in spite of tenacious efforts to re-establish his authority, Tam was compelled to resign on 17 December.[41]

Some days later the Prime Minister designate, Prince Buu Loc, announced his intention of forming a Government which would be 'representative, efficacious, and stable'. The creation of such a government proved, however, an arduous under-taking since representative Vietnamese, who were of the opinion that elections to a National Assembly could not be long delayed, hesitated to compromise themselves by serving in a transition government. In consequence the cabinet which Prince Buu Loc finally presented to the head of the state on 11 January con-tained an unduly high proportion of ministers who were normally resident in France. These ministers were in many cases well fitted to participate in the forthcoming negotiations with France, but their residence abroad disqualified them in the eyes of their countrymen from assuming responsibility for the con-duct of national affairs.

### OPERATIONS IN THE RED RIVER DELTA

In the meantime Navarre was profiting from the rainy season to carry out a series of operations designed to improve security conditions in the Red river delta area, while bases and

---

[40] *Le Monde*, 1 Dec. 1953.
[41] Rumours which originated in Dalat indicated that Nguyen De himself was a candidate for the premiership.

communications in the Viet Minh zone continued to be subjected to attack. The most spectacular of these operations was
an airborne raid—*Opération Hirondelle*—which was intended to
destroy important stocks of war material stored in limestone
caves near Lang Son. On 17 July three battalions of parachute
troops occupied Lang Son itself and the caves without encountering more than sporadic opposition, and destroyed some 5,000
tons of weapons, ammunition, explosives, and petrol. When its
mission had been completed this force set off for the coast some
sixty miles away, while a mobile group advanced inland to
meet it. The junction of the two forces took place without
incident; and by the 20th the units had returned to their bases
in the delta.[42]

During the following month the evacuation by air of the
garrison of the entrenched camp at Na San was completed
successfully. The garrison, which had gradually been reduced
to a strength of about 5,000, was brought back to the delta
between 8 and 13 August, while dumps of ammunition and
other stores which the French had been compelled to abandon
were later bombed and destroyed: this delicate operation was
completed without provoking any reaction from the Viet Minh
forces surrounding the camp, who had been deluded into
believing that the French were preparing a sortie in the direction of Hoa Binh.

However, the successful evacuation of Na San appears to
have led the French to underestimate the dangers involved in
maintaining isolated garrisons in inaccessible mountainous
country, with the result that their belief in the advantages to be
derived from an 'aeroterrestrial' base remained unimpaired,
and plans were made to set up a similar base at Dien Bien Phu
in the Thai province of Lai Chau.[43] On 20 November, Dien

[42] The allegation was subsequently to be made that the operation had been
timed to coincide with French negotiations for increased military aid and financial
assistance in Washington, where the success of the raid served to refute American
criticism of French defensive strategy (*Combat*, 22 July 1953). An allegation of a
similar nature was to be made later in the year, when operations both in the south
of the Red river delta and against Lao Kay were ascribed to the necessity of
satisfying American demands for aggressive action (Servan-Schreiber in *Le
Monde*, 27 Oct. 1953).

[43] Navarre, p. 157. Navarre was to claim that the establishment of a base at
Dien Bien Phu, which had been recommended by his predecessor, Salan, and by
General Cogny, the General Commanding in North Vietnam, was essential to the
defence of North Laos. This claim was based on the fact that Dien Bien Phu,
which is situated astride the main invasion route passing through Tuan Giao and

Bien Phu, which had remained in Viet Minh hands since the offensive of the previous year, was reoccupied by a force of six parachute battalions, and immediate steps were then taken to establish an entrenched camp around the airstrip, which was situated on a plateau measuring ten by five and a half miles and ringed by thickly-wooded hills. This plateau, which represents a unique natural feature in the surrounding sea of mountains, allowed the Expeditionary Corps full scope to entrench itself behind minefields and barbed wire, in a labyrinth of strong-points, look-out posts, trenches, communication centres, messes, and underground dug-outs which displayed in perfected form the subterranean conception of the 'aeroterrestrial' base evolved at Na San.

The reoccupation of Dien Bien Phu had been preceded in September by a resumption of the annual 'mopping-up' operations in the Red river delta, the operations being directed on this occasion to expelling Viet Minh regular and regional units from their accustomed haunts in the Thai Binh area, and to destroying the villages in which they had established their bases.[44] On 15 October the French launched a major raid in the direction of Phu Nho Quan. The raid was intended to forestall an attempt by the 320th Viet Minh Division, which was quartered in that area, to infiltrate through Phu Ly into the region of Hung Yen and Hai Duong, but in face of the stiff resistance encountered, the French Union troops failed to retain possession of the town, and withdrew to the delta.[45]

Meanwhile the Viet Minh divisions had started to regroup to

down the valley of the Nam Ou to Luang Prabang, represents the last and the most suitable position where resistance can be offered to an invading force. But in spite of Navarre's insistence on the imperious necessity that had led him to decide to defend this remote and inaccessible plateau, insufficient consideration appears to have been given to the fact that the 187 miles separating Dien Bien Phu from Hanoi would put the camp outside the range of most of the available fighter aircraft and place an undue strain on the transport planes which would be required to supply the garrison. Moreover the inability of the garrison to operate outside the defence perimeter and thereby to impede the passage of Viet Minh troops and supplies—an inability which had been demonstrated at Hoa Binh, and again at Na San—was to immobilize most of the crack French units during the impending Viet Minh offensive.

[44] These operations, which were only partially successful, revealed a disquieting improvement in the tactics and the aggressive spirit of the Viet Minh regional units.

[45] During this operation casualties estimated at 3,000 were inflicted on Division 320, which was incapacitated by these losses from operational activities for two months (Navarre, p. 101).

the north of the Red river delta in the Phu Tho–Yen Bay–Thai Nguyen area, and in the region of Vinh and Ha Tinh in North Annam. Anticipating a general offensive designed to cut communications between Hanoi and Haiphong, the French Command proceeded to mass their available reserves in Tongking.

On 28 November information was received that two of the Viet Minh divisions stationed to the north of the delta were preparing to move into North-West Tongking, where Lai Chau and Dien Bien Phu represented the remaining French outposts. Navarre then decided to centre the defence of the region on the entrenched camp at Dien Bien Phu, which was to be held 'at all costs'.[46] The decision was also taken to evacuate the garrison and the civilian population from Lai Chau, the capital of the Thai chieftain Deo Van Long, which, in spite of the grandiose nature of its site, would have proved indefensible in the event of a major attack. French Union troops were therefore evacuated by air to Dien Bien Phu between 5 and 8 December, while the Thai units either withdrew on foot to the entrenched camp or took to the hills.

After the move of the two Viet Minh divisions, a third division, together with elements of a fourth, and the Viet Minh 'Heavy' Division,[47] which had still been awaiting its equipment during the previous campaigning season, now took the road which led from the base areas to the north of the Red river delta, through Tuan Giao to Dien Bien Phu, where a Viet Minh force estimated at thirty-three battalions had assembled by the beginning of January. The ability now shown by the Viet Minh to maintain the bulk of their operational forces for a period of months in wild mountainous country was to surprise the French Command, who had consistently tended to underrate the enemy, basing their assessment of Viet Minh capacities on their showing during the previous campaigning season.[48]

[46] Laniel, p. 38.

[47] The Viet Minh had started to form a 'Heavy' Division in 1951. It was armed with mountain guns, heavy and medium mortars, and comprised a regiment equipped with heavy artillery which had originally represented American aid to Chiang Kai-shek.

[48] Laniel, p. 45. This logistic achievement must be ascribed principally to the efforts and devotion of the civilian population in the Viet Minh zone who were to provide both the porters to shift supplies and also the labour gangs to extend and repair the communications system. A labour force was engaged in repairing road communications from Cao Bang and Lang Son through the Viet Minh base areas around Thai Nguyen and Tuyen Quang to Yen Bay, whence a track had

By the beginning of January the unexpected ability that the
Viet Minh were displaying to transport food supplies, ammunition, and even heavy artillery to the mountainous region around
Dien Bien Phu aroused Navarre's misgivings and caused him
to ask for additional aircraft with which to counter the mounting threat to the entrenched camp, a request that received
partial, if tardy, satisfaction. Meanwhile a Viet Minh force
consisting of a division and a regiment concentrated in the Vinh
area had launched an offensive across the Annam chain on
20 December 1953 and, proceeding by paths used by their
emissaries and smugglers, they surprised and overwhelmed the
garrisons of the small posts in the path of their advance. On
28 December advance units of this force reached the Mekong
and occupied Thakhek, severing by their occupation of this
town road and river communications between North and South
Laos. French Union reinforcements were dispatched, however,
to Seno near Savannakhet, with the result that the Viet Minh
failed to capture this important air base between 5 and 9
January 1954. The Viet Minh then abandoned Thakhek and
dispersed their forces among the limestone hills to the east of
the town, while some units proceeded south, where they either
joined forces with the bands operating from the Bolovens
plateau or else infiltrated into Cambodia.

When the enemy offensive had spent itself in Central Laos,
Navarre decided to proceed with an important operation which
had been planned to take place during the winter campaigning
season. This operation—*Opération Atlante*—was designed to
evict enemy forces from the Viet Minh Military Interzone or
*Lien Khu* V, whence an attack had been launched against
An Khe in Southern Annam in the previous year. The existence
of this dissident area, where the Viet Minh had now succeeded
in equipping 12 regular and from 5 to 6 regional battalions,
constituted a permanent threat to the upland regions of South
Annam, to the French base at Tourane, and even to Cochin-
China itself.[49] On 20 January, therefore, a Franco-Vietnamese

been driven across difficult country to the existing road (*Route Provinciale* 41) at
Son La. From Son La supplies were forwarded to an advance base at Tuan Giao,
situated twenty-five miles from Dien Bien Phu. The creation of this route, covering a distance of some 220 miles, enabled supplies to be carried, wheeled on
bicycles, or transported by Molotov trucks to within a short distance of the Viet
Minh positions around Dien Bien Phu.

[49] Navarre was later to justify his decision to launch *Opération Atlante* on the

force advanced northwards from Nha Trang on an operation
which revealed both the poor quality of the recently raised and
summarily trained light battalions and the inability of the
Mobile Administrative Groups for Operational Purposes
(GAMO) under the direction of Pham Van Giao, the swash-
buckling Governor of Central Vietnam, to reorganize the
administration of the occupied territory. In spite of landings
at Tuy Hoa and Qui Nhon, and the absence of many of the
Viet Minh regular units from the area, the rate of advance was
slow; the occupation of the territory between Nha Trang and
Qui Nhon, where the advance of the Franco-Vietnamese force
was stopped, was not completed until the beginning of March.
Meanwhile the Viet Minh forces in the Interzone had launched
a counter-offensive on 28 January, across the upland region of
South Annam in the direction of the important centre of
Kontum, threatening Pleiku and An Khe in the course of their
advance.

The confused military situation in other parts of Indochina
had not prevented the Viet Minh, however, from completing
their preparations for a general assault on Dien Bien Phu, and
on the night of 25–26 January troop and artillery movements
around the camp led the garrison to suppose that such an
assault was imminent.[50] Nevertheless the attack failed to take
place, while Viet Minh Division 308—the 'Iron' Division—left
the perimeter of the camp some days later and set out on a
raid in the direction of Luang Prabang. The troops, barefoot,
lightly equipped, and carrying a sling of cooked rice, advanced
in three columns, at the rate of some twenty miles a day, upon
the royal capital, which was once more hurriedly put into a
state of defence. By 3 February these troops, proceeding down
the valley of the Nam Ou river, were reported to have reached
a point some ninety miles to the north of Luang Prabang, while
the garrisons of the defence posts along their route had either
been overwhelmed or were attempting by unfrequented tracks
to rejoin French positions to the south. But although Viet Minh

grounds that the troops employed—with the exception of a Mobile Group of
North African troops—were unsuitable for service in Tongking, while the aircraft
engaged in providing support were unable, either for technical or mechanical
reasons, to be employed on flights to Dien Bien Phu (Navarre, p. 176 n.4).

[50] The postponement was ascribed to the advice of a Chinese, or more probably
Sino-Soviet, Military Mission, who were reported at that date to be inspecting
the Viet Minh positions (ibid. p. 210 n.).

advance parties arrived some five days later within twenty miles of the capital, the enemy columns halted and on the 23rd returned posthaste to Dien Bien Phu.

The failure of the 'Iron' Division to attain its presumed objective has been ascribed both to the success that had attended Franco-Laotian attempts to discover and destroy the stocks of paddy accumulated in the course of the previous year by Viet Minh agents along the invasion route, and to the rapidity with which the garrison of Luang Prabang had been reinforced. The feint in the direction of the royal capital had, however, resulted in a further dispersal of French Union troops throughout Indochina, where units of the Foreign Legion and parachute troops continued to be shuttled during these critical months between areas where danger appeared most imminent, while the commitments of French aircraft were increased to a point where they threatened to exceed their capacities. In fact at the beginning of March fifteen different airfields were serving as operational bases, of which only seven were equipped for that purpose, while three of the remainder—those at Pleiku, Xieng Khouang, and Dien Bien Phu—were wholly dependent on transport aircraft for supplies.[51] The effect of this dispersal was to reduce maintenance and repair facilities and, in spite of the heroic efforts of a hard-pressed ground staff, to curtail the number of aircraft available for operational purposes.[52] Moreover air crews and ground staff were estimated at that time to be one-third under strength.

The Americans, who were generally critical of the Expeditionary Corps' failure to service their equipment, had insisted prior to the Viet Minh offensive that increases in personnel should precede the supply of additional aircraft,[53] but faced with the French Air Ministry's inability to provide more than a fraction of the additional ground staff required (700 out of 4,000), they agreed towards the end of January 1954 to send 1,200 ground staff to Indochina in order to assist the French in the task of maintenance and repair.[54]

---

[51] Chassin, p. 203.

[52] Before the battle of Dien Bien Phu aircraft in the Indochinese theatre of war comprised 75 transport planes—increased to 100 at the beginning of February— 48 bombers, and 112 fighter-bombers (Navarre, pp. 107–8).

[53] Ibid. pp. 108–9.

[54] J. and S. Alsop in *NYHT*, 27 Jan. 1954.

# XVI

# Dien Bien Phu and the Berlin Conference

In November 1953 an important debate on European policy took place in the French National Assembly when it was expected that the Assembly would ratify the European Defence Community Treaty of 1952. During the debate a Soviet Note was delivered to the Allied Governments announcing Russia's acceptance of a proposal which had been made five months earlier for a four-power conference to discuss the unification and demilitarization of Germany, on the understanding that the Russian delegate would there raise the question of convening a five-power conference, to which Communist China should be invited. This tardy acceptance of the Allied proposal aroused hopes that some acceptable alternative would be found to the ratification of the controversial EDC Treaty and enabled the opponents of EDC to carry another innocuous motion expressing general agreement with the Government's policy of constructing a unified Europe.

Some days after this debate Joseph Laniel, the Prime Minister, and Georges Bidault, the Minister for Foreign Affairs, left France to attend a meeting with President Dwight Eisenhower and Sir Winston Churchill in Bermuda. Here the three western powers reached agreement on an agenda for the forthcoming four-power conference and on the necessity of maintaining a common front, while the discussions also revealed a readiness on the part of the American Government to shoulder an increasing proportion of French military expenditure in Indochina and, in particular, to provide instructors and training facilities for the armies of the Associate States.

On 25 January 1954 the Foreign Ministers of the four powers met in Berlin, but Bidault appears to have had some reason to suppose that the ostensible purpose of the Conference was a secondary consideration to Vyacheslav Molotov, who was proposing to offer the good offices of his Government to arrange an armistice in Indochina in exchange for a French undertaking to abandon EDC.[1] Before he left for Berlin, therefore,

[1] Chinese Communist support for this Soviet proposal was probably obtained before Ho Chi Minh's replies to the *Expressen* questionnaire had been forwarded in

Bidault is reported to have assured his colleagues in the cabinet that although the Soviet Union would be given every guarantee in regard to EDC, no suggestion could be entertained that France should agree to withdraw from this organization in exchange for a 'concession in this, or in any other continent'.[2] In spite of these bold words, however, Bidault seems to have been aware that his Government, which was under increasing pressure to conclude an armistice, was counting on his ingenuity to enlist Soviet assistance in arranging for discussions to be opened with the Viet Minh without alienating J. F. Dulles.[3]

The Soviet desire to sabotage, and the American intention to defend EDC at the Berlin Conference were thus to ensure such a flattering reception for the French delegation that Bidault's speech at the opening session was compared by Dulles to an oration by Abraham Lincoln. Next day Bidault dined privately with Molotov, who appears to have been sardonically amused by the French predicament, and was alleged to have offered his good offices to arrange for armistice discussions to be opened with the Viet Minh.[4]

However, the discussions at the Conference soon revealed that Molotov did not intend that agreement should be reached either on the unification or the demilitarization of Germany, and that his principal purpose in coming to Berlin was to attempt to substitute for EDC a comprehensive European security pact, from which the United States would be excluded. The task of refuting Russian allegations and of revealing the true nature of Molotov's proposals devolved principally upon Bidault, who managed to attract American sympathy by his 'steadfast and loyal support' of Dulles's theses.[5]

Finally, when the negotiations had revealed that no basis existed for an agreement on European issues, the delegates proceeded

November of the previous year through the channel of the Viet Minh diplomatic mission in Peking. Evidence is available that this support was based on recognition that further intervention in the internal affairs of neighbouring countries should be postponed until the Communist régime in China had been consolidated (speech by Chen Yun, *NCNA*, 5 Mar. 1954). Moreover the Peking Government must have been aware that the increase in American aid to French Union forces in Indochina threatened to involve China in hostilities on behalf of the Viet Minh in a distant area where her forces would be handicapped by dependence on extended and inadequate lines of communication.

[2] *Le Monde*, 21 Jan. 1954.
[3] *NYT*, 6 Feb. 1954.
[4] Ibid. 12 Feb. 1954.
[5] *CSM*, 18 Feb. 1954.

to examine Molotov's proposal for a five-power conference in restricted sessions. Bidault's impatience to discuss this question had already been noted by the Soviet Foreign Minister, who expressed his willingness to accord priority to this item, 'if the Far East conference was a matter of such great urgency for France'.[6] Although Molotov had originally proposed that the five-power conference should deal with a wide agenda, it was finally decided to limit the discussions to Korea and Indochina, but Dulles, who had at first insisted that proof of Chinese Communist good intentions in regard to Korea must be provided before he would consent to discuss, even in principle, other issues,[7] maintained his refusal to allow Communist China to be included among the 'inviting powers'. A diplomatic formula was therefore agreed upon which specified that 'neither the invitation to, nor the holding of, the above-mentioned conference shall be deemed to imply diplomatic recognition in any case where it has not already been accorded'.[8] On 18 February it was finally proposed that the conference should be held at Geneva in April.[9]

American support for the proposal had been accorded with considerable reluctance, and Dulles, whose distrust of Communist intentions had in no way diminished, warned Bidault at the end of the Berlin Conference that, as the American experience in Korea had shown that a display of readiness to negotiate on the part of the Communists was usually the prelude to a renewed offensive, the Expeditionary Corps would be well advised to make preparations to meet a general assault.[10]

On his return to Washington the Secretary of State clarified the American attitude towards the Geneva Conference and gave further vent to his misgivings in a broadcast in which he declared that he had 'told Mr. Molotov flatly' that he would not agree to meet the Chinese Communists 'unless it was expressly agreed and put in writing that no United States recognition would be involved'. Indeed, he assured his audience that the

---

[6] *CSM*, 11 Feb. 1954.

[7] Ibid. 18 Feb. 1954.

[8] Cmd. 9080, p. 180.

[9] Molotov is reported to have been aware that the prospect of such a conference would be sufficient to deter the French National Assembly from ratifying the EDC Treaty (Roger Massip in *Figaro*, 20–21 Feb. 1954).

[10] *Le Monde*, 1 July 1954.

'Communist régime would not come to Geneva to be honoured by us but rather to account before the bar of world opinion' for her role in the Korean and Indochinese wars.[11] This uncompromising approach, which appeared to be based more on moral than on military considerations, caused irritation in Moscow, where 'certain American personages' were accused of seeking to create a state of political feeling at Geneva, which would render 'fruitful, calm and profitable discussions very difficult'.[12]

### THE ATTACK ON DIEN BIEN PHU

The Viet Minh appear to have been dismayed by the decision that had been reached in Berlin, since although Ho Chi Minh's replies to the *Expressen* questionnaire had revealed an apparent readiness to negotiate, he seems on this occasion to have lent his authority to a Sino-Soviet manoeuvre which was not considered by the Viet Minh leaders to be in their best interest.

Consequently Viet Minh broadcast commentaries tended at first to discount the prevalent rumour of impending negotiations, but when these rumours proved to be well-founded incredulity gave place to anger and dismay, since although they were now confident that victory lay within their grasp, the Viet Minh Command were aware that it would not be sufficiently decisive to enable them to dictate the conditions which would alone in some measure justify the toll in lives and material destruction exacted by the long war. However, Communist discipline, which must have been fortified by the realization of the extent of their dependence on Chinese war material and technical aid, enabled the Viet Minh leaders to master their 'reactionary' resentment and to resign themselves to the necessity of accepting a compromise solution based on a partition of the country.

Nevertheless the prospect of armistice negotiations encouraged Vo Nguyen Giap, who was supported in this by the Chinese Communists, to throw all available forces into the struggle during the intervening weeks in an attempt to extend Viet Minh control over Indochinese territory and to inflict a spectacular defeat upon the Expeditionary Corps. The capture

[11] *DSB*, 8 Mar. 1954.
[12] *Le Monde* (quoting *Pravda*), 2 Mar. 1954.

of the entrenched camp at Dien Bien Phu, which contained many of the best French units, offered the prospect of such a victory.

The camp, which now resembled a collection of fortified hill villages in Africa or Afghanistan—an illusion heightened by the varied racial origins of the garrison—consisted of a central position composed of five separate strong-points situated to the south-east and west of the airstrip, the approaches to which were guarded to the north and north-east by two outposts located at a distance of 1½ and 2 miles respectively from the central position, while an eighth strong-point was situated 4 miles to the south at the extremity of a secondary airstrip which had been laid down after the reoccupation of the plateau. These strong-points, which had been named after ladies of whose company the garrison were deprived, had been progressively reinforced, until on 13 March they contained a force of 12 battalions, a squadron of 10 tanks, which had been flown in piecemeal and reassembled on the spot, artillery including 105 and 155 mm. guns and 120 mm. mortars, and six fighter aircraft, which, together with observation planes and a helicopter, were based on the airstrip.[13]

On 19 February 1954 the defences were inspected by René Pleven, Minister for National Defence, who was accompanied by Marc Jacquet, Secretary of State for Indochinese Affairs, and General Paul Ely, Chief of the General Staff.[14] After the party returned to France Ely submitted a report in which he described Dien Bien Phu as an 'extremely strong position, which could only be attacked by a very powerful force'. Moreover even in the event of such an attack, Ely considered that the advantage would probably lie with the defenders.[15] The Prime Minister, Laniel, appears to have been sufficiently encouraged by these findings to reveal, in the course of a debate on 5 March, the somewhat unrealistic conditions on which the French Government would be prepared to reopen negotiations with the

[13] Navarre, p. 213.

[14] Pleven had been responsible both for fixing the advantageous exchange-rate for the Indochinese piastre in December 1945 and for the appointment of de Lattre in 1950. He had also arranged for Admiral Cabanier, the permanent Under-Secretary at the Ministry of National Defence, to visit Indochina in December 1953 with the secret mission of ascertaining Navarre's opinion on the advisability of taking immediate steps to negotiate a cease-fire (Laniel, p. 41).

[15] Ibid. p. 78.

Viet Minh. These conditions included the evacuation of Laos, Cambodia, and South Vietnam by Viet Minh troops, and the creation of a no man's land around the Red river delta.[16]

Pleven, however, does not appear to have shared the optimism of his military advisers. Although he was able to assure the National Assembly that he had found the Dien Bien Phu garrison confident in the strength of its position and well equipped to repulse attack, he confided privately to the Prime Minister that he viewed the prospect of such an attack with misgivings, describing the Expeditionary Corps as 'exhausted' and the general military situation as essentially 'precarious'. He consequently recommended that the Government should neglect no steps to ensure the success of the Geneva Conference and suggested that, to avoid the possibility of future misunderstanding with the Americans, Ely should be sent to Washington 'in order to inform our allies very exactly of the real military prospects'.[17]

Ely's departure was precipitated by a Viet Minh attack on the Dien Bien Phu garrison on the nights of 13–14, and 14–15 March respectively, which resulted in the fall of the advance positions 'Béatrice' and 'Gabrielle'. Although the attack had been expected, the weight of the preliminary bombardment, in which the 105 mm. guns of the 'Heavy' Division went into action for the first time, stunned the defenders of 'Béatrice', and after the death of the commanding officer and of the second in command, the position was overwhelmed by waves of fanatical assailants.[18] On 14–15 March the attack on the position 'Gabrielle', which had been repulsed on the previous night, was resumed. The artillery fire preceding this attack again demonstrated that the French were not prepared to resist bombardment by 105 mm. guns. The assault was carried out with great bravery by Viet Minh troops, who in spite of heavy casualties continued to emerge from trenches dug clandestinely to the fringes of the barbed-wire entanglements, which 'volunteers for death' demolished with plastic charges. The defences were finally breached, and although a counter-attack launched at

[16] *L'Année Politique, 1954,* pp. 565–8.
[17] Laniel, pp. 79–80. Pleven also recognized that the cessation of Chinese military aid was a prerequisite for any attempt to overcome Viet Minh resistance (*Le Monde,* 9 Apr. 1954).
[18] Viet Minh artillery at Dien Bien Phu comprised 20 75-mm. and 20 105-mm. guns, which were supported by a large number of heavy mortars (Navarre, p. 218).

dawn from the main defence positions around the airstrip succeeded in rescuing the remnants of the garrison, who had taken refuge in the southern section of the defences, 'Gabrielle' itself was abandoned.

The fall of 'Béatrice' and 'Gabrielle', preceded by the intervention, for the first time in the history of the war, of Viet Minh artillery, had an adverse effect upon the morale of the garrison, and during an attack on the night of 17–18 March a Thai battalion deserted, with the result that a third defence position on the north-west salient of the camp, that of 'Anne-Marie', had to be evacuated. Although the garrison soon recovered from its dismay and proceeded to strengthen the defences against artillery fire, while a sortie was carried out against nests of anti-aircraft guns installed in villages about a mile outside the defences, the attacks nevertheless revealed that the French decision to establish an entrenched camp at Dien Bien Phu was based on a miscalculation. For it had been erroneously assumed that the airstrip, which was situated some six to seven miles from the summits of the hills enclosing the saucer-like plain, would be out of range of gunfire and that Viet Minh attempts to install guns and anti-aircraft batteries on the slopes commanding the camp would be prevented by French counter-batteries and by air attack. But probably acting on the advice of Chinese military advisers the Viet Minh proceeded to install their guns separately in heavily camouflaged positions excavated in the hillsides, which proved difficult to locate. As a result the Viet Minh were soon able to render the airstrip, on which the garrison depended for supplies and for the evacuation of the wounded, unserviceable, and further attempts by aircraft to land at Dien Bien Phu had to be abandoned after 26 March.[19]

The garrison continued to be reinforced and supplied by parachute, but the Viet Minh now proceeded to install their anti-aircraft batteries in ever closer proximity to the dropping zones which the aircraft employed on these dangerous missions were compelled to approach on a fixed course and at a low altitude.[20] Moreover the French Command had made a further

[19] The officer commanding the French artillery at Dien Bien Phu, realizing the catastrophic implications of this miscalculation, committed suicide after the loss of the defence position 'Gabrielle' (Frédéric-Dupont, p. 133).

[20] Viet Minh anti-aircraft guns at Dien Bien Phu consisted of 100 heavy machine-guns and 16 37-mm. guns, and in March an anti-aircraft regiment

miscalculation. Basing their assessment on detailed and accurate reports received through their intelligence channels, they had estimated, on 9 March, that the supplies of ammunition laboriously assembled around the entrenched camp would limit the Viet Minh offensive to attacks on two or three defence positions, which could be kept up for five or six days.[21] But during the month of March the volume of Chinese military aid doubled, while the arrival of a consignment of 500 Molotov trucks facilitated the onward passage of supplies to Dien Bien Phu.[22]

Consequently the defenders of the camp, which had been garrisoned and supplied to resist an attack of limited duration, were subjected to a protracted siege lasting fifty-six days, their resistance within the shrinking perimeter of the defences being inspired by the knowledge that the fall of Dien Bien Phu would represent a decisive defeat for the Expeditionary Corps.

Their resolution was to be matched by that of the French Command, who encouraged the garrison by their readiness to commit the remaining parachute battalions to the battle. After the loss of 'Béatrice' and 'Gabrielle' the decision was taken to dispatch further reinforcements which were being held in reserve at Hanoi; and two parachute battalions were dropped over the camp on 14 and 16 March, but they proved insufficient to enable the French to reoccupy the lost positions.

The defence of the camp was also seriously handicapped by the lack of aircraft and in particular by the shortage of air crews needed for large-scale and sustained operations of this nature. The entire fleet of transport aircraft, consisting of 100 Dakotas, were engaged in supplying the garrison, their commitments in other parts of Indochina being assumed by aircraft of the local civil air lines. In addition, sixteen American cargo aircraft—Fairchild Packets—operated by American civil air crews belonging to General Chennault's civilian air fleet—the 'Flying Tigers'—were also engaged in parachuting supplies until the last days of the siege, when the dangers involved on this operation caused them to be withdrawn.[23] The resistance of the

arrived from China with a further 64 37-mm. guns (Navarre, p. 218).

[21] Ibid. p. 218.
[22] Ibid. p. 243 n.
[23] The Fairchild Packet is capable of transporting a load of 6 tons compared with the load of 2½ tons which can be carried by a Dakota.

garrison was supported at the same time by two-thirds of the bomber and fighter-bomber force, but although an average of 75–80 of these aircraft was available daily for 'strikes' against enemy positions and for raids on enemy communications, neither their numbers nor their capacities, which restricted them to the employment of 100 lb. bombs, were sufficient to deal a crippling blow to the Viet Minh forces.

### DULLES'S PLAN FOR UNITED ACTION

The failure of the defence to silence the enemy artillery and to expel the nests of anti-aircraft guns from the vicinity of the airstrip appears to have convinced the military authorities in Paris at an early date that the fate of the garrison was sealed.[24] Ely, who had arrived in Washington on 20 March, therefore proceeded to draw the attention of the President, Admiral Radford, Dulles, and the Pentagon to the catastrophic implications of this situation.

His efforts proved successful. In an address to the Overseas Press Club of America on 29 March, Dulles stated that 'the imposition on Southeast Asia' of Communism 'should be met by united action. This might involve serious risks. But these risks are far less than those that will face us a few years from now if we dare not be resolute today.'[25] This speech caused some uneasiness in London, and on 1 April Anthony Eden, the Foreign Secretary, instructed Sir Roger Makins, the British Ambassador in Washington, to point out to Dulles that a refusal to entertain the possibility of a stalemate in Indochina would add to the difficulty of reaching tripartite agreement should the Allies be forced to compromise with the Communists at Geneva, and to inform him that the British Government considered that partition represented the least damaging alternative solution. This suggestion was met by the objection that, after carefully examining the implications of partition, the United States Government had reached the conclusion that it would merely provide a respite and would not lead the Communists to abandon their plans to dominate South East Asia. Dulles considered that the best way to avert such a catastrophe would be to deprive the Viet Minh of further military supplies by

[24] Frédéric-Dupont, pp. 136–7.
[25] *DSB*, 12 Apr. 1954, p. 540.

the threat of joint naval and air action against the China coast. Some days later Dulles approached the French and British Governments with the proposal that the countries threatened by recent developments in Indochina should issue a solemn declaration announcing their readiness to take concerted action to stop Chinese intervention and that they should at the same time set about organizing the collective defence of South East Asia. These proposals aroused Eden's misgivings; in an appreciation circulated to his colleagues in the Government he expressed the opinion that the mere threat of retaliation was unlikely to stop the Chinese from assisting the Viet Minh, with the result that the signatories of the declaration would be faced with the alternative either of implementing their threat, or of taking no further action. He then pointed out that whereas in the opinion of the Chiefs of Staff neither a coastal blockade nor air attacks on China's communications system were likely to prove militarily effective, such aggressive action would give China every excuse for invoking the Sino-Soviet Treaty and might lead to a world war, a possibility which the United States Government had apparently failed to take into account. But although he considered that no steps should be taken to form an *ad hoc* coalition for the purpose of preventing further intervention by China until the results of the Geneva Conference were known, Eden welcomed the American proposal in regard to collective defence and thought that it would be useful to acquaint the United States Government with British views on this matter at an early stage.[26]

Meanwhile, General Ely had been sufficiently encouraged by his reception to send an emissary to General Navarre with instructions to inform him that the scale of Chinese Communist intervention in the fighting at Dien Bien Phu justified, in the opinion of the Pentagon, American retaliatory action, and to request his opinion on the probable effect of such action on the outcome of the fighting.[27]

[26] Anthony Eden, *Full Circle* (1960), pp. 91–93.

[27] Chinese intervention in Tongking at this stage of the war included, in addition to the provision of war material, the presence of a Chinese general with a staff of twenty at Viet Minh military headquarters, and Chinese military advisers were present at divisional level. Chinese were also driving the Molotov trucks, now estimated at 1,000, which were being used to bring supplies to Dien Bien Phu, and the 37-mm. anti-aircraft guns around the camp were reported to be manned by Chinese crews (Navarre, p. 243 n.).

Navarre replied that rapid and massive intervention by American aircraft could still save the garrison.[28]

On 4 April Ely returned to Paris, where he immediately informed the Prime Minister that he had received 'a very definite impression' in Washington that the American Government would be prepared to entertain a French request for a massive air 'strike'.[29] On receiving this information the French Government requested that a force of heavy bombers should be sent to attack objectives around Dien Bien Phu.[30]

Meanwhile a plan—'Operation Vulture'—had been worked out in Hanoi and Saigon between representatives of the American Command in the Pacific and the French General Staff, which provided for a force of 300 carrier-based fighter-bomber aircraft, supported by 60 heavy bombers from Philippine airfields, to raid Viet Minh communications and their advance base at Tuan Giao.[31] On this occasion, however, the plans of the Pentagon and of the French General Staff seem to have misjudged the intentions of the politicians; for consultations between Dulles and Radford on the one hand and representatives of Congress on the other revealed the existence of opposition to an action which threatened to involve the United States in another war on the Korean pattern. Indeed, the representatives of Congress are reported to have advised the Secretary of State that, in conformity with his original proposal, he should first ascertain the nature of the support that the United States could expect to receive from her allies for 'united action' in South East Asia.

On 11 April Dulles arrived in London for talks, which took place on the two following days. In these discussions Dulles showed grave concern at the turn events were taking in Indochina, where he discounted the chances of a French victory at Dien Bien Phu. He disclosed also that the United States Government had thought of taking independent action, but had finally given up the idea and decided that such action must be dependent on a French undertaking to grant the Associate States real independence within the French Union and on an assurance of Allied support. He therefore wanted to see an *ad hoc* coalition

[28] Navarre, pp. 242–3.
[29] Laniel, pp. 83–84.
[30] Ibid. p. 85.
[31] Navarre, p. 244.

formed, which might provide the nucleus for a South East Asia defence organization, as a first step.

This approach to the situation perturbed Eden, who pointed out that any suggestion of Allied intervention, military or otherwise, or of any warning announcement before Geneva, would require extremely careful consideration, and also questioned the assumption that the situation in Indochina could be re-established merely by military means, and he advised Dulles to wait until the Communists had had a chance to put forward their proposals at the Conference. He emphasized that India and the other Asian Commonwealth members should on no account be excluded from the proposed coalition, but Dulles expressed the hope that any indication that India might be invited to join would be avoided.[32]

However, the joint announcement issued after the talks contained no reference to these fundamental differences, and merely stated that 'we are ready to take part, with the other countries principally concerned, in an examination of the possibility of establishing a collective defence, within the framework of the Charter of the United Nations, to assure the peace, security and freedom of South-East Asia and the Western Pacific'.[33]

During his visit Dulles mentioned that, in response to a suggestion made three weeks previously by the United States' Chiefs of Staff in favour of an intervention by American naval and air forces, aircraft-carriers had been sent to the Indochina coast from Manila. However, he gave an assurance that the United States did not intend to act without first finding out whether its allies, especially the United Kingdom, Australia, and New Zealand, took an equally grave view of the situation. Nevertheless, the presence of these vessels in Indochinese waters revealed Dulles's determination to do his utmost to save Dien Bien Phu. Further proof of this was provided later in Paris, where he is reported to have hinted that an attack by American

[32] Eden's suggestion that India and other Asian countries should be given an opportunity to join the coalition was prompted by a sense of responsibility towards fellow members of the Commonwealth, and, also, by his belief that the inclusion of these countries would increase the chances of success at Geneva. For he calculated that China would be unwilling, at that stage, to align India against her, and would make considerable efforts to conciliate Asian opinion in general (Eden, p. 97).

[33] Ibid. pp. 97–98.

aircraft using atomic bombs might yet save the beleaguered garrison.[34]

On his return to Washington Dulles, ignoring British objections, proceeded to carry out his plan for the formation of an *ad hoc* coalition; and on 16 April Makins reported that a meeting of the Ambassadors of the United Kingdom, Australia, New Zealand, France, the Philippines, Thailand, and the Associate States had been convened with the object of setting up an informal working group to study the collective defence of South East Asia. Eden, fearing that a 'get together' of this nature would be resented by the Asian Commonwealth countries and prejudice the chances of success at Geneva, instructed Makins to tell Dulles that the United Kingdom could not be represented; although this decision is reported to have angered Dulles, who regarded it as an attempt to back out of the agreement in principle arrived at in London, he undertook nevertheless to confine the agenda at this meeting to a general briefing conference on the coming negotiations at Geneva.[35]

THE BELEAGUERED FRENCH GARRISON

After the attack on the night of 17–18 March, the Dien Bien Phu garrison was afforded some respite as the Viet Minh were now engaged in constructing a system of trenches which they extended at night zig-zag fashion across the plain towards the French defences, and in moving up their artillery and anti-aircraft batteries in preparation for a renewed onslaught. The French Union troops sought to counter these activities by filling in the enemy trenches, by sorties against enemy gun positions, and by efforts to strengthen the defences, while French aircraft attempted to burn with Napalm the thick tropical forest which covered the surrounding hills and provided cover for troop concentrations, gun positions, and supply dumps.

On 3 March the Viet Minh preparations were sufficiently far advanced for them to launch an attack, which was maintained for five successive nights, on the eastern perimeter of the

---

[34] J. R. Tournoux, *Secrets d'État* (1960), pp. 48–49. Two United States aircraft-c  ᵗers anchored off Haiphong at that time were rumoured to be loaded with atomᵢc bombs destined for that purpose (Eden, pp. 51 ff).

[35] Ibid. p. 99.

camp, and in spite of repeated counter-attacks they succeeded in gaining a foothold in the defences which enabled them to install anti-aircraft guns within a mile of the airstrip. Although a third battalion of parachute troops was dispatched from Hanoi on 4 April, the position of the garrison was now desperate, for the Viet Minh were engaged in mining and isolating the strong-points on the perimeter of the defences, while they subjected the dropping zone on which the French depended for their supplies to intense and accurate gunfire.

However, the arrival of a fourth battalion of reinforcements on 11 and 12 April enabled the garrison to recapture a vital strong-point on the eastern defence perimeter after a violent engagement.

Meanwhile the Viet Minh refusal to allow the evacuation of wounded from the camp was adding to the distress of the garrison since the medical facilities and personnel were woefully inadequate to deal with the increasing number of casualties, who were consigned to await the outcome of the interminable siege in damp and ill-lit tunnels.[36] French resistance continued to be sustained, however, by French and American air crews who supplied the camp with food and ammunition: a task which was performed with admirable tenacity in the face of increasingly heavy anti-aircraft fire and in spite of the decreasing size of the dropping-zones, pilots of these transport aircraft being frequently required to carry out three missions a day over difficult mountain country under unfavourable weather conditions.[37] While the transport planes performed this vital task, bomber and fighter-bomber aircraft were engaged in attacking enemy gun positions, troop concentrations, bases, and communications, but in spite of the unremitting efforts of air crews and ground staff, neither the number of aircraft engaged in these operations nor the destructive power of their bombs were sufficient to deter an enemy operating under good natural cover, expert in the use of camouflage, and well drilled in the evasive action to be taken in the event of air attack. This air support contributed, however, to maintain the morale of

[36] Between 13 March and 7 May 3,000 of the garrison were treated for wounds, while 1,000 surgical operations were performed. The mortality rate among the wounded was 12 per cent. (Navarre, p. 224 n.).

[37] 20 per cent. of the supplies parachuted to the garrison are estimated to have fallen into Viet Minh hands, and during the last days of the siege the percentage rose to 30 per cent. (ibid. p. 234).

the defenders, who must also have drawn some encouragement from the readiness of the French Command to reinforce the camp[38] since after five battalions of reserves had been committed to the battle, the garrison continued to receive volunteers, who personified the spirit of self-sacrifice, solidarity and comradeship which served to cement and inspire the heterogeneous Expeditionary Corps.[39]

Meanwhile, the progress of the siege was being followed with close attention throughout Indochina; and even in Saigon, where officials and representatives of business interests had become inured and somewhat indifferent to the changing fortunes of the war, a sense of disquiet tended to pervade the European quarter at nightfall, where the obsessive thought was present in many minds that the darkness which favoured Viet Minh assaults would also be closing in upon the trapped garrison. If resident Europeans were united in their concern for the fate of the French Union troops at Dien Bien Phu, many Vietnamese nationalists, who were aware that they could expect short shrift at Viet Minh hands, remained nevertheless divided in their attitude. Although one-third of the garrison was composed of Vietnamese troops, these nationalists appeared unable to suppress a feeling of jubilation, inspired by the conviction that on this isolated plateau in North-West Tongking the military fiascos which had led to the conquest and the national and personal humiliations endured during eighty years of foreign occupation were being avenged. This feeling was increased by the belief that a demonstration was also being afforded that the disadvantages under which the peoples of Chinese culture laboured in their dealings with European nations had now been overcome.

In France concern for the fate of the garrison was tempered, in some quarters, by the calculation that if resistance should be unduly prolonged the American Government might be tempted to intervene directly, and prejudice thereby the outcome of the forthcoming Conference at Geneva. This attitude was expressed by Christian Pineau, an influential Socialist

[38] On 2 May a fifth battalion of parachute troops was dispatched from Hanoi to Dien Bien Phu.

[39] 1,800 members of the Expeditionary Corps volunteered at this late stage in the battle for service at Dien Bien Phu. These volunteers included 800 metropolitan French, 450 Foreign Legionaries, 400 North Africans, and 150 Vietnamese (Navarre, p. 237).

deputy who took it upon himself to declare to journalists in
New York on 19 April that he was not in favour of direct
American intervention in Indochina on the grounds that it
would constitute a threat to world peace, adding that in his
opinion the reopening of negotiations with Ho Chi Minh
represented the only possible solution to the Indochinese problem.[40] This attempt to discourage the implementation of
Dulles's proposal for 'united action' on behalf of French Union
troops at Dien Bien Phu was ably supported by a section of the
French press which, ignoring France's moral obligations towards the garrison and towards the Vietnamese nationalists
who were providing the bulk of French Union casualties, appeared to be waiting, with ill-concealed impatience, for the
fulfilment of their gloomy prophecies in regard to the outcome
of the siege.

NEGOTIATIONS FOR THE INDEPENDENCE OF VIETNAM

Although the deterioration in the military situation and the
prospect of negotiations with the Viet Minh rendered the 'completion' of Vietnamese independence and sovereignty a matter
of somewhat academic interest, the Prime Minister, Prince Buu
Loc, together with an important delegation, had arrived in
Paris on 3 March, to negotiate a settlement of Vietnamese
claims on the basis of the French Government's 'solemn
declaration' of 3 July 1953.

The opening of these negotiations took place when a debate
was in progress in the French National Assembly on the Indochinese situation.

This debate was closed by the adoption of a resolution which
expressed satisfaction at the decision to convene a conference at
Geneva for the purpose of finding a way to end the conflict
and, after recalling that the conflict had been sustained on
behalf of the French Union to which the Associate States had
voluntarily adhered, proceeded to advise the Governments
of these states that, if they should completely repudiate their
past agreements, France for her part would consider herself to
be no longer bound by her obligations towards them.[41] The
negotiations which opened under such unfavourable auspices

[40] Frédéric-Dupont, pp. 142–3.
[41] *J.O.*, Débats parlementaires, 9 Mar. 1954, p. 764 (Cole, p. 138).

made little progress, for the French insisted that a Committee should be set up to examine a Vietnamese proposal that two treaties should be negotiated: one to define the 'total' independence that Vietnam was to be granted, and the other the nature of Vietnam's future association with France, and the implications of this proposal were to give rise to exhaustive and interminable discussions, which seemed principally designed to put off Vietnam's accession to 'total' independence until the Geneva Conference had opened.

On 10 April Bao Dai, who was aware both of the desperate plight of the garrison at Dien Bien Phu and of the desire of an important section of French political opinion for an armistice, left Saigon for France with the intention of hastening the conclusion of the negotiations. Before he left he signed two decrees which showed the Government's intention to increase the national contribution towards the common war effort.

The first of the decrees set up a War Cabinet, the membership of which was restricted to the Prime Minister, the Ministers of the Interior and National Defence, the Chief of the General Staff, and Bao Dai's principal private secretary, who held ministerial rank. This Cabinet was empowered 'to take all necessary measures to intensify and to co-ordinate national activities directed towards the prosecution of the war'.[42]

The second decree, which was promulgated after Bao Dai had left for France, formally incorporated the militia forces of the Cochin-Chinese sects in the national army. This measure displeased the Cao Dai and Hoa Hao leaders, whose autonomy had hitherto been based on French subsidies and military supplies. Their displeasure was voiced by Cao Dai 'General' Nguyen Thanh Phuong, who had succeeded 'General' Nguyen Van Thanh at the head of the sect's militia forces in March 1953, and Phuong, whose tendency to indulge in futile political agitation had already aroused some misgivings, bluntly declared that he would not allow the units under his command to be incorporated with the national army.[43] His truculent attitude

---

[42] *Bull. du Haut Commissariat du Viet-Nam en France*, No. 73, 15 Apr. 1954. On 12 April the War Cabinet issued a decree mobilizing the entire male population between the ages of 20 and 25. This decree, which affected 150,000 Vietnamese, was extensively evaded by the conscripts, who preferred, at this nadir of Franco-Vietnamese fortunes, to avoid military service by concealment, by flight, or by enlisting in the sects' militia forces.

[43] *Le Monde*, 16 Apr. 1954.

threatened for a time to lead to wholesale defections from the sect's militia forces, but wiser counsels prevailed, and Phuong was finally persuaded to retract his challenge to the Government's authority, his statement being ascribed to a 'misunderstanding'.

The month of April was also marked by the announcement of the appointment of a Binh Xuyen nominee, Lai Huu Sang, to the post of director-general of the Saigon–Cholon police and security services. Sang's appointment was followed by the resignation of several hundred police and security agents, who proceeded to enlist in the national army, to which their former director, Mai Huu Xuan, had been transferred with the rank of General,[44] their action being inspired by the well-founded apprehension that, as they had compromised themselves by their previous efforts to combat the activities of the Binh Xuyen group, they would now be delivered into the hands of their triumphant enemies. It can occasion no surprise, therefore, that an appointment which entrusted the responsibility for public security in Saigon–Cholon to an armed group, whose fortunes were founded upon the very activities which they would now be required to combat, should have given rise to the rumour that this scandalous appointment had been preceded by a generous cash payment to the Prime Minister.[45]

Meanwhile the Committee set up in Paris to examine the Vietnamese proposal on the form that the agreement should take, had been in session for a full seven weeks when it was decided that this proposal should be embodied in a joint declaration.[46]

The signature on 28 April of this Franco-Vietnamese declaration, which recognized the 'total independence' of Vietnam, enabled the delegates to proceed rapidly with the task of

[44] Ibid. 5 May 1954.

[45] *L'Humanité*, 24 Dec. 1954. Although the decision to appoint Lai Huu Sang appears to have been made by Prince Buu Loc, Bao Dai approved the Prime Minister's action. His approval may have been based on the calculation that Binh Xuyen control of security in Saigon–Cholon would present certain advantages since the Binh Xuyen 'General', Le Van Vien, who possessed a capacity for friendship and a code of loyalty commonly found among those who prey upon society, was personally attached to Bao Dai. He could be relied upon, therefore, during the critical months ahead, to combat subversive activities. But whatever motive may have prompted Bao Dai's approval, insufficient consideration was given to the inference that would be drawn abroad from an appointment which appeared to offer conclusive proof of the moral bankruptcy of the régime.

[46] Text in *The Times*, 29 Apr. 1954 (*L'Année Politique, 1954*, p. 569).

21

drawing up the treaties, but the dilatory course of the initial proceedings, in the absence of any fundamental divergence of views, had exasperated and alarmed Bao Dai, who divined the French desire to delay recognition of Vietnamese independence until the Geneva Conference had begun. On the eve of this Conference, therefore, a communiqué was issued on 25 April by the imperial cabinet which defined the attitude of the head of the state and of his Government towards the association with France and the impending negotiations.

After deploring that the treaties which were to confirm Vietnamese independence and to establish the limits of Vietnam's future association with France had not been signed before the opening of the Geneva Conference, the communiqué declared that the Government's decision not to insist that this phase of the negotiations should be concluded by the signing of these treaties was based on the consideration that, in certain respects, Vietnam had not received the effective guarantees in regard to her independence and unity to which, in accordance with the principles that had been laid down, her status as a free and equal partner entitled her.

With regard to Vietnamese unity [continued the communiqué] it is known that various plans have been drawn up which would entail a partition of Vietnam. Such solutions may offer certain specious advantages of a diplomatic nature, but their adoption would present extremely grave disadvantage and dangers for the future. . . . Vietnam would never be prepared to consider the possibility of negotiations in which France, violating the basic principles of the French Union from which her authority is derived, were to negotiate with those who are in rebellion against the Vietnamese nation or with hostile powers, thereby disregarding or sacrificing her partner.

Whatever may happen neither the head of the state nor the Vietnamese Government will consider themselves bound by decisions which by running counter to national independence and unity would violate the rights of peoples and reward aggression, contrary to the principles of the United Nations Charter and to democratic ideals.[47]

This vigorous statement produced a reply from Marc Jacquet, the Secretary of State for Indochinese Affairs, who expressed astonishment that the good faith of the French

[47] *Le Monde*, 27 Apr. 1954.

Government should be questioned and drew attention to the fact that the Foreign Minister had discussed the implications of the Geneva Conference with representatives of the Associate States on the previous day. Nevertheless, Bao Dai's fear of an impending threat to national unity proved to be well founded.

Meanwhile the French press, stressing nationalist divisions, gave good coverage to political agitation in Saigon, where Ngo Dinh Nhu[48] and the Movement for National Union and Peace were demanding the immediate formation of a representative government, the rapid organization of general elections, and a constitution.[49]

## THE FALL OF DIEN BIEN PHU

During the latter half of April the French positions at Dien Bien Phu continued to be subjected to harassing gunfire and to night attacks, while Viet Minh sappers proceeded to enmesh the camp in an increasingly complex maze of trenches. These tactics confined the garrison within ever narrower limits and further reduced the dropping zones on which they depended for supplies. By the end of the month the Viet Minh, in spite of sustained attacks on their communications, had completed their preparations for a general assault, which was delivered on the night of 1–2 May by a force estimated to consist of two divisions. In this attack breaches were made in the defence perimeter, and the Viet Minh were able to maintain their pressure in spite of French counter-attacks. Although torrential rain, which transformed the camp into a quagmire and added to the discomforts of the living and to the difficulty of disposing of the dead, afforded the garrison some respite, the attack was resumed on the night of 6–7 May. This final assault overwhelmed the remaining French positions, while a gallant attempt on the following night by the garrison of the outlying position to the south—'Isabelle'—to effect a sortie ended in inevitable disaster.

The fall of Dien Bien Phu was generally considered in France and Indochina to have decided the outcome of the war since

[48] Max Arnaud in ibid., 13 Mar. 1954.
[49] The Movement for National Union and Peace, which had been abandoned at this stage by its principal supporters, was composed of Cao Dai 'General' Nguyen Thanh Phuong and Nguyen Ton Hoan, the representative of a Dai Viet splinter group (*Bull. du Haut Commissariat du Viet-Nam en France*, No. 71, 15 Mar. 1954, p. 419).

although Navarre insisted in the Order of the Day announcing the fall of the camp that the fight would continue, France's inability to dispatch the necessary reinforcements rendered an armistice inevitable.[50] When the news was received in Paris, general instructions were drafted by the Chiefs of Staff and approved by the Committee for National Defence in regard to the action which should now be taken. These instructions were entrusted to Ely, the Chief of the French General Staff, who was dispatched, together with Salan, to Saigon.

The principal considerations which had inspired the Chiefs of Staff in drawing up these instructions had been the necessity of ensuring the safety of the Expeditionary Corps. Navarre therefore was ordered to withdraw French Union garrisons from the regions to the south and west of the Red river delta, a delay of from ten to fifteen days being allowed for carrying out this operation. Arrangements were also to be put in hand to withdraw the Expeditionary Corps within the Haiphong redoubt, which had been heavily fortified in 1951. Preparations for the evacuation of Tongking were to be accompanied by the pacification of the territory to the south of the 18th parallel with a view to facilitating the defence of Annam and Cochin-China.

These orders were, however, criticized by Navarre, who questioned the probability of an imminent offensive by the decimated and exhausted Viet Minh divisions on the Red river delta, and objected that the French Union garrisons would be accompanied in their precipitate retreat from the outlying areas to the south and west by thousands of refugees under con-

---

[50] The argument can be advanced that the siege had not been entirely to French disadvantage. While French Union forces had lost 16,000 officers and men, including seven battalions of the parachute troops on whom the defence of Indochinese territory principally depended, the casualties inflicted on the Viet Minh regular units were estimated to have amounted to at least 20,000 killed and wounded (Navarre, pp. 228-9). But such an argument ignores the fact that the capture of the entrenched camp had revealed the fallacious assumptions on which French strategy had been based. For undue reliance had been placed on the defence of fortified watch-towers, defence posts, strong-posts, and concrete fortifications: a reliance which had found its ultimate expression in the creation of the 'aero-terrestrial' base. Dien Bien Phu had demonstrated, however, that the possession of artillery and air support no longer afforded sufficient protection against Viet Minh attacks. In consequence the precarious equilibrium which had confined the French Union forces to the towns and to the vicinity of their defence positions, while the Viet Minh were left in control of most of the countryside, had now been broken to Viet Minh advantage.

ditions calculated to encourage the offensive which the National Defence Committee were anxious to forestall.[51] But Navarre's objections were ignored and on their return to France Ely and Salan submitted a report which stressed the critical nature of the situation and the need, if the fighting should continue, of sending conscripts to serve in Indochina.[52]

On 3 June Ely's appointment as Commissioner General and Commander-in-Chief of French Union forces in Indochina was announced and, in view of the overwhelming demands that these dual functions would be likely to make upon his time and stamina, Salan was delegated to accompany him as his military deputy.

Before he left Indochina Navarre denied, in a letter addressed to the troops, that the defence of Laos, which had led to the setting up of an entrenched camp at Dien Bien Phu, had been imposed for political reasons or that any choice of strategy had been dictated by 'higher authority'.[53] But if he was prepared to exonerate the French Government from the charge proffered by French journalists that strategy had been laid down in Paris,[54] Navarre returned to France with legitimate grievances against the politicians who had proved incapable of imposing a consistent policy, together with the sacrifices that such a policy would have demanded, and had begrudged the Expeditionary Corps the reinforcements and supplies, which might have enabled victory to be won at an earlier stage of the war.[55]

[51] The regions that were to be evacuated included the Vicariates of Phat Diem and Bui Chu, which had provided the best recruits for the French Union forces, including many volunteers for the parachute battalions.

[52] The confidential section of this report was published in the weekly newspaper *L'Express*.

[53] *The Times*, 8 June 1954.

[54] Guillain, *La Fin des illusions*, p. 67.

[55] Navarre's grievances, which amounted to an indictment of the régime, had been summarized by a French journalist after the fall of Dien Bien Phu, as follows: 'The Dien Bien Phu drama' is 'a tragic illustration of what must be termed the basic weakness of the French governing class, which has been socially identified, since the Revolution, with the bourgeoisie. . . .

'What most characterizes [this class] both in the spheres of domestic and foreign policy, is a consistent refusal to make the timely and spontaneous concessions that justice demands, and to wait for such concessions to be extorted by force—or by the threat of force—with the result that a higher price has had to be paid for a less satisfactory solution. . . . This short-sighted policy leads to a paradoxical situation where the men in public life who would consider themselves dishonoured by the spontaneous concession of some advantage in a frontier dispute, or by the surrender of a few square miles of colonial territory, are prepared, on occasion, to make concessions that are wholly unjustified: a policy which was illustrated in

Indeed considerable sympathy must be felt for Navarre, who had been called upon to shoulder the blame for a defeat which the victory of the Chinese Communists and the defensive nature of French strategy probably rendered inevitable. Nevertheless the wisdom of appointing a general to command French Union troops in Indochina whose career had been devoted principally to the collection and assessment of military intelligence may be open to question. Although he possessed a precise appreciation of the difficulties with which he was confronted, Navarre lacked the robust self-assurance which might have enabled him to acquire the confidence of the troops, the loyalty of his subordinates, and the support of a critical press. Moreover his readiness to sacrifice, with almost hysterical abandon, the surviving parachute battalions at a stage in the siege when the fate of the garrison was sealed must arouse doubts concerning his temperamental fitness to discharge the crushing responsibilities with which he had been entrusted, while his critical attitude towards Vietnamese troops, for whose deficiencies the French were themselves principally to blame, reveals an embarrassing lack of generosity.[56] This attitude is revealed by the fact that whereas the Vietnamese authorities were to claim that more than 6,000 Vietnamese officers and men, belonging for the most part to the crack parachute battalions, had taken part in the defence of Dien Bien Phu,[57] Navarre's acknowledgement of these considerable services was confined to a lament that during the concluding phase of the war the proportion of Vietnamese serving 'even in the best battalions' was far too high.[58]

1917, when the defection of Russia having compelled us to seek other allies, French deputies advocated the unconditional transfer of Indochina to Japan in order to secure that country's wholehearted co-operation on the side of the Western democracies' (Maurice Vaussard in *Le Monde*, 13 May 1954).

[56] In a press interview on 8 June 1954 Navarre attributed greater military importance to the failure of *Opération Atlante*, for which he blamed the lack of patriotism and aggressive spirit of the raw Vietnamese light battalions, than to the fall of Dien Bien Phu (*Le Populaire*, 9 June 1954).

[57] *Bull. du Haut Commissariat du Viet-Nam en France*, No. 75, 15 May 1954.

[58] Navarre, p. 252.

# XVII

# The Geneva Conference

J. F. DULLES, who was to lead the American delegation, left Washington on 20 April with the intention of first attending a meeting of the North Atlantic Council which was to take place in Paris on the 23rd.

On 23 April Dulles received an urgent appeal for help from Bidault, the French Foreign Minister, who said that, unless a powerful air-strike by American carrier-based planes was carried out within twelve hours, all hope of saving the Dien Bien Phu garrison must be abandoned. That evening Dulles cornered Eden and told him this grave news, adding that, if Eden felt able to stand with him, he would advise the President to ask Congress to approve a declaration of the United States' intention to support France in Indochina: a declaration which would apparently enable Eisenhower to authorize an air-strike in support of the Dien Bien Phu garrison.[1] But Eden questioned the effectiveness of an air-strike at this late stage in the siege and discounted American fears of an imminent and general collapse of French resistance.

On the following afternoon the two ministers met again to discuss the situation. Dulles began by saying that the French had warned him of their intention to abandon the struggle unless assistance was forthcoming for the Dien Bien Phu garrison; and although he now admitted that the approval of Congress could not be obtained in time to save the situation, he thought it essential to show that France had powerful allies, who were prepared to stand by her in the emergency. Eden, however, maintained his objections to Dulles's proposal, pointing out that precipitate action might lead to a world war. Finally, it was agreed that Bidault should be asked to clear up the existing discrepancy between the American and the British assessment of the military situation. Accordingly a meeting took place later that afternoon at the Quai d'Orsay. Here Eden's misgivings in regard to American intentions were increased still further, for not only did Dulles apparently assume

[1] Tournoux, p. 55.

that the British Government was in some way committed to armed intervention, but he produced the draft of a letter, which he proposed to send to Bidault officially, announcing the readiness of his Government to move American forces into Indochina if France and the other Allies so desired; and, although this offer appears to have taken Bidault aback, he agreed, after hesitating for some minutes, to give the proposal official consideration.[2] Faced with Dulles's evident determination to enlist British support for armed intervention, Eden decided to return to London immediately and consult with his colleagues.

Next day an emergency Cabinet meeting was held at which it was agreed that no undertaking should be given in regard to military intervention before the Geneva Conference. The Government decided, however, to join in guaranteeing any settlement reached, or in considering other forms of joint action should the Conference fail to produce a settlement. This decision was maintained despite a final *démarche* by the French Ambassador, René Massigli, who called on Eden in the afternoon and told him that if the United Kingdom would join with France's allies in immediately declaring their common determination to check the expansion of Communism in South East Asia, and to use 'eventual military means' for that purpose, President Eisenhower, for his part, would seek Congressional approval for intervention: a step which would be followed by an air-strike in support of the Dien Bien Phu garrison on 28 April.[3]

Meanwhile the French Government, who may have wished to allay suspicions that France might be tempted to purchase the safety of the Expeditionary Corps in exchange for an agreement with the Russians to abandon EDC, had authorized Bidault to initial on its behalf the Convention on Co-operation

---

[2] Although the French Government was morally bound to do everything in its power to relieve the Dien Bien Phu garrison, and had repeatedly impressed upon the Americans that their salvation depended upon a massive air-strike, Bidault must have been aware that the official dispatch of American armed forces to Indochina would internationalize the war, and thereby destroy all hope of a negotiated settlement being reached at Geneva: this probably accounted for his hesitation.

[3] Eden, p. 106. The French Ambassador in Washington, Henri Bonnet, seems to have formed the opinion, however, that Eisenhower did not share Dulles's views on military intervention in Indochina, and would have been reluctant to sanction such a course of action (Tournoux, pp. 53–54).

of Vietnam, measures were taken to hasten the arrival of the Indochinese delegations and to overcome Bao Dai's reluctance to agree to nationalist representation.

On 28 April Marc Jacquet, the French Secretary of State for Indochinese Affairs, visited Bao Dai at Cannes to inform him of the wishes of the French Government, and on the 30th a joint message was addressed to him by Bidault, Dulles, and Eden expressing their desire to consult with a representative of the head of the state of Vietnam on the work of the Geneva Conference. At the same time, tendentious articles started to appear in the French press insinuating that the delay in evacuating the wounded from Dien Bien Phu was due to Bao Dai's refusal to allow Vietnamese representation at the Geneva Conference. Finally Bao Dai, whose conduct throughout the negotiations would seem to have been based on the belief that American opposition would prevent the conclusion of an armistice, agreed that the Minister for Foreign Affairs, Nguyen Quoc Dinh, who was engaged in negotiating with the French Government in Paris, should go to Geneva in order to discuss the question of Vietnamese representation with the three Foreign Ministers; during this discussion Dinh agreed to nationalist and also to Viet Minh participation in the Conference. He emphasized, however, that the presence of this last delegation would not constitute recognition of a Viet Minh state or government, and that the Vietnamese Government reserved its right to refuse to subscribe to any decision prejudicial to national independence, liberty, or unity. On 3 May, therefore, a formal invitation was sent both to the Nationalist Government and to the Government of the Democratic Republic of Vietnam.

The Government of the Democratic Republic seemed to have been anticipating such an invitation, and on the following day its delegation arrived from Berlin under the leadership of Pham Van Dong, who had been the principal Viet Minh representative at the Fontainebleau Conference. Dong, who was now deputy Prime Minister and Minister for Foreign Affairs *ad interim*, soon revealed that neither the passage of years nor the hardships of life in the Viet Minh zone had changed his somewhat truculent approach to a conference table, and bluntly declared on his arrival that a particularly important task facing the Conference would be the restoration of peace in Indochina on the basis of the recognition of the national rights of the peoples of Vietnam, the Khmer, and Pathet Lao.[9]

Meanwhile the Laniel Government was under constant attack in the National Assembly, where a vigilant opposition under the leadership of Mendès-France were resolved that Bidault's pride and scruples should not be permitted to impede a settlement; after a debate on 9 May, it was generally recognized that the Government's survival now depended on the rapid progress of the impending negotiations.[10]

On 8 May the Indochina phase of the Geneva Conference had opened under singularly unpropitious circumstances, the garrison at Dien Bien Phu having succumbed on the previous day. At this session Bidault made a speech in which, after paying tribute to the heroism displayed by French Union troops at Dien Bien Phu, he put forward a number of proposals for an armistice. These were that the Viet Minh regular and irregular forces which had invaded Cambodia and Laos should be evacuated, and that in Vietnam regular units of the opposing forces should regroup in predetermined areas, while irregular elements should be disarmed and prisoners of war and interned civilians liberated. Bidault also recommended that these troop movements should be supervised by international commissions and that the agreements should be guaranteed by the Governments participating in the Conference.

Pham Van Dong, whose brusque manner and embittered attitude did not appear to conceal diplomatic ability of a high order, confined himself in his opening speech to repeating his demand that representatives of the 'Khmer' and 'Pathet Lao' resistance governments should be invited to take part in the work of the Conference. In spite of his insistence that the governments whose claims to recognition were thus advanced had 'liberated vast areas of their national territory' and 'exerted all their efforts in creating a democratic Power and in raising the living standard of the population in liberated

[9] *Figaro*, 5 May 1954.
[10] On 6 May Eden and Bedell Smith had assured Bidault of their strong support if the French Government was able to clear its policy, concert it with their allies, and present it at the opening meeting of the Indochina phase of the Conference; a task complicated by the internal difficulties facing the French Government and by Bidault's despairing belief that he held no cards in his hand or, at most, a 'two of clubs' and a 'three of spades' (Eden, p. 115).

areas',[11] the fallacious nature of these claims was promptly pilloried by Sam Sary, the head of the Cambodian delegation, who denied all knowledge either of a 'Free Government of Free Khmer' or of the location of the vast if unspecified territories where its writ was alleged to run. Phoui Sananikone, the head of the Laotian delegation, after pointing out that the Lao Issara movement had dissolved itself voluntarily in October 1949, observed with equal vigour that 'this so-called Pathet Lao', under the leadership of an expatriate prince, represented 'absolutely nothing' and, indeed, that 'it would be almost comic to recognize him as representing anybody'.[12]

Dong, who was unabashed by the ridicule with which his pretensions had been treated, revealed two days later the Viet Minh conditions for a cease-fire. These were the recognition by France of the sovereignty and independence of Vietnam over the whole national territory as well as the sovereignty and independence of 'Khmer and Pathet Lao', and an agreement for the withdrawal of all foreign troops from the territories of the three states, where free general elections would then be held under the supervision of local committees. The elections would be preceded by the convening of Advisory Conferences to discuss the necessary arrangements between representatives of the Governments of the two parties in Vietnam and of 'Khmer and Pathet Lao'. These proposals were accompanied by a declaration of Viet Minh readiness to examine the question of the Democratic Republic of Vietnam's future association with the French Union and to recognize France's economic and cultural interests in Indochina.[13]

Dong's confused proposals caused surprise and dismay, but Anthony Eden, the British Foreign Secretary, who had already discussed with Molotov the implication of the Viet Minh demand for 'Khmer and Pathet Lao' representation, was sufficiently encouraged by the Soviet Foreign Minister's conciliatory attitude[14] to persist in his attempts to prevent the work of the Conference from being blocked by the Viet Minh attitude. He therefore intervened in the debate on 10 May and, after refuting certain allegations which Dong had made in

[11] Cmd. 9186, pp. 112-13.
[12] Ibid. pp. 114-16.
[13] Ibid. pp. 116-18.
[14] Roger Massip in *Figaro*, 11 May 1954.

regard to American and French predatory designs, he recommended Bidault's plan to the attention of the delegates and proposed that the armistice should be based on the separation and subsequent concentration of the opposing forces within distinct and clearly defined zones under some supervisory organization. Two days later Eden again intervened during the third plenary session to discourage flights of dialectic materialistic fancy on the part of Chou En-lai and to urge the delegates to consider the French proposals.

Also during this session Nguyen Quoc Dinh, the Vietnamese Foreign Minister, whose delegation had symbolically established its residence outside Geneva at Saint-Julien-en-Genevois, submitted the proposals of his Government for an armistice. Dinh recognized that the restoration of peace would entail a political and a military settlement, but although he declared that the Vietnamese delegation would be prepared to examine any plan submitted in good faith, he stipulated that the military settlement must exclude any proposal that would lead either directly or indirectly to a permanent or temporary, *de facto* or *de jure*, partition of the national territory, and he insisted that provision must be made for international supervision of the execution of the cease-fire terms. Dinh also specified that the political settlement must accord recognition to the principle that the only state entitled to represent Vietnam legally was the state of which Bao Dai was the head; although he expressed willingness to allow free elections to be held throughout the national territory as soon as the Security Council were satisfied that the Government's authority had been established and conditions of freedom were fulfilled, he insisted that these elections must be internationally supervised by representatives of the United Nations.[15]

At this stage in the Conference the negotiations appeared to have reached an impasse, but on 14 May Molotov, after a tirade against American aggressive designs in South East Asia, made an unexpected concession proposing that any agreement on the cessation of hostilities should include provisions for the setting up of a supervisory commission composed of representatives of neutral countries. If the credit for this concession was ascribed by the press to Eden,[16] Molotov's tirade appears to

[15] Cmd. 9186, pp. 123-4.
[16] *CSM*, 14 May 1954.

have been occasioned by Dulles's activities, for the divergences and uncertainties of the Western democracies perplexed and disquieted the Soviet representatives, who were inclined to suspect that some concerted plan of action must underlie such apparent incoherence.

However, on this occasion Soviet perplexity was fully shared by the French and British representatives. Whereas French morale had been adversely affected, on 12 May, by reports of a press conference in Washington at which Dulles was reported to have declared that the retention of Indochina was not essential to the defence of South East Asia,[17] the British delegation, for their part, were astonished to read in the Swiss morning papers some days later that Franco-American discussions had taken place on the possibility of military intervention by the United States in Indochina. Moreover, inquiries about the truth of this report were met evasively, until Bidault's principal adviser, R. de Margerie, furtively produced a document setting out the conditions under which the United States would be prepared to intervene in Indochina either after the breakdown of the Conference, or earlier if the French so desired. Later that day the arrival of the *New York Herald Tribune*, giving full details of these negotiations, enabled Eden to raise the matter officially with the head of the American delegation, who deplored Washington's failure to keep the matter secret and sought to mollify Eden by assuring him that the discussions had been confined to the provision of assistance with military training. Although Bidault was to give an undertaking two days later that no request for American intervention would be made while the Conference was still in session, Eden discounted the American thesis that the threat of intervention would incline the Chinese to compromise, and objected that the publicity given to these 'noises off' could prejudice the chances of a settlement.[18]

On 17 May the delegates met for the first time in restricted session and decided that priority should be accorded to the military aspects of the settlement, while the recommendation was made that private discussions should take place between the French and Viet Minh delegations to solve the difficulties that had arisen over the evacuation of the French wounded

[17] *Le Monde*, 13 May 1954.
[18] Eden, pp. 119–20.

from Dien Bien Phu.[19] These discussions in restricted session again revealed an unexpectedly co-operative approach to the problems confronting the Conference on the part of the Soviet Foreign Minister. Nevertheless further proof of Washington's distrust of the proceedings was provided on 19 May, when the French and British were shown a statement prepared by the United States' delegation proposing that restricted sessions should be brought to an end and plenary sessions resumed; and only Eden's plea for patience and Bidault's assurance that its adoption would lead to the fall of the French Government stopped the United States delegation from putting this proposal to the Conference.[20] During the ensuing discussions further progress was stopped by the stubborn insistence of the Communist delegates that 'Pathet Lao and Khmer' should be recognized as *de facto* governments. Finally, a Soviet proposal was adopted towards the end of the week that discussions should be confined to a five-point plan.[21]

These restricted sessions left the press free to devote their attention to activities on the fringe of the Conference. Thus it was noted that when Bidault dined with Bao Dai on 18 May Jacquet, who was then at Geneva, did not accompany him. Rumours that Jacquet was out of favour were confirmed two days later by his resignation, his functions being taken over by Frédéric-Dupont, a deputy with long experience of Indochinese affairs, who was given the portfolio of Minister for the Associate States.[22]

[19] The French refusal to establish non-official contacts with the Viet Minh delegation had been based on the consideration that such contacts would represent the first step towards the *de facto* recognition of the Democratic Republic. The evacuation of the French wounded, which had been the subject of a local agreement between the two Commands, had been stopped following Viet Minh insistence that during the operation the road, *Route Provinciale* 41, from Dien Bien Phu, which the Viet Minh were themselves using in order to move their forces back to the south-east fringe of the Red river delta, should not be subject to observation or attack by French aircraft.

[20] Eden, p. 120.

[21] Molotov's five-point plan covered the following aspects of a settlement: (1) the cease-fire, (2) the allocation of zones in which the hostile forces should be grouped, (3) measures to prevent the arrival of reinforcements after the cease-fire, (4) the creation of a supervisory body to control the execution of these arrangements, and (5) the form of guarantee required to ensure the implementation of a settlement (*Manchester Guardian*, 22 May 1954).

[22] Following the publication in the French weekly newspaper *L'Express* of the confidential report submitted by Generals Ely and Salan on their return from Indochina, in which pessimistic conclusions were drawn in regard to the military

Meanwhile the French Government continued to be harassed by interpellations in the National Assembly, and on 13 May its Indochinese policy was endorsed by the narrow majority of two votes. French uneasiness in regard to the outcome of the negotiations was increased, moreover, by press reports indicating that in spite of Molotov's conciliatory attitude, relations between the Soviet and French delegations were strained, as the Russians were perturbed by reports of Franco-American discussions on the Indochinese situation and resented Bidault's persistent refusal to contact the Viet Minh delegation.[23]

On 29 May the deadlock was again broken by Eden, who had conferred privately with Molotov on the previous evening. After this meeting the Communist delegates waived their insistence on 'Khmer and Pathet Lao' representation and agreed, during a restricted session, that contacts should be established between the two Commands in Indochina and that military discussions should take place in Geneva between French and Viet Minh representatives to decide the location of the zones in which French Union and Viet Minh troops should regroup after a cease-fire.

When these representatives met on 1 June, the Viet Minh showed a marked reluctance to confine the discussions to the agenda and caused irritation by their tendency to lecture the French on their conduct in Indochina. However, private conversations between the French and Viet Minh officers engaged in the discussions seemed to indicate some readiness on the part of the Viet Minh to negotiate a cease-fire, a readiness which was ascribed to the losses that their regular forces had suffered at Dien Bien Phu, to the exhaustion of the population in the Viet Minh zone, and also to the threat of direct and massive American intervention.

On the eve of another crucial debate in the French National Assembly one of the French military representatives who was in touch with a Viet Minh officer was instructed to find out whether the Viet Minh were in fact prepared to negotiate an armistice on the basis of partition. This approach was well

situation, the office of the newspaper was raided. The raid produced evidence that Jacquet was in close touch with the editorial staff. Thereupon Laniel, the Prime Minister, who had received the Secretary of State's personal assurance some time before that he was not in contact with this newspaper, asked him for his resignation (Laniel, pp. 95–96).

[23] *Le Monde*, 18 May 1954.

received, and on the evening of 10 June an unofficial meeting took place, in the course of which Ta Quang Buu, the Viet Minh Vice-Minister for National Defence, declared that his Government would be prepared to accept an armistice, on the basis of a regroupment of the opposing forces in North and South Vietnam respectively, and the partition of the country in the vicinity of Hué.[24]

Meanwhile the work of the Conference had again been impeded by failure to reach agreement on the composition of the international commission which would be charged with supervising the execution of the terms of an armistice agreement and also by Communist insistence that decisions by this commission should be unanimous. At the beginning of June Molotov paid a brief visit to Moscow, and on his return the rumour became current that he intended to propose that a four-power conference should be held after the Geneva Conference, to discuss the organization of European security, acceptance of this proposal being the condition on which he would be prepared to restrain the Viet Minh from launching an offensive on the Red river delta. This rumour, which was ascribed to the Russian desire to embarrass the French Government and to encourage the opposition in the French National Assembly in the impending debate on Indochina, led Bidault again to deny categorically that his Government would be prepared to trade French adherence to EDC against Russian assistance in securing acceptable terms for a cease-fire agreement in Indochina.[25]

On his return from Moscow Molotov had also proposed that a plenary session should be held, and in view of the procedure adopted in these sessions it was presumed that the Soviet Foreign Minister intended to make an announcement to which he wished maximum publicity to be given.[26] At this plenary session, which was held on 8 June, the main interest therefore centred on Molotov's speech. The Soviet Foreign Minister soon revealed the motive that had prompted his proposal by making a virulent personal attack upon the French Foreign Minister, which was presumably designed to assist Mendès-France to overthrow the Laniel Government by persuading hesitant

[24] Frédéric-Dupont, pp. 154–6.
[25] *The Times*, 7 June 1954.
[26] Ibid.

deputies that under the leadership of Bidault the French delegation would be incapable of reaching a settlement.[27]

Molotov's desire for a change of Government in France was fulfilled: after Mendès-France's attack on Bidault's conduct of Indochinese affairs and dilatory approach to the negotiations at Geneva the outcome of the debate in the National Assembly was unfavourable to the Government, which failed to carry a motion of confidence on 12 June. In accordance with French constitutional practice, Mendès-France was then charged by the President of the Republic with the task of forming a new Government, and on 17 June this Government was formally invested by a large majority.

During the speech in which he outlined his programme Mendès-France declared that his Government adhered to the Western Alliance, and undertook to submit definite proposals in regard to EDC to the National Assembly before the parliamentary recess.[28] He also announced his intention of resigning if he should fail to conclude an honourable peace in Indochina by 20 July. This undertaking, which appeared to be a demagogic gesture designed to attract popular support, caused general surprise. Moreover in view of persistent Soviet inferences that such an armistice could only be arranged in exchange for a French undertaking to abandon EDC, the calculation that might underlie this wager was of a nature to arouse misgivings among the supporters of an integrated Europe, since the delicate balance between the supporters and opponents of EDC made it probable that an adroit Prime Minister, if he were not encumbered by excessive scruples, would be able to sabotage the ratification of the Paris Treaty. Mendès-France's confidence in his ability to secure an armistice must have been fortified, however, by Molotov's timely attack on his predecessor and also by the revelation of Viet Minh readiness to agree to acceptable armistice terms.[29]

The news of Mendès-France's investiture was well received

[27] Ibid. 14 June 1954 and Frédéric-Dupont, p. 153.

[28] Text in L'Année Politique, 1954, pp. 521-3.

[29] Mendès-France was subsequently to deny in the National Assembly that he had been accurately informed, prior to his investiture, of the terms which the Viet Minh had proposed on the night of 10-11 June. But this statement is challenged by Frédéric-Dupont, Minister for the Associate States in the Laniel Government, who claims to have personally given the Prime Minister designate particulars of the Viet Minh proposals (Frédéric-Dupont, pp. 160-1 and 167-71).

at Geneva where Chou En-lai had proposed, on 16 June, the evacuation of all foreign troops from Laos and Cambodia following bilateral military talks between the Viet Minh and representatives of the two Governments concerned. This proposal, which represented the withdrawal of the Communist demand that a cease-fire agreement should be negotiated with 'Khmer and Pathet Lao' representatives, was regarded as an important step forward. On 19 June the Conference reached agreement that representatives of the two Commands in Laos and Cambodia should study the questions relating to the cessation of hostilities in their territories, the talks to be held either in Geneva or in the country concerned. The military representatives taking part in these negotiations were instructed to report to the Conference on the progress that had been achieved in three weeks, and during the interval the heads of the British, Soviet, and American delegations returned to their respective capitals.

Eden broke his journey to have luncheon with Mendès-France in Paris, where he urged the new Prime Minister to have an early meeting with Chou En-lai and also, if he felt able to do so, with Pham Van Dong. On his return to London Eden again set out, four days later, in company with Sir Winston Churchill, for Washington. Here he found Dulles in a somewhat chastened mood and apparently resigned to the partition of Vietnam, provided the French could be persuaded to abandon their economic stranglehold over the country, a prerequisite which he considered essential for the survival of a régime in the non-Communist part of the country; and although he considered that the United States would be most unlikely to guarantee any settlement reached at Geneva, he agreed nevertheless that it would be useful for Mendès-France's guidance during the final negotiations, if the maximum concessions which the United States and the United Kingdom would be prepared to countenance were decided upon. A document was drawn up, therefore, setting out the conditions for an acceptable settlement.[30]

Meanwhile, Mendès-France had profited from the lull in the Conference to meet Chou En-lai in Berne: a visit officially ascribed to his desire to thank the Swiss President in person for the hospitality which the French delegation was receiving at

[30] Eden, pp. 131–3.

Geneva. Their exchange of views was described as frank and friendly.[31] Mendès-France's evident impatience to establish personal contact with the head of the Chinese delegation was however noted with misgivings in Washington, where fears were expressed that the meeting might prejudice the success of the impending negotiations for a South East Asian Security Pact.[32]

Meanwhile Mendès-France, who had announced in the National Assembly that his last act before resignation would be to obtain approval for the dispatch of conscripts to Indochina, proceeded to make ostensible preparations for the continued prosecution of the war and, as an earnest of his intentions, gave instructions for French troops stationed in Germany to be inoculated against yellow fever.[33]

### THE FIRST INDEPENDENT VIETNAMESE GOVERNMENT

While international attention remained focused on the proceedings at Geneva, the initialing, on 4 June, of the treaties[34] which finally established Vietnamese independence and the nature of the Vietnamese future association with France received little publicity. The completion of these negotiations was followed by reports of the imminent resignation of the Buu Loc Government, and Ngo Dinh Diem, whose uncompromising insistence on the equivalent of dominion status had prevented his acceptance of the premiership in 1948, was mentioned as his probable successor, the selection of this somewhat enigmatic personage being apparently inspired by the consideration that he would be best able to ensure American support for a régime faced with the prospect of imminent collapse.[35] On the resignation

[31] *The Times*, 28 June 1954.
[32] *Le Monde*, 24 June 1954.
[33] Frédéric-Dupont, p. 163.
[34] Text in *L'Année Politique, 1954*, pp. 572–3.
[35] After leaving Vietnam in 1950 Diem had lived for two years with the Maryknoll Fathers at Lakewood, New Jersey, where his presence and fitness for high office appear to have been noticed by the influential Cardinal Spellman. In the meantime, his family and friends, and in particular Ngo Dinh Nhu, continued to assist the exile and to keep him informed of developments, while they canvassed his claims to the Premiership and extolled his reputation for moral integrity and financial disinterest. In June 1953 Diem left the United States for Europe, where, after a brief stay in France, he took up residence as a tertiary member of the Benedictine Order in the monastery of St. Andrew at Bruges (*Tablet*, 10 Aug. 1954). But his stay in Belgium was brief, and in May 1954 he returned to Paris.

of Buu Loc on 19 June, Ngo Dinh Diem was accordingly entrusted with the mission of forming the new Government, and as the French decision to evacuate Tongking and the Viet Minh readiness to accept partition were now common knowledge, his moral courage in accepting office at this juncture is worthy of tribute:[36] in the southern half of the country, where the Bao Dai régime was to be allowed to subsist, the loyalty of the armed forces and the competence of the administrative service were alike open to question, while the Government, without adequate financial resources, would be required to combat the danger of collapse, to counter the threat of internal disruption, and to cope with an influx of refugees from Tongking, where close acquaintance with Viet Minh methods would be likely to prevent any undue confidence being placed in an amnesty. To strengthen Diem's hand, therefore, Bao Dai decided to invest him with full civil and military powers.[37]

On 24 June Diem arrived in Saigon. He was welcomed at the airfield[38] by some 500 people, including personal friends, Roman Catholic priests, village notables with goatee beards, and in the front rank an old gentleman with a red turban, royal blue tunic, and bare feet shod in wooden pattens, representing the Catholic communities of Annam who were to provide the new Government with some semblance of popular support.[39] Diem also received an enthusiastic message from Mgr. Pham Ngoc Chi, the Apostolic Vicar of Bui Chu, assuring him of the support 'unto death' of the 1½ million Roman Catholics in the north,[40] but Chi was generally considered on this occasion to have exceeded his authority since Roman Catholics in Tongking, where Diem represented a little-known personage from Annam, were divided in their attitude to the new Prime Minister. Moreover in spite of Bao Dai's exhorta-

[36] NYT, 1 May 1954 and Combat, 19–20 June 1954.

[37] Vietnamese aware of Diem's dubious loyalty had attempted to dissuade Bao Dai from making this appointment, but Bao Dai, who had been nurtured on legends extolling the loyalty of senior mandarins to the Emperor, dismissed these warnings on the grounds that those proffering such advice did not belong to the official caste, and were therefore not in a position to question Diem's loyalty.

[38] Diem's arrival coincided with a period of national mourning in protest against the intention of the negotiators at Geneva to partition the country. The absence of popular enthusiasm must be ascribed to the fact that Diem was practically unknown in South Vietnam.

[39] Clos in Le Monde, 27–28 June 1954.

[40] Georges Naidenoff in Missi, 10 Nov. 1954.

tions to nationalists to rally to the new Prime Minister,[41] Diem seemed reluctant to play the part assigned to him, and with innate sectarian prejudice let it be known that former ministers would be excluded from his cabinet.[42]

The consultations which preceded the formation of the first Government of an independent Vietnam were therefore prolonged. Although they revealed the existence of a measure of goodwill towards a Prime Minister who was prepared to undertake the desperate task of preventing the disintegration of the state, Diem's membership of the mandarin class, whose haughtiness and greed had been partially responsible for the popular rising in 1945, his adherence to an unpopular religious minority, and his constricted timidity of manner were not designed to appeal either to the robust adventurers who controlled the forces of organized nationalism in South Vietnam or to those members of the middle class who had hitherto refused to participate in nationalist governments. The Government finally constituted on 5 July was thus composed of the Prime Minister's personal supporters and members of the Ngo Dinh clan.

A dramatic situation faced the new ministers, for during the last days of June the French garrison at An Khe had been withdrawn, losing in the course of their retreat artillery, transport, and a large number of their effectives. The evacuation of this town opened up the southern half of the mountainous region of Central Vietnam to enemy infiltration and provided Viet Minh units with access to Cambodia and Cochin-China.[43] On 1 July the French Command, acting in conformity with the instructions of the National Defence Committee, also ordered the evacuation of outlying positions in the Red river delta and of the French-controlled zone in South Tongking. The withdrawal, which was known as Opération Auvergne, caused a panic among the population, who thus found themselves abandoned without warning to the Viet Minh, and many of those who had

[41] *Combat*, 19–20 June 1954.

[42] Leroy, p. 185. These former ministers included, together with venal and incompetent men, patriotic and courageous Vietnamese who, conscious of the pressing Communist danger, had been prepared to attempt the reconstruction of the Vietnamese state on a basis that Diem had rejected as inadequate.

[43] Navarre (pp. 279–80) claims that the Viet Minh forces operating from *Lien Khu* V possessed neither the armament nor the reserves which would have enabled them to capture An Khe. In consequence, the Viet Minh Command had decided prior to the French evacuation to withdraw their units to the base areas.

compromised themselves by supporting the Bao Dai régime were compelled to evacuate their homes and villages in haste and confusion.

The refugees included Mgr. Le Huu Tu, the Apostolic Vicar of Phat Diem, who had been seized with alarm when the French intention to withdraw became apparent and, abandoning in haste both his vicariate and his militia guards, escaped from Phat Diem by sea.[44] His colleague, Pham Ngoc Chi, whose vicariate was not immediately exposed to Viet Minh incursions, was, however, able to leave Bui Chu at the head of an imposing contingent comprising the diocesan priests and part of the population.

By 4 July the French Union troops had completed their regroupment along the road and railway linking Hanoi with the port of Haiphong and in the coastal area stretching eastward from Haiphong. But the refugees proved a source of grave embarrassment to the provincial administrators, who were unable to provide them with the necessary food and shelter. In order to relieve the congestion in the French zone, it was therefore decided to evacuate a number of Vietnamese troops, together with their dependants, to Nha Trang and Saigon.

Meanwhile the Vietnamese Government, who do not appear to have been forewarned of an operation which vitally affected an important section of the population, decided to set up a Committee for the Defence of the North. This Committee was invested with the powers hitherto exercised by the Governor, and instructed to prepare the defence of Hanoi in the event of a French withdrawal. However, these orders were later amended, with the result that the Committee directed its activities to the organization of reception centres for the refugees, who were later, with French assistance, transferred to the south.

After the completion of *Opération Auvergne* the Viet Minh and the Franco-Vietnamese military representatives met, in conformity with the decision reached at the Geneva Conference, in order to discuss arrangements for a cease-fire. The meeting had been delayed for some days by the Viet Minh refusal to agree to nationalist representation, but after the dispute had been referred to Geneva it was decided that three nationalist representatives should be included in the French

[44] Tu had been officially sentenced to death on five separate occasions by the Viet Minh.

delegation. As these nationalist representatives were, however, expressly forbidden to discuss matters relating either to an armistice or to a regroupment of military units, their role was confined to that of observers.[45]

The Conference met at Trung Giao in Viet Minh-controlled territory to the north of Hanoi on 3 July, and after a formal opening in the presence of French and Viet Minh press correspondents, the delegates proceeded to discuss, in closed session, the exchange of prisoners of war. Two days later a communiqué was issued stating that agreement had been reached for the first exchange of prisoners to take place on the 14th.[46] A further communiqué announced that priority was to be given to the exchange of wounded and of prisoners in poor physical condition. Agreement was also reached that immediate measures should be taken to improve the lot of those confined in prison camps: these measures included an increase in rations and the arrangement of facilities for the dispatch of medicines, while an undertaking was given that prisoners should no longer be subjected to physical exploitation or to moral pressure.[47]

This communiqué was welcomed in France since in the absence of any supervision by representatives of the International Red Cross organization the fate of prisoners of war had been a source of grave anxiety, inspired by the knowledge that prisoners, who were confined in the unhealthy jungles of North Vietnam, received rations which represented slow starvation, were deprived of medical care, and were subjected to Communist indoctrination. These conditions, which were partly due to shortages in the Viet Minh zone but also to the contempt for human life displayed by the Viet Minh Command in their conduct of the war, were found to have exacted a terrible toll. The President of the French Red Cross estimated in October that 65 per cent. of the inmates of Viet Minh prisoner-of-war camps had died in captivity.[48]

[45] Clos in Le Monde, 7 July 1954.
[46] L'Humanité, 6 July 1954.
[47] Le Populaire, 12 July 1954.
[48] Figaro, 7 Oct. 1954. In September Ely announced in Saigon that while 9,886 prisoners had been released, those missing or those who had died in captivity included 4,995 French, 5,349 Foreign Legionaries, 2,074 Algerians, 2,907 Moroccans, 63 Tunisians, and 1,041 Equatorial Africans, while some 23,000 Vietnamese had disappeared (ibid. 20 Sept. 1954). These figures were subsequently amended in a joint statement by the Ministries of National Defence and for the Associate States, in which it was stated that 14,905 prisoners had been released, including

After the conclusion of the agreement on the exchange of prisoners the delegates at Trung Giao proceeded to examine the manner in which the military forces should be regrouped after a cease-fire. These discussions progressed favourably, the French delegation insisting merely on the retention of an extensive bridgehead around Haiphong for the evacuation of their forces.

## THE ARMISTICE AGREEMENTS

On the eve of the resumption of plenary sessions at Geneva there were indications that neither Dulles nor Bedell Smith, the Under-Secretary of State, would be returning to lead the American delegation, a decision which was ascribed to the fear that the presence of a member of the Government at Geneva might be interpreted as a sign of American readiness to ratify an agreement that formally recognized a territorial extension of Communist influence by force of arms. The absence of American ministerial representation at the concluding phase of the Conference was however viewed with misgivings by the French and British Governments on the grounds that the withdrawal of American support would be interpreted as evidence of basic disagreements among the members of the Western Alliance. But in spite of a *démarche* by the French Ambassador in Washington, on the eve of the resumption of the discussions Dulles publicly confirmed that neither he nor Bedell Smith would be returning to take part in the Conference unless some evidence of Communist goodwill were provided. This decision was discussed by Mendès-France and Eden, after the latter's return to Geneva on 12 July, and it was decided that the French Prime Minister should invite the American Secretary of State to fly to Paris for a tripartite meeting.

Dulles promptly accepted this invitation and left for Paris that evening. During the discussions Mendès-France managed to dispel his suspicions that there would inevitably be some departure from the conditions laid down in Washington, and a document setting out the position adopted by the French and United States Governments was then drawn up, signed, and exchanged, Eden expressing the general approval of the British Government in a separate letter. On his return to Washington,

2,118 Vietnamese, while 2,840 metropolitan French remained unaccounted for (*Le Monde*, 21–22 Nov. 1954).

therefore, Dulles announced that a 'formula for constructive Allied unity' had been found,[49] which would have a beneficial effect on the Conference negotiations. The agreement on this formula also enabled him to recommend that Bedell Smith should return to Geneva.[50] His brief visit to Paris had likewise provided Dulles with an opportunity to discuss EDC with the French Prime Minister. He is reported to have expressed astonishment that the French Government should again have deferred the ratification of the Paris Treaty, but Mendès-France, who possessed a gift for lucid exposition, was able to persuade him that the American assumption that a majority existed for the ratification of the treaty was ill-founded, and that the French Government's decision to seek an acceptable compromise was entirely justified. Indeed so convincing did Mendès-France prove in his analysis of the state of French political opinion that Dulles is reported to have returned to Washington considerably incensed at the ineptitude of his advisers.[51]

This improvised tripartite meeting had, however, aroused the misgivings of the Soviet delegation, with the result that the Tass agency distributed among press correspondents in Geneva a statement in which Dulles's journey was described as another attempt by 'aggressive circles in the United States' to wreck the Conference and to bring pressure to bear on France and Great Britain.[52] The suspicions aroused by Mendès-France's readiness not only to confer with Dulles but even, it was alleged, to discuss with him the ratification of the obnoxious Paris Treaty were soon to be dispelled, however, by his patent anxiety to secure a settlement.

The Foreign Ministers who now returned to Geneva for the resumption of the plenary sessions included Dr. Tran Van Do, who held the portfolio of Foreign Affairs in the newly constituted Vietnamese Nationalist Government. Tran Van Do, who had long deplored the prevarication and subterfuge to which the French authorities had resorted in their attempts to prevent, and later to delay, the creation of a 'Nationalist' state, was to play his thankless part in a manner which stressed the

[49] *NYT*, 16 July 1954.
[50] Eden, pp. 138–9.
[51] André Fontaine in *Le Monde*, 17 July 1954.
[52] *The Times*, 19 July 1954.

element of tragedy implicit in a Conference that the French Prime Minister is reported to have described with distasteful flippancy as a 'stock-clearance sale'.[53] Shortly after his arrival, prompted perhaps by the supposition that the head of the Viet Minh delegation would share his objections to partition, Tran Van Do called on Pham Van Dong, but Dong, who had resigned himself to this solution, is reported to have confined the discussion to generalities. Indeed, the Viet Minh leader appears to have been principally preoccupied at that time with obtaining, in return for his agreement to abandon the 'Khmer Resistance Movement', the establishment of an autonomous 'Pathet Lao' régime in the Laotian provinces of Sam Neua and Phong Saly. However, on 18 July, after a homeric argument with Chou En-lai, Mendès-France obtained an undertaking from the latter that he would cease to support these Viet Minh claims. Chou En-lai's 'betrayal' is reported to have reduced Dong to a state of suppressed fury and to have clouded subsequent relations between the Viet Minh and Chinese delegations.[54]

Meanwhile the negotiations, which were conducted during the final stage of the Conference either in restricted sessions or by informal contacts between the delegates, continued to make good progress, but the somewhat furtive nature of these proceedings, which included frequent meetings between Mendès-France and Pham Van Dong, finally alarmed Tran Van Do, who had been left to wander disconsolately on the fringes of the Conference. On 17 July, therefore, he addressed a note to Mendès-France in which he complained that the French Command in Indochina had ordered the evacuation of zones vital to the defence and existence of a free Vietnam without fighting and despite protests, leaving the Vietnamese delegation at Geneva to discover from the newspapers and tardy communications that the French delegation had agreed to evacuate to the south all Vietnamese units stationed to the north of the 18th parallel.[55] This démarche merely evoked from the French delegation an expression of pained surprise at 'this unexpected move'.[56]

[53] Fontaine in Le Monde, 18–19 July 1954.
[54] Roger Massip in Figaro, 24–25 July 1954.
[55] Observer, 18 July 1954.
[56] Manchester Guardian, 19 July 1954.

Next day the Vietnamese Foreign Minister intervened, during a restricted session, and declared that his Government would refuse to subscribe to any cease-fire agreements partitioning the country,[57] while he drew the attention of the delegates to the original Nationalist proposals,[58] but on 20 July he informed the French Prime Minister with sorrowful dignity that his Government would not oppose the impending armistice, in spite of the fact that it considered such an armistice to be both catastrophic and immoral.[59]

In the early hours of the 21st Armistice Agreements covering the territory of Vietnam and Laos respectively were signed by General Deltiel on behalf of Ely, and by Ta Quang Buu, the Viet Minh Vice-Minister for National Defence; the Armistice Agreement for Cambodia was signed some six hours later by Tep Phan, Cambodian Minister for Foreign Affairs, the delay being caused by his brusque decision to insist on his Government's retaining the right to establish bases on Cambodian soil for the military forces of foreign powers. After feverish discussions, however, in which Molotov displayed an amused tolerance, this demand was qualified by the restriction of this right to a situation in which Cambodian security was threatened.

The final plenary session was held that afternoon. At this session eight of the nine participating heads of delegations adopted by verbal assent a Final Declaration of intention, by which the Conference took note of the agreements which ended hostilities in Cambodia, Laos, and Vietnam and set up an international organization to supervise the execution of the provisions. The heads of delegations also agreed in the name of their Governments to consult one another on any question referred to them by the International Supervisory Commission in order to study such measures as might prove necessary to ensure the respect of the agreements. Bedell Smith, representing the American delegation, made a unilateral declaration in which he stated that the Government of the United States took note of the Agreements and declared that it would refrain from the threat or the use of force to disturb them, and 'would view any renewal of aggression in violation of the aforesaid

[57] *NYHT*, 19 July 1954.
[58] *Le Monde*, 20 July 1954.
[59] Ibid. 22 July 1954.

Agreements with grave concern and as seriously threatening international peace and security'.[60]

The session was marked by two further interventions by the Vietnamese Foreign Minister, in which he protested 'against the hasty conclusion of an Armistice by the French High Command alone' and proposed that the Vietnamese Government's objections and reservations should be incorporated in the Final Declaration. His protest was brusquely dismissed by Mendès-France and firmly overruled by Eden in his capacity as chairman of the plenary session.[61] The Conference ended amid a flurry of mutual congratulations, while Molotov, giving further proof of the unusual amiability which had distinguished Soviet behaviour throughout the proceedings, paid a fulsome compliment to Eden, stressing the latter's outstanding services and role in the Conference, a role which Molotov insisted 'cannot be exaggerated'.[62]

In spite of the fact that the Conference had resulted in an armistice on terms which were unexpectedly favourable to France, the proceedings aroused misgivings among some observers, which Molotov's final tribute to the British Foreign Minister, with its hint of some undefined ironic undertone, did little to allay. This reaction appears to have been due to some suspicion that Mendès-France, in his patent desire to score a personal triumph, had been tempted to come to a tacit understanding with the Soviet representative by which, in return for Molotov's assistance in securing an armistice in Indochina on acceptable terms, he had given some undertaking in regard to France's proposed participation in EDC, a *quid pro quo* which Bidault had stoutly rejected.[63] The French Prime Minister's subsequent action in regard to the ratification of the Paris Treaty did little to allay the suspicion that some understanding had, in fact, been given, for after the rejection, in August, at the Brussels meeting of the Defence Community of additional protocols which he had personally drafted, Mendès-France arranged for a debate on the Paris Treaty to take place in the National Assembly on 30 August; during this

[60] Cmd. 9239, pp. 6–7.
[61] *Daily Telegraph*, 22 July 1954.
[62] Cmd. 9239, p. 8.
[63] Jean Wetz in *Le Monde*, 13 July 1954; Jacques Fauvet in ibid. 23 July 1954; *Manchester Guardian*, 23 July 1954.

debate the proposed European Defence Community was implicitly and ignominiously rejected on a mere question of procedure.[64]

[64] Mendès-France proposed seven amendments to the Paris Treaty, including the suspension of any clause of supra-nationality for eight years, the maintenance of a right to veto, and the limitation of the integration of the European Armies to the covering forces (i.e. to the forces stationed in Germany). 'The protagonists of the European Defence Community never forgave M. Mendès-France what they called "the crime of 30 August". Six months later they overthrew him, ostensibly on his North African policy, but in reality because they considered him responsible for the defeat of E.D.C.' (D. Lerner and R. Aron, *France Defeats E.D.C.* (1957), pp. 162–3.)

# XVIII

# The Aftermath

AFTER the Geneva Agreements had been signed the Military Commission at Trung Giao was entrusted with the task of bringing the war to an end, and on 23 July the dates were announced on which the cease-fire would become effective in the three regions of Vietnam, Laos, and Cambodia respectively. However, the Armistice Agreements, which had been hastily drawn up in order to comply with Mendès-France's self-imposed time-limit, were carelessly drafted, and in the case of Vietnam the validity of the agreement itself was open to question since it had been negotiated and signed by representatives of the Commander-in-Chief of the French Union Forces in Indochina, in spite of the protests of the Saigon Government which, as the authority charged with the civil administration of the southern zone, would be responsible for the execution of some of its provisions.

By the terms of this agreement Vietnam was to be provisionally partitioned at the 17th parallel, arrangements being made for general elections to be held under international supervision throughout the national territory in July 1956. These elections were to be preceded by consultations, which were to take place after 20 July 1955, between 'the competent representative authorities of the two zones'. The decision to fix the military demarcation line at the 17th parallel had, however, placed the bulk of the population under Communist control,[1] and although Mendès-France was to declare in the National Assembly that the liberal policies and economic prosperity in the south would compensate in the general elections for this disparity,[2] Vietnamese nationalists, who were better acquainted with Communist methods than the French Prime Minister, were inclined to discount this assumption.

The Armistice Agreement laid down that French Union forces were to withdraw from Hanoi within 80 days, and from

---

[1] The population of the northern zone was estimated to outnumber that of the southern zone by some 3 million (Frédéric-Dupont, p. 205).
[2] Ibid. pp. 210–11.

# THE AFTERMATH 339

Hai Duong within 100 days, while 300 days were to be allowed for the final evacuation of the Expeditionary Corps from the Haiphong area. The evacuation of Viet Minh forces from South and Central Vietnam was to conform to a similar timetable, the Viet Minh being allocated for the purpose of assembling their forces the areas in South Vietnam which they controlled in the Plaine des Joncs and in the mangrove swamps around Point Ca Mau, and in Central Vietnam the provinces of Quang Ngai and Binh Dinh, forming part of *Lien Khu* V.

These arrangements were completed by an undertaking that the two parties to the agreement would refrain from reprisals or discrimination against persons or organizations on account of their activities during the hostilities, and that the democratic liberties of such persons would be guaranteed. Instructions were also to be issued to local authorities to permit and help civilians residing in a district controlled by one party who wished to go and live in the zone assigned to the other party, to do so, this authorization being restricted, however, to the period of 300 days which had been assigned for the completion of troop movements. Both parties likewise undertook not to introduce into Vietnam troop reinforcements, arms, munitions, or other war material, and to refrain from establishing new military bases, the maintenance of military bases under the control of a foreign state and the contracting of military alliances also being expressly precluded.

The agreement on the cessation of hostilities in Cambodia, which contained somewhat similar provisions, had been negotiated directly between a representative of Norodom Sihanouk, in his capacity as Commander-in-Chief of the Khmer national armed forces, and the Viet Minh Vice-Minister of National Defence, acting on behalf of the Commander-in-Chief of the Khmer resistance forces, and the Commander-in-Chief of the Viet Minh military units.[3] By the terms of this agreement the armed forces and military combatant personnel of the French Union, together with combatant formations of all types which had entered Cambodia

[3] The difference in procedure was due to the fact that the autonomy of the national army, under the operational command of the king, had been formally recognized by the French Command in October of the previous year, when French Union troops, with the exception of three Cambodian battalions which were transferred to the Khmer National Army, had evacuated the national territory on the right bank of the river Mekong.

from other countries or regions of the peninsula, and all foreign elements (or Cambodians not natives of Cambodia) in military formations of any kind or holding supervisory functions in political, military, administrative, economic, financial, or social bodies in liaison with the Viet Minh military units were to be withdrawn within 90 days, while Khmer resistance forces were to be demobilized on the spot and integrated without discrimination with the national community.

While the Cambodian Armistice Agreement was to lead to the rapid dispersal of the armed bands, operating for the most part in remote parts of the country or in the frontier regions, the agreement on the cessation of hostilities in Laos, which was signed by the representative of the Commander-in-Chief of the French Union Forces in Indochina and by the Viet Minh Vice-Minister of National Defence on behalf of the 'Commander-in-Chief' of the fighting units of Pathet Lao and the 'Commander-in-Chief' of the People's Army of Vietnam, proved less satisfactory. The agreement authorized the French Command, however, to maintain a limited number of officers and n.c.o.'s in Laos for the purpose of training the national army and also to retain the use of two bases, one at Seno and the other in the Mekong valley either in the province of Vientiane or downstream from Vientiane. A period of 120 days was allowed for the withdrawal and transfer of the personnel, supplies, and equipment of French Union forces and Vietnamese People's Volunteers to provisional assembly areas, while provision was also made for a special convention which would safeguard the position of those 'volunteers' who had been settled in Laos before the hostilities.[4] In addition to these arrangements, twelve provisional assembly areas, one to each province, were to be set aside for fighting units of Pathet Lao. These units, except for those military personnel who wished to be demobilized on the spot, were then to move, pending a political settlement, into the provinces of Phong Saly and Sam Neua, a corridor of territory being reserved for their use across the adjoining province of Luang Prabang.

In view of Pham Van Dong's insistence, however, that these two provinces should be handed over to the Pathet Lao, fears were expressed that such ill-defined and extensive concessions

---

[4] These Vietnamese 'volunteers' were reported to form an important part of the Pathet Lao forces.

would be exploited in order to establish Pathet Lao control over these areas, fears which proved to be well founded. Moreover the Laotian Government had also undertaken, in a declaration issued at the close of the Geneva Conference, to 'promulgate measures to provide [pending general elections] for special representation in the Royal Administration of the provinces of Phong Saly and Sam Neua . . . of the interests of Laotian nationals who did not support the Royal forces during hostilities'.[5] This generous intention provided an opportunity to prevaricate and to impede thereby the re-establishment of the royal authority in these provinces.

The supervision of the terms of the three Armistice Agreements was entrusted to three International Commissions, composed of representatives of Canada, Poland, and India, under the chairmanship of the Indian representative. These Commissions were to set up fixed and mobile inspection teams, composed of an equal number of officers from each of the three participating states. The teams were to operate throughout Indochina at ports and airfields, in regions bordering land and sea frontiers and, with the exception of Cambodia, at the demarcation lines between regrouping and demilitarized zones. Their duties included the prevention of the entry of troop reinforcements and war material, with the exception of troops relieving units of the Expeditionary Corps up to battalion strength which had completed their overseas service.[6]

## THE EXODUS FROM NORTH VIETNAM

It was perhaps appropriate that a war which had been officially defined as a 'pacification' should be ended by agreements reflecting the confusion of thought which had been allowed to subsist throughout the conflict. This confusion had been reflected in French military communiqués which, by consistently stressing the French role in operations, tended to obscure the major contribution that was being made both by the Vietnamese themselves and by French Union troops.[7] But

[5] Cmd. 9239, p. 41.
[6] Ibid.
[7] The losses of the French Expeditionary Corps in killed, dead, and missing from 1945 to 1 July 1954 were made up as follows: French, 20,685; Foreign Legion, 11,620; African, 15,229; and indigenous regulars, 26,666 (U.S. Information Service, *France: Facts and Figures*, Mar. 1955, pp. 39–40).

if a tendency to appropriate an undue share of operational credit reveals some lack of generosity, the French Command had been compelled to adapt the tenor of their communiqués, and the conduct of the war itself to political considerations, even to the point of mounting operations to facilitate the vote of military credits in the National Assembly or to obtain increased grants of American aid.[8]

Such official reticence in regard to certain aspects of the war had resulted in some credence being attached to Communist propaganda, which had persistently and grotesquely ascribed both the origins and protracted nature of the war to the activities of French financiers who, in collusion with certain political groups, were engaged in recouping themselves for their losses under the protection of well-paid mercenaries with criminal records. Rates of pay, however, could not explain the unbroken morale of the French-officered Expeditionary Corps and the courage displayed by French Union troops engaged in dangerous and inconclusive operations in the Red river delta, or occupying defence posts isolated in the midst of a hostile population or located in inaccessible regions, where survival might depend, in the last resort, on the unfailing readiness of the aircraft crews and parachute battalions to endure fatigue and danger in their defence. Whereas the morale of French Union troops had been fortified by the knowledge that, in the event of death or injury, some measure of assistance would be forthcoming for themselves and their dependants, the readiness to resist the Viet Minh shown by the ill-equipped guards who assured the defence of their native villages in Tongking, by the Thai partisans in the mountainous region of North Indochina, and by the members of the various militia formations had been based on the knowledge that no other course of action was open to those who wished to defend their religious beliefs and established customs.

The extent of this popular opposition to Viet Minh rule was revealed after the signing of the cease-fire agreement. Although the French authorities anticipated that wealthy Vietnamese, and those who had served the Bao Dai régime would be unlikely to remain in Tongking, the possibility of a massive

---

[8] Estimated total French appropriations for military purposes in Indochina from 1946–54: $7,594,284,714. Estimated total U.S. aid through France and directly to the state of Vietnam before 30 June 1954: $4,169,284,000 (Cole, p. 259).

exodus was discounted. In consequence, the French authorities who had undertaken to evacuate Vietnamese civilians from Tongking estimated that they would be required to provide transport for some 30,000 refugees, but it was soon apparent that this figure represented a gross underestimate. By the beginning of August 70,000 applications for passages to South Vietnam had been received.

Ngo Dinh Diem, who had exhorted the population of North Vietnam in a speech at Hanoi on 3 August 'to rally the South in order to continue the struggle for independence and liberty',[9] then sent a personal message to President Eisenhower requesting American assistance in the evacuation of civilians and an urgent appeal was issued to friendly nations and to international philanthropic organizations for assistance in the provision of relief for the destitute refugees, who were now arriving in large numbers in South Vietnam. The American response was prompt, and orders were immediately given to the Seventh Fleet to sail for Indochina, while an assurance was provided that aid would be forthcoming.

Meanwhile, in order to meet the immediate emergency, the Saigon Government obtained an advance of 500 million piastres from the Indochinese Bank of Issue, a sum equivalent to the combined monthly pay of the civil service and the armed forces. This sum was then used to buy essential supplies and to set up reception centres in schools and public buildings in Saigon–Cholon. The refugees for whom these arrangements were made came for the most part from the Roman Catholic villages in Tongking, where entire communities, under the leadership of their parish priest, in many cases took a collective decision to move south. This decision was based on the knowledge that under the Viet Minh, with whom the villagers were well acquainted, the continued practice of their religion would be attended by insuperable difficulties.

The movement, which had been started in somewhat impetuous fashion at the beginning of the month by the Apostolic Vicars of Phat Diem and Bui Chu, had attained considerable proportions by 26 July, when French missionaries in Hanoi reported that the Roman Catholic communities established to the north and west were arriving daily in the town. Although the movement had been officially encouraged by the Prime

[9] *Le Monde*, 4 Aug. 1954.

Minister, by the Vietnamese Catholic hierarchy, and by the
local authorities, the evacuation was not actively promoted
either by the Vatican or by the Paris Foreign Mission Society,
which had instructed missionaries to remain at their post;
instructions which were stressed by the decision of Mgr. Dooley,
the Apostolic Delegate, to remain in Hanoi. By the beginning
of September a total of 260,000 Tongkingese, including 110,000
soldiers and their families, had been evacuated to South
Vietnam, where civilian refugees were accommodated in
reception centres and paid an allowance of 12 piastres a day.[10]
During the months of September and October the exodus continued and an average of 10,000 refugees was estimated to be
embarking daily at Haiphong.

The influx of such numbers into Saigon–Cholon, where the
available accommodation was limited, soon threatened to
create a catastrophic situation, but the crisis was surmounted
largely through the devoted efforts of a group of Vietnamese
whose activities had hitherto been confined to relief work on
behalf of the Vietnamese Red Cross. These men, with the
support of Pham Ngoc Chi, started to move refugees to the
countryside, transporting whole village communities with a
minimum of equipment to the province of Bien Hao, where
they were required, under the direction of the parish priest, to
clear the site of their future village, to build their church and
huts with the timber, bamboo, and palm-leaves that were to
hand, and to plant vegetables. By the beginning of October
it was estimated that 40,000 refugees had been established in
the province.[11] Great was the despair, however, of these
reluctant pioneers from the thickly populated plains of Tongking when they were thus unceremoniously dumped on the
fringe of a tropical forest teeming with dangers which were both
imaginary and real, and where the felling of timber and the
cultivation of manioc would henceforth replace the accustomed
labour in the rice fields.[12]

[10] Clos in *Le Monde*, 2 Oct. 1954.
[11] Ibid.
[12] Although the settlement of the Cochin-Chinese provinces had been pursued
in somewhat similar fashion under the Nguyen lords of Hué, who had arranged
for the implantation of communities of soldiers and felons whose services could best
be employed on the frontiers, the proposed site of these villages had at least been
reconnoitred and selected after careful consideration of its natural advantages.
The haphazard construction of villages along the main roads in Bien Hoa province, where even the water-supply was not in all cases assured, represented a new

The area available for these settlements was restricted by the fact that in the autumn of 1954 the Government exercised only nominal control over the countryside, since the withdrawal of the Viet Minh regular units to the assembly areas in the Plaine des Joncs and around Point Ca Mau had encouraged the sects' militia forces to infiltrate into the evacuated areas, with the result that Cochin-China remained in a state of anarchy. In consequence, although the sparsely populated Transbassac contained a vast number of abandoned paddy fields, which the leaders of the Hoa Hao sect, who now controlled most of this area, were prepared to place at the disposal of the refugees, the dangers to which settlers would be exposed at the hands of the savage and xenophobic adepts of a 'restored Buddhism' prevented the adoption of such a solution.

On 17 September an Office for Refugees was set up under a Commissioner General, who was given the rank of Secretary of State.[13] Meanwhile the arrival of these refugees was viewed with considerable dismay by the population as the Cochin-Chinese, who possess the spontaneity and somewhat feckless temperament which stems from the relatively easy conditions of life in the rich and under-populated Mekong delta, were afraid that the frugal, hard-working, and calculating northerners would now oust them from the positions of profit and power which they regarded as their birthright. Moreover the religion of the refugees increased the undesirable nature of the invasion in Cochin-Chinese eyes, since the possibility could not be ignored that the Roman Catholic Prime Minister might use the refugees to secure his hold on political power and to establish a Christian state in South Vietnam. The somewhat tactless fashion in which relief was distributed did little to dissipate these popular misgivings: whereas the requirements of Roman Catholics, who composed 80 per cent. of the refugees, were accorded priority, those Cochin-Chinese who had been living

development in the secular expansion of the Vietnamese race. The despair of the Tongkingese villagers was matched by that of the French Forestry Commissioners at the prospect of the devastation that the indiscriminate felling of timber would cause in this well-wooded province.

[13] In spite of the decision to set up this Office the distribution of gifts in kind and of large sums of money received from abroad provided the unscrupulous and the rapacious with opportunities for personal gain which are reported to have been fully exploited (*The Times*, 23 Sept. 1954). Even the dissident Cao Dai 'General' Trinh Minh The was to profit from this, being awarded a contract to erect attap huts for 10,000 refugees.

in a state of destitution in the Viet Minh zone received little assistance from the Government.[14]

## AMERICAN SUPPORT FOR NGO DINH DIEM

In the meantime Ngo Dinh Diem was disappointing his supporters by his failure to provide the firm leadership which the situation demanded. His failure to act was accompanied, moreover, by a stubborn refusal to delegate any of the power with which he had been invested, so that the Government's authority was practically confined to the Gia Long Palace.[15] The Prime Minister's inertia, combined with reports of his administrative incapacity, aroused widespread criticism,[16] and, in the middle of August his brother, Mgr. Ngo Dinh Thuc, the shrewd Apostolic Vicar of Vinh Long, is reported to have advised him, in view of the mounting tension and the absence of popular support, to resign.[17]

Such a decision would have caused no surprise, for the nationalist groups and personalities, freed from the restraint which the French authorities had hitherto exercised over their activities, were now preparing to give free rein to their anarchic propensities in the disintegrating and truncated state. In the impending struggle for power the chances of a Roman Catholic mandarin from Hué, who displayed a congenital inability either to compromise or to act, appeared to be slight. Moreover Diem could count neither on the support of the police and security services nor on the loyalty of the armed forces, while he had alienated the sympathy of the French authorities by a censorious refusal to forget old grievances. But although he may have appeared, in the isolation of his official residence, to be at the mercy of any incident, Diem was to prove that he held nevertheless a trump card. This was the

[14] This aid had, however, been provided for the most part from Roman Catholic sources.

[15] After the final decision of the French authorities to hand over the High Commissioner's residence to the Vietnamese on 7 September, the Government's authority was extended to include the building and grounds of the Palais Norodom, which became the Prime Minister's official residence.

[16] Diem's success in concealing this incapacity in the course of his career may have been due to the fact that, even if they occupied positions of importance at Hué under the Protectorate, mandarins were merely required to endorse the decisions of the French colonial administrators.

[17] *Daily Telegraph*, 10 Aug. 1954.

assurance of unqualified and unfaltering American support, which assumed the form of a threat to withhold the economic aid and financial support on which the survival of the state depended in the event of a successful attempt to oust him from the premiership.[18]

The American decision to intervene repeatedly and decisively in support of the Diem Government appears to have been inspired by the Prime Minister's reputation for integrity and patriotism, which had been sedulously built up by relations and friends during his absence abroad. Indeed the possession of such qualities by a Vietnamese Prime Minister must have seemed eminently desirable both to the personnel of the American Embassy in Saigon and to itinerant American senators, who were bewildered and frequently outraged by the baffling complexity of the local intrigues, by the scale of the financial scandals, and by the saddening evidence that the exploitation of vice and the pursuit of crime could be attended by substantial financial rewards. Moreover, in view of the existing state of confusion, the selection of a 'providential man' appeared to be an essential prerequisite for an attempt to salvage a nationalist state in South Vietnam.

The original decision to support the Prime Minister appears to have been based merely on the assumption that he was the man best qualified to hold the premiership. But in the ensuing months of plot and counterplot, during which Diem was to cling with the immobility and tenacity of a limpet to his head-quarters in the Palais Norodom, American officials became emotionally involved in a struggle the outcome of which was to saddle the American Government with some moral respon-sibility for investing the Prime Minister, his family, and his clients with control of the state's administrative machinery. Moreover, this investiture was secured not only in the face of resistance by the sects and armed groups, whose assimilation would have represented the first task of any responsible govern-ment, but also in spite of opposition from the army and from the vast majority of those Vietnamese whose services on behalf of the nationalist cause would seem to have entitled them to play some part in the creation of an independent state.

---

[18] Clos in *Le Monde*, 23 Sept. 1954; M. Olivier-Lacamp in *Figaro*, 9 Dec. 1954.

### OPPOSITION TO DIEM

Military opposition assumed the form of a personal feud which appeared to be based on mutual antipathy between General Nguyen Van Hinh, the Chief of Staff, and Diem. The sly and complex Prime Minister, with his capacity for sustained rancour and his preference for the oblique approach, must have recognized an adversary in the young Chief of Staff, who had acquired during his service with the French air force the informal manners and easy self-confidence of his colleagues and whose frankness could be termed on occasion a lack of tact. In consequence relations between Diem, who had retained the portfolio of National Defence, and Hinh soon became strained. Diem, whose qualifications to discharge the functions of Defence Minister were not apparent, expressed his dissatisfaction at the inefficient state of military administration and deplored that in the recruitment for the armed forces quality should have been sacrificed to numbers; Hinh, counterattacking, reproached Diem with his ultra-conservatism and with his failure to understand the revolutionary changes which had taken place during his long absence abroad. In Hinh's opinion this had led Diem, in spite of paying lip-service to democratic institutions and practices, to prefer the outmoded conceptions of government which had brought disaster upon the Empire of Annam.[19]

On 11 September this mutual recrimination led Diem to arrange for a seat to be reserved for Hinh on board an aircraft which was due to leave Saigon for France the following day. When he was informed of his abrupt dismissal and virtual banishment Hinh, whose services would seem to have entitled him to more considerate treatment, cancelled the reservation and announced that he intended to remain in Vietnam for the time being. This high-handed action on the part of a Prime

---

[19] P.-Albin Martel in *Le Monde*, 19 Nov. 1954; *France-Soir*, 27 Nov. 1954. Hinh's assessment of the Prime Minister's shortcomings were to be echoed in March of the following year by Joseph Alsop: 'This descendant of a great mandarin family [wrote this influential American journalist] is narrow, obstinate, and petty. He is so unwilling to delegate authority that in Indo-China's death agony he deals personally with the issuance of passport visas. Above all, he is completely out of contact with the broad mass of his people and the political realities of his country. . . . The roots of Diem, moreover, are in the dead and gone court of Hue. In modern Indo-China, except for his connection with the small Catholic minority, Diem is effectively rootless ' (*NYHT*, 31 Mar. 1955).

Minister who had apparently been engaged during the war years in enlisting American support for his claim to govern Vietnam aroused the army's resentment and provoked demonstrations of sympathy and support for the Chief of Staff, and after a second refusal by Hinh to leave for Europe, the situation in Saigon seemed to presage an imminent military coup d'état. The security guards at the Palais Norodom were reinforced by a detachment of police militia from Annam, but Hinh demonstrated the strength of his position by ordering troops and armoured vehicles to patrol in the town. Nevertheless, in spite of the support that he was receiving, Hinh soon showed considerable reluctance to assume responsibility for an action which might have unpredictable consequences and sought to temporize, while he demonstrated his defiance of the Prime Minister's authority by a boyish prank, which took the form of ostentatiously driving about the town on a powerful motorcycle to which a placard announcing his 'expulsion' had been affixed.

Meanwhile the leaders of the Cochin-Chinese sects met in conclave, on the 16th, to decide on the attitude that they should adopt. At the end of this meeting a manifesto was issued in which the sects officially dissociated themselves from the Prime Minister and proclaimed the need for a democratic and representative government capable of reforming the régime, liberating the country from foreign domination, and improving the lot of the people by the enactment of measures to combat the prevalent poverty and illiteracy.[20] The following day Diem provided Hinh with a further excuse to postpone action by nominating General Nguyen Van Xuan to the Ministry of National Defence. This appointment had the desired effect, and Hinh declared that although the army maintained its opposition to the Diem Government, their affection and respect for the person of the new Defence Minister would deter them from taking any immediate action against the Prime Minister. Hinh also sent a telegram to Bao Dai inviting him to arbitrate in the difference that had arisen between the Prime

[20] Raymond Cartier in *Paris Match*, 25 Sept.–2 Oct. 1954. Both Binh Xuyen 'General' Vien and Hoa Hao 'Generalissimo' Soai were illiterate. But whereas Soai in an expansive mood would occasionally attempt to sign his name, Vien possessed a working knowledge of arithmetic which enabled him to calculate adroitly the takings at the 'Grand Monde' and at the other establishments from which he derived his ample revenue.

Minister and himself, an action which Diem termed that of a rebel.

On 20 September Diem's isolation was completed by the resignation of nine out of the fifteen ministers in his cabinet, but he appears to have been sustained at this stage by a mystic faith in the predestined role with which, in default of a popular mandate, he had been divinely invested, and he refused to accept the evidence that his leadership had been decisively rejected both by representative nationalists in South Vietnam and even by some of his personal supporters.

His self-confidence proved to be justified since the American Embassy now intervened decisively and informed Hinh that in the event of a military coup d'état economic and military aid would be stopped.[21] The knowledge that the forcible eviction of the Prime Minister from his official residence would deprive the armed forces of their pay, together with his reluctance to cause further bloodshed, provided Hinh with the argument, which he may have been subconsciously seeking, against a resort to force. Moreover the temporizing reply which he received from Bao Dai was also clearly designed to discourage any such hasty action.

In an attempt to end the stalemate in Saigon, Bao Dai had sent for the Binh Xuyen General, Le Van Vien, and on the 19th Vien returned from Cannes with instructions to form a coalition Government with the Cao Dai and Hoa Hao leaders who had signed the manifesto of 16 September. The ensuing negotiations proved abortive, however, as Cao Dai 'General' Nguyen Thanh Phuong and the Hoa Hao 'Generalissimo' Tran Van Soai presented demands which were unacceptable to Le Van Vien, who roundly accused his partners in a succession of ephemeral 'United Fronts' with the intention of selling their services to the Prime Minister.

This accusation was well founded. When the negotiations had broken down Phuong and Soai promptly contacted Diem, and on the 24th the formation of an enlarged Government was announced in which Diem retained, in addition to the premiership, the portfolio of the Ministry of the Interior and, after Xuan's refusal to serve in the new Cabinet, that of National Defence as well. The Government in which Phuong and Soai were ministers without portfolio and at the same time members

[21] Clos in *Le Monde*, 23 Sept. 1954.

of the National Defence Committee, contained four representatives each of the Hoa Hao and Cao Dai sects.

This surprising change in the political fortunes of the Prime Minister was ascribed both to a natural reluctance on the part of the Cao Dai and Hoa Hao leaders to concede precedence to the Binh Xuyen 'General' and also to the refusal of the latter to finance his partners, who were now faced with the loss of the French subsidies which enabled them to pay their troops.[22] But if South Vietnam was spared the humiliation of a Government under the premiership of an illiterate war-lord, the new cabinet represented merely a temporary alliance between mutually hostile elements, and possessed neither the unity nor the authority to stem the rising tide of anarchy which was threatening to engulf the country.

Meanwhile the American decision to support Diem was strengthened by a report presented to the Senate's Foreign Relations Committee on 15 October, which had been prepared by Senator Mike Mansfield after a two months' study tour through Indochina. Mansfield, after noting that Diem had 'a reputation throughout Vietnam for intense nationalism and equally intense incorruptibility', stigmatized 'the incredible campaign of subversion by intrigue', 'the conspiracy of non-cooperation and sabotage', which had hitherto prevented him from implementing 'his constructive programme which consists of the elimination of some of the most brazen aspects of corruption and social inequity'. In conclusion the Senator proposed that the policy of supporting Diem's Government, 'based on the sound principles of national independence, an end to corruption and internal amelioration', should be pursued, while he recommended that in the event of a change of Government 'the United States should consider an immediate suspension of all aid to Vietnam and French Union forces there, except that of a humanitarian nature, preliminary to a complete reappraisal of our present policies in Free Vietnam'.[23]

Senator Mansfield's forthright comments and unqualified

[22] References by well informed journalists in Saigon to the important, if unspecified, part that the American Embassy had played in the volte-face of Phuong and Soai seem to imply that the Generals were offered some financial inducement to join the Government (Raymond Cartier in *Paris Match*, 25 Sept.–2 Oct. 1954 and Clos in *Le Monde*, 25 Sept. 1954).

[23] U.S. Senate Commission on Foreign Relations, *Report by Senator Mike Mansfield on a Study Mission to Vietnam, Cambodia, Laos* (Washington, Oct. 1954).

approval of a complex personality and a nebulous political programme, served to confirm the State Department in its determination to persist in the pursuit of a policy based on such impressive moral considerations. Proof of this resolution was afforded on 17 November, when General Lawton Collins, a former American Chief of Staff, arrived in Saigon on a mission of limited duration with the rank of Ambassador Extraordinary and in the capacity of personal representative of President Eisenhower. This important emissary, who was the bearer of a generous instalment of financial aid amounting to $100 million, at once proclaimed the determination of the American Government to provide the Diem Government with unwavering support and added a warning that 'The United States is not interested in training or otherwise aiding a Vietnamese Army which does not give complete and implicit obedience to the Premier'.[24] A means was also found to settle the dispute between Diem and Hinh, by arranging for Bao Dai to summon Hinh to Paris for consultations;[25] and on 29 November a decree was published dismissing him from his post on the grounds that he had made 'regrettable statements'.[26]

The appointment of his successor gave rise, however, to some controversy since the Prime Minister's brother and principal adviser, Ngo Dinh Nhu, and his influential and active wife, Mme Ngo Dinh Nhu, were anxious to appoint to the vacant post an officer, General Le Van Ty, whose professional and moral qualifications were alleged to be open to question, but whose support had apparently been acquired for a scheme by which, in the impending partial demobilization of the armed forces, priority should be given to the demobilization of those elements most opposed to the Diem Government. However, in view of the objections raised both by Ely and Collins to this appointment, a compromise solution was reached, and on 10 December General Nguyen Van Vi, who enjoyed the confidence and the respect of the troops, was appointed to the operational command of the armed forces with the rank of Inspector General, while General Ty was appointed Chief of Staff.[27]

[24] *NYHT*, 18 Nov. 1954.
[25] *Le Monde*, 13 Nov. 1954.
[26] *Bull. du Haut Commissariat du Viet-Nam en France*, No. 87, Dec. 1954, p. 2.
[27] Joseph Alsop in *NYHT*, 8 & 15 Dec. 1954. Mme Nhu first attracted the attention of European press representatives when on 21 September she intervened

Meanwhile, negotiations were taking place in Paris to complete the economic and financial independence of the Associate States. These negotiations had at first been impeded by the resentments, calculations, and fears which had been responsible for the protracted proceedings at the Pau Conference in 1950, but a break-down was averted by a decision at the beginning of September to set up sub-committees entrusted with the task of finding a solution to the various questions at issue. On 21 September agreement was reached to abolish the Inter-State Bank of Issue, and to create a national bank and a national Exchange Control Office in each of the three states.[28] Finally, on 29 and 30 December, thirteen agreements were initialed which gave the Governments of the Associate States full control of their national economy.[29]

By the terms of these agreements an Inter-State Commission was set up to control navigation on the Mekong, and the Indo-chinese Customs Union was abolished and replaced by bilateral agreements covering transit facilities and preferential tariffs, the use of the piastre as a currency common to the three states being abandoned.[30] The existing parity between the national currencies which were now to replace the common currency, and between these currencies and the French franc, was to be maintained, however, by common consent until October 1955, in order to facilitate the forthcoming financial operations, including the replacement of the common currency. The signing of these agreements had been preceded, on 3 December, by the promulgation of a decree setting up a National Bank of Vietnam. The haste with which this bank was established was due to the fact that payments of American financial aid were to be made directly to the Saigon Government as from 1 January 1955, since during Franco-American discussions in

in an incident between a procession of refugees who were proceeding to the Palais Norodom with a banner proclaiming the loyalty of the population of North Vietnam to Diem and a detachment of Binh Xuyen-controlled police, who had started to disperse these unfortunate individuals with bursts of submachine fire. On this occasion, Mme Nhu, who is alleged to have been responsible for organizing the procession, was observed to rush into the mêlée with a passionate courage, which recalled the legendary ardour of the Trung sisters (R. Cartier in *Paris Match*, 2–9 Oct. 1954).

[28] *NYT*, 22 Sept. 1954.
[29] *Notes et Études Documentaires*, No. 1973, 25 Jan. 1955.
[30] Vietnam retained the piastre as the currency unit, while Cambodia and Laos adopted the 'riel' and the 'kip' respectively.

Washington in September it had been agreed that American financial aid to the Associate States should no longer be made available through the intermediary of the French authorities.[31]

## NORODOM SIHANOUK'S ABDICATION

The conclusion of these agreements marked the end of Norodom Sihanouk's mission to achieve the independence of Cambodia, and he used the prestige he thereby acquired to discredit Son Ngoc Thanh, whose criticism he resented. An opportunity to humble this troublesome fellow had occurred in November 1954 when Thanh, taking advantage of the amnesty provided for in the Geneva Agreement, had left his hide-out in the Siamese border region to the north of the Great Lake and sent a message to the king in which he protested his loyalty and asked for an audience; but the proffered olive branch was ignored and its sender publicly denounced as a perjured traitor who had not only deserted his sovereign in his hour of need but had actually imperilled his life by calling in question the sincerity of his attempts to win national independence. This put an end to Thanh's hope that he would be allowed to re-enter the political arena, and he retired discomfited to Siam.

During the following year Norodom Sihanouk was to complete the rout of the opposition by spiking the guns of the Democratic Party, which looked to Thanh for leadership. The opening move was made on 24 January 1955, when the king proclaimed in a message addressed to his people that national independence was 'total and final and cannot be excelled' and, after ascribing his success in this bold enterprise to an ardent desire to save 'our country and our peoples from death and disintegration, which certain groups of politicians endeavoured by every means to achieve', announced that Cambodians would be asked to pass judgement on his mission by a referendum to be held on 7 February, which would be followed by general elections to the National Assembly on 17 April. The

---

[31] The vital factor that American financial aid represented may be gauged by the fact that whereas public revenue for the year 1955 was expected to amount to 50 milliard piastres, it was estimated that public expenditure would exceed 187 milliard piastres (Olivier-Lacamp in *Figaro*, 9 Dec. 1954).

message ended with the statement that an all-party Government would be formed immediately to make the necessary arrangements.[32]

The referendum, in which the electorate were asked to say whether the royal mission had been accomplished to their satisfaction, resulted in 925,667 affirmative to 1,834 negative votes. This evidence of overwhelming popular support is reported to have led the royal entourage, disturbed at the prospect of a Democrat victory in the impending elections, to arrange for delegations to be sent by boat, lorry, or bus from the surrounding countryside to Phnom Penh, with petitions urging the king to refrain from alienating any of his prerogatives, and to cancel the elections on the grounds that the deputies neglected their constituencies and had forfeited the confidence of the electors. Norodom Sihanouk, who appears to have been unaware that his good faith was being abused, was impressed by this evidence of widespread discontent with the incompetence and corruption inherent in 'Government by party', and assured these country folk that he would see to it that elections were held on a reformed basis which would allow for direct participation of the people in the business of government without 'intermediaries'.[33]

On 19 February, representatives of the diplomatic corps and the International Control Commission were summoned to the palace to hear the king outline proposals for constitutional reform. These included the abolition of the system whereby party candidates without residential qualifications had been elected to represent single-member constituencies, and its replacement by the indirect election of deputies by Mayors of Communes comprised within a district (Srok), sitting as an electoral college, candidates for their part being required to stand as individuals and not as representatives of a political party, and to have been resident in a constituency for at least three years. The reforms also provided for direct control of the executive by the king and for changes in the legislature, including the creation of a Consultative Committee of twenty members nominated by, and directly responsible to,

[32] Cmd. 9534, p. 32. The all-party composition of this Government was impaired by the exclusion of the Democrats due to their decision to refer the question to a party congress which met after the Government had been formed.

[33] Ibid. p. 13.

24

the king, which would be required to initiate and draft legislation and to prepare the budget; and for the restriction of the powers vested in the National Assembly to those of approving bills, passing the budget, and voting for the dismissal of a Secretary of State on the grounds of misconduct or incompetence. In the event of a difference of opinion persisting between the Government and the National Assembly, the latter body would be dissolved. Finally, the king informed his audience that a referendum would be held in order to obtain supra-constitutional approval for the implementation of these reforms.[34]

The royal intention of revoking the constitution by supra-constitutional means and reverting to absolutism took the diplomatic corps aback, and the International Control Commission for their part were quick to appreciate that insistence on a three-year residential qualification would automatically debar the Khmer Issaraks from offering themselves as parliamentary candidates and thereby infringe Article 6 of the Geneva Agreement, under which the Government had undertaken to allow all Cambodian citizens to participate freely as electors or candidates in the general elections. Nevertheless, in spite of petitions from individual members of the Democratic Party, who saw their hopes dashed by the royal proposals, the Commission decided to take no action until they had received the official text of the king's speech, and contented themselves in the meantime with asking their respective Governments for guidance. Their reluctance to interfere in an internal affair was justified on 28 February, when the Prime Minister, Leng Ngeth, informed them that elections would be held after all under the existing constitution: a change of plan apparently inspired by the misgivings of certain ministers and court officials in regard to the royal proposals, and by signs of unrest among the pupils attending the Phnom Penh secondary school, whose support of the Democratic Party had long been a source of irritation and grievance to the sensitive monarch. But although he thus yielded to the advice of his entourage, Norodom Sihanouk had not given up his intention of checkmating the Democratic Party in their bid for power, and on 2 March he abdicated in favour of his parents, Prince Norodom Suramit and Princess Kossaman.

[34] Cmd. 9534, pp. 13–14.

In a broadcast speech announcing this decision, the ex-king petulantly ascribed his abdication to the obstacles, calumnies, and difficulties placed in his path by certain personalities, intellectuals, and privileged people, who had not hesitated to contact foreigners on the fallacious pretext that he was sabotaging certain articles of the Geneva Agreement, and he specifically accused Thanh's Democratic Party, 'which is opposed to me', of having encouraged the students of schools and colleges to display their hostility to his policies, 'even though I am very interested in education'.[35]

The abdication of a sovereign whose conduct of national affairs had just been approved by the overwhelming majority of his subjects aroused general surprise and caused dismay in Phnom Penh, particularly among the members of the International Control Commission, who were at pains to disclaim any responsibility for the ex-king's decision. But Norodom Sihanouk's action was probably inspired by the realization that unless he was able to intervene personally in the campaign, elections under the existing constitution would result in a victory for the Democratic Party, which had an efficient party machine and enjoyed great popularity on account of its consistent refusal to compromise with the French.

On 15 March an official communiqué announced the Government's decision not to proceed with the proposed referendum on constitutional reform, and to postpone the elections until 11 September. This delay was sufficient to enable Norodom Sihanouk to sponsor the formation of a party, the 'Sangkum Ryaster Niyum' or Popular Socialist Community, which became known as the 'Sangkum', and the Sangkum, after appointing Norodom Sihanouk as its 'Supreme Councillor', set out to rally all right-thinking Cambodians to the support of his policies. Norodom Sihanouk for his part campaigned actively in behalf of Sangkum candidates, and availed himself of the opportunity to tax their opponents with disloyalty to the monarchy and collusion with the Communists. Besides the services of their popular and influential Supreme Councillor, the Sangkum could also count on official assistance, including the use of those means of influencing public opinion and disseminating news normally at the disposal of the Government, with the result that their candidates received 82 per cent.

[35] Ibid. pp. 37–38.

of the votes on polling day, and captured all the seats in the National Assembly. Having thus eliminated the Democrat opposition, Norodom Sihanouk himself assumed the office of Prime Minister on 26 September.

# XIX

# The Take-Over in North Vietnam

THE scale of the evacuations to the south surprised the Viet Minh, and after officially ascribing the movement to the deliberate spreading of false rumours,[1] instructions were issued that Roman Catholic communities should be treated with circumspection. But a tendency on the part of petty officials to ignore these instructions provoked a further wave of departures,[2] after which the authorities resorted to vexatious measures and sought to retain the physically fit by force. Nevertheless, in spite of incidents and affrays between the refugees and Viet Minh officials and troops, the flight of the population continued, while fugitives from the Viet Minh provinces in North Annam also started to arrive at Haiphong after perilous escapes in fishing boats or even on frail bamboo rafts.[3]

While the refugees assembled near Haiphong, preparations went forward for the evacuation of Hanoi which, by the terms of the Armistice Agreement, was to be completed by 9 October. These were attended by the confusion and heartbreak which are inseparable from such occasions, and as the French Expeditionary Corps shifted their equipment and stores by road and rail to Haiphong, many families whose roots were deep in Tongkingese soil prepared to abandon their homes and property and to emigrate to the south.

Meanwhile the Committee for the Defence of the North,

[1] These rumours are reported to have included assertions to the effect that God had gone south and that those who remained in the north would be exposing themselves to the danger of losing their soul and to certain death at the hands of the Americans attacking with atomic bombs (extract from report by Giap during the 4th session of the National Assembly, March 1955).

[2] Clos in *Le Monde*, 2 Oct. 1954.

[3] Among those who now attempted to escape from the Viet Minh a particularly inclement fate was reserved for the Thai partisans who had been operating at the time of the armistice to the east of Lao Kay. Whereas those who rallied to the Viet Minh were imprisoned and 're-educated', the remainder, who endeavoured—in accordance with instructions by the French Command—to reach Laotian territory were 'deliberately massacred en route'. In particular, Ely specifically accused the Viet Minh of destroying a party of these refugees numbering 1,400 and including women and children (*Courrier du Viet-Nam*, No. 8, July 1955, quoting Ely's reply to Viet Minh accusations).

which had been set up by the Saigon Government after the evacuation of South-West Tongking by French Union troops, extended the range of its activities to include the dismantling and subsequent disposal or shipment to Saigon of equipment in the administrative buildings, broadcasting station, hospitals, and university which the French had formally handed over to the nationalist Government. Since Mendès-France, with the scant regard for Vietnamese interests which characterized his conduct of the negotiations at Geneva, had undertaken to transfer this equipment intact to the Viet Minh, the operation must have given the Committee particular satisfaction.[4]

The evacuation of Hanoi was preceded by an incident on the evening of 10 September, when an attempt was made to demolish with plastic charges an ancient pagoda—the Mot Cot —which rises on a single column in a small ornamental lake near the west gate of the citadel. This attempt, which is reported to have been carried out by two Vietnamese officers, had, however, merely a symbolic significance as the pagoda was built, according to the calculations of the geomancers, on the spot at which the lines of magnetic force that held together the Vietnamese provinces converged. Its destruction, which represented the seal upon this union, thus symbolized the irrevocable nature of the impending partition.

On 2 October a meeting took place at Phu Lo to make final arrangements for the official hand-over of Hanoi. The Viet Minh proved, however, to be in an exacting and suspicious mood, for their uneasiness had been aroused both by the fact that Ely was paying a visit to Washington and also by the setting up, at the Manila Conference on 8 September, of a South East Asia Defence Treaty Organization which represented a counterpart to the North Atlantic Treaty Organization. At this meeting the Viet Minh demanded that the French engineers responsible for the municipal services, including water, electricity, and public transport, should remain behind, a demand inspired by lack of confidence in their own ability to

---

[4] The value of the equipment removed in this way was later estimated at 265 million francs, this sum being paid by the French to the Hanoi Government as compensation for its loss (Frédéric-Dupont, p. 232). It included all the contents of the Hanoi Broadcasting Station, more than 80 per cent. of the equipment at the Post Office, 40 per cent. of the material at the Public Works Dept., half the books at the University Library, and much laboratory equipment including the radium at the Cancer Institute.

maintain these essential services without assistance,[5] but they were reluctant to give any written undertaking in regard either to the treatment that these technicians would receive or to the degree of freedom that they would be allowed. Finally, agreement was reached that French engineers should continue to be responsible for these services until the end of the year, while the French authorities also undertook to supply the Hanoi power station with coal in exchange for electric current which was to be relayed to Haiphong.

Besides these arrangements, the Viet Minh agreed to set aside a sum in convertible Bank of Indochina piastres to pay the salaries of French personnel who would be remaining at the École Française d'Extrême Orient and at the Radium and Pasteur Institutes.[6]

On 3 October the headquarters of the French Command in North Vietnam were officially transferred to Haiphong, and on the same day parties of Viet Minh civil servants and police started to arrive in Hanoi. The Hanoi perimeter had been divided for the purposes of the evacuation into sectors, and on 6 October the first of these sectors, comprising the adjacent town of Ha Dong, was handed over, under the supervision of the Control Commission's mobile teams, to a detachment of the 308th Viet Minh Division—the 'Iron Division'—which had been given the honour of occupying the town in recognition of its outstanding part in the siege of Dien Bien Phu. Three days later the French flag was ceremoniously lowered for the last time in the Mangin stadium and entrusted for safe keeping to Colonel d'Argence, the Commander of the Hanoi citadel, who, in recognition of his long and distinguished service in Indochina, had been accorded the honour of being the last French soldier to leave the town.

When the last French troops had withdrawn d'Argence himself set out on foot across Doumer bridge, leaving behind him the old capital of Tongking, which had been transformed, in the space of seventy years, by the vision and determination of successive Governors-General into the replica of a French provincial town. This exotic legacy which the French Protectorate left to the Democratic Republic of Vietnam, with its

---

[5] Towns in the Viet Minh zone had been systematically destroyed and even in some cases erased.

[6] *Le Monde*, 14 Oct. 1954.

Cathedral, handsome public buildings, and mastodon-like bank, with its amenities, quiet tree-lined avenues, and European-style villas, must have filled the Viet Minh troops who were to take possession of the town next day with an uneasy sense of intrusion.

After a night of curfew the troops of the 308th Division, who had been massing in the suburbs, marched into the town, where the appropriate flags—a yellow star on a red ground—had been put out under the watchful eye of the political cadres—or *Can Bo*—who had been busy for some days past in drawing up lists of households and in directing the population to contact the Committees which had been set up in each of the city wards. In spite of the importance of the occasion, however, French onlookers, who could recall the popular enthusiasm displayed during the years 1945 and 1946, were surprised at the comparative indifference shown by the crowd.

The march-past was led by delegations from the civilian associations. These were followed by an infantry regiment advancing in columns of threes; and although the soldiers appeared dwarfed by their helmets of latania palm-leaves and wore loose and shabby green cloth uniforms with no distinguishing marks, their youth, brilliant smiles, and engaging habit of clapping their own legendary achievements—in spite of the fact that they had been encumbered in some cases with bunches of gladioli—should have warmed the hearts even of a population who were celebrating their fourth liberation in the short space of nine years. However public enthusiasm may have been damped by the impression that these demonstrations represented a performance by some well-drilled chorus, and that all capacity for the spontaneous expression of emotion had been crushed in these youthful robots, who had been tried to the limit of human endurance and whose every action and utterance had been subjected to searching scrutiny and to 'auto-criticism' designed to find out and eradicate deviations in thought and behaviour. The troops who were parading through Hanoi that day belonged to a dedicated army, which possessed conformity but no originality of thought, and an austere morality.

The infantry regiment included 'volunteers for death' carrying explosive charges designed to blow a path through the barbed-wire entanglements with which the French garrisons had tried to protect their posts and towers; a detachment of the Women's Auxiliary Corps, composed of girls with their hair in plaits and dressed in bulky, indeterminate garb, brought up the rear of each company. The parade was closed by 50 Molotov trucks, towing anti-aircraft and mountain guns and 105-mm. guns captured at Dien Bien Phu.

The troops and their civilian supporters marched to the Mangin stadium where they were addressed by General Vuong Thua Vu, the Commander of the 308th Division who had been appointed chairman of the Hanoi Administrative Committee.[7] When the parade was over the realization was to dawn upon the population that the 308th Division had brought with them into Hanoi that day, together with the glory of a long and victorious war, the boredom, suspicion, and fear which are the hall-marks of a Communist state.

This atmosphere was created by enmeshing the population in the system of surveillance and control which had been set up and perfected in the Viet Minh-controlled areas. The population was divided into cells of twelve members, each member being considered individually responsible for the acts and mental processes of the other eleven. They were expected to rise at dawn to the sound of the bugle and to the prospect of collective physical exercises, while their presence was required two or three times a week at meetings where 'auto-criticism' was practised and current events expounded in the light of Marxist doctrine. Their enslavement was completed by obligatory membership of one of the many associations founded on the possession of a common profession, sex, or age. Besides these general arrangements, workers were required both to emulate the exploits of 'national heroes of the labour front' and to devote their brief leisure to unpaid work on behalf of the community.

But if the entire population were to be harassed, dragooned, and deprived of all privacy and leisure, the worst fate awaited the educated middle class. Most of these persons who had had the temerity to remain in Hanoi belonged to that category of citizen who had refused to co-operate with the Bao Dai régime, and thus anticipated that their past expressions of sympathy for, and little services on behalf of, the Viet Minh would now qualify them for posts in the Administrative Service commensurate with their talents and academic qualifications. Such

[7] Sylvère Galard and René Vital in *Paris Match*, 16–23 & 23–30 Oct. 1955.

pretensions were not, however, of a nature to enlist the sympathies of those who had been discharging, without the requisite educational diplomas, administrative functions in the Viet Minh zone. In consequence these unfortunate fence-sitters were now exposed to the malevolent attentions of the *Can Bo*; and, when the slights and persecutions to which they were subjected aroused their resentment, they were informed that they had been classified as 'irrecoverable'. They were then sent in many cases, together with other unemployed, to work as navvies either on the reconstruction of the Hanoi–Lang Son railway track or on one of the other projects for which manpower was urgently required.

Forcible enrolment in labour gangs also was to be the fate of many Hanoi shopkeepers, who were now to lose their means of livelihood as they were unable to replace their goods and at the same time were required to pay taxes on stock in hand which amounted, for some categories of merchandise, to 50 per cent. of its value.

The popular discontent aroused by such tyranny was effectively countered, however, by the omnipresence of agents and informers. The surveillance and denunciation of neighbours, friends and parents were encouraged, children, for whom President Ho Chi Minh has always demonstrated the most tender affection, being widely employed for these distasteful and demoralizing tasks.[8]

Although the occupation of Hanoi appeared to mark the end of the French presence, some survivors remained, including the staff of the Lycée Albert Sarraut—which opened in less commodious premises for a new scholastic year in October—six missionaries, six French nationals belonging to Roman Catholic religious orders, a professor of medicine, the Director of the École Française d'Extrême Orient, the Curator of the Hanoi Museum, and the Director of the Pasteur Institute, together with their assistants. A few French technicians and engineers had also stayed on, at the request of the Viet Minh authorities, to ensure the maintenance of the municipal services, while traffic control at the Hanoi airfield continued to be a French responsibility until the end of the year.

The interests of this small community were represented by a

Delegation-General, known as the Sainteny Mission, which was entrusted with general responsibility for safeguarding French property and for maintaining French cultural and economic interests in North Vietnam, but as no reciprocity of representation had been granted the Democratic Republic in Paris, the exact status of the mission remained undefined. The appointment of Jean Sainteny as head of the Delegation caused surprise since after his return to France in 1947 Sainteny had retired from public service with the rank of 'Colonial Governor'.[9] His decision to accept the post appears to have been due to a belief that his personal acquaintance with the Viet Minh leaders, and in particular his past friendship with Ho Chi Minh, would enable him to render useful service.

Sainteny left Paris towards the end of August with instructions to acquaint himself with local conditions and then to return and report his findings to the French Prime Minister. On his arrival in Hanoi Sainteny, whose retention of a *nom de guerre*[10] presupposes a romantic temperament, announced that his Government desired French cultural, commercial, and industrial ties with North Vietnam to be maintained. This expression of concern in regard to the future of French interests in North Vietnam was justified since in spite of the destruction of many French-owned mines, mills, and factories, the French retained considerable commercial and industrial interests in the area.[11] However, the Armistice Agreement contained no provision for their safeguard, Pham Van Dong having merely assured Mendès-France, in a letter the wording of which recalled in disquieting fashion a similar missive addressed to the British Government before the Communist occupation of Shanghai, that French industrial concerns would be allowed to continue their activities.

[9] *Le Monde*, 8–9 Aug. 1954.
[10] Alias Jean Roger.
[11] The High Commissioner's Office in Saigon had estimated earlier in the year that 150 French-owned commercial and industrial concerns remained in operation in North Vietnam and that 55 per cent. of the import-export trade continued to be handled by French business houses. The principal French interests included the open-cast coal mines in the Hon Gay–Campha area, the Portland Cement Factory and glass works at Haiphong, the cotton mill at Nam Dinh, breweries and distilleries, mechanical engineering workshops and ship repair yards, public utility companies, including the Water and Electric Light Companies in Hanoi and Haiphong and public transport in Hanoi, port services in Haiphong, and the Yunnan railway (*Le Monde*, 2 Aug. 1954).

After some initial hesitation, and in the absence of any definite undertaking on the part of the Viet Minh, the representatives of French commercial and industrial interests in Hanoi decided, therefore, to evacuate their personnel, files, and movable equipment and to await the outcome of the negotiations before taking any final decision in regard to their interests within the Haiphong perimeter. Sainteny, who returned to Hanoi on 9 October, thus sought to hasten the conclusion of an agreement which would safeguard the future of these French interests. He was inspired in his endeavours by the conviction that the maintenance of French interests would prevent the isolation of the area from the non-Communist world and facilitate attempts, to which Mendès-France attached particular importance, to develop contacts with Communist Governments, and in particular with the Chinese Communist Government, through their diplomatic missions in Hanoi. He was also personally persuaded that a demonstration of the ability of capitalist enterprises to survive under a Communist régime would have a far-reaching and beneficial effect upon future economic relations with the Communist bloc.

The negotiations continued to be impeded, however, by the Viet Minh refusal to provide the definite guarantees which, after the spoliations in Shanghai, were now considered essential before any decision could be made to leave movable industrial plant in territory destined to come under Communist control. Moreover the reluctance of French commercial and industrial undertakings to remain in North Vietnam was increased by the success that had attended their efforts to amortize their capital investments and also by the fear that the maintenance of their activities in the territory of the Democratic Republic would entail their inclusion in an American 'black list' and reprisals by the Government of South Vietnam. The final decision to resist Sainteny's blandishments and discreet pressure by the French Government—who, however, refused to underwrite the financial risks involved in the proposed experiment in economic coexistence—[12] appears to have been clinched by the calculation that exports from North Vietnam would be unlikely to provide sufficient foreign exchange for profits to be repatriated to France. Consequently, although an agreement was signed in December 1954, which provided certain assurances of a general

[12] Frédéric-Dupont, p. 233.

nature, industrial plant continued to be dismantled and shipped out of Haiphong.

However, the agreement at least enabled the 'Charbonnages du Tonkin' to conclude an arrangement with the Hanoi Government by which, in exchange for the surrender of the company's plant and mining concessions around Hon Gay and Campha, the Hanoi Government undertook to pay the company 1 million tons of coal, the delivery of which was to be spread over a period of fifteen years.[13]

### THE DEMOCRATIC REPUBLIC OF VIETNAM

After the French evacuation of Hanoi the Viet Minh leaders, whose demise had in some cases been reported and whose disagreements and rivalries had long been a subject of speculation and rumour, emerged from their hide-outs in the Viet Bac and returned in almost clandestine fashion to the town. On 12 October General Giap inspected the garrison and visited the citadel and the power station, where he talked with the French technicians in charge. Some days later a cabinet meeting was held, which was presided over by Ho Chi Minh, who later received representatives of the Hanoi community.

On the 17th the Government of the Democratic Republic welcomed its first official visitor in the person of the Indian Prime Minister, Jawaharlal Nehru, who was on his way to Peking. The visit enabled Nehru to renew his acquaintance with Ho Chi Minh, whom he had met at the time of the Fontainebleau Conference in Paris, and to greet the Indian representatives on the International Commission.[14] In a joint statement issued next day Ho announced that his Government 'believed

[13] *Le Monde*, 4 June 1955. The French-owned public transport company operating in the Hanoi area were also able to sell their interests in June 1955 to the Hanoi Administrative Committee for the sum of 300 million francs payable by instalments over a period of twenty-five years.

[14] Although fixed teams comprising an equal number of Canadian, Indian, and Polish officers had been installed during the previous month at Lao Kay and Lang Son, which were the principal 'points of entry' from China, the French Command at Haiphong were critical of the Commission's attempts to prevent the entry of war material. Indeed, Cogny, who commanded French Union troops in North Vietnam, informed a French parliamentary mission in November that deliveries of war material from China between 20 July and 1 November had enabled the Viet Minh to treble the number of their heavy units. These deliveries were alleged to include 180 105-mm. howitzers, 340 75-mm. recoilless guns, 80 75-mm. guns, and 470 mortars (Frédéric-Dupont, p. 206).

fully in the five principles which had been agreed upon between the Prime Ministers of China and India and wished to
apply them in the relations of Vietnam with Laos and Cambodia, as well as with other countries'.[15]

On the following day Sainteny was received by Ho Chi Minh
in the former Governor-General's palace on the outskirts of the
town, where he had himself been confined in 1945. Sainteny,
who remained to luncheon, found that his friend had retained
a preference for an informal mode of life and a taste for American tobacco.

Indeed Ho, who had devoted thirty years of his life to clandestine activities, appears to have found his representative role
and official duties somewhat irksome. His next public appearance was delayed until 1 January 1955 when he was the central
figure at a demonstration in which 200,000 persons were
estimated to have taken part[16] to celebrate the tenth anniversary of the founding of the Democratic Republic. However,
although he was reported to prefer living in an unpretentious
house in Ha Dong rather than in the pompous Italianate
villa of the French Governor-General, Ho occasionally turned
up unannounced at official receptions, where he was accustomed to explain his appearance by saying that he had 'by
chance' heard that guests were present. This withdrawn
existence was appropriate enough to an avuncular figure who
had acquired, in the eyes of the adoring Vietnamese, a status
that was semi-divine.

Meanwhile the economic situation in which the Democratic
Republic had been placed by the partition of the country was
causing Ho Chi Minh, in his capacity as President and Prime
Minister, grave concern. Under the terms of the Armistice
Agreement North Vietnam had been deprived both of the
paddy surplus of the Mekong delta and of the production of the
Cochin-China rubber plantations, which would have procured
some of the foreign exchange urgently needed to repair the
war-ravaged economy and the wrecked communications

[15] *NYT*, 19 Oct. 1954. The 'five principles of peaceful coexistence' which had
been formulated in the course of negotiations between the Indian and Chinese
Governments on the subject of Tibet, were mutual respect for each other's territorial integrity and national sovereignty, non-aggression, non-interference in the
internal affairs of other states, equality of rights and reciprocity, and peaceful
coexistence.
[16] *Le Monde*, 4 Mar. 1955.

system. There was also an acute shortage of petroleum products, which came under the ban of strategic exports. The loss of these assets forced the Hanoi Government to undertake the immense task of reconstruction by methods based on a ruthless exploitation of labour.

The success of the Hanoi Government's endeavours was dependent, in last resort, on the ability of the countries composing the Communist bloc to provide some economic aid and technical assistance. These countries were represented in Hanoi by a Chinese Ambassador, who had accompanied the Viet Minh authorities on their return to the capital, a Soviet Ambassador, whose arrival was announced in October, and a Polish Ambassador, who presented his credentials at the end of the year. These diplomatic missions were reinforced in the course of 1955 by the arrival of diplomatic representatives from East Germany, Czechoslovakia, Rumania, Bulgaria, and Hungary.

In December 1954 evidence that aid and assistance would be forthcoming was provided when an agreement was signed in Peking by which the Chinese Government undertook to provide equipment to repair road and rail communications and water-conservancy works throughout North Vietnam and to restore postal and telegraph communications between the two countries.[17] The agreement also provided for the dispatch of Chinese technicians to operate local airfields and meteorological stations.

This assistance was first used to repair the railway line from Hanoi to Lang Son. These repairs, on which 80,000 coolies were employed under deplorable conditions, represented a considerable undertaking. Most of the rails and steel sleepers had been sacrificed to the needs of the Viet Minh war industry, thirty-three bridges had been destroyed, and a third of the permanent way had either been incorporated in the surrounding paddy fields or had been cut at short intervals by deep trenches.[18]

The completion of the repairs and the conversion of the railway to the Chinese gauge[19] was celebrated on 4 March. Repairs to the Yunnan railway were also put in hand, and by

[17] NYT, 29 Dec. 1954; The Times, 15 & 29 Dec. 1954.
[18] L'Humanité, 23 Nov. 1954.
[19] Le Monde, 11 Feb. & 5 Mar. 1955.

November 1955 the rails had been relaid to Vietri,[20] a town situated at the confluence of the Clear and Red rivers.

Nevertheless, the economic situation in North Vietnam remained critical; so that no opportunity was neglected to press for the implementation of the provision in the Final Declaration of the Geneva Conference in regard to the holding of general elections in July 1956. This demand was formulated by Pham Van Dong, the Viet Minh Deputy Prime Minister and Minister for Foreign Affairs, when he visited New Delhi at Nehru's invitation on 8 April 1955. At the end of this visit Nehru and Dong reaffirmed in a joint communiqué that the agreements reached at Geneva had the full support of their respective Governments, who shared the view that free elections should be held in Vietnam and national unity re-established in the manner laid down at Geneva.[21]

The completion of the military withdrawals and transfers in May provided Dong with a further occasion to announce the readiness of his Government to send delegates to attend a consultative conference with representatives of the Saigon Government to discuss the organization of general elections.[22]

On 22 June his initiative was supported by a joint declaration issued during Nehru's visit to Moscow, in which the Indian Prime Minister and Marshal Bulganin, Chairman of the Soviet Council of Ministers, stressed the responsibility incurred by those Governments which had been represented at the Geneva Conference to ensure that the provisions of the agreements were carried out.

The Saigon Government did not acknowledge Dong's proposal for some weeks. Finally, on 16 July, President Ngo Dinh Diem declared in a broadcast statement that the Nationalist Government did not consider itself bound in any way by the Geneva Agreements, which had been signed against the will of the Vietnamese people. Although he did not reject the principle of free elections as a means to end partition, he demanded as a preliminary condition that the Viet Minh should cease to violate their obligations and afford proof of their readiness to place national interests before those of their Communist creed.[23]

[20] *Combat*, 3–4 Dec. 1955.
[21] *The Hindu*, 11 Apr. 1955 (Cole, pp. 236–7).
[22] Viet-Nam News Agency, 6 June 1955.
[23] Vietnam Embassy, Washington, Press and Information Service, 22 July 1955 (Cole, pp. 226–7).

The next day a public demonstration in support of the Prime Minister's stand took place in Saigon, in which delegations from the civil service, surviving political groups, trade unions, and refugees took part.

Dong reacted promptly and dispatched notes to the Saigon and French Governments and to the International Commission demanding the convention of a consultative conference. The British Secretary of State for Foreign Affairs, who had assured the House of Commons on 14 July that the Government had repeatedly advised the Saigon Government to arrange for consultations with the Viet Minh about holding elections,[24] then instructed the Ambassador in Saigon to approach Diem, in concert with his French colleague, and obtain an undertaking that his Government would confer with representatives from Hanoi.[25]

However, this *démarche* elicited no immediate response from the Prime Minister, whose ability to postpone decisions and whose reluctance to make concessions had hitherto stood him in good stead. Finally, an official statement was issued on 9 August in which Diem maintained that the principle of free elections was a democratic and peaceful institution but that his Government believed 'that conditions of freedom of life and voting must be assured beforehand'.[26] This uncompromising reply appears to have angered Pham Van Dong, who appealed to Eden and to Molotov, in their capacity as joint chairmen of the Geneva Conference, 'to take all the necessary measures to ensure that the Geneva agreements were respected'.[27] At this stage Nehru again intervened and wrote to Eden and Molotov expressing the hope that the Saigon Government could be induced to adopt a more co-operative attitude.[28]

[24] H.C. Deb., vol. 544, col. 161 (*Written Answers*).
[25] Vietnam Embassy, Washington, Press and Information Service, 19 Aug. 1955.
[26] Ibid. (Cole, pp. 227–8).
[27] *NCNA*, 16 Sept. 1955.
[28] *NYT*, 27 Aug. 1955. In his assessment of the situation in Vietnam Nehru had consistently tended to discount the fact that to millions of Vietnamese a Communist régime was abhorrent. This attitude had been revealed on the eve of the Geneva Conference when he had declared in the Indian Parliament that 'the conflict in Indo-China is in its origin and essential character a movement of resistance to colonialism and the attempts to deal with such resistance by the traditional methods of suppression and divide-and-rule. Foreign intervention has made the issue more complex, but it nevertheless remains basically anti-colonial

However help for Diem was on the way, and on 30 August Dulles declared in the course of a press conference that the American Government was in agreement with Diem and supported his contention that conditions in North Vietnam ruled out the possibility of holding free elections.[29] This may have encouraged Diem to issue a communiqué on 21 September, in which he declared bluntly that 'there can be no question of a conference, even less of negotiations' with the Hanoi Government.[30]

Although Dong approached Molotov again in November with a request that measures should be concerted with the British Government to ensure that the Geneva Agreements were respected,[31] his plea proved ineffectual as the Soviet Government, whose policy was now directed to easing international tensions, was reluctant to resort to coercive measures.

### THE ECONOMIC SITUATION

Meanwhile the food situation in North Vietnam had become so critical by January 1955 that the Hanoi Government was compelled to restrict the consumption of rice by the urban population.[32] The shortage was ascribed to floods in the previous autumn, which had ruined the crop in the rich province of Thanh Hoa, while the withdrawal of the Expeditionary Corps, together with the flight of many Roman Catholic village communities, had prevented the paddy in the Red river delta from being harvested with the usual care. This short-fall in the December crop had, moreover, been followed by a drought which now threatened to diminish the yield in June.[33] Faced with the threat of famine and with a catastrophic deterioration in the economic situation, the Hanoi Government appears to have resigned itself at this stage to the necessity of making an urgent appeal for aid to its Chinese and Russian allies. This decision was probably made with some reluctance, as the Government was aware that exclusive dependence on Chinese

and nationalist in character' (India, House of the People Deb., 24 Apr. 1954, vol. 4, No. 52, pp. 5574–83).

[29] *NYHT*, 31 Aug. 1955.
[30] *The Times*, 22 Sept. 1955.
[31] *NCNA*, 7 Dec. 1955.
[32] *Le Monde*, 20 Jan. 1955.
[33] *Figaro*, 9 June 1955.

and Russian aid would reduce the status of North Vietnam to that of a satellite state, or even to that of an outlying Chinese province. Moreover, the Viet Minh leaders, who had spent seven years in the isolation of the Viet Bac, had emerged from their long retreat with an imperfect appreciation of the state of affairs in the outside world and with considerable illusions in regard to their own importance on the international chequer board. These illusions had been voiced by Ho Chi Minh in December of the previous year when, adopting the theories of his friend Sainteny, he declared, in an interview with a British journalist, that Viet Minh policy in international affairs would be primarily devoted to bridging the gap between China and the Western nations.[34]

However, the inability of the French Government to provide economic assistance,[35] the refusal of the southern régime to trade with the North, and the maintenance of an American embargo on the sale of industrial products and strategic commodities to Communist countries seem to have convinced Ho that this policy must be sacrificed to the pressing demands of the economic situation. In consequence, on 22 June he left suddenly at the head of an important delegation, comprising the Ministers of Finance, Industry and Commerce, Education, Agriculture, and Health, for Peking and Moscow.[36] At the Peking airfield Mao Tse-tung was present in person to greet him, a courtesy which was due both to the head of a friendly state and also to a senior Communist personage who, after playing some part in the beginnings of the Communist movement in China, had transferred his activities with notable success to South East Asia. The negotiations were concluded on 7 July by a joint communiqué whereby the Government of the People's Republic of China undertook to give the Democratic Republic of Vietnam economic aid to the value of 800 million Chinese yuan[37] (about £120 million). Chinese technicians were also to be sent to Vietnam, Vietnamese workers were

[34] Denis Bloodworth in *Observer*, 2 Jan. 1955.
[35] A barter agreement was signed in October for the exchange of a milliard francs worth of goods.
[36] *Sunday Times*, 24 June 1955.
[37] *NCNA*, 8 July 1955 (RIIA, *Documents, 1955*, pp. 475–9). This aid was to include machinery to equip textile mills, tanneries, paper mills, and factories for the production of pharmaceutical goods, electrical equipment, and agricultural implements.

to serve as apprentices in Chinese factories, and cultural exchanges between the two countries were to be encouraged, while the Chinese undertook to provide North Vietnam with material and apparatus for cultural, educational, and health work.

Ho Chi Minh then left by air for Russia, breaking the journey at Irkutsk, where the party visited the site of a hydro-electric scheme on the shores of Lake Baikal, and at Sverdlovsk, where Ho spoke Russian with men employed at the heavy engineering works.[38] The party reached Moscow on the 12th. Here the President addressed the crowd which had assembled to greet him and, stressing the plight of the Vietnamese economy, expressed confidence that his Government would be assisted by the Soviet Union and 'other fraternal countries' in the task of reconstructing a democratic and independent country.[39]

This confidence was justified. On the 18th, when the Viet-namese delegation was already on their way back to Hanoi, a joint communiqué was issued which announced that the Soviet Government had allocated the sum of 400 million roubles (about £36 million) to assist in raising the living standards of the population and in restoring the economy of the Democratic Republic of Vietnam.[40] The Soviet Government also under-took to accept Vietnamese for training at Russian universities and technical schools, to assist in setting up technical training establishments and to give technical aid in carrying out geological surveys and implementing measures for combating infectious diseases.[41] On 22 July Ho returned to Hanoi, where he assured the crowd which had assembled to welcome him that no strings were attached to the aid and technical assistance which had been obtained.

Although the Viet Minh leader's pilgrimage to Peking and Moscow had secured some assistance in the immense task of reconstruction, the material lot of the population remained

[38] *Combat*, 12 July 1955.
[39] *Soviet News*, 14 July 1955.
[40] Part of this sum was to be used to restore or reconstruct factories and public utilities.
[41] *NCNA*, 18 July 1955 (RIIA, *Documents, 1955*, pp. 279–82). Russian engineers were later to install plant at iron mines in the province of Cao Bang, and after the departure of the surviving French engineers in December 1955, to operate the coal mines at Hon Gay and Campha (*Combat*, 4 Dec. 1955). Russian engineers were also reported at the end of the year to be drawing up plans for the erection of tea factories in North Vietnam (*Hindu*, 6 Jan. 1956).

unenviable. The agreements covered the Government's minimum requirements for capital equipment and services, but no arrangements had been made for the provision of food. However, the threat of famine was averted by a three-cornered deal early in 1955 involving shipments of Burmese rice to Haiphong in return for deliveries of Russian industrial equipment to Rangoon. Barter and aid agreements were also signed during 1955 with Czechoslovakia, Hungary, Poland, and Rumania, these countries undertaking to supply capital equipment, pharmaceutical products, medical assistance, and technicians either in exchange for raw materials or as a free gift.

## LAND REFORM AND MASS MOBILIZATION

While the gravity of the economic situation in North Vietnam was the main preoccupation of the authorities, the political situation had not been entirely neglected. On 30 December 1954 the Government had been reinforced by the appointment to minor posts of three senior officials from South Vietnam and of one senior official from *Lien Khu* V (South-Central Vietnam). Further evidence of political activity was provided in January 1955, when the Lien Viet Front, which had been reconstituted in 1951 to include the surviving members of the Viet Minh League,[42] held its third Congress and expressed the wish that its membership should be further increased with a view to the organization on a nation-wide scale of a campaign for the elections.[43] Its transformation into an even broader organization, the Fatherland Front, took place in September, the Front being of so comprehensive a nature that the deliberations of its Central Executive Committee of eighty-one members had to be directed by a more manageable steering committee.

The Lien Viet Congress was followed by the fourth session of the National Assembly on 20 March 1955. This body, which had been elected in 1946 on a three-year mandate, proceeded to record its unanimous approval of every aspect of government policy on which its opinion was solicited. It approved the Geneva Agreements and measures dealing with agrarian reform, and passed three resolutions: on the consolidation of

[42] See above, pp. 228-9.
[43] *Le Monde*, 13 Jan. 1955.

national defence, the land reform policy, and on religious freedom.[44]

In December 1953, on the occasion of the National Assembly's third plenary session, the delegates had also been required to ratify a land reform law.[45] This law effected no drastic change in land tenure; it merely reduced rents and interest rates, wiped out certain categories of debts, declared a moratorium on others, and vested the title to land in nationalist ownership in the landless peasants who were engaged in its cultivation. The conservative nature of this reform appears to have been inspired by the fear that any drastic attempt to reapportion agricultural holdings would have an adverse effect upon production, but the Viet Minh intention to effect a radical land reform at a later date was revealed by a decree in April 1953, defining the stages by which a 'Mass Mobilization Movement' was to be organized.

This Movement, which was modelled on methods evolved by the Chinese Communists, was designed to eradicate the 'landlord' class from village communities. It was to be initiated by the deliberate creation of a feeling of hostility towards landlords, who were to be pilloried by Viet Minh propagandists and portrayed as heartless and perverse parasites. Poorer members of the community were to be encouraged in the course of public meetings to recall or invent incidents in which the conduct of their richer neighbours had been open to criticism. When popular hatred had been sufficiently aroused by these methods, the village community was to be classified into 'landlords', 'rich farmers', 'middle-class' peasants, and 'poor' peasants. This operation, which was euphemistically termed 'land reform', was to be concluded by the arraignment before their less wealthy neighbours of the unfortunate individuals in the 'landlord' category, who were to be stripped of their holdings and, as the occasion demanded, either murdered or sent to forced labour camps.

Since circumstances did not appear to be favourable to implement this decree early in 1953, in September of that year the Central Executive Committee of the Lao Dong Party issued

[44] NCNA, 27 Mar. 1955. A Thai–Meo autonomous area was set up in May 1955 covering the provinces of Lai Chau and Son La in North-West Vietnam (Viet-Nam News Agency, 8 May 1955).

[45] Vietnam Agrarian Reform Law, adopted 4 Dec. 1953 (Hanoi, 1955).

a new directive on 'Mass Mobilization and its new relations with rich farmers' in which Viet Minh officials were reminded that current policy was based, on the political plane, on acting in concert with the rich peasants and, on the economic plane, on respecting their property and leaving them 'free to live'.[46] Truong Chinh, the Secretary General of the Lao Dong Party, who was regarded as the party's official theoretician, was aware, however, that the Communist tenure of power in China was based on the support of the 'poor peasants', who by benefiting from a redistribution of land carried out by these methods had become morally involved in the maintenance of the régime. Accordingly, he took advantage of the platform provided by an Agricultural Production Conference in Hanoi on 13 November 1955, to set in motion the 'Fifth Crucial Wave of Mass Mobilization': the 'wave' having been preceded by a census of the population and by the promulgation of a Population Classification Decree designed to hasten the rate of its advance.[47] Nevertheless, with doctrinaire rigidity Truong Chinh had decreed that the procedure adopted should conform exactly to the Chinese Communist pattern, without taking into account the fact that in Tongking the percentage of landholdings cultivated by their owners was higher than that in any other Asian country, 61 per cent. of these holdings being estimated at less than an acre. On 13 December it was officially announced that: 'During twenty days more than 100,000 persons belonging to all the social classes in Hanoi had participated in the trial of the landlords of villages surrounding the capital'.[48] The reality which underlay this and subsequent claims to the effect that more than 10½ million peasants had been 'liberated from the feudal yoke' was revealed, however, in the course of the following year, when mounting discontent led Ho Chi Minh to confess, in an open letter on 18 August, that 'mistakes' had been made in the implementation of agrarian reform.

These 'mistakes' had been committed by the Communist cadres in charge of this operation who, when they were faced with the disconcerting discovery that no landlords existed in many of the delta villages, had proceeded to create such a class

[46] *Voix du Viet-Nam*, 22 Sept. 1953.
[47] Viet-Nam News Agency, 19 Nov. 1955.
[48] *Voix du Viet-Nam*, 13 Dec. 1955.

by resorting to murder and torture, in order to wring the statutory confessions of past ill-treatment of tenant farmers from villagers who either cultivated their own meagre holdings or in some cases possessed no land at all. The cost in lives and suffering of this sombre farce was revealed in December 1956, when 12,000 victims of the operation were released from the forced labour camps to which they had been unjustly condemned, the number of those who had been murdered was unofficially estimated at between ten and fifteen thousand.[49] The protagonist of Chinese Communist methods who had been responsible for setting in motion the 'Fifth Crucial Wave of Mass Mobilization' was, however, allowed to go into temporary retirement, his functions being taken over by Ho Chi Minh, whose popularity was exploited to deflect popular indignation from the Democratic Republic's ill-informed attempt at agrarian reform.

[49] Tibor Mende in *Figaro*, 30–31 Mar. 1957 and Georges Chaffard in *Le Monde*, 6–7 Jan. 1957.

# XX

# Changes of Front

ON 5 January 1955 Cardinal Spellman, the Archbishop of New York, arrived in Saigon to inspect the relief work being done on behalf of the Roman Catholic refugees. Some official embarrassment appears to have been felt that the visit of this eminent personage, who was generally believed to be one of Diem's staunchest and most influential supporters, should have taken place before the notorious gambling establishments and brothels in Saigon–Cholon[1] had been closed. However, negotiations for the surrender of the gambling concession were in their final stage, and on 9 January it was announced that the gambling rooms at the 'Grand Monde' in Cholon, and at the secondary establishment, the 'Cloche d'Or', in Saigon,[2] would close at the end of the week.

The Government's decision to cancel the concession was wise. The facilities provided by the Binh Xuyen 'General' for the Vietnamese to indulge their passion for games of chance had led to recurrent public scandals and domestic dramas and to a progressive impoverishment of the working class.[3] 'General' Le Van Vien, who realized that the return of peaceful conditions and Vietnam's future dependence on American aid would entail certain readjustments in his way of life, seems to have accepted the decision with equanimity, pocketing the sum paid in compensation, merely with an expression of regret that the Government should be prepared to forgo such an important source of revenue.

His example was not followed, however, by his Cao Dai and Hoa Hao colleagues, who were themselves about to lose the

[1] The world's largest brothel—the Hall of Mirrors with 600 inmates—had recently been added to the attractions at the Grand Monde, the cost being met, it was alleged, by the misappropriation of funds representing American financial aid to South Vietnam (*NYHT*, 11 Jan. 1955 and *Figaro*, 24 Dec. 1954).

[2] *Le Populaire*, 10 Jan. 1955. Le Van Vien was the head of a consortium which had purchased the gambling concession in Saigon–Cholon in 1949. Binh Xuyen troops were also responsible for public security in the two gambling establishments.

[3] The equivalent of 100 milliard francs (some £100 million) were estimated to have changed hands in the course of the preceding eight years across the tables at the Grand Monde and the Cloche d'Or (*Combat*, 18 Jan. 1955).

subsidies on which they depended to pay their inflated militia forces.[4] These subsidies stopped on 11 February, when the French Command officially handed over administrative responsibility for the Vietnamese armed forces to the Saigon Government, but after this the President still refused to reveal his intentions in regard to the sects' militia forces, and on 12 February the Secretary of State for National Defence confined himself to the statement that they would become part of the national army.[5] Since the Government had announced in January that the strength of the army was to be reduced from 270,000 to 100,000,[6] this statement failed to satisfy the sects' leaders. Thus the loss of the French subsidies faced the Cao Dai and Hoa Hao leaders with the alternative either of waiting for their unpaid troops to disband or of taking immediate steps to promote the formation of a Government which would prove more sympathetic to their problems.

Diem's readiness to provoke a trial of strength with the sects appears to have been based both on his congenital inability to compromise and on the shrewd calculation that he would be able to exploit the internal dissensions of his adversaries in order to avoid a general settlement. His confidence that such a policy would prove successful had been strengthened on 14 January, when Tran Van Soai's Chief of Staff, Nguyen Van Hué, after accusing the Hoa Hao 'Generalissimo' of being 'greedy' and a 'traitor to the nation', had requested that the troops who recognized his authority should be integrated with the national army.[7] Hué's example was followed at the end of the month by the dissident Cao Dai 'General', Trinh Minh The,[8] who announced his intention of rallying to the support of the Government,[9] in the course of Diem's visit to a refugee

[4] At the beginning of 1955 the strength of the Cao Dai and Hoa Hao militia forces was estimated at 25,000 and 20,000 respectively, or about twice the number of troops which the sects were officially allowed to maintain under arms under the terms of past agreements with the French Command (*Combat*, 1 Apr. 1955 and Leroy, p. 128).

[5] *Courrier du Viet-Nam,* No. 7, Mar. 1955.

[6] *NYT*, 20 Jan. 1955.

[7] *NYHT*, 17 Jan. 1955.

[8] *NYT*, 1 Feb. 1955.

[9] After the failure of the French attempt in 1952 to encircle and destroy his force, The had transferred his headquarters to the sacred mountain—the Nui Ba Den near Tay Ninh. Installed in this eyrie, he was well placed to draw his supplies from the 'Holy See' and to maintain contact with nationalists in Saigon. Although he appears to have devoted himself principally, during this time of waiting, to the

settlement near Ben Cau, which had been constructed by the Caodaist force and paid for out of official funds. The, who was present together with a small contingent of dissident Caodaists to welcome the Prime Minister, revealed in the course of a short speech of welcome that his decision to 'cooperate' with the Government was inspired by the considerable success Diem had achieved in his struggle against the agents of 'colonialism' and 'Communism' and also by the hope that the Prime Minister would now justify his reputation for incorruptibility by instituting proceedings against traitors and peculators whose fortune had been acquired by robbing and exploiting the people.[10] On 13 February The, who had been promoted to the rank of General in the Vietnamese army, made a triumphant entry into Saigon at the head of his black-garbed troops[11] and marched past representatives of the Government and the diplomatic corps some of whom may have recalled the outrages perpetrated by this disquieting young man in 1952.[12] His example was followed by another Hoa Hao leader on 22 February, when 'General' Nguyen Giac Ngo also announced his decision to support Diem.[13]

Meanwhile a state of great confusion prevailed over wide

business of training and equipping his band, The attracted attention in 1953 by kidnapping the Caodaist General-cum-Archbishop, Tran Quang Vinh, forcing him to disgorge, with an appropriate expression of repentance, some ill-gotten piastres, and in the following year he kidnapped the Commissioner-General for Refugees himself, whose ransom is reported to have been paid out of the official funds at his disposal. Finally, The's men had captured and brutally murdered two French officers in the Tay Ninh area in December 1954.

[10] *Courrier du Viet-Nam*, No. 7, Mar. 1955 and *Combat*, 1 Feb. 1955. The's hope had been partially fulfilled earlier in the month when an attempt had been made to arrest Pham Van Giao, the ex-Governor of Central Vietnam, but Giao, apprised of this intention, had hurriedly left for France. In February further evidence of the Prime Minister's 'purity' and 'intransigence' was provided by the arrest of Tam's mistress, Mme Le Thi Gioi. Mme Gioi, who was sentenced to five years imprisonment for bribery and the misuse of official funds, is reported to have caused a sensation in court by roundly accusing the active and prominent Mme Ngo Dinh Nhu of indulging in similar activities on a far more extensive scale.

[11] *NYHT*, 14 Feb. 1955.

[12] The size of the contingent which The produced for enrolment in the national army caused surprise, but these troops are reported to have included 1,000 ex-Viet Minh who had joined The's force to avoid evacuation to North Vietnam (Clos in *Le Monde*, 3 June 1955).

[13] *Combat*, 23 Feb. 1955.

areas of Cochin-China, where the Viet Minh political cadres and regional troops who had secretly remained behind continued to be obeyed by the population.[14] The unrest was increased by the undisciplined behaviour of the sects, affrays taking place continually between Cao Dai and Hoa Hao armed bands who were attempting to establish their control over former Viet Minh territory in the Plaine des Joncs and the Transbassac. In this scramble by the sects to extend the boundaries of their respective zones, the Hoa Hao were at an advantage since in August 1954 Hoa Hao 'General' Le Quang Vinh, alias Ba Cut, had abandoned his headquarters at Thot Not in the province of Long Xuyen and taken to the maquis at the head of 3,000 men.[15]

His defection, which was believed to have been connived at by the Hoa Hao 'Generalissimo', had led to fighting between Hoa Hao irregulars and units of the national army, and after an attempt—*Opération Écaille*—to reduce his force had proved abortive and negotiations had broken down, Ba Cut attacked a battalion of government troops near Long Xuyen on 3 January 1955.[16] However, in spite of the disturbed state of West Cochin-China, government troops proceeded at the beginning of February to occupy the Ca Mau peninsula following the evacuation of the Viet Minh regular units to the north, and on the 19th Diem himself paid an official visit to this outlying region.

While South Vietnam thus drifted into a state of anarchy, Bao Dai, whose declared intention of returning to Saigon had been consistently discouraged by the American State Department,[17] was viewing the trend of events with misgivings inspired by the fear that the sects, who by a strange sequence of

[14] Leroy, pp. 174–5. At the end of February 1955 French intelligence reports indicated that, with the exception of the territory controlled by the sects, from 60 to 90 per cent. of the villages in the southern zone were subject to Viet Minh influence and control (*NYHT*, 1 Mar. 1955).

[15] This was the fifth occasion on which Ba Cut had taken to the maquis since 1947. Hitherto he had been able to negotiate his return on advantageous terms, rejoining the French-controlled zone with the disarming grin of a schoolboy who had carried out some successful prank: an illusion increased by the protuberant ears and defective teeth of the culprit.

[16] *Le Populaire*, 3 Feb. 1955. The failure of *Opération Écaille* was ascribed to the fact that Ba Cut had received a copy of the plan, possibly from Hoa Hao 'General' Tran Van Soai, who was at that time a member of the National Defence Committee.

[17] *Le Monde* and *Manchester Guardian*, 30 Apr. 1955.

events had become the champions of the popular demand for a broadly-based and liberal government, would be unable to oppose any effective resistance to President Diem's demand that they should place themselves unreservedly in his hands trusting to his generosity and sense of justice.[18] Finally, in February 1955, Bao Dai sent his cousin, Prince Vinh Canh, to Saigon with instructions to urge upon the sects the need for unity.[19] This advice was followed, and after protracted negotiations of a more or less secret nature it was announced, at the beginning of March, that the Cao Dai and Hoa Hao sects and the Binh Xuyen resistance group had signed a non-aggression pact, which was completed by a 'spiritual union between the three sects'—designed, in the words of Cao Dai 'General' Nguyen Thanh Phuong, 'to protect the country and to serve the people'.[20] On 4 March the Cao Dai Superior, Pham Cong Tac, issued a proclamation in which he demanded in the name of this 'spiritual union', now described as a 'united front of nationalist forces', the constitution of a strong democratic government composed of honest men.[21]

Bao Dai's role in the formation of this 'united front' had not escaped the attention of the American Government or of the press, and he is reported to have received a personal letter from President Eisenhower on 9 March reaffirming that American policy was based on support for President Ngo Dinh Diem.[22] This *démarche* was followed by press articles attacking the monarch, which culminated in the following salvo from the representative of the *New York Times* in Saigon:

There can be no pretense of political respectability in South Vietnam [declared this journalist] until the moral dead weight of Bao Dai, so-called Emperor and Chief of State, is shed. . . . He has collaborated successively with the Japanese, the Communists and the French Colonial Administration. He now lives on France's Riviera happily spending the proceeds of his sordid profiteering and enjoying the prestige of diplomatic recognition as head of tormented Vietnam. It is appalling that this situation should be permitted to prevail. . . . Bao Dai rests on democracy's conscience about

[18] David Schoenbrun, in *Colliers*, 30 Sept. 1955.
[19] Clos in *Le Monde*, 22 Mar. 1955.
[20] Ibid. 5 Mar. 1955.
[21] Ibid.
[22] *NYT*, 11 Mar. 1955.

as comfortably as the putrefying albatross tied around the neck of Coleridge's Ancient Mariner.[23]

Such violent abuse appears to have taken Bao Dai aback. Although he expressed his approval of the desire for unity revealed by the setting up of a united front, he also sought to deflect American anger by sending a message to Diem expressing his satisfaction with his services.[24]

But the formation of the 'united front of nationalist forces' was to provide further and conclusive proof that the sects were incapable of sinking their differences. On 7 March General Trinh Minh The, whose decision to join the front had caused a sensation, changed his mind and announced that he would continue to 'co-operate' with Diem, a change of front which he attributed to the sudden realization that he was unable to belong to an organization 'which did not support the Government'.[25] Meanwhile Diem began to take precautionary measures, and it was announced on 1 March that three battalions of Nung militia troops had arrived in Saigon from Phan Thiet.[26] The Saigon garrison were further reinforced that month by the arrival of two battalions of Tongkingese parachute troops from Nha Trang.[27] Their arrival proved timely, as on 21 March the 'united front of nationalist forces', alarmed at the prospect of mass desertions among their unpaid troops, presented the Prime Minister with an ultimatum demanding the formation of a government of national union within five days.

On the 24th Diem broadcast an explanation of his refusal to agree to the sects' 'request'.[28] This explanation was accompanied by an invitation couched in general terms to representa-

---

[23] C. L. Sulzberger in *NYT*, 14 Mar. 1955.

[24] *NYHT* and *Le Populaire*, 16 Mar. 1955.

[25] *Le Monde*, 8 Mar. 1955. Hoa Hao 'General' Ba Cut declared bluntly, however, that The's decision had been clinched by a cash payment (*Le Populaire*, 22 Mar. 1955) alleged to amount to 20 million piastres (Joseph Alsop in *NYHT*, 31 Mar. 1955).

[26] *Le Monde*, 11 Mar. 1955. These Nung battalions had been evacuated from Tongking where they had been responsible for the security of an autonomous zone around Mon Cay which was directly attached to the Crown of Annam. The Nungs are of mixed stock, being descended from Hakkas, who had invaded the territory in the nineteenth century and inter-married with the predominantly Muong population.

[27] *Daily Telegraph*, 24 Mar. 1955.

[28] Viet-Nam Embassy, Washington, Press and Information Service, vol. 1, No. 4, Apr. 1955.

tives of the military groups to reconsider with him the problems arising out of the demobilization of their forces, but this invitation did not disarm suspicions in regard to the Prime Minister's intention, and following the expiration of the ultimatum the Hoa Hao and Cao Dai representatives resigned from the Government.

Diem's refusal to comply with the ultimatum did not, however, lead to an outbreak of hostilities. The Hoa Hao, who controlled the ferries and river traffic in the delta, contented themselves with holding up food supplies for Saigon–Cholon, and the Binh Xuyen proceeded to entrench themselves in the police and security headquarters and in other requisitioned buildings in Saigon–Cholon. Diem then ordered paratroops under the command of Colonel Cao Van Tri to stand by to take over the police headquarters in the Boulevard Gallieni at the boundary of Saigon and Cholon and the security headquarters in Saigon. The occupation of police headquarters was carried out without difficulty, as the Binh Xuyen troops withdrew and established themselves in an adjacent building, but the Binh Xuyen commandos refused to evacuate the Security Service headquarters and on the 28th the Prime Minister, whose readiness to accept a trial of strength was causing general dismay, ordered Colonel Tri to attack the building.[29] This attack was later countermanded at the instance of General Paul Ely, the French Commander-in-Chief, who objected to the operation on the grounds that French lives and property would be endangered. The outbreak of fighting had merely been postponed, however, until the night of the 29–30th when an affray took place around the police headquarters.

After the fighting, in which civilians were a target for both sides, had lasted for four hours, the French Command were able to arrange for a cease-fire,[30] but this action was resented by Diem, who suspected the French of secretly supporting the sects, a suspicion apparently founded on a rumour that the Binh Xuyen had received French tactical advice during the fighting and on the fact that the French Command had refused to provide the national army with extra supplies of ammunition

---

[29] Pierre Dubard in *Figaro*, 12 May 1955.

[30] The casualties were army and police: 6 killed, 34 wounded; Binh Xuyen: 10 killed, 20 wounded; civilians: 10 killed, 58 wounded (Clos in *Le Monde*, 31 Mar. 1955).

and fuel or with transport to move the parachute battalions from Nha Trang to Saigon.[31] General Lawton Collins, however, the American Ambassador Extraordinary, is reported to have approved Ely's action and to have betrayed increasing misgivings in regard to a policy directed to imposing upon the population of South Vietnam a Prime Minister whose leadership aroused such widespread opposition.[32]

These misgivings were shared by the bulk of Diem's supporters, who were nonplussed by his refusal to seek some compromise with the sects by which further bloodshed would be avoided. Their attitude was to have little effect upon the course of events since after the cease-fire the direction of affairs was assumed by a junta comprising the Prime Minister, his brothers Ngo Dinh Nhu and Ngo Dinh Luyen, and their nephew by marriage, Tran Trung Dung.[33] This family junta was assisted by American advisers who were referred to enigmatically by French press correspondents as 'the Americans who have an office in the Palais Norodom',[34] or as the 'young Colonels' attached to 'certain American services'.[35]

These Americans were a Colonel Lansdale, who with an assistant had been given office accommodation at the palace, where their facilities for access to the Prime Minister were causing the French authorities some concern since Lansdale was credited with pronounced 'anti-colonialist' views and with some important but unspecified part in building up the authority and popularity of the Filipino President, Ramon Magsaysay.[36] Rumours were thus soon rife that the advice which Lansdale was giving Diem ran counter to the American Ambassador's encouragement of Ely's efforts to prevent the outbreak of civil war. But, if the American attitude appeared ambiguous, the French themselves were believed to be in two minds about the situation. This belief was based on reports that Commissioner-General's staff was split into pro- and anti-Diem

[31] Clos in *Le Monde*, 7 Apr. 1955.

[32] Dubard in *Figaro*, 12 May 1955.

[33] The junta's uncompromising approach to the situation was summed up on 6 April by an official spokesman in the following words: 'We have the support of the entire population, who are imploring us to get rid of the Binh Xuyen bandits' (*Le Monde*, 7 Apr. 1955).

[34] Dubard in *Figaro*, 2 May 1955.

[35] Guillain in *Le Monde*, 18 May 1955.

[36] Amoureux, *Croix sur l'Indochine* (1955), p. 90 and Tibor Mende in *Figaro*, 29 Mar. 1957.

factions, while the activities of certain French officers gave rise to a suspicion that the Expeditionary Corps was providing the sects with unofficial support in their opposition to the Prime Minister.

On 31 March the junta acquired another ally in the person of the Cao Dai Commander-in-Chief, General Nguyen Thanh Phuong, who rallied to the Prime Minister in exchange for an undertaking to incorporate his troops with the army. This pact was sealed by a parade of Cao Dai troops in the grounds of the Palais Norodom, at which Phuong, under the watchful eye of Trinh Minh The, proclaimed his loyalty to Diem.[37] Since, however, Phuong had neglected to inform the Cao Dai Superior of his intention, Pham Cong Tac caused some confusion next day by flatly denying that the sect's militia forces had been transferred to the Government.[38]

Meanwhile the junta, encouraged by this success, now sought to complete the isolation of the Binh Xuyen by purchasing the support of the Hoa Hao leaders, but on 23 April a communiqué issued in the name of the 'united front of nationalist forces' announced that Hoa Hao 'Generals' Tran Van Soai, Lam Thanh Nguyen, and 'Ba Cut' had rejected this approach, which had been baited with an offer of 100 million piastres.[39]

During the month of April the population of Saigon–Cholon became accustomed to the presence of armed and hostile forces in their midst. But in spite of this public unconcern, the defence preparations by Binh Xuyen commando units at Security Service headquarters put a stop to the routine examination of passports at the airfield and port, while the military occupation of the adjacent Ministry of Finance and of police headquarters and the port office led to further administrative confusion. Finally Diem, who must have been outraged by the element of farce implicit in the situation, on 24 April dismissed the Binh Xuyen's nominee, Lai Huu Sang, from the post of director-general of the Security Service and appointed an army officer,

[37] *Combat*, 1 Apr. 1955. Although Phuong's decision is reported to have been inspired by fear of mass desertions among his unpaid troops, The's influence over his volatile and emotive colleague is likely to have been the decisive factor in this change of front.

[38] *Scotsman*, 2 Apr. 1955.

[39] Diem's emissaries were more favourably received, however, by Hoa Hao 'General' Nguyen Giac Ngo, who appears to have later altered his decision to rally to the support of the Prime Minister out of deference to the wishes of his colleagues.

26

Colonel Nguyen Ngo Le, to replace him, while all members of the service were ordered to report within 48 hours on pain of court martial at a new headquarters which Colonel Le was instructed to set up.[40] The gravity of the situation created by this decree was increased by a further announcement next day that when this time-limit had expired Binh Xuyen troops would no longer be allowed to circulate in Saigon–Cholon.

On the 28th fighting broke out at midday in the Boulevard Gallieni[41] and spread down the Boulevard towards the bridge which spanned the Arroyo Chinois and linked the Binh Xuyen General's headquarters with Cholon and also northwards to the Lycée Petrus Ky, which was garrisoned by Binh Xuyen troops. Mortars were used in the battle, setting fire to attap huts built on waste land near the battle area, and at 1.15 p.m. four shells exploded in the grounds of the Palais Norodom.[42] The French Command again attempted to arrange a cease-fire, but abandoned these efforts during the afternoon when the decision was taken to limit French action to safeguarding the European community in Saigon.

Meanwhile the Palace junta was taking every precaution to ensure the success of this operation, and although four battalions of paratroops and an armoured car squadron were engaged in the fighting, while some fourteen battalions were being held in reserve, orders were given for further reinforcements to be sent from Annam. The Binh Xuyen, who were estimated to have some 2,000 troops in Saigon–Cholon entrenched in requisitioned buildings ill-adapted to resist attack, began after some initial confusion to oppose a spirited resistance to attempts to expel them from the lycée, from a cinema, and from a printing works commanding the approach to their headquarters, but Le Van Vien, probably acting on the assumption that the

---

[40] *NYT*, 27 Apr. 1955. Le, who was a native of Annam, was to be assisted in his task by General Mai Huu Xuan, who had been summarily dismissed from the post of Director-General in April of the previous year. As he was able to call upon the services of those members of the Security Services and police force who had been transferred to the armed forces at that time and were now eager to settle old scores with the Binh Xuyen, Xuan proved a useful ally.

[41] The fighting is alleged to have been provoked by the action of paratroops proceeding down the Boulevard in two trucks, who opened fire on a Binh Xuyen commando unit in occupation of an adjacent building.

[42] Diem was to claim, however, in his speech to the Free World on 8 May, that 'peace was lost in Saigon only when the Binh Xuyen fired mortar shells on the government palace in the very heart of the town' (Vietnam Embassy, Washington, Press and Information Service, 13 May 1955).

French would stop the fighting, failed to direct the resistance of his troops and refused to commit his reserves, numbering some 4,000, to the battle. Accordingly in the early hours of the morning the lycée, the last of the three centres of resistance remaining in Binh Xuyen hands, fell to the paratroops, who then made preparations to advance on Vien's headquarters.

The occupation of these headquarters, from which Vien had decamped at dawn to rejoin his reserves, was delayed for some hours by the collapse of the bridge across the Arroyo Chinois, which had been partially destroyed by the explosion of a stray mortar shell setting off demolition charges, an accident which also caused grave embarrassment to the Binh Xuyen troops withdrawing from Cholon. In the afternoon fighting again broke out around the 'Grand Monde', where isolated groups of Binh Xuyen continued to resist the advance of the government troops. However, by midnight, their resistance had been overcome and the victors were rewarded by the discovery of a large sum of money in the Binh Xuyen 'General's' villa, overlooked by the late occupants in their hurried flight.[43]

The swift collapse of Binh Xuyen resistance confounded the nationalist pundits who had foretold that the struggle would be prolonged and inconclusive, but the combative qualities which the group had once shown in skirmishes with the French Expeditionary Corps and with the Viet Minh had been sapped by the nature of the activities in which they had been indulging since 1949. The exploitation of the gambling concession and of prostitution, the collection of tithes on paddy, rubber, fish, and coal, the exaction of protection money from the owners of bars, shops, and public transport, together with the time-honoured custom of blackmailing the wealthy Chinese community, had proved of such absorbing interest that military training had been neglected.

Although the eviction of the Binh Xuyen from Cholon might be ascribed to their ignorance of the technique of street fighting, to the poor quality of their officers, and to the inadequate and heterogeneous nature of their armament and equipment, the readiness of the national army to fight in defence of a Prime Minister whose authority they had decisively rejected in the

---

[43] The total casualties incurred in the course of the fighting were 500 killed and 2,000 wounded, while it was estimated that 20,000 had been rendered homeless (*Le Monde*, 30 Apr. 1955).

autumn of the previous year caused general surprise. This seems to have been due to the dislike felt by the regular units for the Cochin-Chinese militia bodies who had long flouted their authority and questioned their courage and virility, and to the fact that the troops engaged in the operation had not been directly involved in the events culminating in General Hinh's dismissal in the previous autumn.

### OPERATIONS AGAINST THE SECTS

The outbreak of fighting in Cholon finally aroused Bao Dai to action, and on 2 April he announced his intention of summoning without delay the principal representatives of Vietnamese opinion to France, 'far from the theatre of over violent passions', in order to discuss the situation. This announcement was followed by a decree nominating General Nguyen Van Vi as Commander-in-Chief of the armed forces and investing him with the full military powers hitherto exercised by the Prime Minister. Nguyen Van Hinh was also ordered to proceed to Vietnam with instructions to contact the leaders of the sects.

These decisions would seem to have met with the French Government's approval; on the 29th the Prime Minister, Edgar Faure, declared at a press conference that 'it would appear that for some time past his (Ngo Dinh Diem's) government has not been well adapted to discharge the mission with which it has been entrusted,[44] but the American Government, whose efforts had been directed to forestalling any attempt by Bao Dai to reassert his authority, continued to back Diem.[45] Indeed the violent reaction of the American press to the course of events in South Vietnam would certainly have rendered any modification of American policy extremely difficult. Whereas on 23 March the *New York Herald Tribune* merely informed its readers that the United States would be unlikely to give financial backing to any movement which tended to undermine Diem's authority, the report of the outbreak of fighting was greeted by an explosion of indignation against the corrupt and venal elements in the pay of French colonialist interests who had presumed to take up arms against an honest,

---

[44] *Le Monde*, 30 Apr. 1955.
[45] On 20 April a press report from Saigon alleged that Dulles had turned down a French proposal that Diem should be replaced (*Combat*, 21 Apr. 1955).

CHANGES OF FRONT

391

ascetic, idealistic, anti-Communist, and Roman Catholic Prime Minister.[46]

Further support for this assessment of the situation was forthcoming on 30 April, when the *New York Times* published a statement by Generals Phuong, The, and Ngo portraying General Vi as a traitor and a French puppet and ascribing 'the trouble' to French machinations inspired by a desire 'to hang on to colonialism in Vietnam'. However, the success of the operation against the Binh Xuyen smoothed over this difference of opinion and by 29 April Diem's position had been sufficiently reinforced for him to refuse to obey Bao Dai's message recalling him to France, a refusal in which he persisted on receiving a second and a more peremptory summons. Moreover Bao Dai's tardy attempt to reassert his authority, and in particular his decision to invest Vi with full military powers, convinced the junta that the time had come to bring about a change of régime.[47]

A plan was then drawn up in concert with Cao Dai 'Generals' Phuong and The, designed to give such a change the appearance of popular support.[48] On the afternoon of the 30th the rumour spread that an interesting meeting would take place at four o'clock in the Town Hall. This meeting, which was alleged to constitute a General Assembly of the 'democratic revolutionary forces of the nation', was attended by some 200 delegates claiming to represent eighteen political parties.[49]

In conformity with Viet Minh precedents these delegates elected a Revolutionary Committee,[50] who then got the Assembly to approve a number of important measures, including the repudiation of Bao Dai, the dismissal of the Government, and the formation of a national Government under Ngo Dinh Diem, who was charged with the specific tasks of restoring order and security, obtaining the withdrawal of the French

[46] N. Chatelain in *Figaro*, 4 May 1955.

[47] Clos in *Le Monde*, 3 May 1955.

[48] The had aroused considerable alarm on the afternoon of the 28th by infiltrating armed groups of his supporters into the residential quarter of Saigon.

[49] Most of the political parties existed in the imagination of their representatives or consisted of the personal following of obscure political agitators (Clos in *Le Monde*, 3 May 1955).

[50] Those elected to this Revolutionary Committee included, besides Phuong and The, two former Viet Minh political commissars, two personalities with contacts in French 'Stalinist' and 'Trotskyist' circles respectively, and two 'ultra nationalists' from Tongking (Clos in ibid. 4 May 1955).

Expeditionary Corps, and organizing elections to a National Assembly. The Assembly then adjourned, while the Revolutionary Committee went to the Palais Norodom.

The welcome which the Committee received can only be surmised from the subsequent course of events. Later that evening certain foreign press correspondents were hastily summoned to hear an important declaration. They found the palace full of militia troops, and their suspicions that a coup d'état had taken place were confirmed by the discovery that Generals Nguyen Van Vi and Le Van Ty were being held under the surveillance of Phuong and The. The declaration which the correspondents had been summoned to hear was read in stumbling fashion by Vi, who announced that he repudiated Bao Dai's authority and supported the Revolutionary Committee's decision that French colonialist power in Vietnam must be liquidated.[51] After this humiliating scene Vi, who had apparently walked unarmed, unescorted, and unsuspecting into The's clutches, was set free by the action of the local paratroop commander, Colonel Cao Van Tri, who telephoned to the Prime Minister and informed him bluntly that if the Generals were not liberated within one hour his troops would storm the palace.

When their captives had been freed, the Revolutionary Committee decided to establish their headquarters in the Palais Norodom and to remain in constant session. Their deliberations resulted in the appearance next day of a manifesto appealing to the free democratic nations to support the Revolutionary Committee in their attempt to frustrate a plot by 'traitorous henchmen' to sell South Vietnam to the French colonialists by bringing about a civil war. The manifesto ended with an assurance that the Revolutionary Committee were united 'with various nations' in their determination to wipe out colonialism and oppose Communism, even if bloodshed were to ensue.[52]

On the following morning Generals Vi and Ty were again the central figures at a press conference which was held, on this occasion, at military headquarters. After confirming that his previous statement had been made under duress, Vi announced that, although the Prime Minister was in the hands of a

[51] Clos in *Le Monde*, 3 May 1955.
[52] *Voice of Free Viet-Nam*, 1 May 1955.

Revolutionary Committee, the gravity of this situation was lessened by the fact that he could count personally on the loyal support of 90 per cent. of the army. This assessment of the balance of forces served to confirm that Vi was no match for adversaries employing the subtle tactics evolved at the court of Hué: as soon as the press conference was over General Le Van Ty, accompanied by Colonel Duong Van Minh, the Commander of the Saigon–Cholon garrison, and a Colonel Tran Van Don left military headquarters for the Palais Norodom, where Diem welcomed these recruits by promoting Ty to the rank of lieutenant-general and the colonels to the rank of brigadier-general.

Although their decision was later attributed to the receipt of a message from Washington assuring Diem of American support and encouraging him to persist in the course of action on which he had embarked, this change of front by officers whose conduct appeared to be inspired by such practical motives surprised even case-hardened press correspondents in Saigon.[53] Ty then conferred with the Revolutionary Committee and after these discussions a communiqué was issued announcing that the 'General Assembly of the democratic revolutionary forces of the nation' would back up the army and support him.[54] Faced with these defections, Vi left that afternoon for Dalat, where he could rely on the loyalty of the Imperial Guard.

Having successfully disposed of Vi's claims to command the armed forces, the junta next turned their attention to the task of expelling the Binh Xuyen from their positions to the south of Saigon–Cholon and decided, probably on Ngo Dinh Nhu's recommendation, to place General Trinh Minh The in virtual command of this operation,[55] but The, whose activities had hitherto been confined to isolated affrays with the Viet Minh or with French Union troops and to the perpetration of terrorist outrages, was killed on 3 May on the Tan Thuan bridge, when a motor-boat which had entered the Arroyo Chinois from the Saigon river hoisted the Binh Xuyen flag, turned about, and sprayed the bridge with machine-gun fire. Although The's

[53] On 1 May a State Dept. spokesman again reaffirmed that the American Government continued to support Diem in his capacity as head of the legitimate Government in Saigon (*NYHT*, 2 May 1955).

[54] Clos in *Le Monde*, 3 May 1955.

[55] *NYHT*, 4 May 1955.

death was officially ascribed to Binh Xuyen marksmanship, the fact that he had been shot from behind and that the wound was powder-blackened gave rise to a belief that he had in fact been assassinated at point-blank range by one of his entourage. The murderer's identity and motives remained, however, a subject for speculation, the victim's fanaticism, terrorist methods, and ruthless ambition having made him many enemies.

The was given a state funeral at which Diem caused some surprise by fainting before the bier. This display of emotion on the part of a Prime Minister whose appearance usually reflected dignified self-satisfaction, may have been inspired by distress at the death of a general who had served him well, or it may have represented a natural physical reaction after a period of strain, perhaps combined with a feeling of relief at the removal of a dangerous ally possessed of a capacity for ruthless action. Undoubtedly The, whose decision to co-operate with the Government had been based on the assumption that the Prime Minister would resolutely oppose 'colonialism' and peculation, would have reacted with his customary violence when confronted with increasingly circumstantial rumours that Diem's family were exploiting their position to enrich themselves on a substantial scale.[56]

The's death enabled the junta to neutralize the Revolutionary Committee, whose pretensions were arousing alarm and confusion, and after prolonged discussions they were persuaded to evacuate the Palais Norodom. The Committee's pretensions were further deflated by convening an 'official' Congress in Saigon on 5 May. Although the representative capacity of the delegates, who were for the most part civil servants, was open to question and the debates were confused and inconclusive, the proceedings served to reassure opinion abroad.[57] The Revolutionary Committee reacted to this by

[56] Georges Chaffard in *Le Monde*, 5 Jan. 1957. Rumours of the Prime Minister's purchase of land in South America and remittances to a banking account in Switzerland may certainly be ascribed to the malevolence of the opposition, while reports of the acquisition of property in Paris, including that of the Cinema Rex in the Champs Élysées by the Ngo Dinh Nhus may well stem from the same tainted source. But the origin of the funds which were to enable the mortal remains of Diem's murdered brother, Ngo Dinh Khoi, to be housed at Hué in a style befitting a deceased emperor aroused the legitimate curiosity of those acquainted with the former modest circumstances of the Ngo Dinh family.

[57] Clos in ibid. 6 May 1955.

holding a rival Congress which also met in Saigon on 5 May. Some 400 delegates attended, but the fact that their mandate was clearly derived from their association with the Cao Dai military leaders effectively disposed of the Committee's claim to represent a widespread revolutionary movement.[58]

When the rival Congresses had dispersed, Diem reconstituted his depleted cabinet; the list of members which was published on 10 May revealed that out of the thirteen selected for office six were obscure officials. Meanwhile the government troops engaged in clearing the Binh Xuyen zone to the south of Saigon–Cholon had been encountering little resistance since Le Van Vien had decided to withdraw his remaining battalions to the Rung Sat, a region of mangrove swamps near the estuary of the Saigon river. The Vietnamese Command contented themselves with sealing off the approaches to this area and waited for the hardships of life in this mosquito-ridden maze of tidal waterways to weaken Binh Xuyen resistance and for deserters to provide them with intelligence on their military dispositions.

The expulsion of the Binh Xuyen from Saigon–Cholon now enabled the Government to turn its attention to the task of reducing the Hoa Hao sect, and on 24 May Diem's emissaries again approached Tran Van Soai with the offer of a large sum of money.[59]

Although he would probably have been prepared to accept this offer, Soai was no longer in a position to do so, since at a meeting of the sect's leaders at Cai Von the decision had been reached to resist the Government: a decision which is reported to have been endorsed with particular reluctance by Soai's wife, Mme Le Thi Gam, who was fearful of jeopardizing the wealth which she had amassed. This meeting had been attended by Nguyen Van Hinh, who had left France on 29 April with orders to contact the leaders of the Cochin-Chinese sects on behalf of Bao Dai,[60] but the collapse of Binh Xuyen resistance had led Hinh to change his itinerary and to disembark at Phnom Penh. On 19 May Hinh was reported to have left Phnom Penh on his return journey to France,[61] but the route

[58] The Revolutionary Committee played no further part in shaping the course of events and were persuaded to vote their own dissolution in January of the following year.

[59] Le Monde, 26 May 1955.

[60] Yves Desjacques in Figaro, 27 May 1955.

[61] The Times, 16 May 1955.

which he took lay through West Cochin-China, where he was reported to have set up his headquarters on board a sampan in the vicinity of Soc Trang.

Reports of Hinh's return to South Vietnam failed, however, to provoke defections among the military units, who were then completing their preparations for an offensive against the Hoa Hao. The Hoa Hao forces, aware of these preparations, abandoned their posts and bases on 25 May and, after setting fire to their hutments and to the stores which they were compelled to leave behind, they took to the maquis. The government offensive was launched on 5 June, when units of the national army under Duong Van Minh, supported by amphibious vehicles, attacked Hoa Hao forces in the Can Tho area. Five Hoa Hao battalions surrendered and on the 18th General Nguyen Giac Ngo, who had followed his colleagues into the maquis with some reluctance, again rallied to the Government.

Meanwhile Tran Van Soai had transferred his headquarters from Cai Von to the Seven Mountains near the Cambodian frontier where Hoa Hao 'General' Lam Thanh Nguyen, the war-lord of Chau Doc, had built up stocks of food and war material ready for such an emergency, and here he was joined by Hinh and Vi.[62] Hoa Hao resistance in this remote region proved, however, to be short-lived; on 19 June, Soai, Vi, and Hinh were compelled to seek refuge in Cambodia, while Lam Thanh Nguyen took the road to Saigon and made his submission to Diem.[63] Thus by the beginning of July organized opposition to the Government in West Cochin-China was confined to the activities of the force under the command of Ba Cut, who continued to hold out until April of the following year.[64]

In September the operations against the Binh Xuyen were resumed, and after some weeks' skirmishing the government troops succeeded in expelling Le Van Vien's forces from the Rung Sat. The Binh Xuyen General himself, however, eluded his pursuers and was spirited away to France. This offensive

[62] Hinh is reported to have received at this juncture a message from Bao Dai instructing him to return to France (Desjacques in *Figaro*, 27 May 1955).

[63] 'Generalissimo' Tran Van Soai himself rallied to Diem in February 1956, placing his troops entirely at the Government's disposal in their fight against 'Communism' and 'colonialism' (*Le Monde*, 4–5 March 1956).

[64] In April 1956 Ba Cut was arrested near Minh's headquarters at Long Xuyen, having ventured there apparently on the erroneous assumption that he had been granted a safe-conduct to discuss surrender terms. He was guillotined at Can Tho in July (ibid. 14 July 1956).

marked the end of large-scale operations against the sects as Cao Dai autonomy was suppressed without bloodshed through the action of General Phuong, who on the night of 5–6 October disarmed 300 troops belonging to the 'Papal Guard' and arrested the 'Pope's' two daughters on the charge of exploiting the people, an operation which he completed two days later by deposing the 'Pope'. Pham Cong Tac remained at Tay Ninh until February of the following year, when he fled to Phnom Penh to avoid capture by government troops who were preparing to occupy the 'Holy See' allegedly at the invitation of the sect's high dignitaries.[65]

## THE REPUBLIC OF VIETNAM

On 28 May 1955 Diem paid an official visit to the province of Binh Dinh, which had served as an assembly area for Viet Minh troops in Southern Annam. The Prime Minister, who had hitherto had few opportunities to tour the provinces, is reported to have been agreeably surprised by the warmth of the reception which he received from the destitute population of this former Viet Minh zone, in whose eyes he must have appeared as the harbinger of better times, but popular unrest had been reported from other parts of Annam, and in March seven battalions had taken part in an operation against a dissident force established some twelve miles to the west of Quang Tri in the foothills of the Annam chain. This force, which was made up of local militia and police, adherents of certain nationalist political groups, and some of Hinh's supporters, had taken up arms against the local administrative authorities, whose activities were directed by the Prime Minister's third brother, Ngo Dinh Can, who occupied an all-powerful, but ambiguous position in Annam similar to that held by Ngo Dinh Nhu in Cochin-China.[66]

The Prime Minister's official visit to Annam was followed by

[65] Nguyen Thanh Phuong was himself arrested in 1957 on a number of charges, including that of being party to the murder of one Ho Han Son, a former member of the Revolutionary Committee and Viet Minh political commissar, whose body was found at the bottom of a well near Cao Dai military headquarters.

[66] *Le Monde*, 9 Mar. 1955 and *Figaro*, 10 Mar. 1955. Ngo Dinh Can, who had earned Diem's gratitude by caring for their widowed mother, Mme Ngo Dinh Kha, during the war years, possessed the ability to outmanoeuvre political opponents and the preference for repressive methods displayed by Nhu in his successful efforts to maintain his brother in power.

a disturbance in Hué sponsored by a revolutionary committee under Can's direction. The disturbance was designed to mark the final rejection of Bao Dai's authority and culminated in the symbolic gesture of forcing open the central doors of the triple gateway into the Imperial city, an entrance reserved for the exclusive use of the Emperor. On 15 June, recourse was had to the archaic procedure of summoning a meeting of the imperial family, who proclaimed the dethronement of the Emperor and entrusted the direction of the national destinies to Ngo Dinh Diem.[67]

Finally, on 7 July the Government revealed the action which they proposed to take to bring about an official change of régime, and fixed 23 October as the date of a national referendum to decide the issue. The campaign preceding this referendum was conducted with such a cynical disregard for decency and democratic principles that even the Viet Minh professed to be shocked. Whereas Bao Dai himself was given no opportunity to defend himself, the government-controlled press proceeded to overwhelm him with scurrilous abuse, special editions of the local newspapers being devoted to giving very biased accounts of his life. This press campaign was supported by broadcasts and by posters and effigies depicting Bao Dai as a gambler, or associating him with a pig's head or in the process of caressing a woman with a sack of piastres on his back. In addition police agents and canvassers went from door to door explaining the unpleasant consequences which failure to vote would be likely to entail.

On the day of the referendum polling centres were placed under police surveillance and electors were presented with a ballot paper giving them the choice of voting either for Diem, who was pictured among a group of modern young people against a propitious red background, and democracy, or else for Bao Dai, who was portrayed in old-fashioned robes against an unlucky green background;[68] as an additional precaution, the count was made by government officials without any form of supervision. Under such conditions Diem's victory at the polls was assured, but the final results surpassed even the most

[67] Bao Dai's mother, the widow of the Emperor Khai Dinh, was driven from her home and deprived of the means of communicating with her son by Can's 'revolutionaries' (D. Schoenbrun in *Colliers*, 30 Sept. 1955).
[68] *Figaro* and *Le Monde*, 25 Oct. 1955.

sanguine expectations, as the votes cast in some cases exceeded the number of names on the electoral roll.[69]

On 26 October 1955 the Republic of Vietnam was solemnly proclaimed. The circumstances seemed favourable to the new régime as although Diem had chosen to defeat rather than to come to terms with his adversaries, these tactics had led to a rapid return of peaceful conditions to the countryside, while his refusal to comply with the provisions of the Geneva Agreement had evoked protests but no reprisals.[70] Moreover, the liquidation of the Bank of Indochina's remaining assets[71] and the impending withdrawal of the Expeditionary Corps, which was to be completed by April of the following year, clearly revealed the French intention to abstain from further intervention in Vietnamese internal affairs.

In spite of such a propitious climate and the prospect of unstinted American assistance and financial aid, the proclamation of the Republic aroused misgivings in some quarters, which were to be expressed by Max Clos, the representative of *Le Monde*, on 1 December.

Oddly enough [wrote this well-informed journalist] M. Diem has borrowed from his enemies what is most reprehensible in their methods: the denial of freedom of opinion, the deification of the man who incarnates the régime and also that form of hypocrisy which attributes to the 'people's will' measures taken against those whom one considers as political opponents. . . . The Viet Minh dictatorship is at least as odious as that of M. Diem. But it can show results in the political and economic fields. It is up to Diemism to show concrete achievements. This has not yet been done in South Vietnam.[72]

---

[69] *L'Humanité*, 28 Oct. 1955. In Saigon–Cholon, where Mai Huu Xuan was in charge of proceedings, 450,000 electors cast 605,025 votes (*Figaro*, 25 Oct. 1955). The final results were: Ngo Dinh Diem and democracy, 5,721,735; Bao Dai, 63,017.

[70] Diem's political opponents would probably have proved more co-operative, since Bao Dai's desire to lift the mortgage on the national future represented by partition and the Cochin-Chinese politicians' naïve confidence in their ability to hold their own with the Viet Minh leaders would have been likely to result in some disastrous compromise.

[71] Ngo Dinh Luyen conducted these negotiations on behalf of the Government; they were concluded to the satisfaction of both parties on 21 October.

[72] Clos's expulsion from Saigon had already been reported in *Le Monde* of 19 Nov. 1955.

## THE PATHET LAO AND THE ROYAL LAOTIAN GOVERNMENT

Whereas conditions in South Vietnam and Cambodia had improved by the autumn of 1955, the situation in Laos remained unsatisfactory. This was due to the Pathet Lao contention that the allocation of the provinces of Phong Saly and Sam Neua as a final regroupment area for their forces implied that these provinces had been placed under their control, pending the political settlement for which provision had also been made in the Geneva Agreement: an argument which they bolstered up with a claim to have expelled all Franco-Laotian troops from these areas in March 1953. Both this contention and this assertion were disputed, however, by the Franco-Laotian authorities, who pointed out that the sovereignty of the Royal Government over the national territory had been recognized at Geneva and argued that the provision made in the agreement for Pathet Lao forces to be stationed in provisional assembly areas in each of the twelve provinces effectively disposed of their claim to exclusive control over these two provinces, where Franco-Laotian commando units had continued to operate up till August 1954.

The International Commission for Supervision and Control, who finally assembled in Vientiane at the beginning of October 1954, were thus faced with a complex and delicate situation; and their difficulties were to be increased by the mountainous nature of the country, the uncertain weather conditions, and the absence of transport, and even of an adequate communications system: a state of affairs which is described in their first interim report as follows:

There is no railway in Laos. The road system has deteriorated as a result of long years of war and the monsoon rains. Bridges demolished and culverts washed away make even existing stretches of road unusable, particularly during the monsoon. In most parts of the northern provinces of Phong Saly and Sam Neua, there are only pony tracks and footpaths over jungle-clad hills.[73]

While the International Commission were thus getting ready to assume their duties, a joint armistice committee had been set up, in accordance with the provisions of the Geneva Agreement, to arrange and supervise the withdrawal of foreign

[73] Cmd. 9445, p.3.

troops from Laotian soil. This committee, which was made up of representatives of the Franco-Laotian and of the Viet Minh–Pathet Lao Commands respectively, established its headquarters at Khang Khay, a locality situated on the Tran Ninh plateau some twenty miles north-west of Xieng Khouang. Here a decision was reached towards the end of August to appoint and station joint commissions in Middle and Lower Laos respectively, and to set up combined groups to supervise troop movements. This decision was followed by an agreement on 30 August fixing the respective areas where the French Union, Viet Minh, and Pathet Lao units should regroup provisionally, and the routes to be followed by these units in their subsequent withdrawal either from the country or, in the case of the Pathet Lao, to the provinces of Phong Saly and Sam Neua.

The troops involved in these withdrawals were estimated to include 10,000 Viet Minh regional and 3,000 Pathet Lao troops, while the French for their part were required to withdraw 3,000 from the 8,000 troops stationed in Laos on 6 August, and to transfer the remainder either to their Military Training Mission or to their base at Seno for garrison and maintenance duties. But subsequent attempts by the combined groups and by the teams set up by the International Commission to supervise the withdrawal of these troops were impeded by the nature of the terrain, the monsoon weather and, in the case of the Viet Minh and Pathet Lao units, by the absence of badges or distinguishing marks; and this failure to check troop movements soon gave rise to reports that Communist agents were being left behind and young men were being recruited and abducted for political indoctrination either to North Vietnam or to the Pathet Lao zone in the north. Nevertheless French Union and Viet Minh troops had completed their withdrawal, and Pathet Lao units had regrouped in the provinces of Phong Saly and Sam Neua, by 19 November.

After the implementation of the military clauses of the Geneva Agreement, the need for a political settlement which would enable the Pathet Lao units to be disbanded and the royal authority re-established throughout the country became urgent. Moreover hopes that such a settlement would soon be reached had been encouraged by discussions between the Laotian Prime Minister, Prince Souvanna Phouma, and his half-brother, Prince Souphannouvong, at Khang Khay in early

September, for on his return to Vientiane the Prime Minister had expressed his conviction that a settlement would soon be reached, and discounted the belief that the Pathet Lao leader was a convinced Communist. But the assassination of the Laotian Defence Minister, Kou Voravong, on 19 September, led to the resignation of Souvanna Phouma's Government, and his successor, Katay Sasorith, in view of the maintenance of Pathet Lao claims to control the provinces of Phong Saly and Sam Neua, showed less optimism about the prospects of a settlement. Finally, on 3 December 1954, the International Commission recommended that representatives of the Royal Government and of the Pathet Lao should meet and try to find a basis for an agreement. Both parties accepted this recommendation, and in January 1955 a 'Consultative Political Conference' met at the airfield, the Plaine-des-Jarres, on the Tran Ninh plateau, where agreement was reached to settle by negotiation all questions concerning the independence of the country. The ensuing negotiations proved laborious, but on 9 March a joint undertaking was given that neither party would permit any hostile acts, particularly those of a military nature, to be carried out against the other. It was, also, agreed that further meetings should take place in Vientiane. Here the negotiations soon reached an impasse, due, it was alleged by the Royal Government, to the fact that the Pathet Lao 'consider themselves still under the authority of the Vietminh High Command and as having conquered the provinces of Phong Saly and Sam Neua',[74] and on 25 April the royal delegation withdrew from the conference.

Meanwhile the Royal Government had decided to adhere to their original intention, and to hold general elections on 28 August 1955. This decision displeased the Pathet Lao, who summoned the Royal Government on 6 June to 'stop immediately the illegal elections, stop immediately the despatch of forces to attack the two provinces, and resume immediately the political conference'.[75] But the Royal Government ignored these demands, and merely informed the International Commission that the situation in the provinces of Phong Saly and Sam Neua would prevent elections being held there. The deadlock was finally resolved on 10 June by a vote in the National

[74] Cmd. 9630, p. 9.
[75] Ibid. p. 11.

Assembly in favour of postponing the elections until 25 December, or the last day on which they could still be held constitutionally. The International Commission then again intervened and called upon both parties to reopen the negotiations; in response to this appeal talks were resumed in Vientiane on 15 July. But Pathet Lao insistence on important amendments to the electoral law, and the maintenance of their claims to exclusive administrative control in the disputed provinces until after the elections, led to the suspension of these talks on 5 September.

Meanwhile arrangements had been made for the Prime Minister, Katay Sasorith, and Prince Souphannouvong to meet and discuss the situation at Xieng Khouang on 30 September. At Souphannouvong's request the place of meeting was later changed to Rangoon. However, the choice of 'neutral' territory had little effect upon the course of the negotiations, and although an agreement for a cease-fire was signed on 11 October, little progress was made towards a settlement. At the end of the month the negotiations were resumed in Vientiane, where it soon became apparent that an agreement would not be reached in time for the Pathet Lao to take part in the elections.

During the latter half of the year the situation in the northern province had continued to deteriorate, despite the efforts made to settle the recurrent incidents by members of the International Commission, who travelled by helicopter through rifle fire to the trouble-spots, and clashes were taking place on an increasing scale between national troops and Pathet Lao forces, plentifully supplied with ammunition. These clashes culminated on 5 December in a full-scale but unsuccessful attack by three Pathet Lao battalions on posts held by the National Army near Muong Peun in Sam Neua province. From the spring of 1956 onwards the situation began to improve, due perhaps to the general requirements of Communist strategy and also to the return to power, on 21 March, of Souphannouvong's brother, Prince Souvanna Phouma, who announced in a speech setting out the Government's programme that priority would be given to the task of reaching a settlement with the Pathet Lao. This prompted Souphannouvong to send a letter to the Prime Minister on 22 April, reminding him that at a time when the relaxation in international tensions offered good prospects for

27

world peace, it was incumbent on them 'to find timely measures required for a full and rigorous implementation of the Geneva Agreement aimed at restoring Peace, perfecting Independence, realizing Democracy and unifying our country',[76] and proposing that they should meet again to continue the promising talks begun at Khang Khay in September 1954.

The meeting took place in Vientiane at the beginning of August 1956 'in an atmosphere of entire cordiality and of good mutual understanding';[77] and on the 5th and 10th respectively joint declarations were issued outlining the basis of a general settlement and setting out the concessions mutually decided upon.[78] These included an undertaking on the part of the Royal Government to pursue a neutralist foreign policy and in the internal sphere to allow the Pathet Lao movement to continue to pursue its activities as a political party, to hold complementary elections, and to set up a Government of national union in which the Pathet Lao would be represented.[79] In return for these concessions, the Pathet Lao for their part agreed to hand over the two provinces to the royal authorities and to place their troops under the orders of the National High Command. Finally, both parties recognized the need for a 'cease-fire' and agreed to set up a joint political and a joint military committee to work out the details of the proposed settlement.

After concluding these negotiations, the Prime Minister set out without loss of time for Peking and Hanoi, presumably with the intention of obtaining Communist support for the proposed settlement since he announced in Peking his Government's intention to pursue a policy of 'peace and neutrality', and signed in Hanoi a joint statement with the Prime Minister of the Democratic Republic of Vietnam, Pham Van Dong, to the effect that future relations between the two countries should be governed by the 'five principles of coexistence'.

Meanwhile the 'cease-fire' had been held up by the delay in appointing the Joint Military Committee, whose creation had

[76] Cmnd. 314, p. 54, annex. 6.

[77] Ibid. p. 55.

[78] Ibid. pp. 54 and 56.

[79] The Royal Government undertook (1) to follow the path of peace and neutrality; (2) to sincerely apply the five principles of peaceful coexistence; (3) to maintain good relations with all countries, in particular with 'neighbouring countries'; (4) to refrain from adhering to any military alliance; and (5) to allow no country to establish military bases on Lao territory other than those provided for in the Geneva Agreement (ibid. p. 55).

been decided upon in the declaration of 5 August. This Committee finally met towards the end of September, and on 31 October agreement was reached on the measures to be taken to end hostilities. Two days later another agreement was signed laying down the principles which were to govern foreign policy. This stressed the need to establish diplomatic relations and to promote economic and cultural exchanges with 'immediate neighbouring countries'[80] and thereby confirmed the priority attached by the Pathet Lao to the alignment of their country with Communist China and North Vietnam. But although further agreements were signed on 24 December 1956 and 21 February 1957 respectively, a final settlement continued to be evaded by the Pathet Lao, who appeared in no hurry to hand over the two provinces, where the population were being indoctrinated and organized by Viet Minh and Chinese political cadres.

These prevarications, combined with some uneasiness at Souvanna Phouma's ingenuous belief in the purity of Communist intentions, led to the fall of the Government on 31 May 1957, but subsequent attempts to form a new Government proved abortive, and on 9 August the National Assembly formally invested the outgoing Prime Minister and a coalition Government with office. Souvanna Phouma's return to power was a source of satisfaction to the Pathet Lao, who proposed that the negotiations should be resumed. Finally, on 2 November, agreements were signed covering the re-establishment of the royal administration in the provinces of Phong Saly and Sam Neua, and the integration of the Pathet Lao forces in the National Army.[81] Under these agreements the two provinces were to be administered jointly by royal and Pathet Lao officials, and a total of 1,500 Pathet Lao officers and men were to be incorporated in the National Army, while the remainder, now estimated to number some 5,500, were to be placed on the reserve list and sent to their homes.

The signing of these agreements was followed on 18 November by a ceremony in Vientiane at which Prince Souphannouvong symbolically handed over the two provinces to the Crown Prince, Savang Vatthana, and swore allegiance to the king on behalf of all Pathet Lao officials and troops. Next day the

[80] Ibid. p. 61.
[81] Ibid. pp. 59–67.

formation of a Government of national union was announced under the premiership of Souvanna Phouma, in which Souphannouvong held the portfolio of Town Planning and Reconstruction and another Pathet Lao personality, Phoumi Vongvichit, that of Religious Affairs and Fine Arts.[82]

During the following month royal officials assumed administrative responsibility for Pathet Lao-occupied territory, and while the Viet Minh and Chinese political cadres and military advisers withdrew to 'immediate neighbouring countries', the Pathet Lao troops prepared to be demobilized, or integrated with the National Army. But the guerrilla fighters with their drab uniforms, helmets of latania palm leaves, rubber-soled canvas shoes, and slings of cooked rice, who now converged, accompanied by propaganda units of hard-faced, pigtailed and sullen girls, on the assembly areas[83] seemed rather to belong to the Asian Communist genus than to the gay, elegant, and carefree people whose national independence they had ostensibly been championing.

---

[82] Phoumi Vongvichit, who was Minister of the Interior in the Pathet Lao 'Government', had led the Pathet Lao political delegation at the preceding negotiations. He had formerly held the post of Governor of Xieng Khouang in the Royal Administrative Service.

[83] Richard Hughes in *Sunday Times*, 22 Dec. 1957.

# APPENDIX I

### THE MORAL CLIMATE AND THE SINEWS OF WAR

IN May 1949 General Georges Revers, Chief of the General Staff, was sent to Indochina to report to the French Government on the possible effect on the military situation in Tongking of the Communist victory in China and to see if the military situation called for a change in strategy. At the end of his visit Revers made a statement to the press in which he said that the French must strengthen their means of defence and finish a war that had gone on far too long, but that they must also 'discuss, treat, and try to resolve the situation not in the European way but in the Asian way, the only way that has a chance to succeed'.[1]

The report he submitted to the Government on his return to France, which was not published, contained the finding that the arrival of Chinese Communist troops at the Indochinese frontier would have a serious effect on the general military situation and recommended that the frontier garrisons, and in particular the exposed and isolated garrisons at Cao Bang and Dong Khe, should be withdrawn. Revers also proposed that the defences of the Red river delta should be strengthened, the delta itself pacified and handed over for administrative purposes to the Vietnamese authorities, and that a similar course of action should be taken in the Mekong delta.[2] The report recognized that the execution of these proposals would require the dispatch of reinforcements, including a sufficient number of instructors to train the Vietnamese army, and the replacement of much of the armament and the equipment of the Expeditionary Corps, which had become unserviceable.[3]

These findings appear to have been presented in the form of a memorandum containing certain reflections on the general situation, to which appendices were attached dealing with specific military aspects, including the strength of units and the state of military equipment. While the tactical recommendations served as a basis for subsequent plans for dealing with the persistent deterioration in the military situation, the memorandum itself is reported to have included a devastating assessment of the inadequacy of the support that the French were receiving from the Vietnamese nationalists, and also the specific recommendation that Léon Pignon should be replaced by a military officer of appropriate rank.

The General's report aroused great though brief interest. By the

[1] *Le Monde*, 7 June 1949.
[2] Ibid. 13 July 1949.
[3] Devillers, pp. 448–9.

end of June 1949, however, copies of the memorandum, which was confidential, were known to be circulating in Paris, and on 26 August Pignon complained that extracts were being broadcast verbatim from the Viet Minh transmitting stations.[4] Discreet inquiries were made in order to discover the channel by which the Viet Minh had been able to receive their copy of the memorandum. These were greatly assisted by the discovery, on 20 September, of a copy of the memorandum in the brief-case of a Vietnamese who had been arrested in a Paris omnibus as the result of a fight with a French soldier belonging to the Expeditionary Corps.[5]

The discovery led to a search of a flat occupied by another Vietnamese, Hoang Van Co by name, an acquaintance of the arrested man, and there a further eighty roneo-typed copies of the memorandum were found, together with other incriminating documents. Further inquiries established that Hoang Van Co had received a copy of the memorandum from one Roger Peyré, a Frenchman of dubious commercial antecedents who claimed that he had received it from General Mast, a former Resident-General in Tunisia who was a candidate at that time for Pignon's post.

The responsibility for the ensuing scandal was subsequently ascribed, with some semblance of probability, to the machinations of the Vietnamese Deputy Prime Minister, General Xuan, who was known to be seeking to establish a Vietnamese republic in which he hoped to occupy the position of President.[6] Xuan's desire to set up a republican régime probably sprang from his knowledge that the French Socialist Party (SFIO), in which he now had many friends and acquaintances, was prepared to give 'the Bao Dai solution'—which had been imposed by the MRP—only divided and reluctant support. But whatever his motives, the agent whom Xuan had been employing in Paris happened to be Hoang Van Co.

Both Co and Peyré had reason to suppose that the appointment of Mast might be advantageous, Hoang Van Co to the personal ambitions of Xuan, and Peyré to his own commercial interests in Saigon.

To improve Mast's prospects Peyré, who wielded much occult influence in French political circles and numbered Revers among his acquaintances, had preceded the General on his visit to Indochina, where, acting in a semi-official capacity, he had arranged for Revers to be met by persons of local importance who with one accord recommended that Pignon—who was known to be committed to 'the Bao Dai solution'—should be replaced by a military High Commissioner, and named Mast as an acceptable choice.[7] On

----

[4] P. Parpais in *Le Populaire*, 17 Apr. 1950.
[5] *L'Aurore*, 26 Sept. 1949.
[6] Frédéric-Dupont, p. 97.
[7] Ibid. p. 98.

his return, Peyré obtained from Mast a copy of that portion of the Revers report in which references were made to the conversations that had taken place and circulated it to the politicians whose support he wished to enlist.

The far-reaching and disturbing ramifications of this intrigue, and the knowledge that the Communists were likely to exploit the scandal to the full, prompted Paul Ramadier, the Minister for National Defence, to take measures to discourage further publicity, and seizing on the fact that no 'secret' information had been divulged, he decided to remove Revers from his post and also to retire Mast, a decision which was approved and implemented by René Pleven, who replaced Ramadier at this ministry in October.

But the Socialists, who had reason to think that they had been defamed in a report concerning the incident which had been submitted by the Minister for Overseas Territories, P. Coste-Floret, to Henri Queuille, the outgoing Prime Minister, refused to support this prudent measure, and insisted that a parliamentary Commission should be appointed to inquire into the origins of the leakage.[8] The subsequent inquiry, which received full publicity thanks to the action of the Communist Party's representative, Maurice Kriegel-Valrimont, who successfully circumvented the decision to hold the proceedings in camera by extensive and calculated indiscretions to the press, was attended by a series of incidents that served mainly to discredit the régime.

Although Peyré, presumably with the connivance of the Security Service, was allowed to escape to Brazil, the disappearance during the proceedings of evidence believed to incriminate certain deputies and newspaper editors and the admission that documents relating to the case, described as 'duplicate copies', had been destroyed by fire within the precincts of the Ministry of Interior, all revealed the official determination to conceal the identity of the persons implicated in this affair. Moreover, evidence produced at the proceedings revealed a propensity on the part of senior generals to indulge in political intrigues in order to promote their career, and also a state of rivalry, perhaps more properly described as a state of feud, between the intelligence services attached to the Ministries of Interior and National Defence respectively; while at the same time damaging, and in some cases reckless, accusations were levelled against civil and military officials who were alleged to be involved in illicit currency deals, and against politicians who were accused of having accepted bribes. These disclosures, which revealed the greed and self-interest that seemed to dictate the conduct of some of the prominent figures entrusted with the destinies of the Fourth Republic, appeared at one stage to threaten the very foundations of

[8] Parpais in *Le Populaire*, 17 Apr. 1950.

the régime. However, the length of the proceedings, together with the extravagance of some of the accusations, ended in wearying and confusing the general public, and in June, acting on the findings of the Commission, the Government announced its decision to retire both Revers and Mast, on the grounds that by consorting with and by employing Peyré they had 'offended against the rules of prudence, circumspection and conduct, incumbent on high-ranking officers in positions of trust'.[9]

The inquiry, which had served to show the interplay of politics and finance, and the readiness of a section of the community to traduce the Expeditionary Corps, might have been expected to lower French morale in Indochina, but the officers and n.c.o.'s serving with the Expeditionary Corps, inured to such vagaries of political behaviour, seemed not to attach an undue importance to these revelations. Their indifference was to stand them in good stead since popular impatience with a war which was absorbing so large a proportion of the national revenue was to remain a constant factor throughout the long struggle. This impatience was aggravated by the failure of successive Governments, mainly on account of divided counsels within the Socialist Party, to proceed with the necessary vigour against persistent Communist agitation: agitation which took many forms, including the organization of meetings of protest against the 'dirty' war, exhortations to dock and transport workers to refuse to handle military supplies, and demands, scrawled on walls and bridges throughout the country, for 'peace in Indochina'. These demands were emphasized on occasion by the sabotage of war material, which was often perpetrated by the introduction of iron filings and loose bolts into gear-boxes or damage to ball-bearings, while consignments of parachutes, batteries, and aeronautical equipment were, with suspicious frequency, found to be in a defective condition on their arrival in Indochina.

In addition to the embarrassment, inconvenience, and danger which the Expeditionary Corps suffered from these activities, the military operations in Indochina were constantly being jeopardized by frivolous or deliberate indiscretions in Paris, where the leakage of secret military information from the various ministries was described as 'torrential'.[10] In such a moral climate it was not surprising that an official decision in 1948 that awards for service in Indochina should cease to be gazetted aroused no protest.[11]

---

[9] *The Times*, 22 June 1950.

[10] Navarre, p. 56. With the creation in December 1950 of a Ministry for the Associate States, nine separate ministries were directly concerned in and responsible for some aspect of French activities in Indochina (see also ibid. p. 92).

[11] The status of ex-serviceman, to which considerable advantages attached, was denied until July 1952 to men who had been on active service in Indochina.

By September 1949 the strength of the military contingent from metropolitan France serving in Indochina had been reduced to 44,000 officers, n.c.o.'s, and enlisted men, and these were used mostly to officer or stiffen units, or to fill staff or base appointments.[12] The Expeditionary Corps, which had originally consisted of some paratroop units, the Massu group, and the 9th Colonial Infantry Division, had, following the repatriation of time-expired French elements, become a variegated and composite force, numbering in the autumn of 1950 some 152,000 men:[13] it included units of Moroccan, Algerian, Tunisian, and Senegalese troops, and about a third of the Foreign Legion; an increasing number of Vietnamese were to be found in all branches, including the armoured and paratroop units.[14] The credit for welding this Corps into a fighting force which was able to maintain its morale unbroken throughout a war fought under conditions that were calculated to bring in their train demoralization and despair was due to the French officers and n.c.o.'s who, in the absence of other ideals, were able to infuse into these mercenaries of diverse racial origins a professional soldier's pride in his unit together with respect for a code based on loyalty to comrades, including a moral obligation to go to the assistance of those in danger from enemy attack, to rescue the wounded and retrieve the dead.[15]

In September 1949, besides officers and men of French or French Union origin, 120,000 Indochinese were serving in the nascent national armies, with the units of the Expeditionary Corps, or with auxiliary and partisan formations, and it was estimated that Indochinese were providing the bulk of the total casualties, in the proportion of three to one.[16] Although during the first four years of the war metropolitan French casualties averaged the comparatively small annual total of about 2,500, because of the French directing rôle they included a high proportion of officers and n.c.o.'s.[17] In consequence French losses were to have an effect upon the reorganization of the French army that far exceeded their numerical

[12] In February 1947 the military contingent was composed of 5,001 army officers, including 21 generals, 22,297 n.c.o.'s, and 23,307 enlisted men (French Embassy Press Release, 14 June 1951).
[13] Paul Ramadier in *Bourse Égyptienne*, 18 Nov. 1950.
[14] Georges Marey in *Figaro*, 11 Sept. 1949.
[15] The numerically small military contingent from metropolitan France was supported by strong air force and navy detachments numbering in September 1949 5,000 and 9,000 respectively.
[16] Marey in *Figaro*, 11 Sept. 1949.
[17] By the end of 1949 some 677 French officers had been reported as either killed or missing (*Le Monde*, 20 June 1952) while casualties among n.c.o.'s amounted to 2,608 by 31 March 1951 (French Embassy Press Release, 14 June 1951).

importance.[18] Indeed, the grave implications for the future of the French army of the continuing drain of the Indochinese war may be gauged by the fact that in 1950, when the officer casualties numbered 140, only 440 officer-cadets were in training at the Military Academy of St. Cyr.[19]

The nature of the fighting in Indochina offered junior officers unique opportunities for acquiring operational experience and for assuming responsibilities which would have been considered beyond their capacities in other parts of the French Union. These opportunities induced many junior officers, the entire naval contingent, and many senior officers and civil servants to volunteer for service in Indochina.[20] In some cases these volunteers were inspired by the fact that the local rates of pay and allowances made service in Indochina an attractive proposition for those who were burdened with family responsibilities in France, where accommodation was hard to find and where pay tended to lag behind the price spiral. Moreover the financial prospects were further improved by the favourable exchange-rate of the piastre, which had been fixed by government decree on 25 December 1945 at a parity of 17 French francs,[21] and which offered a handsome premium on money remitted to France for the support of dependants.

The French Government appears to have originally intended that this rate of exchange should offer servicemen an additional inducement to volunteer for service in this distant theatre of war; but in fact it was French financial and commercial interests which derived the chief benefit from a decree appropriately promulgated on Christmas Day. Although an Indochinese Exchange Control Office, which was dependent on its French counterpart and derived its foreign exchange from the French Stabilization Fund, had been set up in Saigon in April 1947, its subsequent attempts to check the traffic in piastres and the flight of capital proved singularly ineffectual. While the office had been provided with a charter to enforce the existing regulations and the provisions contained in financial agreements between the 'franc' area and foreign countries, the requisite legal authority to prevent the transfer of funds to France and other parts of the French Union had been withheld. The Indo-

---

[18] The French army had dispensed with the services of officers who had compromised themselves with the Vichy régime.

[19] Hanson W. Baldwin in *NYT*, 25 Nov. 1952.

[20] Indochina had been administered in pre-war days by an establishment of some 4,000 officials. In 1948, however, at a time when the Viet Minh were in control of most of the Vietnamese countryside, the number of French civil servants had increased to 7,000.

[21] The quotation on the 'black' or parallel market stayed at about 10 French francs to the piastre.

chinese courts consequently refused to regard as an indictable offence attempts to effect such transfers by fraudulent means, even where the means involved the presentation of inaccurate invoices or bills of sale. As a result, officials of the Exchange Control Office, lacking for the most part the necessary qualifications and sense of responsibility for their delicate task, were forced to resort to the arbitrary expedient of inventing regulations which were incapable of being legally enforced, and which, for reasons of political or economic expediency, were continually waived. Under these circumstances officials of the Exchange Control Office were popularly accused of obstructing the transfer of funds by applicants without influence while facilitating the perpetration of frauds and the export of capital by authorizing without demur large transfers by important people and by French and Vietnamese business houses with the necessary political connexions.[22]

The successful exploitation of the favourable exchange-rate, and the increases in the price of certain export commodities, particularly rubber, together with the prompt payment by the French Government of enormous war damage claims amounting to more than 400 milliard francs,[23] enabled French companies with important local interest, and in particular the Bank of Indochina, to amortize their capital investments and to transfer their financial resources and commercial activities, within the space of a few years, to more secure if less profitable regions. The success achieved by the Bank of Indochina in this respect is revealed by a statement made by the Chairman at a general meeting of shareholders in June 1953, in which he claimed that although banking activities in Indochina continued to provide more than half the total profits, the Bank's holdings in Indochina represented, at that date, less than 17 per cent. of its total investments. This claim was fully substantiated in the Bank's balance sheet published on 31 December 1953, in which its capital investments were shown to be divided as follows: Africa 27 per cent., the United States and Latin America 28 per cent., Europe 23 per cent., the Pacific area 4 per cent., and China and South East Asia 18 per cent.[24] This is all the more extraordinary when it is recalled that before 1945 the bulk of the Bank's capital was invested in Indochina, where it had succeeded in building up

[22] Effective control over the movement of funds was further impeded by a facility given to French residents and to Vietnamese who had dependants in France to remit monthly to France by postal order, without prior authorization, a sum equivalent to 25,000 francs. The abuses to which this facility gave rise resulted between July 1948 and July 1950 in the dispatch of more than 600,000 orders for this amount from the Saigon post office alone (J-M. Garraud in *Figaro*, 22–23 July 1950).

[23] *Le Populaire*, 27 Feb. 1951.

[24] *Combat*, 22 July 1954.

a vast latifundia embracing every aspect of the Protectorate's financial, commercial, and industrial life.

The financial and commercial opportunities Indochina offered also proved an irresistible magnet to impecunious Frenchmen wishing to profit from the exchange-rate by founding businesses and import-export agencies in Saigon, with the principal object of obtaining permits to transfer piastres to France, by means which might include the production of falsified and inaccurate invoices, or even the purchase of defective and unsaleable goods.[25] In addition to the substantial profits to be derived from commercial transactions such as these, the smuggling of currency and gold offered further substantial rewards to those who were prepared to indulge in extra-legal operations since the difference between the official and the 'parallel' exchange-rate resulted in a profit of more than 100 per cent. on the sale of smuggled American dollars and gold.[26]

Financial operations of this nature, however, were on a relatively small scale, compared with the arrangements which could also be made by those with the necessary contacts in the world of international finance for a fructifying transfer of funds through the 'free' market at Tangier, and even for the legal purchase of American dollars by an agency of the Bank of Indochina in French Somaliland, where the creation of a 'free' market in this currency in 1949 had been attended by a minimum of publicity. The losses incurred by the French treasury from these transactions were estimated in May 1953 by the left-wing newspaper *Observateur* to have amounted in the space of seven years to 1,000 milliard francs: a loss which *Le Monde* had previously computed at 'more than 100 milliard francs a year'.[27]

During the seven years between Pleven's Christmas Day decree in 1945 and René Mayer's devaluation of the piastre in May 1953, the capacity displayed by the Indochinese 'parallel' currency market to absorb the large amounts of foreign currency and gold involved in such transactions had been increased by a desire on the part of the Sino-Vietnamese middle class to insure against catastrophe by investing in American dollars and in gold, and by Viet Minh requirements for 'hard' currency with which to pay for arms, medicines, and manufactured goods. In view of the discredit that

---

[25] *Le Monde*, 8 May 1953.

[26] An American dollar that had been bought in France for 350 at the official, or 400 francs at the 'parallel', rate could be sold in Indochina for 50 piastres or the equivalent of 850 francs, if arrangements could then be made to transfer this sum to France, while a similar profit could be derived from the sale of smuggled gold (Garraud in *Figaro*, 22–23 July 1950).

[27] *Le Monde*, 5 Dec. 1952.

# 4^I^5

the piastre traffic was bringing upon the war effort, the failure of French Governments to take any effective measures to check it aroused surprise, but was ascribed to the obvious complexity of the problem and to the supposition that 'certain French political groups' were deriving most of their funds from the facility that they enjoyed to arrange financial transfers from Saigon and to obtain approval for the payment in French francs of Indochinese war-damage claims.[28]

In marked contrast to the prosperity of the large French commercial companies, Indochina's adverse balance of trade continued to increase during the war years. The deficit was caused by the increase in imports and decline in exports, due principally to a drastic reduction in the export of rice. This was the result not only of the disturbed state of the countryside but also of Viet Minh control over the Transbassac area, which had formerly provided most of Indochina's annual exportable surplus amounting, in pre-war years, to some 1½ million tons. Their control over the Transbassac enabled the Viet Minh to impose a levy on the peasant producer and also on the Chinese intermediary who shipped the paddy to the mills in Cholon. In 1949, therefore, in order to deprive the enemy of an important source of revenue, the French authorities had decreed an economic blockade of the area, with the result that Indochina's paddy exports declined from 250,000 tons in 1948[29] to 135,000 tons in 1950.

The decline in rice exports made rubber the most important exportable commodity in Indochina's war-torn economy, and in spite of shortage of labour, damage to trees, and raids by Viet Minh bands, the production of the great plantations of South Vietnam and Cambodia continued to rise, reaching in 1952 a total of 61,000 tons, or the equivalent of the quantity that had been exported in an average pre-war year.

The parlous state of the Indochinese economy was matched by the financial plight of the Governments of the Associate States, for although by the conventions of 30 December 1949 Vietnam had been given internal autonomy, the reorganization of the national finances remained subordinate to subsequent agreements between the Associate States. Meanwhile, in order to meet current expenditure, Vietnamese Governments continued to rely on indirect taxation which, together with customs receipts, had formerly provided 70 per cent. of the public revenue. These absurd financial arrangements, under which both the actual revenue and expenditure

[28] J. J. Servan-Schreiber in ibid. 3 Apr. 1953.
[29] J. de Coquet in *Figaro*, 27 May 1949.

of the state were shrouded in obscurity, were perpetuated by a readiness on the part of the French treasury to make the necessary advances to meet a public expenditure unofficially estimated in 1950 to exceed receipts by some 33 milliard francs.[30]

French readiness, after the signing of the Élysée Agreement, to continue the payment of subsidies without insisting on a *quid pro quo*, either in the form of public economies or of a more substantial contribution from the local taxpayer, may have been inspired by a wish to postpone the advent of Vietnamese financial and commercial autonomy. For Indochina ranked, after Algeria and Switzerland, as France's most important market, and absorbed about a third of French textile exports, together with an important percentage of exports of motor cars, bicycles, paper, clocks, watches, pharmaceutical products, flour, tinned food, and wine.[31] The constitution of a government in Saigon having the requisite authority and ability to alter a pattern of trade which was proving extremely advantageous to French industry, and having also power to impose direct taxes on the French business community—a community which held a disproportionately large share of the national wealth—may not have seemed, therefore, altogether desirable either to the French Government or to politically influential commercial interests in France.

The unwelcome necessity of meeting both the cost of the war and of subsidizing the bankrupt Governments of the Associate States was alleviated by increasingly important allocations of American military and economic aid: these were to provide the French treasury with a welcome means of settling the French deficit of payments with the 'dollar' area. The value of these contributions was further enhanced by an undertaking that the provision of military aid from American sources would be restricted to items that were either not manufactured or else were not readily available in France.[32] This was to provide France, between 1950 and 1954, with hundreds of millions of dollars, representing payment for 'off-shore' orders of French manufactured equipment and supplies which were required in Indochina. The scale of these payments is illustrated by the fact that whereas in June 1950 it was announced that American dollar aid to the French forces in Indochina would amount, for the fiscal year ending June 1951, to the comparatively modest sum of $23½ million,[33] the American Government had already decided, five months later, to underwrite the French war effort to the tune of between $300 and $400 million, representing a two-year pro-

---

[30] *Le Monde*, 30 Sept. 1950. The French treasury assumed also the responsibility for the payment of Bao Dai's civil list, at the rate of 51 million francs a month.

[31] Ibid. and *Combat*, 22 July 1954.

[32] Tillman Durdin in *NYT*, 3 Nov. 1950.

[33] *Le Monde*, 2 June 1950.

gramme of aid to French and French Union Forces.[34] This generous allocation, estimated in June 1952 to represent 33 per cent. of the total French expenditure,[35] was further increased during the latter half of the year to cover some 40 per cent. of the total cost of the war, amounting for 1952 to 569 milliard francs.[36]

In September 1953 Joseph Laniel, the French Prime Minister, announced that France was to receive additional dollar grants and supplies of American manufactured arms and military equipment which, together with the aid already allocated, would defray 70 per cent. of France's expenditure on the Indochinese war. Finally, not long before the Geneva Conference, the American Government undertook to underwrite the entire cost of the war, allocating $1,175 million for that purpose. This enormous sum included the payment of subsidies to the Expeditionary Corps totalling $400 million and deliveries of $325 million worth of military supplies, while the sum of $385 million was appropriated for the budgetary support of the Associate States.[37]

While it would be hazardous and presumptuous to ascribe to financial and commercial considerations paramount responsibility for the protracted nature and unsatisfactory conduct of the war—this perhaps was to be found in the long succession of errors and illusions, and the weakening of governmental authority in France,—the inability displayed by successive Governments either to prosecute the war with a will to achieve victory or to hasten, by timely and liberal concessions, the formation of a viable Vietnamese state was to place the French authorities, and also the Expeditionary Corps itself, in a position of inextricable difficulty. Indeed, the morale of individual officers and men must often have been steeled only by the expectation and hope that the expiration of their period of service in Indochina would precede the advent of catastrophe.

[34] *The Times*, 25 Nov. 1950.
[35] *Combat*, 26 June 1952.
[36] *Le Monde*, 18 Dec. 1952.
[37] Homer Bigart in *NYHT*, 18 Dec. 1954.

# APPENDIX II

## ADMINISTRATION AND MILITARY ORGANIZATION
## IN THE VIET MINH ZONE

AFTER their expulsion from Hanoi in December 1941 the Viet Minh
Government retired to the mountainous region stretching northwards from the Red river delta to the Chinese frontier and established their headquarters in the Viet Bac, which was to serve as
their 'Capital Region' for seven and a half years. In the Viet Bac,
which comprised the provinces of Thai Nguyen, Tuyen Quang,
Bac Kan, Yen Bay, and Ha Giang, the government departments
were installed near the town of Thai Nguyen in limestone caves and
obscure villages which provided temporary refuge from the constant
threat of French raids. The presence of the ministers in this inaccessible region, where they were deprived of the means of communication normally at the disposal of a central Government, prevented
them from exercising effective control over those parts of Annam
and Cochin-China where their authority was still recognized. The
central Government's efforts to maintain the cohesion of the
resistance movement had in consequence to be confined to the
promulgation of general instructions on administrative and political
matters, leaving considerable latitude to the regional and local
committees to whom these instructions were addressed.

After the French reoccupation of the Red river delta the areas
which the Viet Minh Government still controlled included, in
addition to the mountainous region of Tongking, the provinces of
Thanh Hoa, Nghe An, and Ha Tinh in North Annam and, except
for the French enclaves around Hué and Tourane, the coastal plains
stretching south to Cape Varella.

In Cochin-China, where they were disputing possession of the
countryside both with the Expeditionary Corps and the militia
forces of the Hoa Hao and Cao Dai sects, the Viet Minh had
established themselves in the forests in the provinces of Thu Dau
Mot and Baria, in the Plaine des Joncs—a vast area of swamp to the
north-west of Saigon—and in the Transbassac, which is the region
on the right bank of the river Bassac stretching down to the mangrove swamps around Ca Mau Point.[1]

---

[1] Under the general provisions of the constitution of the Democratic Republic
of Vietnam the national territory was defined as being composed of the three *ky*,
which was renamed the Bac Bo or North Vietnam, the Trung Bo or Central
Vietnam, and the Nam Bo or South Vietnam. Within these three regions, or Bo,
the administrative units of the province, district and village were retained
(Vietnam News Agency, *Viet-Nam; a New Stage in Her History* (Bangkok, 1947),
pp. 11–12).

While most of their forces, training camps, stores, and workshops were concentrated in the mountainous region of Tongking which, together with the three Communist-held provinces of North Annam, constituted the centre of Viet Minh resistance, South Annam and Cochin-China were semi-autonomous areas which had to provide for their own needs in food and war material and also to assist the war effort in the north. The national territory had at first been divided for military purposes into fourteen zones; but in March 1948 the number of zones, then renamed 'inter-zones' or *lien khu*, were reduced to six and placed under the administrative authority of a Committee the members of which included representatives of the local military command.[2]

Wireless transmission was the chief means of communication between the inter-zones and Viet Minh military headquarters in the Viet Bac, and although official emissaries undertook on occasion the hazardous and exhausting journey from the Viet Bac to the Trung Bo, or to the Plaine des Joncs and the Transbassac, where the Nam Bo Committee lived a precarious and errant existence in the mosquito-ridden swamps, these journeys took much time, whether the traveller followed the course of the river Mekong to Thakhek and thence to Vinh, or made his way along the jungle-infested summits of the Annam chain, where danger in many forms would await him.[3]

The extraordinary difficulties encountered in maintaining contact between the Viet Minh Government in the north and Viet Minh authorities in the south were fertile in misunderstandings, since the Viet Minh Government failed to appreciate the difficulties facing their troops in the Nam Bo and the Trung Bo and were quick to suspect separatist tendencies in these far-off regions. At the beginning of 1949, therefore, two important personages, Pham Ngoc Thach, who had played a part in the Communist seizure of power in Saigon, and Pham Van Dong, the leader of the Viet Minh delegation at the Fontainebleau Conference, were dispatched to the Nam Bo and the Trung Bo respectively to impress upon the authorities in those areas the need for stricter conformity with official policies. But in spite of the fact that Thach's visit was backed up by a personal message from Ho Chi Minh himself, complaining that the Nam Bo Committee had neglected the political indoctrination of

[2] Two of these inter-zones comprised the mountainous and upland regions of the Bac Bo respectively, while the third was constituted by the Red river delta itself. The Trung Bo was partitioned into two inter-zones, of which one consisted of the territory to the north and the other of the territory to the south of Hué, while the whole of the Nam Bo was included in Inter-Zone VI.

[3] The maintenance of French coastal patrols appears to have stopped attempts to reach the Bac Bo or the Nam Bo by sea.

the forces under their command and had failed to eradicate 'individualism',[4] the Viet Minh forces in that region, with their more expansive and optimistic temperament, reflecting the easier living conditions and sunnier climate of Cochin-China, continued to fall short of the austere standards set by the formal and reserved Tongkingese.

Although 'nationalist' supernumeraries were allowed to retain some of the ministerial portfolios, the Communist leaders continued throughout the war to maintain and reinforce their exclusive control over the resistance movement, striving always to perfect a system by which surviving vestiges of 'individualism' might be removed from the Vietnamese character. The indoctrination of the rural population with Marxist theory was effected through the medium of communal meetings held once or twice a week, attended by the entire adult village community. At these meetings the tenets of Marxism and government instructions were expounded by the Communist cadres, while the villagers themselves were encouraged to 'analyse' the causes of any deficiency in agricultural production, particularly if this could be ascribed to outmoded feudal conceptions, and to denounce also the presence in their midst of discontented elements and malingerers.

In September 1945 a campaign had been launched under the slogan 'war against ignorance' to abolish the illiteracy which was a legacy of French rule. This campaign appears to have been inspired by a genuine desire to remove an unjust handicap from a people who had retained a deep respect for learning, the acquisition of which had formerly given all classes the opportunity of an administrative career. Nevertheless these admirable and rather feverish efforts seem also to have been prompted by the calculation that a literate people would more readily absorb Communist propaganda:[5] a calculation based on the knowledge that the printed and written word were regarded almost with veneration by the rural population who believed that such an extravagant medium of communication must enshrine unquestioned truth. Ingenious methods were devised to induce even the aged, the idle, and the obtuse to learn to recognize the letters of the alphabet and to decipher a prescribed number of words written in the romanized script bequeathed by the Jesuit missionaries. In 1949 it was officially announced that the object of the campaign had been achieved, and that 6½ million Vietnamese had been taught to read.

Meanwhile as well as attending classes and frequent village meet-

[4] *Combat*, 23–24 July 1949.
[5] M. Perchet, 'La Propagande Viet-Minh', *Indochine Sud-est Asiatique*, No. 21, Sept. 1953.

ings, usually held during the hours of darkness, the rural population were required to maintain under cultivation the pre-war average, to pay taxes in kind amounting to between 50 and 70 per cent. of the local agricultural production, to meet financial levies for specific purposes, and to contribute towards forced loans. As the long war pursued its course, the conscription of hordes of porters for the transport of military supplies and of labour gangs to repair recurrent damage to communications resulting from air attacks also made increasingly heavy demands upon the time and resources of the population. At length, in November 1949, a government decree mobilized the entire population aged between 18 and 45. The labour force thus made available received no pay, scant rations, and small thanks from the vainglorious Commander-in-Chief and yet, by its exertions and readiness to face injury and death, this force was able to lay the foundations of final victory.[6]

The extravagant nature of Viet Minh propaganda, combined with the histrionic nature of the proceedings at the meetings that they were required to attend, soon reduced the population to a state of sceptical indifference towards the cynically exaggerated claims with which the Communist cadres sought to stimulate their flagging energies, but any overt expression of discontent would have been foolhardy and vain. For the Viet Minh had enmeshed the population, collectively under a hierarchy of nominated 'Administrative and Resistance Committees', and individually in one or more of the many associations to which all members of the community were required to belong. These associations were based on the possession of a common occupation, profession, or sex, and were again controlled by Communist cadres who arranged for frequent meetings at which the attitude and behaviour of individual members were often the subject of debate. The activities of these associations thus completed the mobilization of the physical and moral resources of the community, while the inquisitorial methods employed to discipline members provided the authorities with an additional means of controlling a potentially restive population.[7]

However, in spite of these intolerable conditions, there were relatively very few refugees and deserters from Viet Minh-controlled territory, this reluctance on the part of the population to abandon

[6] The capacity of the rural population to meet these exactions had been increased by the fact that after the disturbances in August 1945, which had in certain localities assumed the aspect of a traditional agrarian revolt, some redistribution of land had occurred, with the result that tenant farmers in many cases no longer paid rent. In July 1949 Viet Minh Government decrees had recognized this state of affairs by granting 'provisional possession of land to the tiller' and by imposing a general reduction of 25 per cent. on all agricultural rents (André Clermont, 'L'Économie Viet-Minh', ibid., No. 19, June-July 1953.
[7] Claude Guigues, 'Troika et Autocritique Viet-Minh', ibid. No. 27, Mar. 1954.

areas where they were exposed to such pitiless exploitation being attributed to the efficiency of the system of surveillance, to the attachment of Vietnamese to their native villages, and to the popular conviction that the struggle in which they were engaged would, in spite of the terrible sacrifices involved, figure honourably in the national annals.

At first, therefore, refugees consisted of those whose health had been undermined by privation and those who had incurred Viet Minh displeasure, but the arrival, in December 1949, of the Chinese Communist armies at the frontier, which was followed by increasing evidence of the Communist nature of the Viet Minh régime, led to some defections among nationalists who considered that a resurgent China represented a greater threat to independence than the inept and inconclusive attempts by the French to perpetuate an outmoded domination. These defectors were joined by others, who had either realized that their social origins would exclude them from most forms of employment in a Communist state or had been outraged by crude official attempts to distort history and tamper with scientific truth.

While the Viet Minh Government was attempting to overcome the physical difficulties under which it laboured, the training of the military units was pursued with vigour. As the Viet Minh conception of the war was based on the principles that Mao Tse-tung had laid down for successful resistance by a semi-colonial and semi-feudal nation to an attack by an industrialized enemy, stress was laid on the protracted nature of the struggle and on the fact that it would be divided into three phases. The first of these phases had been represented by the French occupation of the principal towns and lines of communication, while the second was a stalemate during which the Viet Minh raided the French-occupied centres and lines of communications and proceeded to build up their regular units. These units would then launch a final victorious counter-offensive. During the second phase of the war Viet Minh regional troops were thus required both to oppose French attempts to pacify the countryside and to protect the base areas where the regular units were being trained.

The recruitment of these regional troops was on a territorial basis, each district being required to raise a company, and each province a battalion: these troops then operated in sections, companies and, on occasion, as a battalion, in the region where they had been raised. Their training included instruction in the use of the rifle, submachine gun, and mortar, in the handling of explosives and grenades, and in the laying and removal of mines.

In addition to their defensive activities, regional troops were also given a limited offensive role, including night attacks on local objectives and operations designed to screen the movement of regular units through their area. These offensive activities gave French Union forces a good deal of trouble, for the ability of these lightly armed regional troops, dressed in the traditional garb of the Vietnamese peasant, to move by night across the paddy fields, where their presence during daylight hours was unlikely to arouse suspicion, favoured the element of surprise on which the success of their operations generally depended.

Another contributory factor to the success of these operations was the practice of French Union troops, when they were stationed outside the delta towns, of withdrawing at nightfall into fortified positions leaving the countryside to the enemy, who profited from the hours of darkness to enter the villages left without protection and to launch surprise attacks on isolated strong-points, to lay mines and to damage road surfaces. When the French attempted to counter these nocturnal activities by the construction along the main roads and rivers of fortified watch-towers built in such a way that garrisons were within visual range of each other, the elusive but ever-present Viet Minh were sometimes able to come to an understanding with the poorly paid militia troops in occupation of these watch-towers who had often brought with them a clutter of domestic impedimenta designed to provide the solace of family life.[8]

The heavy casualties sustained by the regional troops in the course of their operations were made good from the ranks of the village militia which comprised, in principle, the valid male population of every village. These militia units were given the limited task of obstructing attempts by French Union troops to occupy their native villages, but they were sometimes required to assist regional and regular troops farther afield. The obstructive tactics to which the village militia resorted proved most effective in disputed territory on the fringes of the Red river delta where, after the French evacuation of Cao Bang and Lang Son in the autumn of 1950, some villages were used by regular and regional units as temporary bases from which to conduct their operations. These villages were honey-combed with tunnels and subterranean hiding-places and usually protected by a thorn hedge, a ditch set with bamboo spikes, and a thick earth rampart pierced with loop-holes, while their approaches were protected by booby-traps, including camouflaged pits planted

[8] These watch-towers, which were to form a distinctive feature of the French-occupied zone, were usually built by impressed labour. They were constructed in many cases of bricks from abandoned dwellings and isolated pagodas and their dimensions appeared to depend on the whim of the constructors; they were crowned by a tiled conical roof and protected in many cases both by an outer palisade and a mattress of tree-trunks and surrounded by barbed-wire entanglements of varying depth and complexity.

with spikes. In the event of an attack militia units from neighbouring villages, where 'women beat drums and shouted support', were supposed, in theory, to hasten to the assistance of the defenders.[9]

The methods employed to form and train the regular units had been evolved by the Chinese Communists. Recruits graduated as a rule through the ranks of the village militia and the regional units where they received some elementary training, including instruction in the use and maintenance of weapons. The unusual conditions under which they operated, due to the superiority of French armament and to French control of the communications system and undisputed mastery of the air, were reflected in the importance given in military training to night exercises and the use of camouflage, so that regular troops acquired an uncanny ability to remain invisible during daylight hours—which they frequently spent during operations in the Red river delta buried up to their neck in the paddy fields—and to travel at night across a terrain often intersected by dykes and watercourses. A third of the time allocated for training was set apart for basic instructions in Vietnamese history and geography, Marxist theory, and the careful study of the messages promulgated by President Ho Chi Minh and Giap to the Vietnamese people and the Viet Minh army respectively.

When the first part of their training had been completed, recruits were introduced to the practice of 'self-criticism' on which the homogeneity and discipline of the army were based.[10] 'Self-criticism' was practised in the course of meetings at which the attendance of both the officers and men making up the unit was obligatory. These meetings were presided over either by the Military Commissar or his delegate, who would ensure, after a general debate on such military, political, and even personal matters as were considered to be of general concern, that unanimous agreement was reached on whatever question had been the subject of the discussion.

The presence at these meetings of officers whose personal failings and professional faults might be the object of general criticism revealed the delicate and exacting position of those exercising command in the army of the Democratic Republic since these officers, whose professional qualifications might be limited to the experience that they had acquired in the field, supplemented by brief attendance at one of the military training schools in the Viet Bac, were required to maintain their authority by affording constant proof of their aptitude for command.

The officers were assisted in the discharge of their duties by commissars, who were entrusted specifically with the maintenance

---

[9] *The Times*, 7 July 1951.
[10] Claude Delmas in *Combat*, 14 May 1954.

of morale. These commissars formed a numerically important and influential section of the army—'the Section for Surveillance and Propaganda'—and operated under a hierarchy parallel to that of the military command with agents implanted down to platoon level. In addition to the facilities for surveillance thus provided, the commissars' inquisitorial powers were reinforced by the division of military units into groups or cells of from five to ten members, each member of which was individually responsible for the political rectitude of the other members of the group or cell. At brigade, or inter-zone level, the commissar had at his disposal special police and security detachments, together with a political bureau which was in direct communication with, and responsible to, Viet Minh military headquarters. The commissar's duties were, however, not merely confined to the maintenance of morale, as he shared with the military commander the responsibility for the conduct of operations and was expected to give proof, on all occasions, of a devotion to duty and of moral qualities superior to those of any other officer in the unit. In the event of his failing to fulfil any of these exacting requirements, he would be replaced at the end of a twelve-month appointment, the decision in such a case being reached by a 'self-criticism' meeting attended by the officers and men under his authority.

The military machine which was built up by these methods from the armed bands that the French troops had brushed aside in 1945 in their reoccupation of the towns was finally to prove a match for the heavily equipped Expeditionary Corps itself, but progress in the formation of this army was slow. In the spring of 1949 the Viet Minh Command were still reported to be engaged in regrouping their forces in companies and battalions; by December 1950, however, three operational divisions had been formed and equipped with automatic weapons, mortars, and a few field guns.[11]

While this was going on, the Viet Minh Command, and in particular Giap, were slowly acquiring greater proficiency in the complex art of directing military operations; and it was observed that the Viet Minh infantryman for his part, in spite of the apparent fragility of his physique, displayed extraordinary stamina and a hysterical fury in attack, ascribed by nonplussed French Union troops to over-indulgence in rice wine. These qualities, combined with vivacious intelligence, natural docility, and few physical needs, enabled the Viet Minh Command to fashion an army which was compared subsequently to the military orders of European chivalry, the Knights Templars or Knights Hospitallers, since in between their arduous campaigns these regular troops led a communal life that entailed the sacrifice of all domestic ties, and from which all physical

[11] Jean Lacouture in *Le Monde*, 11 Nov. 1952.

and mental privacy was absent. It is not surprising, therefore, that these soldiers, whose politico-military training had stressed Mao Tse-tung's tenet that in guerrilla warfare the survival of the combatant would depend in the last resort upon the support of the population, should have agreeably surprised the inhabitants of the regions where they were quartered by the meticulous correctness of their behaviour: behaviour which contrasted favourably with the less formal conduct of French Union troops. Indeed the demure attitude of Viet Minh troops towards the population in the mountains of north Indochina gave rise to a legend among the women in this inaccessible region that the Viet Minh had been deprived through some misadventure or in compliance with an inhuman decree, of certain male attributes.

The shortage of arms and military equipment was the chief obstacle to a rapid build-up of the regular units. In December 1947 the equipment of their levies had consisted mainly of the 30,000 rifles and the 1,000 automatic weapons which had served before 9 March 1945 to arm either the Indochinese Guard or the French garrison forces. Any additional weapons in their possession represented arms either originally supplied to their guerrilla bands engaged in fighting the Japanese, or acquired from the Japanese and Chinese nationalist forces by purchase or amicable arrangement, while a few consignments were believed to have reached them from abroad.

Although war material continued to be bought in neighbouring countries, and weapons were occasionally captured from the Expeditionary Corps, the Viet Minh were thus compelled during the early stages of the war to rely on the output of their own workshops. These were to be found throughout Viet Minh-controlled areas in caves and camouflaged huts, but were most numerous and best equipped in the Viet Bac. Remarkable ingenuity was displayed in overcoming the technical difficulties encountered with the result that supplies from this source included rifles, submachine guns, light mortars, and even some types of ammunition.

During the early stages of the war the Viet Minh also made a series of experiments with the object of utilizing available raw material to replace some of the essential commodities of which they had been deprived by the French blockade, means being found to produce a limited quantity of paper and soap, and some pharmaceutical products; the cottage weaving industry which, prior to the importation of French manufactured cotton goods, had provided the population of the confined coastal plains of Annam with a supplementary source of income, was also successfully revived. Nevertheless, in spite of these efforts, military requirements absorbed most of this local production, so that in many localities the civilian population were in a state of destitution.

However, in the absence of clearly demarcated frontiers the French blockade of Viet Minh-controlled territory could only be partially enforced. Viet Minh emissaries and agents were able to penetrate with relative impunity into the French-occupied towns, where manufactured goods and medicines could be purchased in large quantities. The impunity enjoyed by these agents was partly due to the inability of the French authorities to exercise effective control over the large numbers of refugees who had been compelled by the troubled state of the countryside to seek refuge in these centres, and partly to the readiness of many Vietnamese to provide the Viet Minh with some measure of support.[12]

This readiness amounted in some cases to recognition that existing national differences were limited to the methods by which independence could best be achieved, while most families possessed at least one member who had either opted for or had been compelled by force of circumstances to throw in his lot with the Viet Minh. In consequence even those Vietnamese who were not prepared to agree that freedom should be bought at the price of a Communist dictatorship retained a certain regard for their compatriots who had chosen to oppose the French by force of arms.

The task of these agents was, moreover, facilitated by the salutary fear that the Viet Minh Security Service inspired, since this Service, which was staffed by experienced Communist cadres and had informers in the administrative service, in business houses, and in places of amusement, would on occasion arrange for the assassination of those whose activities were considered to constitute an embarrassment. In spite of an occasional misadventure, the Viet Minh were thus able both to procure supplies from the towns and to extort the money to pay for their purchases from the Vietnamese and from the wealthy Chinese who were living under French protection.[13]

Although arms and medicines represented their most urgent requirements, the Viet Minh authorities were also compelled to arrange some redistribution of the available food supplies, particularly in the north, where the bulk of their regular forces were concentrated in barren mountainous country. The Military Commissariat in the Viet Bac were able, however, to procure additional supplies of rice from the province of Thanh Hoa and also from the

[12] In 1951 Saigon–Cholon had a population of 1,603,831, which represented an increase of nearly 1 million in the space of ten years (*Annuaire des États Associés, 1953*, p. 250).

[13] In 1951 the Chinese community in Saigon–Cholon numbered 583,000 (ibid. p. 250).

Red river delta itself, where the operations of foraging parties led to seasonal skirmishes and, in the later stages of the war, to major engagements between Viet Minh units and Franco-Vietnamese forces. In South Vietnam the position was eased by their control over part of the fertile Transbassac, the surplus from this area being available to meet a deficit in less favoured zones in Central and East Cochin-China. In the Viet Minh-occupied provinces of South Annam, however, known as Inter-zone or *Lien Khu V*, where the cultivated area was small, production barely sufficed to feed the local population.

But if by Vietnamese standards vital needs continued to be met in Viet Minh-held territory, the lot of the 10 million inhabitants constituting the population of these areas remained unenviable since with each succeeding year the military juggernaut which Giap was constructing increased its demands upon the civilian population, who were compelled to provide the increasing number of porters required to transport military supplies during the seasonal campaigns, while in the rainy seasons their services were requisitioned in order to shift rice and ammunition to the forward dumps that were being built up in preparation for future military operations.[14]

[14] The implication of these demands can be gauged by the fact that a Viet Minh division, which had a strength of some 12,000 men, required the services of 50,000 porters. These porters, who carried an average load of 45 lb., were able on occasion to increase their capacities by the use of bicycles to which two or even three bundles were attached.

# BIOGRAPHICAL NOTES

LEROY, Col. Jean, whose father owned an estate in the area, assisted the French forces under General Leclerc to reoccupy Cochin-China at the head of a group of partisans. During the uneasy truce which followed the agreement of 6 March 1946 he continued to operate against the Viet Minh and to recruit partisans principally from among the Catholic minority in Ben Tre province. But his attempt to appropriate the name 'Catholic Militia' for his brigades aroused the vigorous opposition of the Apostolic Vicar of Vinh Long, Mgr. Ngo Dinh Thuc, who compelled him to rename the force 'Mobile Units for the Defence of the Christian Communities', or 'UMDC'. Leroy displayed such aptitude for guerrilla warfare, however, that he was encouraged by the French military authorities to undertake the pacification of the Viet Minh-occupied islands adjacent to Ben Tre, and was provided for that purpose with sufficient weapons to equip a force of 7,000 men.

LE VAN VIEN, alias Bay Vien. Alleged to have become outlaw at an early age following death of an opponent in a brawl. Joined bandit gang based on Binh Xuyen area, specializing in hold-ups on roads to south of Cholon. Arrested and sent to penal settlement on island of Poulo Condore, whence he escaped on raft to mainland. Co-operated with Viet Minh, and after death of Binh Xuyen chief Duong Van Duong assumed leadership of the armed group. Appointed Commander of Viet Minh Military Zone to east of Saigon, but following disagreements with Viet Minh Committee for Nambo rallied to Bao Dai in June 1948. Appointed brigadier general in national army April 1952.

NGO DINH DIEM. Born in 1910. Roman Catholic and third son of Ngo Dinh Kha, who held high office at court of Hué. Entered the mandarinate and was serving as governor of Phan Thiet Province when he was appointed Minister of the Interior and head of the secretariat of the Committee for Reforms set up by Bao Dai in 1933. Refused to serve in an official capacity during Japanese occupation and was held captive by the Viet Minh in the mountainous region of Tongking until February 1946, when he declined Ho Chi Minh's offer of a portfolio in the 'Government of Union and Resistance'. Retired to South Vietnam, where he refused to co-operate with the French authorities and declined the office of Prime Minister in the central Provisional Government of May 1948. Left Vietnam and went to United States in 1950. (*Le Monde*, 18 June 1954, and *New York Times*, 26 June 1954.)

NGO DINH NHU was born in 1910. He attended the School of Palaeography and Librarianship in Paris (École des Chartes). In 1945 he escaped from the Viet Minh in Hué and made his way on foot to Saigon. Two years later he started to organize a Roman Catholic Trades Union movement, and in 1952 he was employed as archivist and palaeographer in the Imperial secretariat at Dalat.

NGUYEN DE. Served as Bao Dai's private secretary on the latter's return to Annam in 1932. After the frustration of the then youthful monarch's attempt at constitutional reform De, who had been forced to resign from the Imperial service, devoted his considerable talents to promoting the interests of a Vietnamese commercial firm which successfully invaded the exclusively French preserve of export and import trade. Following the revolutionary disturbances he again appeared in an official capacity as adviser to the Viet Minh delegation at the Fontainebleau Conference, but his employment in this capacity was of a temporary nature, and he was reappointed head of the Imperial secretariat in 1950. His resumption of his former post marked the ascendancy in the Imperial entourage of a man who possessed considerable intellectual affinity with the head of the state, for both De and Bao Dai were endowed with subtlety of mind and intelligence of a high order. Moreover De, who was industrious and adept at divining Bao Dai's wishes, soon rendered himself indispensable by the efficiency with which he discharged his functions and by the legerdemain he displayed—however at some cost to Imperial prestige—in engineering increases to the generous civil list and in the acquisition of elephants, and even aeroplanes, which had momentarily aroused Bao Dai's acquisitive instincts.

NGUYEN VAN HINH, General. Son of Nguyen Van Tam (q.v.). In 1938 obtained a commission in the French air force. During the war rose to the rank of Wing Commander and married a Frenchwoman who later directed the Women's Auxiliary Corps attached to the nationalist army with cheerful and broadminded gusto.

NGUYEN VAN TAM. Held the portfolio of Public Security in the Governments of Drs. Thinh and Hoach, and had distinguished himself as a protagonist of Cochin-Chinese autonomy. The son of a small shopkeeper at Tay Ninh, he had succeeded, in spite of the modesty of his beginnings, by dint of energy, determination, and industry, in obtaining a diploma in law and administration at Hanoi University, and prior to the Japanese *coup de force* he was responsible for the administration of a district which lies between the Plaine des Joncs and one of the mouths of the river Mekong, where he acquired some local notoriety by the ferocity of the methods he used in November 1940 to suppress the Communist-inspired disturbances originating in the district. After the *coup de force* of 9 March 1945 Tam was arrested and tortured by the Japanese, and two of his young sons were murdered by the Viet Minh during the rising that occurred later in the year. Following his release, he assisted the French forces under General Leclerc in the pacification of Cochin-China, and was subsequently appointed Administrator of Tan An province (*Le Monde*, 5 June 1952), being the first Vietnamese since the French conquest to occupy such a post.

PHAM VAN DONG. Belonged to a family with a tradition of service in the mandarinate, but in spite of this conservative background he opted at the age of 19 for a revolutionary career, joining the Vietnamese exiles in Canton where he was enrolled by Ho Chi Minh in the Association of Revolutionary Youth. After receiving instruction in Marxist doctrine and training in revolutionary technique he was sent back to Vietnam with the mission of organizing Communist cells. He was arrested and sentenced to six years imprisonment at the penal settlement on the island of Poulo Condore, where he proved himself a zealous Marxist propagandist among the political prisoners. On his release Dong remained in Vietnam until September 1939 when, following the outlawing of the Indochinese Communist Party, he rejoined Ho Chi Minh in the Chinese province of Kwangsi.

SOUPHANNOUVONG. Born in 1912, the son of Boun Khong, the Viceroy of Luang Prabang. Studied at the School of Civil Engineering in Paris, where he acquired a diploma. On his return to Indochina he got a job with the Trans-Indochinese Railway, and was employed at the railway workshops near Vinh, where his rancour was aroused by the discovery that his French colleagues were paid more than he was. After an absence of twenty years he returned to Laos in 1946 and joined the Lao Issara movement, receiving a slight wound in the course of his escape across the Mekong from French troops.

In 1947 he married the daughter of a Vietnamese employed in the Postal and Telegraph Service at Nha Trang, who was a Communist sympathizer. Following his expulsion from the Lao Issara movement in May 1949 Souphannouvong, with the support of a few dissident Lao Issara adherents, set up a Lao Liberation Committee in the following October, and later moved the headquarters of this Committee from Bangkok to the Viet Minh zone in North Vietnam, whence he was sent to China for a Communist indoctrination course.

SOUVANNA PHOUMA, Prince. Son of Boun Khong, the Viceroy of Luang Prabang and brother of Prince Phetsarath and the Lao dissident leader, Prince Souphannouvong. Born in 1901, he studied engineering in France. He joined the Lao Issara movement in 1945, holding the portfolio of Public Works and Communications in the rebel Government set up in Bangkok. He has held cabinet posts in the Royal Government since February 1950, and was appointed Prime Minister for the first time in the autumn of 1951.

TRAN VAN HUU, who had acquired French citizenship, was by profession an agricultural engineer. He had served in the Cochin-Chinese Dept. of Agriculture from 1915 until 1929 when he had joined, as an agricultural inspector, the staff of the Indochinese Land Bank, a subsidiary of the Bank of Indochina (*Le Monde*, 29 April 1950). He was credited, when employed in the mortgage section, with some responsibility for a harsh policy of foreclosure, which had resulted at the time of the economic depression in the ruin of many Cochin-Chinese families and, it was said, in his own enrichment. Huu was considered to be competent and shrewd and to possess some capacity for adroit political manoeuvre, while he had certainly displayed outstanding ability in the administration of his large fortune, a portion of which he had prudently invested abroad. These qualities were offset, however, by susceptibility to flattery, vanity, and a capacity for tenacious rancour.

TRUONG CHINH, alias Dang Xuan Khu. Was expelled from a primary school at Nam Dinh in 1928. He then attended the School of Commerce in Hanoi, where he joined the Association of Vietnamese Revolutionary Youth and worked on the editorial staff of a newspaper *The Hammer and Sickle*. He was arrested in 1930 and confined in a prison camp at Son La until 1936. On his release, he resumed his political activities and co-operated with a group of Vietnamese who were engaged in producing a newspaper, *Lao Dong*. In 1939 he was again taken into custody for some months, and when he was set at large he joined the Vietnamese Communists who had taken refuge in China. Here he was charged with the task of disseminating propaganda on behalf of the Indochinese Communist Party, of which he was appointed secretary general. Following the official dissolution of the ICP in 1945, he became secretary general of the Association for Marxist Studies. (*Le Monde* of 9 June 1950 and Chesneaux, p. 272.)

VO NGUYEN GIAP, General. While he was still a pupil at the National School in Hué, Giap was sentenced in 1930 to a term of imprisonment for subversive activities. In September 1939, evading an attempt by the French police to arrest him, Giap joined Nguyen Ai Quoc in China. After attending a course on guerrilla warfare at Chinese Communist headquarters in Yenan, he returned to Tongking to recruit guerrilla fighters in the mountainous region. He operated at first with some thirty supporters, who were armed for the most part with flint-lock rifles, but after this brief apprenticeship he joined forces with a local bandit named Chu Van Tan, belonging to one of the tribal minorities, in whose company he soon revealed outstanding ability in the conduct of guerrilla operations, acquiring a considerable reputation among the turbulent and variegated local population for energy, audacity, and ubiquity.

# SELECT BIBLIOGRAPHY

Amoureux, Henri. *Croix sur l'Indochine*. Paris, Domat, 1955.

Bodard, Mag. *Indochine, c'est aussi comme ça*. Paris, Gallimard, 1954.

Briggs, Lawrence Palmer. *The Ancient Khmer Empire*. Philadelphia, 1951.

Brodrick, Allan H. *Little China, the Annamese Lands*. London, Oxford Univ. Press, 1942.

—— *Little Vehicle, Cambodia and Laos*. London, Hutchinson, 1949.

Burchett, Wilfred. *North of the Seventeenth Parallel*. Hanoi, 1956.

Catroux, Georges. *Deux actes du drame indochinois*. Paris, Plon, 1959.

Célerier, Pierre. *Menaces sur le Viet-Nam*. Saigon, 1956.

Chaigneau, Michel Duc. *Souvenirs de Hué*. Shanghai, Éditions Typhon, 1941.

Chappoulie, Henri. *Aux Origines d'une église ; Rome et les missions d'Indochine au XVIIe siècle*. 2 vols. Paris, Bloud and Gay, 1943.

Chassin, L. M. *Aviation indochine*. Paris, Amiot Dumont, 1954.

Chesneaux, Jean. *Contribution à l'histoire de la nation vietnamienne*. Paris, Éditions Sociales, 1956.

Chézal, Guy de. *Parachuté en Indochine*. Paris, Deux Sirènes, 1947.

Cœdès, G. *Les États hindouisés d'Indochine et d'Indonésie*. Paris, F. de Boccard, 1948.

Cole, Allan B., ed. *Conflict in Indo-China and International Repercussions*. New York, Cornell Univ. Press, 1956.

Decoux, Jean. *À la Barre de l'Indochine*. Paris, Plon, 1949.

Despuech, Jacques. *Le Trafic de piastres*. Paris, Éditions des Deux Rives, 1953.

Devillers, Philippe. *Histoire du Viet-Nam de 1940 à 1952*. Paris, Éditions du Seuil, 1952.

Deydier, Henri. *Introduction à la connaissance du Laos*. Saigon, I.F.O.M., 1952.

Dinfreville, Jacques. *L'Opération indochine*. Paris, Éditions Internationales, 1953.

Dorgelès, E. *Sur la route mandarine*. Paris, 1929.

Ducoroy, Maurice. *Ma Trahison en Indochine*. Paris, Les Oeuvres Françaises, 1946.

Eden, Sir A. *Full Circle ; Memoirs of Sir Anthony Eden*. London, Cassell, 1960.

Estirac, Henri. *Je reviens d'Indochine.* Paris, Les Œuvres Françaises, 1946.

Faucher, J-A. and J-L. Febvre. *L'Affaire des fuites.* Paris, E.F.I., 1955.

FitzSimmons, Thomas, ed. *Cambodia; its People, its Society, its Culture.* New Haven, Conn., Hraf Press, 1957.

Frédéric-Dupont. *Mission de la France en Asie.* Paris, Éditions France-Empire, 1956.

Gaudel, André. *L'Indochine française en face du Japon.* Paris, Susse, 1947.

Gaultier, Marcel. *Minh-Mang.* Paris, Larosse, 1935.

Gauthier, Julien. *L'Indochine au travail dans la paix française.* Paris, Eyrolles, 1949.

Gentil, Pierre. *Sursauts de l'Asie: remous du Mekong.* Paris, Lavauzelle, 1950.

Gobron, Gabriel. *History and Philosophy of Caodaism,* trans. by Pham-Xuan-Thai. Saigon, Le-Van-Tan Printing House, 1950.

Goëldhieux, Claude. *Quinze mois prisonnier chez les Viets.* Paris, Julliard, 1953.

Guillain, Robert. *La Fin des illusions; notes d'Indochine, Fèvrier-Juillet 1954.* Paris, Centre d'Études de Politique Étrangère, 1954. (Conference paper, 12th IPR Conference, Kyoto, 1954.)

Herz, Martin F. *A Short History of Cambodia from the Days of Angkor to the Present.* London, Stevens [1958?].

Huard, Pierre, and Maurice Durand. *Connaissance du Viet-Nam.* Paris, Imprimerie Nationale, 1954.

Khoi, Le Thanh. *Le Viet-Nam, Histoire et civilisation.* Paris, Éditions de Minuit, 1955.

Kiem, Thai Van. *Viet-Nam d'hier et d'aujourd'hui.* Tangier, Commercial Transworld Editions, 1956.

Laniel, Joseph. *Le Drame indochinois de Dien-Bien-Phu au pari de Genève.* Paris, Plon, 1957.

Laurent, Arthur. *La Banque de l'Indochine et la piastre.* Paris, Éditions des Deux Rives, 1954.

Le Boulanger, P. *Histoire du Laos français; essai d'une étude chronologique des principautés laotiennes.* Paris, Plon, 1931.

Le Bourgeois, Jacques. *Saigon sans la France, des Japonais au Viet-Minh.* Paris, Plon, 1949.

Lerner, Daniel, and Raymond Aron, eds. *France Defeats E.D.C.* New York, Praeger, 1957.

29

Leroy, Jean. *Un Homme dans la rizière*. Paris, Éditions de Paris, 1955.

Lyautey, L-H-G. *Lettres du Tonkin et de Madagascar, 1893–99*. Paris, Colin, 1920. 2 vols.

Magnenoz, Robert. *De Confucius à Lenine; la montée au pouvoir du parti communiste chinois*. Saigon, Éditions France-Asie, 1951.

Marchand, Jean. *Le Drame indochinois*. Paris, Peyronnet, 1953.

Maybon, Charles B. *Histoire moderne du pays d'Annam, 1592–1820*. Paris, 1920.

Mordal, Jacques. *Marine indochine*. Paris, Amiot Dumont, 1953.

Mordant, Gen. *Au Service de la France en Indochine*. Saigon, 1950.

Mus, Paul. *Le Viet-Nam chez lui*. Paris, Centre d'Études de Politique Étrangère, 1946.

—— *Sociologie d'une guerre*. Paris, Éditions du Seuil, 1952.

Navarre, Henri. *Agonie de l'Indochine*. Paris, Plon, 1950.

Naville, Pierre. *La Guerre du Viet-Nam*. Paris, Éditions de la Revue Internationale, 1949.

Pasquier, Pierre. *L'Annam d'autrefois*. Paris, 1907.

Pavie, Auguste. *À la Conquête des coeurs*. Paris, Bossard, 1921.

Purcell, Victor. *The Chinese in Southeast Asia*. London, Oxford Univ. Press for RIIA, 1951.

Robequain, Charles. *The Economic Development of French Indo-China*. London, Oxford Univ. Press, 1944.

Sabattier, Gen. *Le Destin de L'Indochine; souvenirs et documents, 1941–1951*. Paris, Plon, 1952.

Salisbury-Jones, Sir G. *So Full a Glory*. London, Weidenfeld & Nicolson, 1954.

Sasorith, Katay D. *Le Laos*. Paris, Éditions Berger-Levrault, 1953.

Savani, A. M. *Visages et images du sud Viet-Nam*. Saigon, 1955.

Taboulet, Georges. *La Geste française en Indochine*. 2 vols. Paris, Maisonneuve, 1955.

Thomazi, A. *La Conquête de l'Indochine*. Paris, Payot, 1934.

Tournoux, J. R. *Secrets d'État*. Paris, Plon, 1960.

Viollis, Andrée. *Indochine S.O.S.* Paris, Gallimard, 1931.

Werth, Alexander. *La France depuis la guerre, 1944–57*. Paris, Gallimard, 1957.

'X . . .'. *Le Laos*. Paris, Peyronnet, 1948.

# INDEX

437

Morlière, Gen., 170 f.
Mountbatten, Adm. Lord, 128
Moutet, Maurice, 154, 161 f., 173
MRP, 176, 180 n., 184, 186, 240, 408
Mus, Paul, 179

Nam Bo, 139, 418 f.
Nam II, Gen., 315
Nam Phuong, Empress, 149 n.
Nationalists: before 1945, 73 ff., 112 ff.; after Japanese surrender, 117–18, 126 n., 127; Viet Minh and, 126 n., 127, 145–6, 166–7, 169, 363–4, 422; French attempt to form coalition of, 175 ff., 179, 181–2; weakness of, 195
Navarre, Gen. Henri, 280 n.; appointment of, 263–5; previous career, 263 n.; plan of campaign, 265–7, 268; military operations (1953–4), 283 ff.; and Dien Bien Phu, 284 n., 286–7, 310–12; leaves Indochina, 311; criticism of, 312
Nehru, Jawaharlal, 367, 370 f.
Ngo, see Nguyen Giac Ngo
Ngo Dinh Can, 397–8
Ngo Dinh Diem: early career, 75–76, 429–30; refuses office, 187 n.; premiership, 327–9, 346–52, 380–99; life in exile, 327 n.; character, 329, 346 ff., 390–1, 394 n., 399; and refugees, 343; U.S. support for, 347, 350 ff., 383 f., 386, 390–1, 393; and proposal for elections, 370 ff.; conflict with sects, 380–1, 383 ff.; relations with Bao Dai, 383–4, 390–3, 398–9; family junta, 386; in Annam, 397; and proclamation of Republic, 398–9
Ngo Dinh Luyen, 386, 399 n.
Ngo Dinh Nhu, 276, 282, 309, 327 n., 352, 386 ff., 393 f., 430
Ngo Dinh Nhu, Mme, 352 f.
Ngo Dinh Thuc, Mgr., 276 f., 346, 429
Nguyen Ai Quoc, see Ho Chi Minh
Nguyen Binh, 139, 164
Nguyen De, 250, 283 n., 430
Nguyen dynasty, 20–22, 28 ff.
Nguyen Giac Ngo, 192 n., 381, 387 n., 391, 396
Nguyen Han Tri, 195, 254 n.
Nguyen Ngo Le, Col., 388
Nguyen Phan Long, 200 f., 205, 208
Nguyen Quoc Dinh, 317, 320
Nguyen Thanh Phuong, 306–7, 309 n., 349 ff., 383, 387, 391 f., 397
Nguyen Ton Hoan, 309 n.
Nguyen Tuong Tam, 154 f.
Nguyen Van Hinh, Gen., 248, 253 f., 348–50, 352, 390, 395–6, 397, 430
Nguyen Van Hué, 380

Nguyen Van Tam, 209, 250, 276, 283, 381 n., 430–1
Nguyen Van Thanh, 192 n., 233, 306
Nguyen Van Thinh, 154, 157, 163–5
Nguyen Van Tuong, 47–49.
Nguyen Van Vi, Gen., 352, 390 ff., 396
Nguyen Van Xuan, Col., 165, 182, 184, 187, 189 f., 200, 205, 349 f., 408
Nhu, see Ngo Dinh Nhu
Norodom Sihanouk, Prince, 97 n., 134, 237 f., 271–4, 339, 354–8
Norodom Suramarit, King, 42–44, 68, 97 n., 356
Nungs, the, 384 n.

Office of Strategic Services, 111, 124 f., 132–3, 143
Opium, 71, 121, 150
Oun Kham, King, 51–52, 55–56

Pallu, Father François, 25–26
Partition, 318, 320, 323–4, 326, 338, 359–60; Vietnamese reactions, 308–309, 320, 328, 334 f.
Pathet Lao, 199, 228 ff., 318 f., 322 f., 326, 334, 340 f., 400 ff.
Patti, Major, 124 f., 203 n.
Pau Conference, 209–14, 270
Pavie, Auguste, 50–56
Peaceful coexistence, five principles of, 368, 404 n.
Pellerin, Mgr., 36, 38
Pennequin, Col., 72
Peyré, Roger, 408–10
Pham Ba Truc, 228
Pham Cong Tac, 87–88, 182, 195, 276 f., 383, 387, 397
Pham Ngoc Chi, Mgr., 328, 330, 344
Pham Ngoc Thach, 419
Pham Quynh, 76
Pham Van Bach, 129
Pham Van Dong: and Fontainebleau Conference, 159 ff., 168; and Geneva Conference, 317 ff., 326, 334, 340; assurance about French firms, 365; visits Delhi, 370; and holding of elections, 370 ff.; visits Trung Bo, 419; biographical note, 431
Pham Van Giao, 250, 288, 381 n.
Phan Boi Chau, 73–74, 81 f.
Phan Chau Trinh, 73–74, 79
Phan Ke Toai, 116 f.
Phetsarath, 150–1, 198
Phong Saly, 334, 340 f., 400 ff.
Phoui Sananikone, 319
Phoumi Vongvichit, 406
Phuong, see Nguyen Thanh Phuong
Pigneau de Behaine, Mgr., 28–30
Pignon, Léon, 191 f., 200 ff., 217, 219 ff., 407 f.

# INDEX

443

Pineau, Christian, 304–5
Pleven, René, 122 f., 220, 294 f., 409
Portugal, Portuguese, 10, 23 ff.
Puginier, Mgr., 45

Queuille, Henri, 409

Radford, Adm., 29, 300
Railways, 61, 70, 369–7. *See also* Yunnan Railway
Ramadier, Paul, 409, 411 n.
Raymond, Jean de, 236
Refugees, 329–30, 343–6, 359, 421–2
Revers, Gen. Georges, 215 ff., 225, 407–8
Reynaud, Paul, 270 n., 275 n.
Rhodes, Father Alexandre de, 24 f.
Rice, 61 f., 98 n., 368, 372, 375, 415
Rigault de Genouilly, Adm., 36 ff.
Rivière, Capt., 46–47
Roads, 31, 61, 70, 100
Roman Catholics: number of, 27, 196; persecution of, 32 ff., 49; and French penetration, 38, 46, 48 f.; period of neutrality, 196–7; in Vietnamese forces, 197, 311, 429; flight of to S. Vietnam, 330, 343–4, 345, 359, 372; support for Diem, 328 f.; unpopularity, 345–6
Roosevelt, President, 125 n.
Rubber, 61, 63–64, 66, 368, 415

Sabattier, Gen., 105 f., 111
Saigon: free port, 211–12; population of, 427 n.
Sainteny, Jean, 112, 124 f., 144, 146, 158, 172 f., 365 f., 368, 373
Salan, Gen., 236, 243 ff., 247, 252, 260, 263 ff., 268, 284 n., 310–11, 322 n.
Sam Neua, province of, 260, 334, 340 f., 400 ff.
Sam Sary, 319
Sang, *see* Lai Huu Sang
Sangkum Ryaster Niyum, 357
Sarraut, Albert, 212
Savang Vatthana, Prince, 199, 405
Schuman, Robert, 240
SEATO, 301 f., 316, 360
Sects, *see* Cao Dai; Hoa Hao
Siam, Siamese, 26, 94–95, 135, 210, 274; and Laos, 32, 51 n., 52 ff., 94–95, 151–2, 210
Sieu Heng, 229
Sihanouk, Prince Norodom, *see* Norodom Sihanouk, Prince
Sisavang Vong, King, 150 ff., 261
Six, Father, 197 n.
So, *see* Huynh Phu So
Soai, *see* Tran Van Soai

Son Ngoc Thanh, 98, 134, 238, 271–2, 254, 357
Souphannouvong, Prince, 229, 401, 406, 431–2
Souvanna Phouma, Prince, 401 ff., 405 f., 432
Soviet bloc: recognition of Democratic Republic, 204; barter agreements, 375
Spain, Spanish, 30 n., 37, 39
Spellman, Cardinal, 327 n., 379
Standard of living, 61 n.

Ta Quang Buu, 324, 335, 339 f.
Ta Thu Thau, 84 f., 137 n.
Thach, *see* Pham Ngoc Thach
Thai guerrillas, 263, 342, 359 n.
Thai peoples, 8–9, 10, 51. *See also* Siam
Thai–Meo autonomous area, 376 n.
Thanh, *see* So Ngoc Thanh
The, Col., *see* Trinh Minh The
Thieu Tri, Emperor, 33–35
Thinh, *see* Nguyen Van Thinh
Thuc, *see* Ngo Dinh Truc, Mgr.
Ton Duc Thang, 229–30
Ton That Thuyet, 47–49, 196
Tong, Mgr., 196
Tongking, *see under* War: operations
Tran Quang Vinh, 88, 137, 380 n.
Tran Trong Kim, Prof., 107, 119
Tran Trung Dung, 386
Tran Van Do, Dr., 333 ff.
Tran Van Don, Brig., 393
Tran Van Giau, 84 f., 118, 129 ff., 137, 138–9
Tran Van Huu, 189, 208–9, 215, 232–3, 250, 432
Tran Van Soai, 183, 195, 276 f., 349 ff., 380, 382 n., 387, 395 f.
Trapnell, Gen. Thomas, 281
Tri, Col., *see* Cao Van Tri
Trinh Minh The, 233–4, 345 n., 380–1, 384, 387, 391 ff.
Trinh, *see* Phan Chau Trinh
Trinh princes, 20–21, 28
Trotskyists, 84 f., 118, 137 n.
Trung, *see* Le Van Trung
Trung Bo, 418 f.
Trung sisters, 13
Truong Chinh, 227, 377 f., 432–3
Tu Duc, Emperor, 35, 40 f., 46 f.
Ty, *see* Le Van Ty

Union of Soviet Socialist Republics: diplomatic relations with, 204, 369; and Dien Bien Phu wounded, 315, 322; and holding of elections, 370 ff.; aid from, 374–5. *See also* European Defence Community; Molotov, Vyacheslav